PHILOSOPHY OF LAW AS AN INTEGRAL PART OF PHILOSOPHY

This edited collection considers the work of one of the most important legal philosophers of our time, Professor Gerald J Postema. It includes contributions from expert philosophers of law.

The chapters dig deep into important camps of Postema's rich theoretical project including:

- the value of the rule of law;
- the ideal of integrity in adjudication;
- his works on analogical reasoning;
- the methodology of jurisprudence;
- dialogues with Ronald Dworkin, Joseph Raz, Frederick Schauer and HLA Hart.

The collection includes an original article by Professor Postema, in which he develops his conception of the rule of law and replies to some objections to previous works, and an interview in which he provides a fascinating and unique insight into his philosophy of law.

Philosophy of Law as an Integral Part of Philosophy

Essays on the Jurisprudence of Gerald J Postema

Edited by
Thomas Bustamante
and
Thiago Lopes Decat

•HART•
OXFORD • LONDON • NEW YORK • NEW DELHI • SYDNEY

HART PUBLISHING

Bloomsbury Publishing Plc

Kemp House, Chawley Park, Cumnor Hill, Oxford, OX2 9PH, UK

1385 Broadway, New York, NY 10018, USA

HART PUBLISHING, the Hart/Stag logo, BLOOMSBURY and the Diana logo are trademarks of Bloomsbury Publishing Plc

First published in Great Britain 2020

A catalogue record for this book is available from the British Library.

Library of Congress Cataloging-in-Publication data

Names: Bustamante, Thomas da Rosa de, 1976- editor. | Decat, Thiago Lopes, editor.

Title: Philosophy of law as an integral part of philosophy : essays on the jurisprudence of Gerald J Postema / edited by Thomas Bustamante and Thiago Lopes Decat.

Description: Oxford, UK ; New York, NY : Hart Publishing, an imprint of Bloomsbury Publishing, 2020. | Includes bibliographical references and index.

Identifiers: LCCN 2020032469 (print) | LCCN 2020032470 (ebook) | ISBN 9781509933884 (hardback) | ISBN 9781509933907 (ePDF) | ISBN 9781509933891 (Epub)

Subjects: LCSH: Law—Philosophy. | Rule of law. | Jurisprudence. | Postema, Gerald J.

Classification: LCC K231 .P475 2020 (print) | LCC K231 (ebook) | DDC 340/.1—dc23

LC record available at https://lccn.loc.gov/2020032469

LC ebook record available at https://lccn.loc.gov/2020032470

ISBN: HB: 978-1-50993-388-4
ePDF: 978-1-50993-390-7
ePub: 978-1-50993-389-1

Typeset by Compuscript Ltd, Shannon

Table of Contents

PART IV
METHODOLOGY AND THE NATURE OF JURISPRUDENCE

PART V
POSTEMA'S ANALYSIS OF CONTEMPORARY LEGAL THEORIES

List of Contributors

Guilherme de Almeida is the Lead Researcher at 'Supremo em Números' (FGV Direito Rio) and a PhD candidate in legal philosophy, PUC-Rio. MSSc in legal philosophy, PUC-Rio (2017).

Brian Bix is the Frederick W Thomas Professor of Law and Philosophy at the University of Minnesota. He holds a DPhil (doctorate) from Balliol College, Oxford University, and a JD from Harvard University. His publications include *Jurisprudence: Theory and Context* (8th edn, Sweet & Maxwell 2019); *A Dictionary of Legal Theory* (Oxford University Press 2004); and *Law, Language and Legal Determinacy* (Oxford University Press 1993).

Thomas Bustamante is Professor of Legal Theory at the Federal University of Minas Gerais, Brazil, and Research Productivity Fellow of the National Council for Scientific and Technological Development (CNPq), Brazil. He holds a PhD from the Pontifical Catholic University of Rio de Janeiro. Some of his works in English appear in the *Canadian Journal of Law and Jurisprudence*, *Modern Law Review*, *Jurisprudence*, *Australian Journal of Legal Philosophy* and *German Law Journal*. He has edited the books *Democratizing Constitutional Law: Perspectives on Legal Theory and the Legitimacy of Constitutionalism* (with Bernardo Fernandes, 2016), *Argument Types and Fallacies in Legal Argumentation* (with Christian Dahlman, 2015) and *On the Philosophy of Precedent* (with Carlos Bernal Pulido, 2012).

Thiago Lopes Decat is Professor of Philosophy and Theory of Law at the Federal University of Minas Gerais (UFMG), Brazil. He got his Master's Degree in Philosophy, at UFMG, in the field of 'Logic, Science, Mind and Language', and his PhD in Theory of Law at the Pontifical Catholic University of Minas Gerais. He has had books and articles published in the areas of Legal Theory and Philosophy, and researches subjects concerning rationality, agency, normativity and metaethics applied to law understood as a social practice.

Franklin M Dutra is Professor of Public Law at the Saint Augustine Faculty (FASA), *campus* Sete Lagoas, Brazil, and temporary lecturer of Legal Theory at the Federal University of Rio de Janeiro, Brazil. He has a Research MPhil from the Federal University of Minas Gerais on *Affirmative Actions and John Rawls's Theory of Justice*, and currently is a PhD candidate in Law at the Federal University of Minas Gerais (Brazil).

Andrea Faggion is Associate Professor in the Department of Philosophy at the State University of Londrina, Parana, Brazil. She got her doctorate in philosophy from the State University of Campinas, Sao Paulo, Brazil. Nowadays, her research interests are mainly in political philosophy and analytical jurisprudence. Her main topics of study are the problems of law's normativity, political authority and political obligation. In past years, she developed research in Modern Philosophy, focusing especially on the works of Immanuel Kant. She has published dozens of papers on Kant's philosophy.

Barbara Baum Levenbook is Professor in the Department of Philosophy and Religious Studies at the North Carolina State University. She has been writing and publishing on topics of legal philosophy for over 30 years. Her articles on legal philosophy have appeared in *Legal Theory*, *Law and Philosophy*, *The Canadian Journal of Philosophy*, *Jurisprudence* and law reviews. In other journals, she has published articles on social and political philosophy, on normative ethics and on its intersection with metaphysics. In addition, she has contributed and continues to contribute to philosophical anthologies, including *Oxford Studies in Philosophy of Law* (vol 2) and *The Cambridge Companion to Legal Positivism*. She is a contributing editor to *Jotwell: Jurisprudence* and is the author of an article in *Philosophy of Law: An Encyclopedia*, edited by Christopher Gray. She holds a BA and an MA in philosophy from the University of Rochester and a PhD in philosophy from the University of Arizona.

Margaret Martin is Associate Professor at the Western University, in Canada. She holds a PhD from the University of Cambridge, a MSL from the University of Toronto and got her BA (Hons) and MA from McMaster University. Her thesis was the basis of her monograph *Judging Positivism* (Hart Publishing 2014), and her doctoral studies were supported by the Social Sciences and Humanities Research Council of Canada, the Cambridge Commonwealth Trust and the Overseas Research Scholarship. Her main research interests are legal philosophy, constitutional law and international criminal law.

Saulo de Matos is Professor of Jurisprudence and Philosophy of Law at the Faculty of Law of Federal University of Pará. He obtained his PhD at the Department of Philosophy of Law and Social Philosophy of the University of Göttingen (Germany) and his Master's degree in Law at the University of Heidelberg (Germany).

Dennis Patterson is Board of Governors Professor of Law and Philosophy at Rutgers University and Professor of Legal Philosophy at Surrey Law School, Guildford, UK.

Gerald J Postema is Professor of Philosophy, Emeritus, University of North Carolina at Chapel Hill; Cary C Boshamer Professor of Philosophy and Professor of Law, University of North Carolina at Chapel Hill (1980–2019). Arthur L Goodhart Visiting Professor of Legal Science, Cambridge University (2013–14) and Fellow of Corpus Christi College, Cambridge; Guggenheim Fellow (2005–06); Rockefeller Fellow, Bellagio (2001); Fellow of the Netherlands

Institute for Advanced Studies (1996–97). He holds an honorary doctorate from the University of Athens and has held visiting posts at the European University Institute (Florence), University of Athens, Yale University and University of California, Berkeley. He is author of *Bentham and the Common Law Tradition* (1986, 2019); *Legal Philosophy in the Twentieth Century: The Common Law World* (2011); and editor of *Matthew Hale on the Law of Nature, Reason and the Common Law* (2018).

Dan Priel is a Professor at Osgoode Hall Law School, at York University, Canada.

Fábio Perin Shecaira is Professor of Legal Theory, Faculty of Law of the Federal University of Rio de Janeiro (since 2012). He has a PhD in Philosophy, McMaster University (2012) and has been a Visiting Researcher at Harvard Law School (2011). He has published in English in journals like *History of Philosophy Quarterly*, *Australian Journal of Legal Philosophy*, *Law and Philosophy*, *Informal Logic*, *Ratio Juris* and *Argumentation*.

César Antonio Serbena is Full Professor of Legal Philosophy at the Law School of the Federal University of Paraná (UFPR), in the city of Curitiba, Brazil. He has experience in teaching Law, focusing on the Philosophy of Law, and researching the following subjects: e-justice, legal language, deontic logic, epistemology and analysis of legal reasoning. He is also the Coordinator of the Research Groups: *e-Justice UFPR* and *Foundations of Law*.

Natalina Stamile, having been a post-doctoral researcher and Professor in the Postgraduate Programme in Law at the Federal University of Paraná, Brazil (2016–19), is currently an Associate Lecturer of Philosophy and Legal Informatics at the University of Bergamo, Italy. She completed her PhD in 2012 on the *Legal Theory and European Legal Order* programme at Magna Graecia University, Italy. She has also been a visiting researcher in numerous universities, and the author of essays and articles in different languages. Her main research areas are Theory and Philosophy of Law, Fundamental Rights, Constitutional Justice and Legal Informatics.

Noel Struchiner is Professor of Law and Philosophy at the Pontifical Catholic University of Rio de Janeiro. He holds a 'Productivity Fellow' at CNPq (National Council for Scientific and Technological Development) and is a 'Scientist of the State of Rio de Janeiro Fellow' at FAPERJ (Carlos Chagas Filho Foundation of Research Support of the State of Rio de Janeiro). He has been a Visiting Researcher, Brown University (2012), a Visiting Researcher, Harvard University (2004). PhD in Philosophy, PUC-Rio (2005).

Introduction

THOMAS BUSTAMANTE AND THIAGO LOPES DECAT*

I. THE PURSUIT OF A SOCIABLE JURISPRUDENCE

'I've always regarded philosophy of law as an integral part of philosophy. I believe that one can do philosophy of law well only if one can do philosophy well, and I believe that one can do philosophy well only if one is immersed in the history of philosophy.' This fragment from the Interview with Professor Gerald Postema that you will find in the final chapter of this book tells an important lesson about his jurisprudence and how he conceives the nature of law and legal inquiry. Contemporary jurisprudence has been dominated, ever since the publication of John Austin's *The Province of Jurisprudence Determined*, about halfway through the nineteenth century, by an analytical methodology, which seeks above any other goal to isolate the law and its theoretical discourse from other disciplines such as sociology, history, political theory and moral philosophy.

Jurisprudence has been concerned with borders, limits, separations, distinctions. It has been dominated by a metaphysical talk of essences, nature, causes, necessary and sufficient properties and the like, and by an endeavour to describe the law from a disengaged and external point of view. The proper job of jurisprudence was to reveal the grounds of law, that is, to explain what makes it a distinctive system of rules with its proper and unique normativity, which cannot be confused with the motivating capacity of moral and ethical values. In describing the law, one should argue in value-neutral terms instead of making judgments, evaluations, interpretations. Much of jurisprudence was meant to make sense of 'intuitions' and 'truisms' that one already knows, according to a methodology of conceptual analysis.

The most plausible candidate to explain the nature of law under this theoretical framework is legal positivism, with its insistence on a *reductive* explanation of legal validity that holds that social facts are the ultimate or, for some, exclusive

* The editors would like to thank Professor Postema, the contributing authors and the Brazilian National Council for Scientific Development (CNPq), which financed part of the seminars in which we discussed the chapters (Grant # 305645/2017-0) and has provided a Research Productivity Scholarship to Thomas Bustamante since 2013 (current Grant # 423696/2018-1). Furthermore, they are grateful to Margaret Martin for insightful comments and feedback on this Introduction.

determinants of the content of the law. Yet the claim that the law emerges from authoritative pronouncements of certain persons or institutions is independent from the theoretical framework adduced in the previous paragraph, as Professor Postema has shown in several writings in his prolific career.

One need not accept the methodology that predominates in analytical jurisprudence to uphold the claim that the law is man-made, or that it is posited by an authority, or that it has a conventional or social source. Most medieval legal philosophers, including those that are now uncontroversially associated with the natural law tradition, which is meant to oppose the central tenets of legal positivism, advocated a 'thetic' ('taking the term from the Greek *tithenai* meaning to put, as in *laid down* or *posited*') conception of law that distinguishes the law established by nature (*ius*) from the law that is 'instituted by agreement or mutual consent' (*ius positiva*), normally expressed in a public way in the form of 'rules or measures prescribing right order' (*lex*).[1]

Perhaps the anxiety to classify natural law and legal positivism as competing conceptions of legal validity, as if these two traditions emerged together and were concerned with precisely the same questions, stems from the kind of philosophical temperament that Professor Postema challenged in the quote at the beginning of this introduction.

Postema's jurisprudence is, first and foremost, historically conscious. It aims to understand the law from the perspective of human experience, as a 'sociable science' in the sense of common lawyers like Edward Coke and Matthew Hale. Jurisprudence is 'sociable' for Coke, 'in that it agreeth with the principles and rules of other excellent Sciences, divine and human'.[2] Perhaps the central idea of Professor Postema's intent to rehabilitate the idea of jurisprudence as a sociable science lies in the Renaissance effort to locate jurisprudence 'in concrete human life and experience': jurisprudence was understood according to Accursio's idea of '*vera philosophia*', which was 'neither speculation nor pure prudence, but the point at which the theoretical and the practical intersected'.[3] It attempted neither to subordinate 'practice to theory nor theory to practice' but to integrate them instead.[4]

Another crucial contribution of Professor Postema to our understanding of the nature of law is the thesis, of which he claims to find some traces in Oliver Wendell Holmes, that time 'is intrinsic to law's ordinary mode of operating, to its distinctive mode of normative guidance'.[5] The point applies not only to law

[1] GJ Postema, 'Positivism: Early Foundations' in A Marmor (ed), *The Routledge Companion to Philosophy of Law* (Routledge 2012) 32.

[2] Edward Coke, 7 *Reports* 28a, in S Sheppard (ed), *The Selected Writings and Speeches of Sir Edward Coke* (first published 1608, Liberty Fund 2003) 231–322, quoted in GJ Postema, 'Jurisprudence, The Sociable Science' (2015) 101 *Virginia Law Review* 869.

[3] Postema (n 2) 870.

[4] ibid.

[5] GJ Postema, 'Melody and Law's Mindfulness of Time' (2004) 17 *Ratio Juris* 203, 205.

but to all kinds of intentional action. Intentional action has a temporal texture: 'intended action is an undertaking, governed by a project. To form an intention is to organize a portion of one's time, to give movement or direction to one's involvement in that span of time.'[6] Professor Postema seeks for a model to explain the normativity of law that is based neither on the idea of *nomos* (that roots the normativity of law in a 'supposed rational ordering of reality') nor on the idea of *thesmos* (which 'models law as a system of commands' or authoritative reasons for action). It appeals to a different metaphor, constructed around the idea of melody (*melos*), which 'highlights the temporal dimensions' of the normativity of law:

> Music *takes* time, but not just in the way that healing or sleeping take time; music exists *in* time, but not in the way paintings and sculpture exist in time. Music, melody in particular, is an *ordering* of time. While Michelangelo's *Pietà* exists in time, and it takes time to appreciate it, space is intrinsic to the sculpture; sculpture is a meaningful ordering of space. A performance of Bach's *Erbarme dich* must be located in time and in space (as must every act of human beings), but time is intrinsic to it; music is a meaningful ordering of time.[7]

The right point for us to start our deliberative processes and our philosophical endeavours to interpret or understand the law is *in media res*, rather than *ex ante*. We cannot be satisfied with *a priori* conditions for emergence of norms or with a static account of legal validity. On Bratman's theory of intentional action, to which Professor Postema resorts in order to provide a framework for his analysis of time-dependence in practical deliberation, 'the agent in mid-course typically faces new problems for deliberation', since the deliberation in which she participates 'is framed by three parameters: the intention-plan, current circumstances, and the initial instalments in the execution of the plan. … Rational execution of one's intention depends on integrating these three parameters into deliberation.'[8]

Legal reasoning is thus a reasoning in which one works *in media res* with materials stemming from past political decisions, but also with the present responsibility to direct the future of our community in certain matters. The practice of following judicial precedents, for instance, is a reasoning that 'is always, like Janus, on the threshold of past and future, seeking to integrate them into a normatively meaningful whole'. Melody, for Professor Postema, 'models this kind of integration'.[9]

Law is time-dependent just as much as it is dependent on politics, and jurisprudence must be integrated into political philosophy for similar reasons. The point is not only that the legal system is part of the political system, or that we need to import some concepts from jurisprudence to make sense of our political

[6] ibid 209.
[7] ibid 207.
[8] ibid 209–10.
[9] ibid 214.

theories. It is, instead, that the arguments and submissions of legal philosophers can be 'taken seriously', or play a 'role … in the life of the law and in determining the place that the law occupies in a society', only by 'paying attention to matters that are in the domain of political science (how law is in fact regarded) or political philosophy (how the law ought to be regarded)'.[10] The arguments for or against legal positivism, for instance, 'can be grasped and illuminated only on the basis of certain normative commitments' that have traditionally concerned moral and political philosophy.[11]

Jurisprudence must be regarded as a branch of political philosophy because of its intrinsically critical nature. As Professor Postema explains, summarising Oakeshott's contribution to philosophical jurisprudence, it seeks for 'comprehensive explanations', and 'its bounden duty is to maintain a resolutely critical stance, especially to its own presuppositions and modes of thought'.[12] Fortunately Professor Postema is not alone in this understanding of the character of jurisprudence, understood broadly as legal philosophy. John Finnis, for instance, is also critical of the methodological claim of descriptiveness in analytical philosophers like Kelsen, Hart and Raz. 'It is obvious,' he argues, 'that the differences in description [of the nature of law] derive from differences of opinion, amongst the descriptive theorists, about what is *important* and *significant* in the field of data and experience with which they are all equally and thoroughly familiar.'[13] A good theory of law must be part of a theory of practical reasonableness, must be a theory in which the 'theoretical work' is 'controlled by the adoption … of some practical viewpoint of the standard of relevance and significance in the construction of [a] descriptive analysis'.[14] And Ronald Dworkin, by the same token, regards jurisprudence itself as a constructive interpretation of the legal practice, which tries to 'show legal practice as a whole in its best light, to achieve equilibrium between legal practice as they find it and the best justification of that practice'.[15]

We should not, however, lose sight of the fact that the purpose of jurisprudence is not purely practical. It is theoretical while integrated with the law as a practice: 'The aim of philosophical jurisprudence is not to change the world, but to understand it.'[16] One can find in Professor Postema's philosophy of law an underlying Hegelian mood that invites us to build our theories by focusing on a concrete practice: jurisprudential arguments are 'anchored in the concrete

[10] J Waldron, 'Legal and Political Philosophy' in J Coleman and S Shapiro (eds), *The Oxford Handbook of Jurisprudence & Philosophy of Law* (Oxford University Press 2002) 357.

[11] ibid 369. It comes as no surprise, therefore, that Waldron cites Professor Postema as a leading example of normative jurisprudence of the right kind.

[12] Postema (n 2) 891.

[13] J Finnis, *Natural Law and Natural Rights* (2nd edn, Oxford University Press 2011) 9.

[14] ibid 18.

[15] R Dworkin, *Law's Empire* (Harvard University Press 1986) 90.

[16] Postema (n 2) 897.

experience and practice of law taken in all its richness'.[17] Like Dworkin, Professor Postema advocates that we should look at the practice's history to figure out its point, which is given by the practice itself, and that this point should be a moral point that is a source of critical power for jurisprudence itself. Jurisprudence must be 'truly illuminating while remaining responsibly critical'.[18] Part of our theoretical responsibilities, as philosophers, is to take up this critical attitude, which despite not being meant for purely pragmatic purposes, such as deciding concrete cases, can lead to an improvement in the practice.[19] In a nutshell, jurisprudence, for Professor Postema, is *constitutionally critical*: 'it takes as part of its remit to destabilize stabilities due to ignorance, indolence, insufficient self-awareness, the powerful dynamics of communal thinking, or past victories in the polity or the academy'; it must, moreover, be 'always prepared to be critical of its own performance and the presuppositions on which it rests'.[20]

Another aspect of the idea of sociable science is Professor Postema's defence of a synechist rather than analytic mentality in jurisprudence. While analytic jurisprudence typically seeks 'explanations built on sharp distinctions and deep differences of a kind', a synechist methodology 'is a methodological inclination favouring explanations that focus on continuities rather than those that insist on sharp distinctions'. He borrows this thought from Peirce's synechism, which was employed as a 'principle of explanation':

> The analytic mentality seeks sharp boundaries for the concept of law, essentially distinguishing properties of law that define its nature, and criteria that enable us to know with some confidence when we have law 'properly-so-called' in our observer-analyst field of vision. When it encounters an as-yet unclassified phenomenon, or phenomena about the nature of which we might be genuinely puzzled, among its first inquiry-structuring question is: Is it or is it not proper law? (And, typically, when the answer is not unambiguously 'yes', further inquiry regarding the phenomena is assigned to the large file marked 'for others to explore'). By contrast, the synechist, no less interested in probing the nature of law, looks for continuities and illuminating similarities (and differences that build continuities). The synechist asks, 'What is law like?' and '(How) is this like law?', rather than declaring, 'This isn't like law, so it's not law (properly speaking)'. It seeks understanding by locating, relating, and integrating.[21]

[17] ibid.

[18] ibid.

[19] Professor Postema criticises Dworkin, however, because he thinks that despite Dworkin's 'radical departure from analytic jurisprudence', his theory is 'ironically, cast in a similar professional service role', insofar as it appears to be primarily responsive to the practice of courts: ibid 899. Regardless of the soundness of this critique, however, it remains true that much of Professor Postema's jurisprudence shares Dworkin's philosophical mood to integrate theory and practice, as one can see in Professor Postema's recognition that the value of *integrity* plays a central role in legal and moral reasoning, which is essential to any legitimate actions of the community and its officials or other members. See, for instance, GJ Postema, 'Integrity: Justice in Workclothes' in J Burley (ed), *Ronald Dworkin and His Critics, With Replies by Dworkin* (Blackwell 2004) 294.

[20] Postema (n 2) 896.

[21] ibid 894.

For much of the last couple of centuries, jurisprudence has been segregated into a safe haven of problems that are resolvable with the conceptual armoury of analytical jurisprudence. It claimed 'modesty' for philosophical inquiry and confined itself to a metaphysical realm in which philosophers can make second-order, detached statements about the nature of law and leave it untouched by any critical or evaluative aims. According to a recent and influential work in jurisprudence, 'the key to conceptual analysis is the gathering of truisms about a given entity'.[22] To determine the nature of a thing, we should stick to 'those properties that it *necessarily* has'.[23] But this kind of inquiry, for Professor Postema, misses an important aspect of the point of philosophy itself, and should no longer be pursued. Instead of being satisfied with a neutral description of the 'prevailing views' in a professional practice and a set of intuitions about its nature, philosophers should ask for more: they should make their discipline more 'sociable' in the sense that we explained above, on pain of losing a big part of its point. We beg your pardon for another extended quote:

> Philosophy that proceeds primarily by plumbing and pumping intuitions is inevitably and uncritically in thrall to the present. Philosophical jurisprudence needs critical distance and resources for critical assessment of current understanding of familiar practice, but such distance and resources rarely come from abstraction alone. A grasp of the forces that have shaped the practice and the presuppositions shaping it is more likely to provide the distance and resources needed for the task. It can help us break the tyranny of present intuitions shaped by preconceptions at or behind the horizons of our ordinary vision, and it can help us excavate, identify, articulate, and critically explore them. Locating familiar notions in initially unfamiliar conceptual and historical neighbourhoods often sheds new light on those notions, revealing aspects or links to other notions and problems that we otherwise overlook.[24]

Professor Postema has successfully shown us, in this fragment, an important aspect of the failure that seems to affect the largest part of contemporary jurisprudence, a failure that doomed even some of the most talented jurisprudence scholars in the twentieth century. Legal philosophers' claim to modesty comes at the price of renouncing the most interesting questions a curious student or lawyer might ask about the nature of her enterprise. It seems that jurisprudence has built a prison in which one is confined to a very specific set of questions that often limit, rather than expand, our knowledge of the object of our inquiry. But there is no reason to confine ourselves to this mindset. If you cannot discuss the point, or the value, or the moral, political and social significance, or the efficacy, or the legitimacy or the history of a legal system because the methodology you chose aprioristically remits you to a different discipline, then probably the problem lies in your method rather than in the questions that you asked but that

[22] S Shapiro, *Legality* (Harvard University Press 2011) 18.
[23] ibid 9.
[24] Postema (n 2) 892.

could not be answered by it. Philosophers of law are advised, therefore, not to encapsulate themselves in a disciplinary realm in which they can only confirm their intuitions and repeat what they believe are truisms or necessary truths. They should make their own science more sociable and try to understand it by critically evaluating the concrete practices in which they participate.

The analytical framework that promises us reliable and conceptually correct descriptions is the same one that gives us only incomplete and fragmented answers that sometimes leave us ignorant about the subject matter of our inquiry. We should thus get rid of the analytical framework, rather than our intellectual curiosity. This point applies to much of the predominant tradition in jurisprudence, including its most prominent participant, HLA Hart:

> Hart brought philosophical investigation to analytic jurisprudence, but his insistence on methodological positivism revealed and amplified analytic jurisprudence's 'unsociable' tendency. Indeed, Hart and his descendants were often careful to identify questions not within the domain of legal philosophy and hand them off to other disciplines, never to be entertained again. At the same time, as debates in the latter decades of the century among positivists proceeded down their complex, winding paths, the core of the dominant positivist jurisprudence narrowed dramatically. This trend had reached such a point that by the turn of the century, the current incumbent in Hart's chair of jurisprudence at Oxford, could boldly declare that 'Legal positivism is not a whole theory of law's nature. It is a thesis about legal validity only' (Gardner 2001, 210). We noted in Chapter 10, that the fundamental debate between the two major camps of contemporary positivists – the exclusive positivists and the inclusive positivists – rested solely on contested claims about what is conceptually possible. Both camps were willing to consign a very large number of what we might regard as salient and perhaps very important features of law to the category of the non-conceptual and merely empirical – and thus not matters proper for jurisprudential attention.[25]

Professor Postema's jurisprudence can be regarded as an attempt to revisit and reinterpret some of our thoughts about law without the conceptual method that analytical jurisprudence has imposed upon the students of philosophy of law. We will try to show in the next two sections whether Professor Postema has been successful in this task.

II. PHILOSOPHICAL JURISPRUDENCE AND THE CONCEPT OF LAW

If what we have been saying is correct, Professor Postema's thoughts on philosophical jurisprudence depart from the metaphysical mood that has taken the scene of mainstream legal theory; for understood as a sociable science,

[25] GJ Postema, *A Treatise of Legal Philosophy and General Jurisprudence*, vol 11: *Legal Philosophy in the Twentieth Century: The Common Law World* (Springer 2011) 582.

the scope of jurisprudence cannot be reduced to the pursuit of certain social facts that allow us to give reductive explanations in order to confirm supposed previously shared intuitions. Even so, it is not far-fetched to expect that many commentators would still classify as metaphysical a crucial argument in support of his position, which he shares with Ronald Dworkin.

In the introduction of *Justice in Robes* and in a chapter dedicated to the study of concepts in legal theory, Dworkin highlights the importance of 'distinguishing among different concepts people use to talk about law': (i) the 'doctrinal' concept, which 'we use in stating what the law of some jurisdiction requires or forbids or permits'; (ii) the 'sociological' concept, which 'we use to describe a particular form of political organization', if we want to describe an alien legal system or make a historical narrative of a system that existed in a given time and space; (iii) the 'taxonomic' concept, that 'we use to classify a particular rule or principle as a legal principle rather than a principle of some other kind', as legal positivists often do when they want to distinguish clearly legal and moral obligations; and (iv) the 'aspirational' concept that we use to 'describe a distinct political virtue', like the virtue of 'legality' or the 'rule of law'.[26]

Part of Dworkin's argument is that the concept relevant for jurisprudence is the doctrinal concept of law, which is the concept that figures in our political arguments and to which we resort when we try to figure out our political obligations and the hypotheses in which the state is justified to exercise coercion on someone. The doctrinal concept of law, for Dworkin, can be understood neither as a 'criterial' concept nor as a 'natural kind' concept, as it might be the case for other (non-jurisprudential) uses of the concept of law. People share a criterial concept, for Dworkin, 'only when they agree on a definition – rough or precise – that sets out the criteria for the correct application of the associated term or phrase'.[27] The concept is shared as a matter of strict convention, that is, as a somehow arbitrary agreement in which the reason for a person to use the concept is the fact that other speakers do the same. When you use the concept of 'bachelor', for instance, people can understand what you mean because they share – as a matter of convention – the same criteria of application for the concept at stake. A natural kind concept, in turn, functions in a different way: 'People share some concepts whose instances have a natural physical or biological structure – metals and animals, for example – even though they do not agree about the essential nature of the examples or the criteria they use to identify those examples'.[28] Nonetheless, when we deal with natural kinds, there will always be some type of analysis or experiment that we can conduct in order to verify the properties that these concepts describe. If you have doubts whether a giant feline is a tiger or a leopard, for instance, you can do a DNA test to dispel

[26] R Dworkin, *Justice in Robes* (Belknap 2006) 223.
[27] ibid at 9.
[28] ibid at 10.

your doubts, since there will be some properties in the deep structure of the animal you are considering that makes it the case that it belongs to one natural kind concept rather than the other.

The doctrinal concept of law, which is the concept appropriate for jurisprudence, is, for Dworkin, an 'interpretive' concept. Although people share a practice in which these concepts figure, they can neither 'simply report the criteria people use to identify instances' nor 'simply excavate the deep structure of what people mainly agree are instances'.[29] On the contrary, they must 'construct' the concept with an 'interpretive attitude' that recognises that the concept (or the practice to which it refers) has a valuable point or purpose, and then tries to read that practice in light of this purpose.[30]

Why does Dworkin think that law is an interpretive concept? And why can some observers claim, *contra* Dworkin, that this might be read without violence as a metaphysical claim?

The answer to the first question is that the doctrinal concept of law is a special type of contested concept, whose distinctive feature seems to be that it is sensitive to its moral point, which provides its justification and the standard to interpret it correctly, that is, to make the best available sense of it. Law, for Dworkin, is a constitutively reflexive practice, and the right way to understand this practice is with an interpretive theory that has many important points of overlap with Professor Postema's philosophical jurisprudence.

The answer to the second question, in turn, is that it is a part of the nature of law that it is an argumentative practice, and that some of the arguments needed to explain this practice – or raise and contest claims or propositions about it – are moral arguments. The intrinsically evaluative aspect of law is not a contingent property but rather a necessary feature of the law. That is why a philosopher might insist that Dworkin is making a metaphysical point when he accounts for the doctrinal concept of law. Nonetheless, the substance of the claim matters more than its character. The important point is not the nature of this theoretical claim, whether it is internal, Archimedean, sociological, evaluative or metaphysical. What matters is that it provides part of the explanation of why analytical jurisprudence fails to understand the law well.

We believe that this incursion on Dworkin's account of the different concepts of law is valuable to understand Professor Postema's jurisprudence for two interrelated reasons. First, if Dworkin is right, each type of concept of law is attached to a distinct language game in the sense of Wittgenstein. The 'doctrinal' concept of law is the proper concept for jurisprudence. It is the concept that is at stake when we raise *genuinely philosophical* questions about the law; it is the concept we use when we want to know how the law works, and how it binds us. It is the concept with which we try to answer what rights and duties can be legitimately

[29] ibid at 12.
[30] Dworkin (n 15) 47.

enforced.[31] To put it in the terms of Professor Postema's jurisprudence, it is the kind of concept of law that we use 'in concrete human life and experience', where we need to integrate our theoretical explanations with the practices in which we look for norms and principles to guide ourselves.[32] We seem to have, therefore, an important Wittgensteinean argument in support for a sociable rather than analytical jurisprudence, which constitutes the second reason for comparison between Dworkin and Professor Postema's jurisprudence: part of the grammar that determines the sense of our concept of law is unintelligible if one attempts to grasp it with non-evaluative concepts and with the guidance of the limited sort of questions that the methodology of conceptual analysis can answer.

Does this conclusion apply to Professor Postema? In other words, is sociable jurisprudence a grammar that claims to be appropriate to understand the wealth and comprehensiveness of the concept of law? Consider what Professor Postema said about the historical dimension of law and its philosophical discipline:

> Jurisprudence must pay attention to history because jurisprudence seeks understanding of law, and law and reflection on it not only have a history, but that history is intrinsic to them. Not everything that exists in and through time, and in that sense has a history, is illuminated by study of that history. But law is different. *Law is by nature time-oriented and reflective*.[33]

The claim that 'law is by nature time-oriented and reflective' might be read as a metaphysical claim (if you like). Nonetheless, it is an argument against the attempt to reduce jurisprudence to a metaphysical inquiry. It entails that only *part*, perhaps a small part, of the explanation of the concept of law can be metaphysical, since what explains the failure of analytical jurisprudence is that jurisprudence should not be limited to metaphysical claims.

If we want to achieve a satisfactory understanding of the law we must, therefore, take up the participant's point of view. As Professor Postema has answered in the interview at the end of this book, legal theory

> always must be constructed from the internal point of view, in at least one sense of that phrase. One orienting assumption of legal theory is that law is a social phenomenon, practised by people, which has some impact on their day-to-day lives. In consequence, we can't begin to understand law in any of its various forms that have appeared over time, unless we understand it from the point of view of those who are engaged in it, practising it, or are critics of it.[34]

This is an important insight, which is one of the reasons not only for showing that Professor Postema and Ronald Dworkin are working on similar projects,

[31] D Priel, 'The Place of Legitimacy in Legal Theory' (2011) 57 *McGill Law Journal* 1, 18.
[32] Postema (n 25) 578.
[33] Postema (n 2) 885.
[34] T Bustamante, CA Serbena and N Stamile, 'Interview with Professor Gerald J Postema', ch 14 of this volume.

as some of the chapters of this book have argued, but also, and perhaps more importantly, to explain why Professor Postema's jurisprudence provides very successful accounts of some themes that remained obscure while they were addressed with the methodology of analytical jurisprudence.

Postema's philosophical jurisprudence advises you to avoid ontological absolutism. It is reflective all the way down. It is a practical discipline and requires you to make moral evaluative judgments even when you describe the foundational rules of a legal system.[35] It advises you to avoid abstract descriptions that do not engage with the arguments and assumptions found in the ordinary practice of law. It recommends a more pragmatic attitude, which asks us to look to the future with a reflective responsibility of making sense of the practice we attempt to understand.

III. PHILOSOPHICAL JURISPRUDENCE APPLIED

We believe that Professor Postema's 'sociable' method for philosophical jurisprudence is part of the explanation of the excellence and originality of his works on many aspects of jurisprudence, dismantling common misunderstandings, caricatures and uninteresting conceptual debates that are recurrent in analytical jurisprudence. It explains, for instance, Postema's successful restatement of classical common law jurisprudence, which freed great lawyers like Coke and Hale from the common caricature that depicts their declaratory theory of adjudication as a 'childish fiction' or a 'fairy tale'. The following statement of a prominent English judge is a good example of the caricature:

> There was a time when it was thought almost indecent to suggest that judges make law – they only declare it. Those with a taste for fairy tales seem to have thought that in some Alladin's cave there is hidden the Common Law in all its splendour and that once a judge's appointment there descends on him knowledge of the magic words Open Sesame. Bad decisions are given when the judge had muddled the password and the wrong door opens. But we do not believe in fairy tales anymore.[36]

Constructed from the point of view of analytic jurisprudence, that is, as a detached and external statement that looks at laws as plain facts which are posited by custom or authoritative pronouncements, the declaratory theory may indeed look silly, for the judicial decision that exercises discretion and creates a new precedent can plausibly be described by an external observer as

[35] One cannot claim, therefore, that we resort to a different type of statement when we look at these fundamental rules, as Hart did when he sustained that legal theorists adopt an 'external' point of view when they attempt to understand the rule of recognition of a legal system. See, for instance, GJ Postema, 'Jurisprudence as Practical Philosophy' (1998) 4 *Legal Theory* 329, 337.

[36] Lord Reid, 'The Judge as a Law Maker' (1973) 12 *The Journal of the Society of Public Teachers of Law* 22.

a political fact that settles the law and creates a new norm that is binding upon lower judges in future cases. Professor Postema, however, consistently with his conception of jurisprudence as a sociable theory, would not be tempted by straw men or caricatures of philosophical traditions. He would apply the same principle he mentioned to repeal caricatures of theories of natural law: the 'Silliness Reflection Principle', which holds that 'if a proposition attributed to an author looks silly on its face, it is likely that the silliness lies not in the author or the text but in the attribution'.[37] Nothing can illustrate this better than Professor Postema's generous reconstruction of the tradition of classical common law.

Classical common lawyers did not regard individual precedents as binding legal sources. They thought that past legal decisions matter for determining the outcome of present and future cases, but their impact must be assessed against a long history of customs, statutes and cases that are part of a larger whole. 'It was the general practice of the courts, not the specific decisions or reasoning in a given case, that established the propositions of law.'[38] Common lawyers like St Germain, Hedley, Coke, Davies, Hale and Selden, regardless of their differences and specific theoretical claims, agreed that common law was based on an interdependent mixture of *custom* and *reason*. They did not regard themselves as 'making' the law, as legislatures do when they posit a norm that becomes strictly binding upon their subjects. Legal rules were not seen as the product of authoritative settlement; they were understood, instead, as a sort of social construction that emerged in the same way as the rules of grammar in a spoken language.[39] Common lawyers thought that legal practice was, first and foremost, a historical enterprise. They believed that legal materials were constantly open to further refinement, adjustment and interpretation. Legal changes never were, for these lawyers, a threat to the 'deeper integrity of the common law'.[40] Common law survived as a social practice and should be read on the assumption of a historical *continuity* of this practice. To discover the common law was to engage in this argumentative practice, with a special responsibility to discover the inner rationality of the social practice of law.

The rationality of common law, as Professor Postema explains, was clearly distinguished from the 'natural reason' of philosophers, theologians and scholastic natural lawyers. Classical common lawyers were suspicious of metaphysical formulae and undertook an effort to avoid transcendental arguments about morality, justice or the nature of law. The reason behind classical common law was a form of 'artificial reason' in the sense that it was a reasoning *in the law*, with little room for 'external' principles imported from second-order

[37] Postema (n 2) 892.

[38] GJ Postema, 'Classical Common Law Jurisprudence (Part I)' (2002) 2 *Oxford University Common Law Journal* 155, 161.

[39] GJ Postema, 'Some Roots of Our Notion of Precedent' in L Goldstein (ed), *Precedent in Law* (Oxford University Press 1987) 9, 21–22.

[40] Postema (n 38) 173.

philosophy. If the historical series of decisions, customs and institutional materials extracted from legal practice failed to give one an uncontroversial solution to a given argument, the job of the lawyer was not to consult 'universal moral sources, as a natural lawyers might do, but rather to look longer, harder and deeper into the accumulated fund of experience and example provided by the common law'.[41] The common law's rationality was called an 'artificial' reason because the grounds for evaluating a legal claim were determined from the *internal point of view*.[42] Among other features, legal argumentation was pragmatic, publicly oriented, contextual and discursive.[43]

It was *pragmatic* not only in the sense that it aimed to solve practical problems of social life, but in the more ambitious sense that it was committed to 'settling grounds for decision for today's and future similar cases'.[44] Common law reasoning was Janus-faced. It claimed continuity with the past, but it also looked to the future. Even though it was part of the responsibility of adjudication to discover the law that lay implicit in historical social practices, it was forward-looking in the sense that it was accountable for the juridical consequences that followed from the decision at stake.[45]

It was also *publicly oriented*, because practitioners saw their roles as a 'public mission'. They 'sought to solve problems of social life and resolve its controversies always "with an eye and due regard for justice and a consideration of the commonwealth wherein they live."'[46]

Furthermore, it was *contextual*, for it required a special ability to interpret particular cases, which formed a long historical series and required a special form of analogical reasoning. To interpret the law was to engage with a mode of reasoning that was neither deductive nor inductive but essentially *analogical*. Common lawyers carefully avoided the perils of philosophical particularism and of rule-rationalism. Unlike fashionable forms of contemporary particularism, analogical reasoning in classic common law was 'discursive rather than intuitive; a matter of argument rather than perception or feeling; a form of reasoning, not just a mode of insight'.[47] And unlike rule-rationalism, it was sceptical of the idea that there is always an abstract rule that can bridge the analogies between cases. According to rule-rationalists, 'it is not possible to judge one case relevantly similar to another without the guidance of a rule that brings them under some

[41] ibid 179.

[42] HLA Hart, *The Concept of Law* (2nd edn, Oxford University Press 1994) 89.

[43] GJ Postema, 'Classical Common Law Jurisprudence (Part II)' (2003) 3 *Oxford University Commonwealth Law Journal* 1.

[44] N MacCormick, *Legal Reasoning and Legal Theory* (Clarendon Press 1978) 76.

[45] Postema (n 43). See also N MacCormick, 'On Legal Decisions and their Consequences: From Dewey to Dworkin' (1983) 58 *New York University Law Review* 239, 249–54.

[46] Postema (n 43) 4. The quote within Postema's excerpt is from J Dodderidge, *The English Lawyer* (1631) 242.

[47] GJ Postema, '*A Similibus ad Similia*: Analogical Thinking in Law' in D Edlin (ed), *Common Law Theory* (Cambridge University Press 2007) 102, 110.

category or description', of which the case is nothing but an instance.[48] The problem with this thought, for Professor Postema, is that it ends up in an infinite regress, for if one asks about the foundation of the abstract rule postulated to allow an analogical inference, the need for a further rule emerges again.[49] The kind of analogical reasoning of classic common law can be explained, therefore, according to contemporary forms of *philosophical inferentialism*:

> Analogical reasoning is not a linear process but rather a dynamic one of locating a new case in a network of inferences; reasoning – tracing compatibilities and incompatibilities of reasons and inferences – occurs throughout the process. If we understand it in this way, we can resist the temptation to reduce it either to a form of intuition or of mere rule application.[50]

Finally, classic common law reasoning was essentially *discursive*. Perhaps the reason that led common lawyers like Coke and Hale to disagree with Hobbes is the same reason that motivated, more recently, Dworkin to disagree with Hart. The law was not conceived of as a plain historical fact. The classical common lawyer's notion of the law's 'artificial reason' implied that 'only in the process of argument, regarding concrete cases, in open court subject to reasoned challenge, is the law to be found and forged'.[51]

It comes as no surprise, therefore, that the classic common lawyers lacked a theory of binding legal precedent. Cases and precedents were but brute facts whose impact should be assessed in light of the whole body of laws and the artificial reason that established its content. As Mansfield expressed in one of his famous *dicta*, 'precedent, though it be evidence of law, is not law itself, much less the whole of the law'.[52] For classical common lawyers 'the authority and force of any component of the common law depends on its integration into the framework of the whole and its satisfaction of a shared sense of reasonableness rooted in this framework'.[53]

We believe that Professor Postema's reconstruction of classical common law jurisprudence provides a formidable example of the wealth and depth of his philosophical jurisprudence. Where others see only commands, rules, social facts and, sometimes, straw men, he was able to see a rich and sophisticated theory, which is fully integrated into the professional practice of some of the great lawyers in English history.

The reliance on the method of a sociable jurisprudence explains, in addition, Postema's insightful reinterpretation of the jurisprudence of one of the most important exponents of modern philosophy: Jeremy Bentham. In effect, before

[48] ibid 114.
[49] ibid.
[50] ibid 121.
[51] Postema (n 43) 8.
[52] *Jones v Randall* (1774) Lofft 383, 386; 98 ER 706, 707 (Lord Mansfield), quoted in Postema (n 43) 11.
[53] Postema (n 43) 14.

Postema's incursion on Bentham's philosophy of law, HLA Hart's interpretation of Bentham's jurisprudence was predominant, perhaps almost consensually accepted among jurisprudence scholars.[54] The great merit of Bentham, for Hart, was to 'demystify' the law, clearing it up from the natural law baggage that was found in the jurisprudence of Blackstone and other classical common lawyers.[55] The two branches of Benthamite jurisprudence ('censorial' jurisprudence and 'expository' jurisprudence) seem depicted, thus, as two separate domains, as if the former dealt with the kind of questions that belong to 'other disciplines' and Bentham's contribution to the real problems of jurisprudence laid exclusively in the 'expository' part of his legal theory, in which he presented a proper concept of law with the method that is proper for jurisprudential inquiry.

We believe that part of Hart's mistake was to rely only on the same methodology that he used in his own legal theory, ignoring the connection between the multiple parts of Bentham's sophisticated philosophical system. As Professor Postema explains, Bentham was, like Hobbes, sceptical of the classical common law's idea of a different kind of rationality in the legal realm, for he regarded the principle of utility 'as the sole and sovereign rational decision principle'.[56] Instead of striving to make sense of a confused notion of 'artificial' rationality, like that of classical common lawyers, Bentham 'insisted that judges must be free to respond to the constantly varying demands of utility in particular cases'.[57] Hence, Bentham's jurisprudential project should be regarded as integrated into his political philosophy, since both strands of jurisprudence (expository and censorial) serve the same principle. Bentham's legal positivism is a *political* or *normative* type of positivism, which is based on a normative theory that not only explains the law as it is, but rather defends a positivistic test for identifying a proposition as 'legal' because of salient utility reasons in support of this view.

Professor Postema's philosophical jurisprudence, or 'sociable science' in his philosophically ambitious sense, allowed him to propose an original and successful interpretation of Bentham's classical writings on the nature of law. While other interpreters looked at Bentham without distinguishing his methodology from that of his successor John Austin, and thrilled every time they found one of Bentham's caricatures of classical common law, Professor Postema emphasised not the caricatures or the uncharitable descriptions of this tradition that one can find in some of Bentham's political writings. He sought, instead, to understand the *melody* of Bentham's thoughts, that is, how they evolved, what he intended with them, what context made them arise and, perhaps more importantly, what principle Bentham was following in his jurisprudential project.

[54] HLA Hart, *Essays on Bentham* (Oxford University Press 1982) 21–39.
[55] ibid.
[56] GJ Postema, *Bentham and the Common Law Tradition* (2nd edn, Clarendon 2019) 155.
[57] ibid.

Bentham's legal positivism did not come from nowhere. It also has a history. There are traces of the positivist conception of law in the works of Thomas Hobbes, who raised some of the most powerful criticisms against the jurisprudence of classical common law. In his *Dialogue between a Philosopher and a Student of the Common Laws*, Hobbes responded to Coke's argument of there being a distinctive type of reason in common law. The claim that law had some sort of 'artificial reason' was, for Hobbes, both wrong and obscure. 'It is not wisdom, but authority that makes a law', and there is no such a thing as a specific 'legal reason'.[58] What we got, rather, is only an unqualified form of 'human reason'.

Core among the ideas of Jeremy Bentham was a struggle to carry on with this argument and bring it to a more sophisticated theoretical level. It is true, as Hart acknowledged, that Bentham intended to demystify the law, to free jurisprudence from the aristocratic vocabulary embedded in classical common law, 'to draw aside that curtain of mystery which fiction and formality have spread so extensively over the Law'.[59] Like Hobbes, Bentham was sceptical of the idea of a different kind of rationality in the legal realm. His utilitarianism saw no room for a confused notion of 'artificial' rationality. On his doctrine, 'laws are at bottom nothing but commands, prohibitions or permissions, artefacts of the human will'.[60]

Bentham's departure from the common lawyers' declaratory theory of adjudication followed a political purpose, and in the beginning was not meant to discard a system of binding precedent but rather to develop it. Bentham's contempt for binding judicial precedents emerged only some years after he put forward the first critique against classical common law. As Professor Postema explains, Bentham argued in an early essay (bearing the title '*Law: Common Law vs Statute*') that a model of *stare decisis* could work as a remedy against the flexibility, uncertainty and obscurity that he claimed were typical of the jurisprudence of common law. By adhering to a doctrine of binding precedents, legal practices would be in a better position to comply with the requirements of the principle of utility in adjudication. We can see, in this view,

> as in his account of utilitarian adjudication under a code of laws, an attempt to unite his deep commitment to the sovereignty of the principle of utility with his recognition of the need for a device which can focus public expectations in a way that public knowledge of the practice and direct appeal to utility cannot.[61]

[58] Thomas Hobbes, *A Dialogue Between a Philosopher and a Student of The Common Laws of England* (first published 1681, Liberty Fund 2011) 4.

[59] Jeremy Bentham, 'A Comment on the Commentaries' in JH Burns and HLA Hart (eds), *A Comment on the Commentaries and a Fragment on Government* (first published 1776, Oxford University Press 2009) 124.

[60] Hart (54) 23.

[61] GJ Postema, *Utility, Publicity and Law: Essays on Bentham's Moral and Legal Philosophy* (Oxford University Press 2019) 164.

But it did not take too long for Bentham to realise that a model of *stare decisis* fails to provide an adequate antidote to the perils of judicial reasoning. After observing the practice of English lawyers in a legal system in which precedents were gradually becoming more important as a source of legal reasons, Bentham identified a paradox that Postema referred to as the 'paradox of inflexibility'.[62] The more a judge is constrained by a strict model of *stare decisis*, the more 'legal fictions, abstract and largely empty notions like "reasonableness", "policy", "natural law" and Latinized principles like "*contra bonos mores*" creep into law and the decision-making practices of common law judges'.[63] The practice of binding precedent, therefore, in the mature and more developed version of Bentham's jurisprudence, is regarded as just as toxic and illegitimate as the classical common law jurisprudence, which explicitly adopted the mysterious assumptions of the declaratory theory of law.

These historical developments of Bentham's jurisprudence are largely ignored by those who consider it with the mindset of analytical jurisprudence. The methodology of 'conceptual analysis', which presupposes always a single concept and a 'truth of the matter' to be excavated with some metaphysical apparatus, impoverishes philosophical reasoning and sets artificial boundaries for its tasks. It is Professor Postema's fidelity to his philosophical approach to jurisprudence, which regards it as a sociable science, that explains why he could find in Bentham not only a rebel, but also a genius, a political philosopher whose theory is fully integrated in practice, and whose jurisprudence is fully integrated in his political and moral theory.

It is also this appeal to a philosophical jurisprudence integrated into practice that explains the reach of Professor Postema's criticisms on some of the leading exponents of contemporary legal theory. Even though Professor Postema himself was influenced by Hart's account of law as a conventional social practice, as we can appreciate in his seminal early article on 'coordinating conventions', which emphasised the law's coordinating role in a political community,[64] he was able to find some relevant problems in the jurisprudence of Hart and some of his most influential followers. One of these problems is that Hartian positivism has trouble explaining why and how legal and moral obligations should be sharply distinguished, and how judges can be obligated to apply a content-independent legal rule while citizens and private persons who are under their authority are not. The claim that officials who accept the law from the internal point of view do so just because other officials do the same seems, for Professor Postema, too weak to secure the normative impact that Hart needs the law to exert on their professional activity, whereas the claim that legal officials should coordinate

[62] Postema (n 56) 273–79.

[63] Postema (n 61) 167.

[64] GJ Postema, 'Coordination and Convention at the Foundations of Law' (1982) 11 *The Journal of Legal Studies* 165.

their actions according to content-independent legal reasons regardless of whether citizens are bound to have the same attitude toward these reasons fails because it ignores the important fact that 'rational direction of action through public rules requires communication, and communication entails interdependence among law-makers, law-appliers and law-subjects'.[65]

In his insightful critique of Hart's account of legal normativity, Professor Postema objects to the two alternatives that are available to make sense of Hart's separations between legal and moral obligations and between the acceptance of legal rules by officials and private citizens. First, one should avoid the 'simple convergence thesis', which claims that although it is a fact that judges in a legal system 'all accept the basic criteria of validity, there is nevertheless no uniformity, no distinctive pattern, in the reasons they give for accepting them'.[66] Second, one should not expect much from the 'strict conventionality thesis', which says, rather, that for the authority of law to emerge, 'all that is necessary is that the criteria be accepted and practiced widely' by judges and officials, in such a way that 'self-identified participants themselves recognize the fact that there is a wide range of reasons for acceptance of the criteria of validity, but those reasons are irrelevant to the question of the authority of the criteria'.[67]

Postema believes that these explanations are exposed to familiar objections that emerge from the natural law tradition, which demand normative reasons to motivate citizens and officials to place themselves under the guidance of law. Once again, one can find traces of Postema's dissatisfaction with the method of analytic jurisprudence, which exports problems to other disciplines never to return to them again, erecting 'modesty' to the level of a fundamental virtue of legal philosophy and remaining quietist about some of the most pressing practical problems of jurisprudence.

The impact of Professor Postema's defence of a sociable jurisprudence goes on and on. It explains, for instance, the problem of Raz's attempt to trace a sharp line to divide 'reasoning about law' and 'legal reasoning', which reflects more a commitment to his own concept of law than an actual reconstruction of the practice of adjudication, as it is interpreted by the participants of legal practice from the internal point of view.[68] By the same token, the strict interpretation of the social sources thesis, which requires that legal validity is neatly separated from moral reasons and that we can determine the content of law without making any judgment about its merits, can only be integrated into Raz's theories of legal reasoning and interpretation at the cost of failing to satisfy an important function of law, which is to guide citizens in their practical deliberations. To retain our commitment to analytical jurisprudence and to the method

[65] GJ Postema, 'The Normativity of Law' in R Gavison (ed), *Issues in Contemporary Legal Philosophy: The Influence of HLA Hart* (Oxford University Press 1987) 81, 92.

[66] ibid 96.

[67] ibid.

[68] J Raz, *Ethics in the Public Domain* (Oxford University Press 1994) ch 14.

that requires philosophers to make only 'detached' statements about the necessary properties of law, one ends up turning the law into a normative system with little force of its own, given that citizens would have very little reason to obey the law once it is properly defined, as it were.[69]

In all these debates, Professor Postema intervened with a detailed and insightful interpretation of the main problems of jurisprudence from a practically oriented standpoint. He was especially concerned to integrate concepts and philosophical reflection on law into legal practice, to understand how law works as an important aspect of practical reasoning, which requires for its proper understanding not a strict demarcation of domains but an effective collaboration between disciplines and an account of the connections between law and morality, politics and perhaps other domains in which intentional action plays a role in our lives.

In effect, Professor Postema's philosophical jurisprudence gives us a method for resolving philosophical puzzles and explaining social practices that seems to be more appropriate than traditional accounts, not only in jurisprudence but also in metaethics and some other branches of philosophy. In his discussion of objectivity in law and morality, for instance, Professor Postema successfully showed us the right way to interpret a crucial concept for the legitimacy of law. Explaining the objectivity of legal judgments is not only a theoretical problem but also a fundamental political concern, inasmuch as the law's claim to legitimacy inherently depends on the possibility of objectivity in the legal domain.[70] If law is to guide our conduct, and if we need legitimate norms to have sound reasons to place ourselves under the rule of law, legal judgments must be mind-independent rather than arbitrary; they must be epistemically correct and invariant across judging subjects, for otherwise they will not be able to vindicate the claim to legitimacy that the law needs to make a practical difference in our reasons for action.[71]

If the point of objectivity in legal discourse is to provide an account for the legitimacy of legal judgments, then the quest for objectivity is not a metaphysical quest. Metaphysical concepts of objectivity (which presuppose a 'truth of the matter' and a correspondence theory of truth, such that objective judgments are only those that provide actual representations of some fact that can be said to pre-exist in the world) seem to be outside the scope of a philosophical jurisprudence in Postema's sense. What we need, to vindicate a sensible conception of objectivity that makes sense of our moral and legal arguments, is not a metaphysical demonstration of moral realism or its refutation by their anti-realist

[69] See Postema's sophisticated argument against Raz in GJ Postema, 'Law's Autonomy and Public Practical Reason' in RP George (ed), *The Autonomy of Law: Essays on Legal Positivism* (Clarendon 1996) 79.

[70] GJ Postema, 'Objectivity Fit for Law' in B Leiter (ed), *Objectivity in Law and Morality* (Cambridge University Press 2001) 99, 113–16.

[71] See, on these structuring features of objectivity, ibid 105–12.

opponents. For metaphysical accounts of objectivity, 'there is only one credible conception of objectivity', which is valid across all the different domains of reality.[72] Yet this assumption is precisely what we do not need to devise a plausible account for objectivity of legal judgments.

Postema's conception of objectivity is neither a metaphysical concept, which attempts to make accurate representations that correspond to a factual reality, nor the sort of stipulative concept of objectivity that we find in philosophers who think that we can 'ascribe' some truth-properties to an object even if it does not actually exist in the world. The 'logical' concept of objectivity, proposed by Andrei Marmor, is one such concept. Logical objectivity is defined in terms of assertability, rather than truth. The difference between the metaphysical and the logical concept of objectivity is that while the former is committed to a correspondence theory of truth and a reductive description of 'an object in the world',[73] the latter is compatible with a pluralistic conception of truth. Logical objectivity is tailor-made for philosophical traditions that 'allow for the validity or truth of statements which are not descriptive (or reducible to descriptive) statements'.[74]

The problem with logical objectivity is that it mimics metaphysical objectivity. It is a stipulative concept designed to explain why abstract metaphysical conceptions of morality, like Humean projectivitism, expressivism, emotivism, quasi-realism and the like, can coexist with the philosopher's intuitions about the objectivity of the propositions participants argue for or against in their internal discourses about moral facts. The point seems more to create a logical space for theories that as moral agents we cannot accept than to say something meaningful and important to the participants in moral practices. Many metaethics scholars, therefore, speak only to themselves when they talk about morality, practices, values, norms, judgments or objectivity, since they do not have anything meaningful to say about or to the participants in the practice.[75]

This is not the right conception of objectivity for a philosophical jurisprudence in Professor Postema's sense. An adequate concept of objectivity for law must be, first, a methodological concept, which is concerned more with the epistemic commitments and discursive procedures for making a correct and reliable claim than with a correspondence with prior metaphysical facts. It must also, second, be a form of 'domain-objectivity', or a conception of objectivity moderately sensitive to the internal requirements of each domain, in the sense that

[72] ibid 133.

[73] A Marmor, 'Three Concepts of Objectivity' in A Marmor (ed), *Law and Interpretation: Essays in Legal Philosophy* (Clarendon Press 1995) 177, 185.

[74] ibid 186.

[75] Perhaps it is a disenchantment with this kind of philosophical mood that led Dworkin, for example, to deny the logical space for second-order assertions about morality, which purport to explain morality in terms of other, non-moral, metaphysical facts. See, for instance, Dworkin's long discussion of metaethical Archimedenanism in R Dworkin, 'Objectivity and Truth: You'd Better Believe It' (1996) 25 *Philosophy & Public Affairs* 87.

although the notion of objectivity has some structuring features and requirements that are valid across different domains (like the independence condition, the demonstrability condition, the invariance across different persons condition, and so on), there are also some requirements and relevance conditions for the objectivity of an assertion that are internal to the domain at stake.[76]

So, to come back to the themes at the beginning of this subsection, this is probably what the classical common lawyers meant: the law is an artificial, distinctive domain because the rules and norms that can vindicate our judgments, that can render them objective and intersubjectively reliable, are extracted from the practice of legal argumentation itself, even when these rules, norms and values remain implicit and require a delicate historical, moral or philosophical examination of the practice's basic rules. The ideas of 'objectivity' and 'artificial reason', for Professor Postema, work in tandem. According to Nigel Simmonds, who is also attracted to this view, the common law requires an artificial reason because of the insufficiency of 'natural' reason:

> Reason reveals to us the need for mutually respectful cooperation, and for the conduct of our lives in friendship with others. But it does not offer us a blueprint for our lives together. We disagree about justice; and, on any sound understanding, the prescriptions of justice are plural and potentially competing. In consequence of this, we must devise our own solutions, even though our solutions will still be constrained by circumstance and answerable to very general requirements of reason.[77]

The driving idea of common law's jurisprudence, thus, is the thought that law's reason is internal to law. The claim to reasonableness of legal doctrines 'lay in the fact that they were the products of a distinctive mode of *reasoning*'. Their 'standing and force' comes not because they correspond to transcendental *reason*, but because 'they are *reasoned*, having emerged from and survived a formal and public process of discursive reasoning'.[78]

The disagreement between classical common lawyers and Bentham, for instance, is at bottom a disagreement about how to construct this kind of objectivity. While common lawyers, like Professor Postema, believed that there is an internal rationality of law, constituted in implicit norms that should be made explicit by careful examination, Bentham remained sceptical of this possibility and proposed, in turn, an authoritative account of legality, which is nowadays popular under the rubric of 'normative positivism'.[79] Utility, as politics and morality's fundamental principle, lies behind this choice for legal positivism.

[76] For a similar view, see J Raz, *Engaging Reason* (Oxford University Press 1999) 124–25.

[77] N Simmonds, 'Constitutional Rights, Civility and Artifice' (2019) 78 *Cambridge Law Journal* 175, 177.

[78] GJ Postema, 'Editor's Introduction' in GJ Postema (ed), *Matthew Hale on the Law of Nature, Reason and Common Law* (Oxford University Press 2017) xxvi.

[79] See, for all, J Waldron, 'Normative (or Ethical) Positivism' in J Coleman (ed), *Hart's Postscript: Essays in the Postscript to The Concept of Law* (Oxford University Press 2001) 411. Waldron is probably not correct, however, when he claims that Professor Postema himself is a supporter of normative positivism. See Waldron (n 10) 369.

IV. A NOTE ON ELIMINATIVISM AND THE FUTURE OF LEGAL PHILOSOPHY

We believe that Professor Postema has made a comprehensive, sophisticated, insightful and sound criticism of analytical jurisprudence. His work, either when he deals with general topics like the nature of law and legal philosophy, or when he considers more specific matters like objectivity, integrity, the rule of law, precedents, analogies, practical reason, legal reasoning or critical remarks on particular legal theories, has not left jurisprudence untouched. He fulfils with honours the job that he claims is proper for jurisprudence, which is to engage in critical reflection on legal practice from the internal point of view. Perhaps one of the conclusions that we can reach from this long introduction is that Professor Postema has earned a place in the history of jurisprudence by reconfiguring the field with a more historical, moralised, empirically responsible, comparative and critical method for jurisprudence. He has showed us a new future for jurisprudence, which lies beyond analytical jurisprudence.

It seems that analytical jurisprudence has exhausted its capacity to offer enlightening explanations about the concept of law. But instead of departing from the method of conceptual analysis characteristic of this kind of approach to legal philosophy, some jurisprudence scholars propose to simply stop attempting to formulate a concept of law. It has been argued, for instance, that the Hart–Dworkin debate (or more properly, the debate between positivists and non-positivists on whether legal facts are determined only by social facts or whether other normative considerations also play a part in determining the content of the law) is a 'fly-bottle' that has been preventing us from achieving relevant progress in jurisprudence.[80] The metaphysical question of the law's distinctive normativity should be dropped, for it prevents us from reaching a correct understanding of how the rules of social practices arise and play a relevant role in our lives.

One might think that it is better, perhaps, to accept some sort of eliminativism about the concept of law, to deny the existence of 'law' as a distinctive entity, or the idea of a 'distinctively legal domain of normativity, or quasi-normativity'.[81] If, for instance, legal positivists and non-positivists have a stark disagreement about the grounds of law but cannot extract from such disagreement an interesting conclusion about how we should resolve interpretive legal disputes or adjudicate on concrete cases, why should we insist on providing a concept of law? Why insist on figuring out the real nature of law, if nothing turns on the answer to this difficult philosophical question? For the eliminativist, there may still be many interesting questions in which legal theorists may engage: 'we can say and do a lot with … accounts of legal decision making, legal counsel,

[80] S Hershovitz, 'The End of Jurisprudence' (2015) 124 *Yale Law Journal* 1160.
[81] ibid 1193.

and good governance', but there is no point in insisting on abstract conceptual discussions about what the law is.[82] When we try to explain what happens when a court distinguishes a case from a binding precedent, for instance, it matters not if you think that judges are 'changing' or 'developing' the law, as a legal positivist might claim, or whether they are, as a non-positivist would put it, correcting a legal mistake by retrieving the actual content of the law, which is determined in accordance with moral principles implicit in the relevant legal materials. The question of the fundamental determinants of the content of law, despite the different answers given by positivists and non-positivists, 'must be paraphrased into a moral question about what a person ought to do or a descriptive question about the state's likely responses to people's decisions'.[83]

When we look at the conceptions of legal reasoning and the theories of adjudication offered by prominent legal theorists like Joseph Raz, in the positivist camp, and Ronald Dworkin, in the non-positivist camp, we will probably be struck about how much they share about the point of interpretation, or the need to make moral judgments in hard cases, or the belief in the objectivity of values, or the kind of moral considerations to which a judge may resort in response to the reasons applicable to a case. Their theoretical disagreement about the grounds of law masks an agreement about the role of morality in legal reasoning, since positivists do not claim that social facts are the only kind of considerations that can be employed in court as a ground for a legal decision. The reasoning undertaken by lawyers and judges is pregnant with moral judgments. Legal reasoning, for Raz, comprises more than a reasoning to determine the content of the law, either because the law unintentionally leaves a gap, in which the scope of one's actual obligation is not fully determined, or because the law itself contains a number of 'principles of discretion' that authorise courts to further develop the law.[84] On the standard positivistic view, 'there is much more to legal reasoning than applying the law, and the rest is … quite commonly straightforward moral reasoning'.[85]

The eliminativist may thus have a point. Does it make sense to drop the quest for the nature of law? Should we give up this concept and redirect our efforts to determine the actual moral duties of ordinary citizens and the proper moral obligations of legal officials?

Although many might be tempted to an affirmative answer, a reader who understands the importance of the philosophical jurisprudence of Professor Postema, who regards this domain of thought as genuinely 'sociable' in the sense of the sections above, will not be impressed by the eliminativist view. As Liam Murphy identified, the problem with this kind of controversy about the grounds

[82] L Murphy, *What Makes Law* (Cambridge University Press 2014) 90.
[83] ibid.
[84] J Raz, 'Legal Principles and the Limits of Law' in M Cohen (ed), *Ronald Dworkin & Contemporary Jurisprudence* (Duckworth 1983) 73, 75.
[85] J Raz, *Ethics in the Public Domain* (Clarendon 1994) 332–33.

of law is that 'at the foundations, they depend on intuitions about the proper application of the concept',[86] and yet when we look at the actual practice of law we cannot confirm these intuitions by appealing to what the participants of the practice agree about the features of the law in particular cases.[87]

The main arguments for eliminativism seem to be rooted precisely in the tyranny of intuitions in philosophical discourse about law, or, as Professor Postema would put it, in the lack of historical consciousness, political sensibility and empirical reflection that is typical of twentieth-century analytical jurisprudence. Like lawyers who become sceptics about rules because of their disappointment with formalism,[88] or like the moral philosophers who doubt the possibility of objectivity because of their frustration with moral realism,[89] the eliminativists give up the concept of law because of their disappointment with the modest achievements of analytical jurisprudence. But once we leave the orthodoxy of analytical jurisprudence behind and begin to look for more important things than 'isolating' the law or looking only to what we intuitively perceive as necessary and sufficient features, we can find out important roles for a concept of law. Our jurisprudence might need a concept of law to explain, for instance, the role that legal norms perform in our practical reasoning, which Professor Postema considers, in the interview at the end of this book, one of the important problems that are open for jurisprudence to explain. As Murphy acknowledges, in response to the eliminativist challenge, 'more important than the law's expressive function is the role of law in people's practical lives'.[90] We believe, however, that without a philosophical jurisprudence that possesses the virtues of Professor Postema's studies in philosophy of law, it becomes very difficult to construct an interesting account of the nature of law.

A philosophically reflective concept of law is needed to determine what rights we are entitled to and what duties we have in a political community, that is, what claims we are entitled to stake and what we owe to each other in this community. It matters what the law says, and it matters how we understand the law. To conclude, we need a concept of law, among other things, because we need to know what the law is in order to provide a complete moral justification for our actions, because the concept of law is *politically* important.[91] Part of what makes us responsible moral agents is our duty to justify these actions, even though, as Thomas Scanlon has famously stated, we know from the start that 'working out the terms of moral justification is an unending task'.[92]

[86] Murphy (n 82) 78.
[87] ibid 84.
[88] Hart (n 42) 139.
[89] A Marmor, 'An Essay on the Objectivity of Law' in B Bix (ed), *Analyzing Law: New Essays in Legal Theory* (Clarendon 1998) 3.
[90] Murphy (n 82) 91.
[91] L Murphy, 'The Political Question of the Concept of Law' in J Coleman (ed), *Hart's Postscript: Essays on the Postscript to 'The Concept of Law'* (Oxford University Press 2001) 372.
[92] TM Scanlon, *What We Owe to Each Other* (Belknap 1998) 316.

V. THE CONTENTS OF THE BOOK

The point of this introduction was not only to provide an overview of part of Professor Postema's comprehensive works on law, philosophy, practical reasoning, common law and so on. It was also to provide some context for the reader to assess the following chapters of the book, which attempt to develop some thoughts based on Professor Postema's contributions to jurisprudence. The book is divided into five Parts and 14 chapters, which will be introduced below.

Part I is dedicated to Professor Postema's contribution to the study of the value of the rule of law and is composed of two chapters. In recent scholarship, Professor Postema stressed that the central aspect of the rule of law is that it is about 'law's ruling'. For the law to rule, it must provide protection and recourse against arbitrary exercise of power. But for this protection to be effective, it must be the case that the members of the political community, whether they are officials or lay members, take responsibility for holding each other accountable under law.[93] The rule of law, on Professor Postema's view, is based on an ethos of fidelity, which is of fundamental importance for it to arise. In chapter 1 of the book, Professor Postema deals with a possible objection to this approach. According to the objection, the structures of accountability in a political community tend to undermine an important aspect of this ethos, which is the value of trust: the fact that each member of the community is responsible for holding the others accountable might provide incentives for disintegration and distrust. So the objection is stated thus: if accountability is at the heart of the rule of law, and distrust a consequence of accountability, the rule of law fails in its claim to provide a robust programme of controlling the exercise of power. In response to this objection, which was named as the 'trust challenge', Professor Postema proposes an integrated account of accountability and trust. He argues that it is not necessarily the case that accountability depends on distrust. On the contrary, accountability is a key component of trust-supporting moral and social relationships, such that fidelity and trust are not only compatible but also mutually supporting.

In chapter 2, Franklin Marques Dutra further discusses Professor Postema's account of the rule of law. He intends to bring to the surface in the chapter the fundamental value underlying Professor Postema's account of the rule of law. After a short introduction to Professor Postema's conception of the rule of law, he proposes to characterise Professor Postema's conception as a monist theory according to Liam Murphy's definition, inasmuch as it claims that the duties of officials

[93] See GJ Postema, 'Law's Rule: Reflexivity, Mutual Accountability and the Rule of Law' in Xiaobo Zhai and M Quinn (eds), *Bentham's Theory of Law and Public Opinion* (Cambridge University Press 2014) 7; and GJ Postema, 'Fidelity in Law's Commonwealth' in LM Austin and D Klimchuck (eds), *Private Law and the Rule of Law* (Oxford University Press 2014) 17.

and individual citizens stem from the same source and are guided by the same principle. He argues, once this interpretation is settled, that Professor Postema's conception of the rule of law rests more properly on the demand of equal concern and respect, as stated in Ronald Dworkin's writings, than on Philip Pettit's neo-republican value of freedom as non-domination.

Part II, which is the longest Part in the book, is dedicated to Professor Postema's reflections on interpretation and integrity, particularly in his exchange with Ronald Dworkin. Chapter 3, by Barbara Baum Levenbook, analyses and evaluates Professor Postema's account of integrity, which, like Dworkin, assumes that integrity is a virtue of political communities that is distinct from other values like justice and fairness. Like Dworkin's, his account is premised on a requirement of fidelity to the past political decisions of the community, including the conception of justice that 'fits and unifies these past decisions'. There is, however, according to Levenbook, a distinctive aspect of Professor Postema's idea of integrity, which is the thought that integrity incorporates not only 'respect for the past' but also the idea of 'regret', which entails a need for reaching compromises to accommodate principles that sometimes do not cohere with the best reconstruction of a community's overarching values: 'Regret is consistent with preserving some currency for a morally incorrect decision, but limiting its force.' For this argument to work, the justification of regret would still have to be a moral justification. Integrity must be based both on justice and on *fidelity*, understood as a distinctly legal virtue and an important aspect of the rule of law. Levenbook is sceptical, however, about the possibility of an internal justification for the value of fidelity and the idea of regret. Although Levenbook acknowledges the wealth and sophistication of Professor Postema's account, she is not persuaded that his idea of regret is part of the practice of common law legal systems, and neither is she convinced that justice itself can establish some spheres of local incoherence in a system of moral values.

The remaining chapters of Part II are dedicated to the exchange between Postema and Dworkin on the idea of protestant interpretation. Chapter 4, by Thomas Bustamante, offers an optimistic view about the possibilities of the value of political integrity. Bustamante insists that Dworkin's idea of protestant interpretation is a plausible view. The point of the chapter is not only to offer a response to Professor Postema, but also to reconcile his thoughts with Dworkinian jurisprudence, that is, to show that Professor Postema himself can accept it to provide a justification for some of his recent views about the character of law and interpretation. In an early review of Dworkin's *Law's Empire*, Professor Postema argued that Dworkin's conception of interpretation is problematic because it allows the interpreter to impose her own view upon the practice, without the need to engage with other citizens' interpretations about the point of law. Even if what we interpret is a common practice, Dworkinian interpretations are private judgments. Given that the point of law is logically independent from legal practice, Dworkin's advocacy of protestant interpretation is insufficiently inter-subjective and insufficiently political.[94] To respond to this objection, Bustamante argues that it is possible to read Dworkin in a more charitable way, so that the point of law is given by legal practice itself. Once we consider the role played by history in Dworkin's interpretivism, we can realise that it is similar to Postema's recent views about the principle of the Rule of Law, which provide a successful conception of legality.

In chapter 5, Dennis Patterson responds to this attempt to reconcile Dworkin and Professor Postema. He claims that Dworkin's account of interpretation implies a commitment to a hermeneutical account of meaning found in Continental scholars like Heidegger and Gadamer, which should be replaced by an account of language, meaning and social practices erected on the basis of Wittgenstein's *Philosophical Investigations*. On Patterson's view, there is no room for an intermediate position between these two, and Professor Postema successfully showed that only the latter offers a promising theory of law.

In chapter 6, Brian Bix also defends Professor Postema's views against Dworkinian interpretation. *Contra* Dworkin, his suggestion is that the structure of law, at least in some legal systems like that of the United States, is comparable to a catholic, rather than protestant, division of interpretive competences. No interpreter can rely, if this is correct, on his own judgment about the point and purpose of a legal practice, to use it as a tool to interpret the law. Legal construction is a social and public process, either because of some institutional constraints imposed by the structure of the judicial system, as Robert Cover suggested, or because of the need for authoritative settlement by higher courts.

Part III of the book is focused on Professor Postema's contribution to analogical thinking in legal reasoning. In chapter 7, Thiago Decat engages with Professor Postema's argument on analogical reasoning in common law legal systems. The chapter highlights the unarticulated and implicit theoretical framework behind Professor Postema's formulation and defence of his version of the classical common law conception of analogy in opposition to particularism and rule rationalism. Decat takes Postema's solution to the problems of relevance and of the infinite regress of rules – raised respectively by the first and the second of these conceptions of analogy – to be made possible by an understanding of reasoning that is broadly inferentialist. Combining what Brandom calls 'fundamental pragmatism' with the Kantian/inferentialist idea that making a judgement involves assuming the justificatory responsibility of integrating the (analogical) judgment to other judgments already inferentially articulated, provides the basis for Postema's conception of analogical reasoning's ability to synthesise a sound conception that profits from the insights of the two examined conceptions while eschewing their flaws. In the end, Decat argues that, had Postema made full and explicit use of inferentialist theoretical resources such as the concepts of material inference and of the expressive function of deontological vocabulary,

[94] GJ Postema, 'Protestant Interpretation and Social Practices' (1987) 6 *Law and Philosophy* 283.

his conception could still retain the possibility of bringing analogies to critical assessment in a public forum without the need to posit the division of analytical reasoning in law into a two-stage process. Had Professor Postema dug deeper into the critical question of how the implicit conceptual norms defining the normative conditions for integrating the analogical judgment in an inferential net historically emerge, he would probably arrive at a monist model of analogical reasoning whose historical expressive rationality is able to account for the rational pressure exerted by both particulars and universals in reaching analogies as different aspects of the same one-stage process.

Chapter 8, by Fábio Shecaira, takes a different direction. In response to Professor Postema, Shecaira attempts to rescue the idea of an 'argument from analogy' from the claim that 'strictly speaking, there is no such a thing as an *argument from* analogy, but only *reasoning with* analogy, or rather *analogical reasoning*'.[95] After distinguishing the concepts of 'thinking', 'argument' and 'justification', Shecaira presents two objections to Professor Postema's charge against rule-rationalist interpretations of legal analogy, of the kind that one can find in the arguments of Professor Postema's opponents, like Posner and Dworkin. On the first objection, Postema's interlocutors are not interested in reconstructing how one thinks about the law but rather the argument or justification that they can offer, that is, the cogency of the claims lawyers and judges offer in support of their view when they resort to a legal analogy. On the second objection, in turn, Shecaira argues that Professor Postema's criticism against argumentation scholars fails because it cannot be generalised, for if it were to work against analogical reasoning it would have to work also against any kind of argumentation analysis and informal logic. According to Shecaira, these objections imply that Professor Postema's criticisms do not hit their target.

Part IV of the book discusses, in more depth than this introduction, some further aspects of Professor Postema's methodological claims about the nature of jurisprudence, understood as a sociable science. In chapter 9, by Margaret Martin, Professor Postema's idea that jurisprudence must be understood as practical philosophy is revisited to provide a reinterpretation of Hartian jurisprudence and rescue it from the assumption of value neutrality. For Martin, as for Postema, Hart failed to establish that legal theory can provide a sociological description of law from an external and uncommitted point of view. One of the reasons of Hart's failure to provide an explanation of the normativity of law is the absence of a distinction between different approaches or points of view that can equally be regarded as 'internal' or 'external', in Hart's sense. One of these distinctions is between two agents who might adopt what Hart would describe as an 'external' point of view with regard to the law: the Holmesian 'bad man', who only acts on the basis of a prudential assessment of the consequences that he believes will arise if he follows a law, and the victim of an extremely unjust

[95] Postema (n 47) 121.

legal system. Hart assumes in *The Concept of Law* that the bad man's failure to internalise the law is problematic because there are sound moral reasons to comply with it, so he does not respond to the law appropriately; and he (Hart) resorts to a similar argument, in chapter 9 of his seminal book, when he discusses the law's impact on the victims. The victim cannot have reasons to follow the law because '[t]he law reaches [her], as Postema perceptively notes, in the form of arbitrary power'.[96] According to Martin, Hart's argument seems to be based on a series of moral judgements. Jurisprudence is a practical philosophy, rather than a purely descriptive or conceptual project.

In chapter 10, Dan Priel produces an insightful discussion of the details of Professor Postema's contribution to the intrinsic relevance of time in jurisprudence. For Professor Postema, law, like practical reason in general, has constitutive temporal aspects; it is part of its nature that it not only exists in time, but also exists as an ordering of time. We should avoid, therefore, the idea that jurisprudence can provide an account of the 'nature' of law beyond time and place, as has been fashionable in analytical legal theory. Priel analyses the relevance of time in jurisprudence on three levels: first, law and jurisprudence exist in time, and have a history; second, at least in common law systems, precedent ties present law to its past; and, third, at the most general level, law's authority cannot be understood independently from time. Priel takes a step beyond what Professor Postema has argued in his account of sociable jurisprudence, however, when he submits that these views should fit within a *naturalistic* approach to jurisprudence, to which he subscribes.

Chapter 11, by Saulo de Matos, comes back to the debate between Dworkin and Professor Postema, to discuss their jurisprudential methodologies. Matos believes that Professor Postema's 'sociable jurisprudence' is in the same neighbourhood as Dworkin's 'law as integrity', since they both present plausible objections to analytic jurisprudence. Both can fit easily into the description of a synechist approach to legal theory, for neither subscribes to an essentialist methodology and both are more interested in explaining how the law works or directs our action than excavating necessary properties. Dworkin's well-known comparison between law and literature, for instance, would be a typical application of the Peirce-inspired synechist methodology that Professor Postema defends. The difference that remains between Postema and Dworkin, for the author, is that the former is primarily focused on a sociological or empirical analysis of the concept of law, whereas the latter is primarily concerned with an account of correct or justified assertions about the content of the law.

Part V of the book considers the dialogues between Professor Postema and other contemporary perspectives on jurisprudence. Chapter 12, by Andrea Faggion, presents a response to Professor Postema's objections to HLA Hart's

[96] M Martin, 'Postema on Hart: The Illusion of Value-Neutrality', ch 9 of this volume.

explanation of the normativity of law. She chooses, however, a path that is different from that adopted in this introduction. After describing Professor Postema's early works on social conventions and the foundations of law, on the one hand, and Postema's later works that criticise Hart's views on normativity and advocate a moralised account of practical reasoning and the normativity of law, Faggion argues that the former provide a more robust account of law and legal reasoning, which should not have been abandoned by Professor Postema. She claims, in a nutshell, that law gives reasons for official action but not necessarily for the ordinary citizens and people in general. A narrow account or legal normativity is considered preferable and more likely to provide a plausible jurisprudence.

In chapter 13, finally, Noel Struchiner and Guilherme Almeida revisit the debate between Professor Postema and Frederick Schauer, as well as the objection that the latter fails to establish, in his seminal work *Playing by the Rules*, a stable criterion to differentiate between a 'particularism sensitive to rules' and a mitigated formalism (or 'presumptive positivism'). In his comments on Schauer, Professor Postema claimed that these two positions are 'extensionally equivalent' and lack a psychological difference. To respond to this challenge, the authors revisit recent developments in psychological theory to attack both claims.

The final chapter of the book, chapter 14, contains an interview with Professor Postema conducted by Thomas Bustamante, César Serbena and Natalina Stamile, which offers not only a bird's eye view of the developments of his philosophy of law, but also an account of the most important influences in his career, his views on law, history, professional practice and philosophy, his general assessment of the state of art and a prospect for the future of jurisprudence.

As editors of the book, we are very much indebted to Professor Postema for his generous engagement with the authors and his willingness to listen and to respond to the chapters, and especially the editors' doubts and considerations about his work. We hope that this book will generate even more interest in Professor Postema's brilliant contribution to philosophy and law.

Part I

On the Value of the Rule of Law

1

Fidelity, Accountability and Trust
Tensions at the Heart of the Rule of Law

GERALD J POSTEMA

THE NEOPLATONIST, IAMBLICHUS, included in his own *Exhortation to Philosophy* a long passage from a work by an early Sophist whom we know only as 'Anonymous Iamblichus'. Writing in perhaps the fourth century BCE, the author announces a thesis linking three notions on which this essay will focus. Our anonymous Sophist wrote that since human beings by a necessity of nature must live together, and since living together in a condition of lawlessness (*anomia*) is even worse than living alone, necessity drove them to '*make law their king*'. And he added, 'The first result of lawfulness [*eunomia*] is trust'.[1]

Our author tied together three notions – law, fidelity to law, and trust. If we add *accountability* to the three we have a family of notions from which springs a robust and attractive understanding of the rule of law. Or so I have argued. However, like all families, this one is not without its tensions. It is especially on the alleged tension between accountability and trust that I invite your attention. A few years ago, the Cambridge philosopher, Onora O'Neill, expressed deep concern that the 'culture of accountability' that she saw rapidly growing in Britain had spawned a 'culture of suspicion'.[2] Accountability, she feared, drives out trust; for the demand for accountability stems from distrust, and distrust corrodes community. But then if accountability is at the heart of *eunomia* and distrust is the condition and consequence of accountability, we must conclude

[1] Anonymous Iamblichus, in M Gagarin and P Woodruff (eds), *Early Greek Political Thought from Homer to the Sophists* (Cambridge University Press 1995) 293, 294. Russell Hardin brought this passage to my attention. See R Hardin, 'Trust in Government' in V Braithwaite and M Levi (eds), *Trust and Governance* (Russell Sage Foundation 1998) 9.

[2] O O'Neill, *A Question of Trust* (Cambridge University Press 2000) chs 1–2.

that our anonymous Sophist has led us astray. We should not look to law and its ethos of accountability to hold human communities together, or even to underwrite a robust programme of controlling the exercise of ruling power. I will call this the 'trust challenge'.

If the trust challenge is sound, the rule of law looks to be self-defeating, at least on the understanding of the rule of law that I have sought to defend in recent years.[3] I propose to answer this challenge, but first I will take some time to articulate and motivate the understanding of the ideal of the rule of law that it appears to threaten.

I. RULE OF LAW: THE CORE IDEA

The passage from the anonymous Sophist we began with invokes a line of argument for law that is familiar, especially in the work of philosophers of the modern era, from Hobbes onward. It begins with the observation that human beings, because they are innately social, or because they are unable to supply their needs on their own, or just because they are thrown together, must find some way to live together. But living together puts them in competition and makes them vulnerable to the power of others. Their conflicts may be interest-driven (as Hobbes argues) or principle-driven (as Locke and Kant argue), but in either case they find themselves subject to the arbitrary will of others. So, it is argued, order must be established, conflict defused and protection against the arbitrary exercise of power secured. A system of authority, of political rule, must be established that is powerful enough to protect liberties, minimise violations of interests and lift the yoke of subjection to others. But as our Sophist, along with Hobbes, Locke, Kant and hosts of others have argued, political rule must be exercised *through law*. Liberties and rights must be defined, articulated and secured; conflicts of principle must be adjudicated, not merely silenced; conflicts of interest must be resolved by appeal to established, common norms, not overwhelmed by power.

This suggests the core idea of the rule of law: *when law rules, it provides protection and recourse against the arbitrary exercise of power through the distinctive instrumentalities, powers and practices of – law*. The thought is that a polity is well-ordered when its members are secured against the arbitrary exercise of power, and that law, because of its distinctive features, is especially if not

[3] See GJ Postema, 'Law's Rule: Reflexivity, Mutual Accountability, and the Rule of Law' in Xiaobo Zhai and M Quinn (eds), *Bentham's Theory of Law and Public Opinion* (Cambridge University Press 2014) 7; and GJ Postema, 'Fidelity in Law's Commonwealth' in D Klimchuk (ed), *Private Law and the Rule of Law* (Oxford University Press 2014) 17. *Note*: an expanded version of the present essay, entitled 'Trust, Distrust, and the Rule of Law', is published in PB Miller and M Harding (eds), *Fiduciaries and Trust: Ethics, Politics, Economics and Law* (Cambridge University Press, 2020).

uniquely capable of providing such security. This notion has a distinctive structure. The *organising aim* of the rule of law is control of the exercise of power; the *means* of doing so is the law. Law seeks to constrain the arbitrary exercise of power in advance (protection) and to hold accountable those who exercise power and provide remedies to victims of power exceeding law's limits (recourse). Note five salient features of this notion.

First, the rule of law is a normative ideal, a principle of political morality. It makes demands on, and provides a standard for evaluation of, political communities, their governing structures and associated legal orders. It can be honoured or realised to a greater or lesser extent in a given political community. Moreover, it is a distinctive principle; it is not reducible to democracy, justice or some other dimension of political morality, but it may relate to them in important ways. As a middle-level principle of political morality, it serves deeper values or principles, although which values it is meant to serves is often debated.

Second, it focuses on the exercise of *power* in a polity.[4] The ideal of the rule of law is not simply an ideal *for* institutions of law, as some have argued,[5] holding them to a standard of performance as justice does; rather it makes demands on the structures, practices, means and wielders of power. It demands that they submit to the discipline of law. Such power can take different forms – it can be *political*, wielded by government over the governed, or (broadly speaking) *social* (including economic), wielded by individual or corporate members of the community over other members. Employers' power over workers is well-recognised,[6] but even at a more interpersonal level, arbitrary exercises of power are familiar. Thus, the rule of law advocates both a *mode of governance*, of ordering the exercise of political power, and a *mode of association*, a distinctive way in which members of a polity regard, recognise and relate to each other.

Third, the kind of power that is the focal concern of the rule of law involves the exercise of one agent's will over the will of another. Such power may be coercive, but it need not be; one can be in the power, under the *dominion*, of another in a way that can decisively shape one's choices and actions, without the active intervention of the *dominus*.[7] Moreover, being subject to the power of another

[4] See M Krygier, 'Inside the Rule of Law' (2014) 1 *Rivista de Fiolsofia del Diritto* 77–98.

[5] G Palombella, 'The Rule of Law as an Institutional Ideal' in L Morlino and G Palombella (eds), *Rule of Law and Democracy* (Brill 2010) 3; J Raz, 'The Rule of Law and Its Virtue' in J Raz, *The Authority of Law* (Oxford University Press 1979) 210.

[6] E Anderson, *Private Government: How Employers Rule Our Lives (and Why We Don't Talk about It* (Princeton University Press 2017) xix–xx, 37–41, discusses the many ways employers exercise arbitrary power over their workers. At-will employment, for example, gives employers control over workers' lives at work and off-duty. 'Under the employment-at-will baseline, workers, in effect, cede all of their rights to their employers, except those specifically guaranteed to them by law, for the duration of the employment relationship. Employers' authority over workers, outside of collective bargaining and a few other contexts, … is sweeping, arbitrary, and unaccountable – not subject to notice, process, or appeal' (ibid 53–54).

[7] See, eg, P Pettit, *A Theory of Freedom* (Polity Press 2001) 78, 137; P Pettit, *On the People's Terms* (Cambridge University Press 2012) 1–3, 7.

is not like being subject to the force of gravity or to threats from a menacing animal. Or, more precisely, it is directly or indirectly a matter of the decisions, choices and actions of responsible agents *with respect to* other agents. Power is the manifest capacity embedded in the relationship that makes this impact possible. Exercising and responding to power are ways persons relate to each other, even if at a distance; power relations are in this interpersonal, not merely objective, impersonal relations.[8]

Fourth, the rule of law sets its face against 'arbitrary' power and its exercise. An exercise of power is arbitrary in the sense relevant to the rule of law when it is the expression of the *liberum arbitrium*, the free, unilateral decision or choice of its agent.[9] The act may be reasonable, reasoned or otherwise justified, but it is still arbitrary if it is taken entirely at the will or pleasure of the agent. Actions that may be assessable in the abstract in light of relevant norms or standards, may still be arbitrary in the sense relevant here if the agent is not answerable *to someone* for them. Arbitrary power is unilateral power. The relationship between the wielder of power and his object makes the former's perspective the only practically relevant perspective on his action. He answers only to his own *arbitrium*. Like Zeus, according to Aeschylus, he 'sends accounts to no one's audit for the deeds he does'.[10] Arbitrary power is not necessarily unreasoned, or unpredictable, or even in a strict sense unruly; rather, it is unaccountable, exercised strictly at the pleasure of its agent. Moreover, because the agent need only attend to his own perspective, the deliberative element in action is emptied of significance as far as his victim is concerned. From the victim's point of view, there is no difference between the power wielder's deliberative perspective and his mere whim; reasoned judgment and mere whim are indistinguishable to the victim.

Discretion is not necessarily arbitrary. Discretion necessarily involves the exercise of judgment. It may also be unguided by norms, and those who exercise it may not be accountable. Yet those two further features, contrary to common opinion, are not essential to discretion. Discretionary judgment may be governed by standards or norms, even if they cannot be expected to generate certain or univocal decisions. The proper exercise of judgment, even if to a degree discretionary, is not necessarily arbitrary, if its deliberative character – its subordination to reasons – is communicated to those affected by the judgment,

[8] This point is not intended to deny, but rather to make room for, the possibility of such power's taking a systemic character, such that no particular individual exercises it over some other particular individual. Thus, it is meant to encompass economic power of those who command wealth and capital over those who have only their labour, even though that power is mediated by what appears to be an impersonal market.

[9] 'An act is perpetrated on an arbitrary basis … if it is subject just to the *arbitrium*, the decision or judgment of the agent; the agent was in a position to choose it or not choose it, at their pleasure': P Pettit, *Republicanism: A Theory of Freedom and Government* (Oxford University Press 1997) 55.

[10] Aeschylus, *Prometheus Bound* in *Aeschylus I*, tr D Grene, eds D Grene and R Lattimore (University of Chicago Press 2013) l. 325.

and those reasons can be brought to bear in assessing the judgment and actions taken under it, by those to whom the agent is accountable. Discretion is arbitrary only if its exercise is not liable to be called to account; only if reasons of an appropriate kind for the exercise of the power can be demanded of those exercising it, especially by those over whom the power is exercised. Some degree of practical judgment is involved in following any norm or rule; arbitrariness of judgment is not.

This brings us to the final salient feature of the rule of law ideal: it insists that the exercise of power be subject to *the distinctive instrumentalities, powers and practices – of law*. The ideal of the rule of law, I have said, is not an ideal *for* institutions, but it does take law and legal institutions as the major instruments in its campaign for control of abuse of power. Law not only mobilises power; it also disciplines judgment and subordinates the power to deliberative forces of law. Aristotle wrote that 'he who bids the law rule … bid[s] … reason alone rule'.[11] Echoing Aristotle, US Supreme Court Justice Brandeis once wrote, 'we look to law to help govern ourselves because we want deliberative forces to prevail over arbitrary ones'.[12] Law is a distinctively *discursive* practice. The quotidian business of the law is the business of making judgments and offering reasons and arguments for and against them. And its characteristic activities take shape through reflective, deliberative articulations of them. The moves in this game are characteristically argumentative, and the discipline mastery of which is necessary for competence in the practice is a certain *discipline of argument*. It is not only through defining its imperatives in rules, but also through its public, discursive aspect, the disciplined practice of public reason that it offers, that law marshals deliberative forces against arbitrary ones.

This thought brings us some distance from Hobbes's argument for the necessity of political rule through law and back to our anonymous Sophist. For in the hands of the Hobbesian sovereign, law is only a *tool* of vertical power. Law rules through subjection of subjects to sovereign power ruling *per leges*. But this does not solve the problem of subjection to the arbitrary will of others; it just shifts the locus of that power. However, the anonymous Sophist argued that *law* is king. The rule of law insists that those who exercise ruling power must themselves be subject to law; it insists not only that they rule *per leges*, but also that their governing be *sub lege*. Johannes Althusius, in the early seventeenth century, put the core idea of the rule of law this way: 'What God is in the world, the navigator in a ship, the driver in a chariot, the director in a chorus, the commander in an army, so *lex* is in the city.'[13] It is superior above all.

The rule of law is all about ruling – the *law's* ruling. Law rules when the interactions among citizens are governed by a law common to them all, where

[11] Aristotle, *Politics*, bk III, ch 16.
[12] *Whitney v California*, 274 US 357, at 375 (Brandeis, J, concurring).
[13] J Althusius, *Politica* (Frederick S Carney, abridged trans, Liberty Fund 1995) X.8 at 82.

exercises of power in the civic domain are held to account under that law. But, equally importantly, law rules when those who hold others to account with respect to that law are themselves governed by it and thereunto held to account. To Juvenal's ancient question *sed quis custodiet ipsos custodies* – who guards the guardians?[14] – the ancient answer, and that of Althusius, was: *the law*. The rule of law ideal holds with Plato, against Hobbes, that law 'is despot over rulers and rulers are slaves of the law'.[15] On this ancient view, the rule of law obtains in a polity just when *law rules* those who purport to rule with law. That is, in a properly ordered polity, *law alone is sovereign*.

A. Fidelity Thesis

This, surely, is a bold claim; no less bold for being of ancient vintage. But of comparable vintage and no less plausibility is the thought that laws do not – indeed, laws *cannot* – rule, that only *people* rule. So, if we are to understand the ideal of the rule of law, and give proper respect for the demands it places on our political communities, we need to take very seriously the question: *how*, if at all, *can* law rule?

Historically, to secure law's ruling, defenders of the rule of law have adopted a strategy with two closely complementary components, although contemporary discussions have focused almost exclusively on just one of them. They devised formal institutions – a structure of clearly articulated, publicly promulgated, prospective general norms and a system of constitutional checks and balances – and they sought to model, encourage and nourish an *ethos* of shared commitments and responsibilities. *Legality* – the system of established rules and institutional checks and balances – was to be underwritten by *fidelity*. Legality was thought to be essential if law's ruling was to be secured, but it could not be sufficient. Formally articulated and fixed rules and counterbalancing institutions cannot eliminate the need for discretion. But discretion, even if guided by law, must be held accountable to the law. Room must be made for a structure of accountability. But to avoid the Hobbesian spectre of a sovereign above the law, an unaccountable accountability holder, this structure must not be hierarchical. It must be reciprocal; a network of accountability rather than a chain of subordination and super ordination. Moreover, if law is to be sovereign, and no one is to be subjected to the arbitrary will of another, then each must be the guardian of each. Moreover, the 'office' of guardian must be open to all, not only to those to whom ruling power has been entrusted. *Ubi ius ibi forum* – wherever there is

[14] Juvenal, *Satires* VI, 347–48.

[15] Plato, *Laws*, bk IV, 715d. Richard Hooker, late in the 16th century, wrote, 'the power of the King … [is so] limited that unto all his proceedings the law itself is a rule': R Hooker, *Of the Laws of Ecclesiastical Polity*, ed AS McGrade (Cambridge University Press 1989) VIII.3.3.

law, and hence agents subject to the law's guidance and governance, there must be a formal or informal forum in which those bound by that law can be held accountable.

This leads us to a fundamental thesis of the rule of law – I call it the *fidelity thesis*:

> Law rules in a political community when its members, official and lay members alike, take responsibility for holding each other accountable under the law.

While the focus of legality is formal and institutional, the focus of fidelity is ethical. It is concerned with the *ethos* of a polity, the mutual understandings and associated practices of a people in a community in which the rule of law is realised. It is an *ethos* in the sense that it consists of practices and relationships embedded in the community. But it is an *ethos*, also, in the sense that these practices have a robust ethical dimension. To clarify this notion of fidelity, we can begin with the Harvard legal theorist Lon Fuller's argument for the moral character of his eight canons of legality.[16] He argued that the rule of law presupposes and nurtures a kind of interdependence and partnership that comprises a set of reciprocal commitments, between government and citizens. Rulers pledge to rule with and to be ruled by law, and citizens, in turn, guide their conduct by and allow it to be judged by the laws that the rulers who govern under this pledge administer. Fuller's idea of fidelity is that of reciprocal compliance with the law.

Drawing on comments of the Scottish Enlightenment writer, Adam Ferguson, we can extend Fuller's idea. Ferguson observed that law's capacity to rule lies in

> the influence of men resolved to be free; of men, who, having adjusted in writing the terms on which they are to live with the state, and with their fellow-subjects, are determined, by their vigilance and spirit, to make these terms be observed.[17]

Only if this vigilance is pursued with 'a spirit [of] … refractory and turbulent zeal,' Ferguson argued, can the effects of the rule of law be secured.[18] Taking our cue from Ferguson, we might say that fidelity is expressed not only in compliance with law and the standards of legality, but also in active taking of responsibility for law's rule. In particular, it involves taking responsibility for holding partners in the relationship to their respective duties, each taking responsibility for other members' exercise of responsibility. Fidelity involves mutual accountability as well as reciprocal compliance. The fidelity thesis implies that to submit to law's rule, which all who exercise power are bound to do, is to submit to and participate in a network of mutual accountability.

[16] L Fuller, *The Morality of Law* (2nd edn Yale University Press 1969). For a reconstruction of Fuller's argument, see GJ Postema, *Legal Philosophy in the Twentieth Century: The Common Law World* (Springer 2011) 153–58.

[17] A Ferguson, *An Essay on the History of Civil Society* (1767), ed Fania Oz-Salzberger (Cambridge University Press 1995) 249.

[18] ibid 160.

Thus, we must think of the rule of law not (merely) as a set of standards for law-making, law-applying and law-enforcing, but also as an ordering of relationships by mutual commitment to a shared and common law, and reciprocal responsibilities with respect to it. Primary among these responsibilities is the mutual responsibility to hold each other accountable under this law. The fidelity thesis holds that the rule of law is robust in a polity when its members, and not merely the legal or ruling elite, take responsibility for holding each other accountable under the law. These commitments hold not only 'vertically', as it were, between the people and the government, but also 'horizontally', among members of the community.

The ideal of the rule of law, then, advocates not only a distinctive *mode of governance*, but equally a *mode of association* – a distinctive social formation, a way in which members of a polity regard, recognise and relate to each other. Law, on this view, not only rules rulers, it also binds the ruled together in a distinctive way. 'What is the *civitas* but a partnership according to *ius*?' wrote Cicero.[19] Johannes Althusius, in the early seventeenth century, gave eloquent expression to this ideal at the opening of his *Politica*. The polity, he wrote, is an 'association of *symbiotes*', participants in a common life who pledge to communicate (share) among themselves what is useful and necessary for their life together, especially *ius*, law.[20] Law is not imposed on these partners; the common rights and responsibilities defined by law are not simply *allocated to* them; neither are they *exchanged between* them as by negotiated bargain. Rather, they are shared amongst and *entrusted to* each other. This sharing involves not only respect for the rights of each other, but also mutual responsibility for holding each other to this common law. Exercising this mutual responsibility for holding each other accountable is one way in which the common bond is expressed, honoured and strengthened, each entrusting their treasures and their responsibilities to each other.

B. Accountability and Trust

This brings us to the third key idea I proposed to explore – trust – and the challenge we encountered at the outset of our discussion. Recall that our anonymous Sophist ventured the thesis that 'The first result of lawfulness [*eunomia*] is trust.' We might say even more strongly that fidelity not only underwrites but also depends on trust. Sociologists who have studied the phenomenon of 'social capital' have argued that trust is a condition of effective government. We might add that trust appears to be at the centre of the fidelity, law's ethos. Fidelity in

[19] '*Quid est enim civitas nisi iuris societas?*': Cicero, *On the Republic*, I.32.49.
[20] Althusius, *Politica*, I, §§1–10, 17–19.

the horizontal or civic dimension depends on a mutual sharing of standing to hold accountable, a standing that involves entrusting to each other the authority to call each other to account. And fidelity in the vertical or political dimension, which involves, inter alia, people holding those who exercise political power accountable to the law that governs that exercise, depends on the combined efforts of the people, and those efforts can be effective only if individual citizens can trust others to join them in the effort.

It is striking that defenders of authoritarian rule, who resolutely reject law's sovereignty, *also* relied on trust at crucial points in their arguments. For example, seventeenth-century defenders of unlimited sovereign prerogatives argued that to restrict sovereign power legally in hopes of eliminating the risk of oppression is futile, indeed irrational. Absolute security, they argued, is impossible. Protection against abuse of power entails *entrusting* that responsibility of protecting to someone or something. Trust is unavoidable and indispensable. Others argued, similarly, that we can protect ourselves from the arbitrary exercise of power by subjecting those who wield that power to authority, but those with such authority must themselves be held accountable by some further authority. But this chain of authority, they argued, must stop somewhere, with someone or some institution with power that cannot be held accountable. At that point, all we can do is *trust* that the power will be exercised responsibly. The question, they argued, is not *whether* to trust someone with final and unaccountable power, but only *where* that power will be located. At some point, eventually, we must abandon accountability – and fall back on trust.

According to this line of thought, trust is directly opposed to accountability. Trust comes into play when all our devices for holding power accountable, devices allegedly expressive of distrust, run out. It is ironic that defenders of the rule of law, and liberal constitutionalism, have rejected these absolutist arguments but have embraced the key premise on which they rest. They insisted that institutions and structures of government, and devices of popular control and accountability, are able to limit sovereign power, but they concede that they do so motivated by a deep and abiding distrust in all who exercise power. This attitude is familiar in the modern history of constitutional theory. The United States Constitution, it is often said, was founded on a principle of distrust of factions and concentrated power.[21] The elaborate structures of checks and balances pitting one institution against and limiting the power of others was meant to reduce the risk of abuse of power. Distrust, it is said, was the driving motive behind their construction and the manifest message of their operation.

The *locus classicus* of this view can be found in Hume's essay, 'Of the Independency of Parliament'. 'Political writers have established it as a maxim,'

[21] See, eg, R Hardin, 'Liberal Distrust' (2002) 10 *European Review* 73.

Hume observed, 'that, in contriving any system of government, and fixing the several checks and controuls of the constitution, every man ought to be supposed to be a *knave*, and to have no other end, in all his actions, than private interest'.[22] Bentham, too, although no friend of constitutional checks and legal limits on the exercise of political power, argued vigorously that the best 'security against misrule' is vigorous criticism by what he called the Public Opinion Tribunal. Indeed, he argued that a free government should enable, encourage and 'cherish' popular resistance to governmental exercise of power.[23] Does this not make the system of 'public responsibility' nothing more than 'a system of *distrust*?', Bentham asked. Yes, indeed, he replied, and for good reason; for 'whom ought we to distrust, if not those to whom is committed great authority, with great temptations to abuse it?'[24] Thus, Onora O'Neill's association of accountability with distrust and suspicion follows in a long tradition, including the rule of law's most ardent defenders and its most resolute critics.

This, then, brings us face to face with the challenge we encountered at the outset. Trust is thought to be a key ingredient in effective governance as well as the glue that keeps together and makes effective efforts at holding power accountable. Yet on the fidelity thesis, a key means of protecting against the arbitrary exercise of power is to subject such exercises to full public scrutiny and robust accountability, accountability that extends in horizontal (civic) as well as vertical (political) dimensions. And, we are told, accountability thrives on distrust and drives out trust. This tension, so the challenge goes, lies at the heart of accountability. Accountability depends on trust and yet drives it out. This is the *trust challenge*.

There are several ways to test and respond to this challenge. One would be to challenge the empirical assumption that that trust is essential to effective government and effective protection against the arbitrary exercise of power. However, I propose to look more closely at the models of accountability and modes of trust relied on by the fidelity thesis to determine whether the challenge is properly directed against it. First, consider the kind of accountability that figures in the fidelity thesis.

[22] D Hume, 'Of the Independency of Parliament' in *Essays Moral, Political and Literary*, ed EF Miller (Liberty Classics 1985) 42, 42–43.

[23] J Bentham, 'On the Liberty of the Press and Public Discussion' in J Bentham, *Works*, ed J Bowring (Edinburgh 1838–43) ii, 287. For Bentham's view of the role of the Public Opinion Tribunal in securing against abuse of power (achieving 'security against misrule'), see GJ Postema, 'The Soul of Justice: Bentham on Publicity, Law and the Rule of Law' in Xiaobo Zhai and Quinn (eds) (n 3) 40, esp 47–55; and GJ Postema, 'Bentham: Theorist of Publicity' in G Gaus and P Turner (eds), *Public Reason in the History of Political Philosophy: Classical Sources and Contemporary Commentaries* (Routledge 2017) 354, 368–71.

[24] J Bentham, *Political Tactics* (*Collected Works*), eds M James, C Blamires and C Pease-Watkin (Clarendon Press 1999) 37.

II. ACCOUNTABILITY FIT FOR THE RULE OF LAW

The concept of accountability embraces many different phenomena that offer us a range of models of accountability. I propose to sketch a model of the kind of accountability fit for the rule of law: a practice that holds some promise for providing protection and recourse against the arbitrary exercise of power in a way that draws on distinctive practices and instrumentalities of the law.

For this purpose, we can understand accountability holding as an *normatively structured, discursive activity*. Accountability can be represented as an interpersonal activity:

> Two parties – an accountability Holder and an account Giver – engaged in an asymmetrical relationship with respect to a Domain of Giver's activity. Holder calls on Giver to provide, in a setting not of his choosing,[25] an Account of Giver's activity in the Domain and the Holder offers an Assessment of the Account given.

The relationship is *discursive* in that:

> The Account makes public (at least to Holder) the activities of Giver in the Domain and explains or justifies them; and Holder's Assessment evaluates Giver's actions in light of the reasons Giver offers for them.

The relationship is *normatively structured* in that:

> Holder has the normative power to call for the Account from Giver (possibly, but not necessarily, backed by some ability to compel it) and Giver is normatively liable to be called, and owes an obligation to Holder, to provide the Account to Holder.
>
> A set of norms defines the powers, claims, and obligations of the accountability relationship, structures the Domain of Giver's activities, and consequently structures Giver's Account and Holder's Assessment.
>
> Thus, Holder's activity, as well as Giver's, is subject to the norms of the relationship and Holder is liable to be held accountable for that activity by Giver or some other party in the accountability network in which Giver and Holder participate.

Accountability fit for the rule of law fills out this sketch. On this model, accountability (i) is a *public* activity; that is, the account is given *in* public, regarding public matters, and given to officers of the public or to the public generally (usually through the mediation of civic associations, organisations or institutions). Moreover, (ii) the norms defining the relationship and the Domain of Giver's activity are the *laws* of the political community. (iii) The discursive,

[25] J Waldron, *Political Political Theory* (Harvard University Press 2016) 169.

reason-giving activity is governed and given content by the *deliberative discipline* of law. (iv) Individual instances of accountability holding, on this model, take place within a network of mutual accountability practices. Each party subject to law submits to and participates in a network of mutual accountability. While each occasion of accountability holding is asymmetrical between Holder and Giver, on other occasions Holder is liable to give an account to some other Holder, perhaps for his calling the initial Giver to account. And these connections form a network, rather than a hierarchical chain. (v) Sanctions or enforcement are not in the foreground of this model of accountability. Holder's power to call Giver to account is normative, not physical. Giver's obligation to provide the account is typically backed by some means of compelling it; however, it is not necessary to this model that there be some means of enforcing Holder's judgment, other than issuing the judgment itself.[26]

There is nothing defective or incomplete about an accountability mechanism that does not build in sanctions to enforce the judgments of accountability holders. When such sanctions are available, they may hover in the background of the practice.[27] It is important that we do not equate subjection to the judgment of another with liability to suffer punishment at Holder's hand. Sanctions are adventitious relative to the activity of demanding and assessing an account. They are additional, external incentives to encourage or compel compliance. (And whether there are good reasons to add them is not settled by the normative structure of accountability alone.) The requirement to provide reasons for the exercise of power appeals to common norms of law and to the presumed commitment Giver and Holder make to these norms. This appeal is effective when Holder's judgment engages Giver's integrity, or at least Giver's concern for Holder's esteem or good offices (or those of the public), which are tied to Giver's presumed commitment to law. Giver may find Holder's adverse and public judgment painful and unwelcome, but that is because Giver takes seriously her commitment to the law and Holder's judgment implicates this commitment.[28]

We can contrast this model of accountability holding fit for the rule of law with other activities that are often regarded as modes of accountability holding. A limiting case would be exercises of power, or threats of them, intended to give a person an external incentive to act in certain ways. Exercises of market power on business enterprises – boycotts or public protests, and the like – are examples. So too are exercises of coercive power, for example by police, where the primary or sole aim is compliance with some norm. Liability to be called to account, we have seen, is not the same as liability to suffer sanctions. Accountability that focuses solely on providing external incentives (especially coercive incentives)

[26] See M Philp, 'Delimiting Democratic Autonomy' (2009) 57 *Political Studies* 34.

[27] See J Braithwaite, 'Institutionalizing Distrust, Enculturating Trust' in Braithwaite and Levi (eds) (n 1) 355.

[28] For a general discussion of such appeals to esteem, see P Pettit and G Brennan, *The Economy of Esteem* (Oxford University Press 2004).

for compliance leaves out of the picture the crucial discursive element of law and threatens to undermine a potentially powerful source of motivation for adherence to the law. It fails to appreciate and make use of the full range of the instrumentalities of the law. The incentives involved in rule of law accountability are, at least in an important respect, internal to the norms to which parties are held accountable, or to mutual commitments comprising fidelity.

Market power and police power, then, are limiting cases of accountability holding for purposes of understanding the rule of law. So too are bureaucratic forms of accountability holding, at least when these forms are limited to reporting and monitoring the activities in a hierarchical structure. 'Managerial accountability,' Onora O'Neill observed, controls performance by setting targets and measuring success or failure in terms of meeting these targets, or, more often, rough (but clear and 'objective') proxies for success or failure, and sanctioning failure and rewarding success.[29] These methods typically are imposed, top-down, leave little room for individual judgment or expert discretion, and rarely give those subject to them opportunities to defend their actions by reference to the general norms. There need be no opportunity for discursive interaction between Giver and Holder.

Moreover, often, bureaucratic norms are not fully public; they are in-house norms determined by the mission of the bureaucratic organisation. One finds this deficiency also in Principal–Agent forms of accountability.[30] In this form of accountability, although the Domain of the agent's activities is structured by norms, the norms are determined by the principal (perhaps within a larger legal framework of the relationship), and the agent's account is owed to the principal just because the agent is doing the principal's business. Moreover, the activity of holding accountable on the Principal–Agent model is hierarchical; reciprocity is not a key element. Partnerships offer a closer analogy to rule of law accountability, since the local asymmetry of any given activity of holding accountable is balanced by reciprocity. The parties are in a non-hierarchical relationship; A's holding B accountable on one occasion may be followed by B's holding A accountable on another. Also, in Partnership relations, sanctions are unlikely to figure in the foreground of the practice. (Dissolution of the partnership will only play a role in the background.) However, the norms of Partnership are not fully public, as they must be in the rule of law model. From this swift survey, we can see that accountability fit for the rule of law is a distinctive kind of accountability, reflecting distinctive features of law and the aims and values of fidelity.

[29] O O'Neill, 'Trust, Trustworthiness, and Accountability' in N Morris and D Vines (eds), *Capital Failure: Rebuilding Trust in Financial Services* (Oxford University Press 2014) 174. O'Neill calls managerial accountability 'unintelligent accountability'. She advocates a more 'intelligent' form of accountability rather than abandoning accountability altogether.

[30] See Jeremy Waldron's discussion of the principal–agent model in Waldron (n 25) ch 8.

III. TRUST AND DISTRUST: INTERPERSONAL DIMENSION

To assess the trust challenge, we also need a nuanced understanding of trust and its complements. Three preliminary points will help to orient our exploration. First, the fidelity thesis maintains that the rule of law is robust in a political community when accountability is vital in both political (vertical) and civic (horizontal) dimensions of community life. The trust challenge concerns the effect of widespread practices of accountability on *political trust* and on *civic trust*. To assess the challenge, we need to understand better these forms of trust. Philosophical discussions of trust in recent years have focused largely on trust in thick, multi-dimensional, interpersonal relations. I, too, will begin with this paradigm, but I will adjust this understanding to accommodate political and civic trust, which arise in relationships that are less personal, thinner, often unidimensional. Interactions among parties to these relationships typically occur at a distance and tend to be mediated by institutions. Political and civic trust is likely to be impersonal in two ways: the relationships in which it figures are not close interpersonal ones, and the party trusted may not be a person at all but rather an institution (and its officials, indirectly) or group of 'unassignable persons'.

Second, we will find it useful to distinguish *trusting* from *entrusting*. Trusting is a *stance* involving a kind of attitude and a disposition that a person takes towards another person, for certain reasons. Trusting person B, A may entrust to B's care something of value to A. Entrusting is a mode of conduct with a communicative dimension – it involves actions that take on meaning for the parties, signalling or enacting the trust. It is possible for a person to *entrust* something of value to another without fully *trusting* that person. (Presently, I will discuss what I call 'proleptic trust'.) In that case, one party *communicates* trust to the other party, but strictly speaking her *trust* is not expressed, because she does not (fully) have such trust, yet. This is possible, because trusting conduct – entrusting – draws on certain public meanings, meanings available in the environment of the parties involved.

The final preliminary point is that although trust and distrust are mutually exclusive, they are not exhaustive of what we might call the trust domain.[31] To *lack* trust is not, necessarily, to *distrust*. Trust and its complement form a spectrum, with full-fledged trust at one end and full distrust at the other, but some interactions among people may not be trust-relevant at all. They fall outside the trust spectrum.

[31] E Ullmann-Margalit, 'Trust, Distrust, and In Between' in R Hardin (ed), *Distrust* (Russell Sage Foundation 2004) 60; PT Lenard, *Trust, Democracy, and Multicultural Challenges* (University of Pennsylvania Press 2012) ch 3.

A. Interpersonal Trust: The Trust Paradigm

Many who have studied trust hold that trust involves a three-place relation: A trusts B to do something in which A has an interest, or involves something that A values. The act of B on which A relies may be quite specific, or it may be understood by both parties to be rather more generic, according to B a degree of discretion in determining how best to fulfil A's trust. Trust may also be more open-ended. A may trust B with respect to matters in a wide domain, or with only some specific matters excluded. In such cases, the trust approximates a two-place relation.

Trust involves a personal stance, not just a cognitive attitude, like prediction, that is directed to or concerns another person and is adopted for certain reasons.[32] This personal stance is complex. If A trusts B then A *relies on* B, more or less voluntarily, with the expectation that B's action on A's behalf will be competent and to A's benefit, where there is some prospect of harm or loss if B does not perform as trusted. If A trusts B, A gives (or is disposed to give) B an opportunity to care for something that A values; she submits something of value to B, and in this way makes herself vulnerable to the actions of a free agent.[33] It is not accurate to say that for A to trust B is nothing more than for A to have certain beliefs about B; nevertheless, trust has a prominent cognitive dimension. Unless it is defective, A's trust rests on beliefs that function as reasons for A to rely on B in the way characteristic of trust. If these beliefs are false, or not sufficient to justify A's reliance on B, then A's trust is misplaced and may be open to moral criticism.

We can distinguish broadly between two kinds of interpersonal trust. *Predictive* trust takes the trustor's reliance on the trusted person as the key feature. This form of trust is relatively thin form of trust and quickly shades off into mere reliance. The only difference from mere reliance is that it concerns persons specifically and not objects, processes or elements of nature – for example, cars, quality-control arrangements for the manufacture of cars or predictable seasonal changes.[34] *Robust* trust builds in further essential, interpersonal conditions, for example appreciation of the trusted person's motivation, in a special way.

Typically, A relies not only on B's competence, but also on B's motivation, but theorists who study trust hold different views about the necessary features of

[32] R Holten, 'Deciding to Trust, Coming to Believe' (1994) 72 *Australian Journal of Philosophy* 63; P Hieronymi, 'Reasons of Trust' (2008) 86 *Australasian Journal of Philosophy* 214.

[33] A Baier, 'Trust and Antitrust' (1986) 96 *Ethics* 231; P Pettit, 'The Cunning of Trust' (1995) 24 *Philosophy and Public Affairs* 202, 208.

[34] T Simpson, 'What is Trust?' (2012) 93 *Pacific Philosophical Quarterly* 550, 565. This is the core notion of trust of many social theorists, eg P Sztompka, *Trust: A Social Theory* (Cambridge University Press 2000).

this motivation. Some, following philosopher Annette Baier, hold that in trusting B, A relies on B's good will; some identify the essential element as something more like a trait of character, namely trustworthiness. Viewed in one way, relying on B's (reputed or demonstrated) good will seems to be a kind of predictive trust, where the basis of the prediction in part looks to evidence of proper motivation. Philip Pettit suggests that these reasons typically include beliefs about B's loyalty, B's character or commitments, or B's prudential considerations.[35] Russell Hardin focuses only on the prudential reasons. Trust, he maintains, is 'encapsulated trust'.[36] A believes that A's interest is encapsulated in B's interest, because it is in B's interest to serve A's interest by doing what A trusts him to do. We can best understand these accounts as accounts of predictive trust.

However, relying on trustworthiness suggests something else, something more interactive between the trustor and the trusted person. To be trustworthy not only seems to involve reliability of a person to do that which another person trusts him to do, but it also involves the trusted person's being trust-responsive. A person is trust-responsive if she takes the fact that another person trusts her to do something in his behalf itself as a salient reason for acting as trusted. Trust that relies on the trusted person's trust-responsiveness is a more robust form of trust. A robustly trusts B when A believes that communicating her reliance on B will trigger B's reasons to do what A trusts him to do (eg, reasons of loyalty, commitment or prudence). That is, B will be motivated in part by A's manifested trust to prove himself trustworthy.[37]

Baier pointed out that the difference between trust and mere reliance is evident in the fact that A reasonably regards B's failure not merely as a *disappointment for* A but as a *betrayal of* A. The relationship is normatively structured, interpersonal and in a morally relevant sense interactive. This seems to be true of robust trust.[38] A manifestly depends on B, expecting in part that her doing so will trigger B's motivation. B's recognition of this manifested trust engages his antecedent reasons for fulfilling A's trust. A's trust manifests her recognition of B as trust-responsive and hence trustworthy. It invites B's recognition of A's vulnerability, and of the valued thing A put in B's care; it also engages B's commitments, his sense of integrity, his sense of himself as trustworthy. Robust trust involves a morally interesting kind of mutual recognition. It is not surprising that we often think trust of this kind engenders an obligation on the trusted party – and why he might resist, or even regard the trust as unwelcome.

This understanding brings trusting and entrusting closer together, because it is A's conduct that is meant to be visible to B and is expected to trigger B's

[35] Pettit (n 33) 208–10.

[36] R Hardin, *Trust and Trustworthiness* (Russell Sage Foundation 2002) ch 1.

[37] Pettit (n 33) 205–07.

[38] I follow here V McGeer and P Pettit, 'The Empowering Theory of Trust' in P Faulkner and T Simpson (eds), *The Philosophy of Trust* (Oxford University Press 2017) 14. See also V McGeer, 'Trust, Hope and Empowerment' (2008) 86 *Australasian Journal of Philosophy* 237.

trust-fulfilling behaviour. However, in some cases, A may trust B privately, without communicating that trust to B. If McGeer and Pettit are correct, this will be a truncated form of trust; it is predictive but not robust trust. More interesting is the case in which A *entrusts* something of value to the care of B while not entirely trusting him, that is, without fully believing in advance that B is fully trustworthy. A may do so hoping that B will take the opportunity to show himself 'trust-responsive'.[39] A's conduct will *communicate* trust, by virtue of the public meaning such conduct typically has, without *manifesting* A's trust, which A does not yet have. We might call it anticipatory, or *proleptic*, trust. There need be nothing sinister, insincere or especially manipulative in A's entrusting behaviour. Entrusting something of value to another *invites* a certain kind of mutual recognition and the interaction rooted in it.

Proleptic trust, and perhaps robust trust more generally, can work only if certain conditions obtain between A and B and in the environment in which A and B interact.[40] First, whether B's motivation in such cases proves trustworthy depends on the reasons that lie behind this motivation. B's own virtue, commitments or sense of integrity may be among his reasons. Often, in addition, the motivation to trust-fulfilling behaviour will depend on the value to B of the good opinion or esteem of A and others in the relevant public. Being in the good graces of A and others may be of value to B because of its contribution to his long-term self-interest. Alternatively, it may be important to B because of his antecedent loyalty to A or others to whom B is related. Or, again, it may be important to B because his trust-fulfilling behaviour implicates his integrity or his commitment to certain principles or norms, and the good opinion of others reflects back to him an assessment of his integrity or commitments that he is inclined to take seriously. It may be difficult to detect the difference in B's motivation of the last two kinds from the outside or even by B himself. Further, B's concern for his own integrity, or at least for the good opinion of others, must be relatively hearty, in the sense that it must not easily yield to countervailing motivations.

Second, A's conduct must communicate A's trust to B and others; so, it must have the public significance of signalling A's reliance and vulnerability, and some expectation of B's good will or trustworthiness. Consequently, the meaning of A's action *as trusting or entrusting* and B's action *as trust fulfilling* must be public to each other and some relevant range of third parties. For this to be true, there must be enough entrusting and trust-fulfilling conduct in the social environment in which A and B interact that their actions can reasonably be taken to have this meaning as entrusting and trust-fulfilling. Additionally, the public context of their interaction will make it possible to interpret B's actions as trust-responsive when they fall short of what A had expected. In some cases it may

[39] Pettit (n 33) 212–17.
[40] I here build on Pettit's discussion of the phenomena of 'trust-responsiveness', ibid 220–25.

be reasonable to read B's falling short not as betrayal but as trust-responsive, especially where B's caring for what A had entrusted to him involves discretion on his part. It must be possible for A and others to regard B's actions as done in good faith within the area of discretion accorded to B, even when they judge what B did to be mistaken.

Third, proleptic trust is not likely to succeed where there are sharp divisions between B and A, or in the social environment in which they interact. Where sharp divisions obtain, B may not care about A's opinion of B's trustworthiness, or may not care about the opinions of others like A. Moreover, for proleptic trust to elicit trust-responsive behaviour, the relationship between A and B must not be such that A's reliance on B is more reasonably seen by B or others as motivated by something other than B's potential trustworthiness; for in that case A's reliance would not be viewed as entrusting conduct. This would be true, for example, if B is forced by some third party to act in A's behalf. Also, the relationship must not be such that there is a manifest and significant inequality of power between A and B. If A holds B in her power, B's action will reasonably be regarded as ingratiating or sycophancy, rather than trust-responsive, or A's conduct will be seen as hypocritical, rather than trusting. And if B holds A in his power, A's reliance and vulnerability will lack the necessary dimension of voluntariness, and likely not seek to engage trust-responsive behaviour. Her reliance will look like acquiescence, not trust. Thus, the manifest presence of strong sanctions for B's behaviour and significant manifest inequalities of power between A and B can make entrusting impossible, and can turn otherwise trust-responsive behaviour into mere compliance. In sum, the social context of potentially trust-relevant behaviour, the social meanings available in that context, can materially affect the possibilities for trusting and trust-responsive conduct.

B. Non-Trust

We may be inclined to think of one's lack of trust in another person to be equivalent to distrust. 'I just don't trust him' sounds like an expression of distrust. But distrust is a distinctive personal stance located at the opposite end of a spectrum of trust-relevant attitudes and dispositions.[41] Of course, it is also possible for one to occupy a position entirely off this spectrum: one may take no trust-relevant attitude to another person. Absence of trust is not a way of regarding another person but the absence of any such regard. A may still rely on B, but for reasons that have nothing to do with B, B's motivation or potential responsiveness to A's reliance. In contrast, *distrust* involves intentional *withholding* of reliance, a refusal to make oneself vulnerable to another person, either on

[41] Ullmann-Margalit (n 31).

some occasion or as a general disposition. If she has no choice but to rely, the reliance of a distrusting person will be unwilling and diffident. (Whether she also manifests these attitudes will depend on the costs to her of doing so.) She will be disposed to withdraw her reliance at the first safe opportunity, or will take all feasible measures to protect herself from the harm that she fears may eventuate. The distrusting person bases her withholding of reliance or diffidence on deep and active suspicion of the other party's incompetence or motivation.[42] If A distrusts B, A believes that B would (or does) treat any entrusting by A with indifference, if not contempt: A not only believes B to be untrustworthy, she also believes B will not only prove not trust-responsive but is likely to act out of ill-will against A or with manifest indifference to A's interests or well-being. This stance colours A's interpretations of B's conduct, insofar as it bears on A's interests. A is strongly inclined to see B's motivations as sinister even when, to others, they might appear innocent. In this respect, the distrusting person tends to be resistant to or to discount evidence of the other party's cooperativeness or benign motivation.[43]

On the spectrum between trust and distrust lie doubt and mistrust. A's trust-relevant stance regarding B may vary in two dimensions. First, A may have more or less confidence in, or more or less doubt about, B's competence, motivation or trust-responsiveness. Second, depending on her confidence or doubt, A may adjust how much of what she values she is willing put in B's hands. At some indeterminate point, A's less than full trust shades into a region of mistrust, characterised by some degree of doubt, which is still distinct from distrust. A, who mistrusts B, may still be willing to rely on B to some extent, still harbouring doubt to some degree. Her reliance will be correspondingly cautious and tentative, perhaps taking some precautions against a worst-case scenario, and taking care about what she puts in B's hands. She may hedge her bets, without closing off opportunities for B to demonstrate his trustworthiness. Thus, one who mistrusts another person is open to further evidence regarding the other party's trustworthiness and trust-responsiveness; perhaps she may be willing to give the other party the benefit of the doubt she still harbours.[44] She may even be willing proleptically to *entrust* something of value to the care of the other person.

C. Beyond the Interpersonal Paradigm: Political and Civic Trust

Looking beyond the interpersonal paradigm, we encounter political trust and civic trust. Political trust, for our purposes, is the trust that those who are subject

[42] PT Lenard, *Trust, Democracy and Multicultural Challenges* (University of Pennsylvania Press 2012) 56.

[43] ibid 57.

[44] ibid 59.

to political power place in those who exercise that power. It involves a form of trust either in governmental institutions or in individuals who hold official positions in those institutions, having very little or any information about them as persons. Civic trust is a form of trust that members of a political community have in other members, or groups of members, or civic associations or institutions. As we noted earlier, trust of these forms is likely to be impersonal, and the relationships in which trust is offered and accepted are thin, distant and often mediated by institutions. So, if A has civic trust in B, A is unlikely personally to encounter B and is unlikely to have any personal knowledge of B's character, commitments, loyalties, general cooperativeness or trust-responsiveness. It is not clear whether we should think of political or civic trust strictly on the model of predictive trust, or whether some features of robust trust are significantly involved in these situations of trust, at least in some important contexts. To better understand political and civic trust, and thus to move towards an answer to the trust challenge we identified earlier, we should look at important forms of *impersonal trust*.

We may distinguish two kinds of such impersonal trust: generalised trust and institutional trust. Generalised trust is found where A adopts a trust-like stance with regard to unassignable members of a group of significant size. In cases like this, trust can shade off into a general confidence regarding the likely competence or motivations of people in the group. This does not have all the key features of interpersonal trust, but some similarities remain. One will not draw evidence one might have of the potential trust-responsiveness of members of the group from personal experience, but rather from commonly known general characteristics of members, or from generalised personal observations of the conduct of some members. A related kind of generalised trust is evident in cases in which A takes a trust-like stance to a particular individual in the absence of substantive interpersonal connection between them. A may be a member of B's group. In that case, A may have some insider, participant attitude that warrants her attributing a degree of trustworthiness to B. Alternatively, A may not be a member of the group, in which case she can only draw on generally available information about the relative trustworthiness of members of B's group, and hence of B. Sometimes A may draw her information from the general climate or cultural milieu in which B lives and interacts with others. I will return to this idea of the 'climate of trust' presently.

Institutional trust can also take one of two forms. Individuals may have *trust in* certain institutions. They trust the institution to perform as designed or advertised, believing that it is likely to be fair, to serve their interests, or to serve important principles or values to which they are committed, despite changes in personnel.[45] We might reasonably regard this form of trust as predictive trust (or in some cases, mere reliance). It is not reasonable to attribute to institutions

[45] Ullman-Margalit (n 31) 72.

the trust-responsiveness characteristic of robust trust. A second kind of institutional trust involves a relation between persons, at least one of whom occupies a role in some institution. This is *institution-dependent trust*. A's trust in B is institution-dependent when A trusts B, who holds an official position in an institution, C, in part based on what A knows about how the C's processes and procedures underwrite B's competence and motivations. On that basis A can count on B, within certain parameters, to act in A's interest, or at least to act fairly when it comes to matters of A's interests. A's trust is akin to personal trust, but more distant and mediated by the institution, C. A's trust in B depends on her trust in the institution in which B is an official, but it extends to something approximating personal trust in B insofar as B acts in his official capacity.

As institution-dependent trust illustrates, trust in institutions does not close off all forms of quasi-personal trust in officials, but rather it may make some such form possible and actually underwrite it, especially in cases where individuals may have no choice but to rely on officials who exercise power over them.[46] This may be especially important for our discussion of the possibilities of trust in political institutions governed by the rule of law. For, as we observed earlier, it is virtually impossible for law and legal institutions to close off all discretion in the exercise of ruling power. Institution-dependent trust may still be possible, and even reasonable, if the institutions (aided perhaps by the ethos of fidelity) work to secure the competence and shape the motivations of those who exercise ruling power.

It appears, then, that political trust combines trust in governmental or legal institutions with institution-dependent trust. Civic trust combines both kinds of generalised trust, perhaps adding in some elements of more robust personal trust. Complements of political and civic trust are also now recognisable. Trust-relevant attitudes across the spectrum are possible, from robust trust through weaker forms of trust, through the range of mistrusting attitudes and conduct, to full and deep distrust.

Finally, I should say a word about what we might call the 'climate' or 'commons' of trust. I have in mind here another form of impersonal trust. A climate of trust (or mistrust or distrust) is a social rather than personal phenomenon. It is not a feature of the attitudes or dispositions of any individuals or aggregate of individuals. It does not exist entirely apart from such attitudes and dispositions, but also it is not strictly reducible to them. It supervenes on them. The climate of trust in a community is a product of the trusting activities, interactions, practices and engagements of members of the community, including the failures of trust, betrayals, corrections and abandonments of trust that their activities comprise. It is rooted in and nourished by the informal norms at work in the community, norms to which members of the community are held by informal means. This complex of interactions and interdependent

[46] P Pettit, 'Republican Theory and Political Trust' in Braithwaite and Levi (eds) (n 1) 313.

expectations, attitudes and dispositions is broadly a matter of common knowledge, although this may be more implicit than explicit to members of the community. They sense the climate and live it, rather than observe, study or manage it. It is the context within which their trusting and entrusting – and their mistrusting and distrusting – take shape. In this climate, conduct gets its public meaning as entrusting or trust-withholding, trust-responsive, trust-fulfilling or trust-betraying. It is from this commons that individuals draw to anticipate and assess the conduct of non-intimate individuals, and on which they depend for the public meaning of their behaviour. It is also from this commons that they draw resources to reinforce social bonds within their circle and to extend trust to those beyond the limits of their narrow circle. It is an important component of what social theorists call 'social capital'.[47] This climate can be rich and robust or thin and weak, it can be narrowly circumscribed, limited to small sub-groups of a political community, or broad and community-wide, embracing many diverse sub-groups in the community.

IV. RESPONSE TO THE TRUST CHALLENGE

With this understanding of accountability fit for the rule of law and of the varieties of trust and its contraries, we are in a position to assess the trust challenge to the fidelity thesis that lies at the heart of my proposed understanding of the rule of law. I shall begin with the challenge addressed to fidelity in the civic, horizontal dimension.

A. Horizontal Accountability and Civic Trust

Recall it was argued that being called to account (in some circumstances) may reasonably be experienced as an insult because it expresses a lack of trust and hence a failure of basic respect. This objection strikes me as fundamentally mistaken. On the contrary, I argue, mutual accountability in the context of interpersonal relations presupposes and expresses trust, rather than distrust or even mistrust, and is likely to build and reinforce it.

The centrality of mutual accountability to moral life and the moral community is a common view among moral philosophers. In the first edition (1759) of his *Theory of Moral Sentiments*, Adam Smith wrote:

> A moral being is an accountable being. An accountable being … is a being that must give an account of its actions to some other, and that consequently must regulate

[47] See R Putnam, *Bowling Alone: The Collapse and Revival of American Community* (Simon & Schuster 2000); see the range of essays on various aspects of 'social capital' in D Castiglione, JW Van Deth and G Wolleb (eds), *The Handbook of Social Capital* (Oxford University Press 2008).

> them according to the good-liking of this other. Man is accountable to God and his fellow creatures. But tho' he is, no doubt, principally accountable to God, in the order of time, he must necessarily conceive of himself as accountable to his fellow creatures.[48]

Kant extended this thesis when he wrote, 'no one can bind another to something without also being subject to a law by which he in turn can be bound in the same way by the other'.[49] According to Kant, to submit to law is, necessarily, to submit to *reciprocal* (or at least *mutual*) accountability. If A claims to bind B and to hold B accountable to this obligation, A is also subject to a network of accountability to others in which B also participates.

In recent work, Stephen Darwall, echoing Kant, has persuasively argued that deontic notions like duty and obligation are categorically different from the idea of a good moral reason for action. Agents who violate their duties or do not fulfil their obligations are liable to moral blame, and 'moral blame comes with an implicit RSVP, an implicit demand for accountability and acknowledgment of the legitimacy of this demand … [Likewise,] guilt reciprocates blame by acknowledging the legitimacy of its implicit demand, and it is itself a form of holding oneself accountable for complying with this demand'.[50] To hold someone accountable for his actions with respect to his obligations to others is not, at the first level of normative communication, to threaten or apply some external incentive to conformity to that obligation. It is, rather, to demand of the obligation-bearer that he make an account of his actions; to encourage the obligation-bearer to take responsibility for his actions, to hold *himself* accountable.[51]

Darwall characterises all of morality in these Smithian-Kantian terms; he calls it 'morality as equal accountability'.[52] 'Moral norms,' he writes, 'regulate a community of equal, mutually accountable, free and rational agents as such, and moral obligations are the demands such agents have standing to address to one another and with which they are mutually accountable for complying.'[53]

Far from giving insult or denying respect, accountability is an expression of respect, provided it is reciprocal. 'Holding someone responsible involves commitment to a form of mutual respect,' Darwall observes, 'since it commits the holder to the idea not just that he has an authority to hold the other responsible,

[48] A Smith, *A Theory of Moral Sentiments*, eds DD Raphael and AL MacFie (Liberty Classics 1982) 111.

[49] I Kant, 'Perpetual Peace' in I Kant, *Practical Philosophy*, tr and ed MJ Gregor (Cambridge University Press 1996) 323, fn † (emphasis deleted).

[50] S Darwall and B Dill, 'Moral Psychology as Accountability' in J D'Arms and D Jacobson (eds), *Moral Psychology and Human Agency: Philosophical Essays on the Science of Ethics* (Oxford University Press 2014) 41, 43.

[51] ibid 44.

[52] S Darwall, *The Second-Person Standpoint* (Harvard University Press 2006) 100–04.

[53] ibid 101. For a similar argument, see RJ Wallace, *The Moral Nexus* (Princeton University Press 2019).

but also that the other can hold himself and others [including the one holding him responsible] responsible as well.'[54] Morality, Darwall argues, is best understood not as a matter of every person's being subjected to an externally imposed, impersonal code of norms, but rather as a norm-structured practice in which each person is and regards himself as accountable to others and they to him. To purport to hold another accountable, under these conditions, is not to exercise unilateral authority or power over the other person, but to acknowledge common participation in the practice of mutual accountability to common governing norms.

Accountability is an expression of respect, provided it is *reciprocal*. Trust plays a key role in the fidelity practice, although it may not do so in structures of bureaucratic or managerial accountability. For in fidelity practice, when one holds another accountable, one acknowledges the authority of the other party to hold oneself accountable. One puts oneself in the hands of the other party, makes oneself vulnerable to her freely exercised judgment, to her 'good-liking', as Smith put it. This entrusting is reciprocal. Acts of accountability-holding may have the properties trust challengers allege when the norms are externally imposed, or where there is no recognisable community between Holder and Giver, and especially where the accountability holding is not mutual, as in bureaucratic orders. In such circumstances, holding accountable another person amounts to subjecting that person to one's power, or demonstrating to her the fact and burden of that subjection. However, the accountability at the centre of fidelity is not like this; it is and must be reciprocal. Civic trust is a condition and a consequence of mutual accountability in the civic association. Where each is the guardian of each, there is no reason for one to regard being called to account as an insult or the expression of distrust.

Thus, regarding the practice of accountability at the horizontal, civic level, we may conclude that, as long as the practice involves mutual submission to and mutual participation in the practice, the practice is not only not threatening to civic trust, but rather presupposes and expresses such trust. Of course, social conditions can undermine or threaten this mutual practice. In a culture otherwise dominated by distrust, it may not be possible for the morality of equal accountability to gain a foothold. In the absence of widely recognisable examples of mutual accountability holding, where normative requirements are impersonal and imposed from above, and demands for compliance are unilateral, it may not be possible to read attempts to hold persons accountable as trust-involving. If the soil of the community's civic culture is poisoned, mutual accountability characteristic of fidelity may not take root. So, we must concede that, under some social conditions, accountability may be read as nothing more

[54] S Darwall, 'Respect and Honor as Accountability' in S Darwall (ed), *Honor, History, and Relationship: Essays in Second-Personal Ethics II* (Oxford University Press 2013) 11, 12–13.

than the exercise of externally imposed power; however, in this climate, fidelity in general could not get a foothold, and, sadly, robust rule of law could not survive. And law itself can survive, if at all, only by depending on the use of coercive force beyond levels few could regard as tolerable.

B. Vertical Accountability and Political Trust

The trust challenge to accountability between citizen and government officials remains to be addressed. Accountability, it is argued, is motivated by and publicly expresses a level of political distrust that is likely to undermine effective government. It drives out trust-responsive behaviour of officials and good faith judgment by officials in contexts in which the exercise of discretion is inevitable and necessary for the good of the polity. Bentham and his like thought this worry was unfounded, because, they thought, distrust – manifest and persistent distrust pursued with 'refractory and turbulent zeal', as Ferguson recommended – of those who wield enormous power is a good thing.[55] However, we do not need to join Bentham and embrace potentially corrosive distrust, because the trust challenge can be met. Accountability does not (necessarily) express distrust and it does not (necessarily) drive out trust; rather, it has the potential to encourage and nourish it.

To begin this defence, we need to recognise that we have in view a mode of relationship between citizens and public officials that stands some distance from thick interpersonal relationships and the trust-relevant attitudes and conduct modelled there. Rarely do citizens address officials directly. Their encounters are mediated by civic associations of many kinds; and these associations themselves may be organised in different ways for different kinds of accountability and for holding accountable different kinds and levels of governmental officials. Likewise, government officials appear in contexts of public accountability in and through a variety of governmental institutions and offices, themselves organised in a variety of ways for different kinds of accountability holding. It is possible, and perhaps in other contexts illuminating, to map out these mediating institutions on the civic and governmental sides of the equation. But I will not pursue that mapping task here, because doing so is not needed for my general argument.

[55] Actually, Bentham's view was much more nuanced than this suggests. In his late constitutional work, he sought to structure governmental institutions so as to, as he put it, 'maximize official aptitude', the most important component of which as 'moral aptitude', the disposition to act manifestly in the public interest. See J Bentham, *Official Aptitude Maximized*, ed P Schofield (Oxford University Press 1993). See also GJ Postema, *Bentham and the Common Law Tradition* (2nd edn, Clarendon Press 2019) ch 11.

There are three conclusions we should draw from this stage setting that will focus our discussion. First, for the most part we are considering matters of impersonal trust and its complements. Moreover, the personal stances that individual citizens or officials take will not be at the centre of our concern; rather, we will focus on their trust-relevant conduct, their entrusting conduct, and their conduct withholding of reliance. Second, the political trust in view here largely takes the shape of institution-dependent trust. Third, we must, again for the most part, consider the publicly recognised meanings, and reasonable inferences from them, of the conduct involved in public accountability-holding activities. Thus, the questions we must consider are: (i) What attitudes and dispositions along the trust–distrust spectrum do accountability-holding activities signal or communicate? (ii) What effect are these likely to have on the conduct and motivations of government officials? Starting with the first question, we can uncover the plausible public meanings of these activities by looking at their publicly acknowledged aims and presuppositions, and at the associations that are reasonably to be drawn between these activities and others seen as similar in motivation and upshot.

To set that stage, we need only recall that accountability mechanisms are recommended as a key component of the strategy of the rule of law that promises protection and recourse against the arbitrary exercise of power, and as an expression of the partnership between those who wield political power and those subject to it. This is viewed publicly as a partnership that involves not only mutual commitments to comply with the law, but also common commitments to hold each other accountable to its terms. Moreover, although the relations between individual officials and individual laypersons will ordinarily be perceived as unequal, the relations between officials and 'the public' (what Bentham aptly called 'the Public Opinion Tribunal'), where rule of law institutions are in place, is not as likely to be so perceived.

In this context, we might articulate the public meaning of the accountability mechanisms as follows. These mechanisms call attention to this shared submission to the law and thus to justification of any exercise of power – civil or political – by reference to our best understanding of the powers, principles and privileges laid out in the law. The public message, communicated through regular activities and practices of accountability holding, calls attention to the reciprocal commitments of citizen and official to govern their actions and exercises of power by their common law. It acknowledges that, even though concentrated governing power is in many respects far greater than the dispersed power of individuals and civic associations, citizens entrusted this power to officials, making themselves vulnerable to official actions and official judgments of them. But they did so because those wielding power also submitted to the law and public judgment of their best efforts to comply with and enforce it. Holding them publicly accountable for actions in the domain of official power as defined by the law provides public officials opportunities to show their good faith in acting out their presumed commitment in circumstances that might otherwise appear to compromise that good faith. Accountability does not rest on the expectation that officials will act to deceive or will abuse the power entrusted to them; neither does it assume that officials will act from malevolent motives against citizens' legally protected interests. But it does acknowledge, realistically, that the temptations of power are significant. Regular, expected calls for officials to give an account of their exercise of the powers entrusted to them protect officials from those temptations and from otherwise not unreasonable interpretations of their actions as ultra vires, taken in bad faith and inconsistent with your commitment.

If this is the prevailing message, and external, coercive sanctions are not immediately involved, or are not constantly in the perception of the public and of officials, then the appeal to the integrity and public spirit of officials, or at least to their interest in the good opinion of others, will be in the foreground. The demand for accountability on a regular, and not personally directed, basis can then reasonably be seen as an invitation to officials to hold themselves accountable, to connect their official duties to values and commitments important to them.

Do accountability mechanisms thus characterised presuppose or express distrust in any significant way? Clearly no. They may be motivated and possibly even express caution, perhaps based on realism about the dynamics of power and a willingness to take certain precautions to avoid some worse-case scenarios. At most, this underlying stance is one of moderate mistrust and may look more like a modest form of trust. But such mistrust, if that is what it is, leaves open the option of genuine proleptic trust. And the activities described above look more like exercises of proleptic trust than resolute refusals to trust. They seem open to, and seek to encourage, trust-responsive behaviour on the part of officials, behaviour that not only demonstrates publicly their good faith, but also allows them to act in ways that maintain their own integrity. There is nothing essentially punitive about holding to account a person to whom great power is entrusted. Accountability just makes manifest that exercises of that power are subject to the deliberative forces of law, and provides a public forum for those deliberative forces to work. In addition, when the accountability mechanisms work reasonably well and are known to do so, and the institutional checks and balances are also doing their work, room is opened up for genuine institution-dependent political trust.

V. CONCLUSION

In discussions of nuclear disarmament, United States' President Reagan famously adopted the mantra 'trust but verify'. The mantra of fidelity should not be 'trust but verify' but rather 'entrust and hold accountable', understanding that the one who calls another to account is also equally accountable. Once we understand the kind of accountability invoked by the fidelity thesis, and the subtle dimensions of civic and political trust and their complements, it is clear, I believe, that the trust challenge can be decisively met. There is not, after all, a deep tension at the heart of our ideal of the rule of law. Vigorous efforts at accountability do not drive out trust, of an important and valuable kind. Rather, such trust is a condition and reasonably hoped-for consequence of it.

2

Equal Concern and Respect as the Foundation of Postema's Notion of the Rule of Law

FRANKLIN M DUTRA*

I. LEGALITY AND FIDELITY AS CONDITIONS FOR THE LAW TO RULE

THE VALUE OF the rule of law stands at a paramount position in Professor Gerald Postema's recent contributions to legal and political philosophy. The central aspects of his conception of the rule of law can be found in his article 'Law's Rule: Reflexivity, Mutual Accountability, and the Rule of Law', on which I intend to comment in this chapter.

Postema believes that the core idea behind the rule of law is 'that the law promises protection and recourse against the arbitrary exercise of power'.[1] Yet this concern about power is not limited to the public exercise of power; rather, it comprises also the arbitrary exercise of power in private relationships. This is what he calls the *societal* or *horizontal* dimension of the law:

> The rule of law at its core promises protection and recourse against the arbitrary exercise of power, but such power can take many different forms, some are political, wielded by those who claim authority to govern or by those governed; some are societal, wielded by parties outside of government over others also outside of government. The rule of law ideal aspires to take all of forms of power exercised in a polity

* I owe the greatest debt to Prof Dr Thomas da Rosa de Bustamante, my academic supervisor, for the countless teachings, opportunities and the priceless comments he made regarding earlier versions of this chapter. Besides, I wish to acknowledge my gratitude to Catherine Minahan for her careful, professional and respectful copy-editing. A draft version of this chapter was presented at the colloquium, 'Dialogues with Gerald Postema', which took place at the 3rd International Conference on Constitutional Law and Political Philosophy, Curitiba, Brazil, 26 October 2017.

[1] GJ Postema, 'Law's Rule: Reflexivity, Mutual Accountability and the Rule of law' in Xiaobo Zhai and M Quinn (eds), *Bentham's Theory of Law and Public Opinion* (Cambridge University Press 2014) 7, 10.

> within its scope. ... This essay will defend the centrality to the rule of law ideal of protecting individuals against power wielded by non-governmental individuals and entities.[2]

With this principle in mind, Postema proposes to revise and supplement the traditional notion of rule of law.[3] He argues that although most commentators focus on the formal and institutional aspects of legality, these features are not enough to sustain a robust conception of the rule of law, inasmuch as this political value implies a more demanding *ethos*, which he designates by the concept of fidelity:

> The rule of law, I maintain, comprises not only *(a) a set of standards for laws and for the conduct of governmental agents*, and *(b) a set of core legal institutions and procedures for administration of these laws*, but also and crucially a third component: *(c) an ethos, a set of relationships and responsibilities rooted in core convictions and commitments*. Law was not meant to be merely an instrument of governance; law was meant to rule governors and citizens alike.[4]

According to Postema, the rule of law cannot fulfil its essential promise if we disregard this ethos of fidelity.[5] The ethos of a society, as Gerald Cohen puts it, 'is the set of sentiments and attitudes in virtue of which its normal practices and informal pressures are what they are'.[6] Postema's notion converges with that one, but also differs from and specifies it, since he channels his attention to the focal point of this ethos, as related to the law:

> The focus of Legality is formal and institutional, but the focus of fidelity is ethical in two ways. First, it is concerned with the ethos or culture of a polity, the mutual understandings and associated practices of people in a community in which the rule of law is realized. Second, it is concerned with the mutual responsibilities borne by members of law's ethos, including the responsibility to hold each other to faithful execution of these responsibilities. Thus, the rule of law is robust in a polity just when its members take responsibility for holding each other, and especially law's officials, to account under the law. Fidelity of citizens and officials alike, properly speaking, is a matter of fidelity neither to law or to government, but rather of fidelity to each other.[7]

As the excerpt shows, the gist of the argument is that the ethos of law requires that 'members, and not merely the legal or ruling elite, take responsibility for holding each other and especially law's officials to account under the law'.[8]

[2] GJ Postema, 'Fidelity in Law's Commonwealth' in LM Austin and D Klimchuck (eds), *Private Law and the Rule of Law* (Oxford University Press 2014) 17, 19–20.

[3] For example, Lon Fuller's canonical principles of inner morality of law or the Razian view, concerned mostly with authority and normativity. See L Fuller, *The Morality of Law* (2nd edn, Yale University Press 1969) 33–94; and J Raz, *The Authority of Law* (2nd edn, Oxford University Press 2009) 210–28.

[4] Postema (n 1) 19 (emphasis added).

[5] ibid 7.

[6] GA Cohen, *Rescuing Justice and Equality* (Harvard University Press 2008) 144.

[7] Postema (n 1) 15–16.

[8] ibid 8.

This point is important for my argument here, for it establishes a relationship between each person directly, so that the whole community assumes certain responsibilities under the rule of law.

The value of the rule of law is about *ruling*, and one of the conditions for the law to rule is that each citizen and official is accountable to the law. Postema is aiming, here, at the conditions for *the law* to rule, instead of aiming at someone's rule. This state of affairs only obtains if no one is unaccountable to the law, for if there were someone in this position, she would be the one ruling instead of the law.

Moreover, Postema argues that accountability relies on 'interpersonal structured normative relationships', which create personal relationships among individuals in a chain of mutual obligations.[9] These relationships arise only when a community internalises the ethos of fidelity, which requires not only a passive form of citizenship, but also a positive attitude: a feeling of participation and of having the right to call for the official's accountability (which is correlative to the official's sense of duty to be accountable).

In the following sections, I explore two interrelated points of Postema's conception of the rule of law. First, I argue that Postema must accept (by implication of his account of the rule of law) that the obligations of individuals and officials stem from a single source. Although these obligations might make a different impact upon each actor, conveying rights and duties not necessarily in the same way, they are grounded in the same core ideal. Second, I turn to the direct relationships among individuals required by Postema's conception. He refers to these bonds among citizens as 'normatively structured interpersonal relationships'. I argue that these relationships play a fundamental role for the ideas of reflexivity and mutual accountability, and help us unveil the core idea underlying the value of the rule of law.

My claim in this chapter is that, insofar as law's ethos allocates rights and duties to both citizens and officials, there must be a fundamental principle underlying these rights and duties. I intend to vindicate this claim on Liam Murphy's distinction between monism and dualism in the realm of principles, pointing out that Postema's ideal rule of law is an instance of the former. Granted this view, I argue that Postema's fundamental principle is not Pettit's conception of freedom as non-domination, as he might claim, but rather a special interpretation of the value of equality. Postema's account of equality is not an understanding of equality as material evenness, but rather the ideal of treating everyone 'as an equal'.[10] Dworkin's formulation of the principle of equal concern and respect seems to be, if I am right, the fundamental principle behind Postema's account of the rule of law.

[9] ibid 13.

[10] R Dworkin, *Taking Rights Seriously* (2nd edn, Harvard University Press 1978) 227.

II. REALMS OF PRINCIPLES: MONISM AND DUALISM

Since Postema's ideal of the rule of law entails rights and duties to citizens and officials, there must be a fundamental principle to sustain it. This is the case even if the principle requires different things from officials and citizens, given that such principle must offer a starting point, not a finishing line.

In order to better understand my claim, I turn to Liam Murphy's idea of monism and dualism in the realms of principles of justice. In advance, it is important to make it clear that Murphy concentrates his writings within the egalitarian debate on distributive justice; more specifically, his monism relates with Rawls's basic structure restriction, namely:

> For us the primary subject of justice is the basic structure of society, or more exactly, the way in which the major social institutions distribute fundamental rights and duties and determine the division of advantages from social cooperation. By major institutions I understand the political constitution and the principal economic and social arrangements.[11]

Murphy follows many of Gerald Cohen's criticism of Rawls,[12] since he is also troubled with the existence of principles of justice that apply only to institutions and which do not concern individual actions. In Murphy's own words:

> [A]ll fundamental normative principles that apply to the design of institutions apply also to the conduct of people. … We should not think of legal, political, and other social institutions as together constituting a separate normative realm, requiring separate normative first principles, but rather primarily as the means that people employ the better to achieve their collective political/moral goals.[13]

According to Murphy, a political theory is based on dualism if it maintains that there are different principles for individuals and institutions (as it is the case, for instance, in Rawls' theory of justice): 'the two practical problems of institutional design and personal conduct require, at the fundamental level, two different kinds of practical principle'.[14] But, instead of dualism, Murphy defends a form of monism, which holds that the evaluation of institutions and individuals must depart from the same fundamental principle.

Murphy thinks that monism is fairly compatible with the existence of non-fundamental principles that apply only to one of these realms. For instance, he finds it quite reasonable for one to argue for the existence of some specific tax law principle like the 'ability to pay'.[15] Furthermore, monism is not violated if

[11] J Rawls, *A Theory of Justice* (rev edn, Harvard University Press 1999) 6.

[12] Cohen (n 6) 116–50.

[13] LB Murphy, 'Institutions and the Demands of Justice' (1998) 27 *Philosophy & Public Affairs* 251, 251–53.

[14] ibid 253.

[15] The Brazilian Constitution of 1988 deploys that principle in its art 145: '§1º. Whenever possible, taxes shall be personal and shall vary with the economic capacity of the taxpayer. To make these

the duties of state officials are not exactly the same as the duties of individuals. On the contrary, what he cannot underwrite is 'that there could be a plausible fundamental normative principle for the evaluation of legal and other institutions that does not apply in the realm of personal conduct'.[16]

It is important to notice that Murphy's thesis intends to strike back at one interpretation of a moral division of labour between citizens and institutions, namely the Rawlsian insight that there should be principles of justice that apply only to the basic structure of society.[17] This argument plays an important role in Rawls' theoretical system, for he presents it as an advantage of justice as fairness when compared to utilitarianism. The point of this chapter, however, is not to analyse if Murphy correctly characterised Rawls as a dualist. Instead, I need only argue that Postema's account of the rule of law could be read as a monist conception of political morality.

Moreover, my reading of Postema's rule of law does not imply its incompatibility with the existence of a plurality of values. As pointed out, what monism claims is that the functional specification of values cannot make sense without a shared moral background.

I hope that this is enough to indicate that one is not logically required to embrace foundationalism[18] in order to embrace a monistic approach to principles of justice and political morality. The version of monism stated here is compatible with non-foundationalism in the following way: 'no specified kind of considered judgment of political justice … is thought to carry the whole weight of public justification'.[19] Therefore, monism can be easily reconciled with the existence of many values, which cohere in a general justification that stems from a fundamental background. In other words, to acknowledge Postema's rule of law as a monist conception implies only that there is a fundamental normative assumption that plays the role of the interpretive vector of his theoretical system as a whole.

Of course, Murphy is immersed in a different debate, but it seems to me that his idea of monism can be applied to our discussion on the rule of law and that Postema would underwrite it. As we might note, Postema's ideal of the rule of law demands an ethos – a mutual sense of accountability from officials and citizens – as a condition for the law to rule. And in his own words, the rule of law is necessarily a 'realized ideal'.[20]

objectives effective, the tax administration may identify the patrimony, income and economic activities of the taxpayer, respecting individual rights, as provided by law.' Translation by the 'Constitute Project', available at www.constituteproject.org/constitution/Brazil_2017.pdf?lang=en.

[16] Murphy (n 13) 253.

[17] J Rawls and E Kelly, *Justice as Fairness: A Restatement* (Belknap 2001) 165.

[18] In a nutshell, foundationalist theories of justification state that 'all knowledge or justified belief rest ultimately on a foundation of noninferential knowledge or justified belief'. A Hasan and R Fumerton, 'Foundationalist Theories of Epistemic Justification' in E Zalta (ed), *The Stanford Encyclopedia of Philosophy* (Fall 2018 edn), available at plato.stanford.edu/entries/justep-foundational/.

[19] Rawls and Kelly (n 17) 31.

[20] Postema (n 1) 18.

It appears, thus, that Postema's account of the rule of law is a form of monism. Throughout his work, he repeatedly maintains that fidelity creates rights and duties for both citizens and officials, emphasising also that it demands a personal and a collective effort:

> Fidelity is the ethos of law; it is first of all a matter of ethics, that is, a matter of personal and collective mutual commitments and the practices that give them concrete content, but institutions are also needed to support and underwrite this ethos. ... But, although fidelity is ultimately a matter of personal commitment and community culture, it can sink deep roots into a community only with the help of civic and legal institutions and practices that facilitate and structure responsible accountability-holding.[21]

Fidelity, for Postema, provides the ground for his notion of mutual accountability, which 'finds its home in a normatively structured interpersonal relationship'.[22] Here, accountability is depicted as presupposing a series of personal relations, in a right-duty logic that links individuals directly. This net of obligations is an essential feature of his ethos of law and, as a consequence, of his notion of the rule of law.

These relationships are expanded in a net of mutual accountability when Postema faces the trade-off between accountability and sovereignty. He maintains that to be accountable to the law means to be subject to another's judgment. Hence, if someone is unaccountable, there can be no rule of law (and this is why accountability must be mutual and reflexive). The only alternative to this scenario is to recognise an 'accountability loop or accountability network'. In other words:

> Law's rule requires submission of all in a polity – officials of all ranks and citizens alike – to the law, but, as we can now see, that entails that all submit to and participate in a network of mutual accountability.[23]

Once again, it seems that this notion brings Postema close to monism, because the net of relationships is direct, binding individuals to each other and not merely to the community or to any formal institutions whatsoever. And again, there must be an underlying principle justifying the net of relationships.

III. BETWEEN NON-DOMINATION AND EQUALITY

If I have made a reliable picture of Professor Postema's conception of the rule of law, and if I could convince others that it is a form of monism, there must be a fundamental principle to ground this account of the rule of law. In other words,

[21] ibid 32–33.
[22] ibid 13.
[23] ibid 28.

there must be a principle that applies equally to individuals and institutions, and that provides a sufficient justification for the political value of the rule of law. One could argue that fidelity itself is the principle I am looking for. Nonetheless, it seems to me that fidelity is a procedural virtue that relies on a substantial basis. I regard it as a procedural virtue because of its character and demands. Fidelity represents a specific public ethic – the ethos of law – shared by persons who see each other as mutually accountable to the law. It exists to make it possible for the law to rule. That is why I see it as a procedural value that relies on a fundamental (substantive) principle. An important question, therefore, arises from this account: what is the fundamental principle required by Postema's conception of the rule of law? Postema had the chance to face this exact question, stated in a draft version of this article, during a colloquium regarding his works.[24] Back then, he did not have enough time to evaluate and reflect properly on the question. Nonetheless, he said that his first intuition would be that his fundamental principle is the principle of non-domination, as stated by Philip Pettit, who understands this principle 'as a condition under which a person is more or less immune, and more or less saliently immune, to interference on an arbitrary basis'.[25]

Pettit's project purports to undertake an examination and critique of the languages of political discussion regarding legitimacy. He intends to revive the long-lasting republican tradition without losing sight of democracy.[26] This is why he reconstructs the ultimate republican values as universal – for every member of a contemporary society, and not only a small ruling elite – as we can read in the following extract:

> I maintain that the traditional, republican ideal of freedom supports and unifies a compelling manifesto of political demands, and that if a state and a society looks after the freedom as non-domination of its members, then most other desiderata will look after themselves.[27]

Pettit thinks his approach overcomes liberalism, because, for a liberal, freedom roughly means non-interference. Certainly, Pettit is well aware that there are many nuances and variations within the liberal tradition. But he maintains that this tradition of thought is usually associated with a negative conception of freedom:

> [L]iberalism has been associated over the two hundred years of its development, and in most of its influential varieties, with the negative conception of freedom as the absence of interference, and with the assumption that there is nothing inherently

[24] Colloquium, 'Dialogues with Gerald Postema', mentioned in the acknowledgements at the beginning of this chapter, which took place at the 3rd International Conference on Constitutional Law and Political Philosophy, Curitiba, Brazil, 26 October 2017.

[25] P Pettit, *Republicanism: A Theory of Freedom and Government* (Clarendon Press 1997) vii.

[26] ibid 4.

[27] ibid 7.

> oppressive about some people having dominating power over others, provided they do not exercise that power and are not likely to exercise it.[28]

Pettit concedes that many of his republican conclusions are quite close to those sustained by left-of-centre liberals. However, he believes that his philosophical bases are less controversial than those of leftist liberals. He believes that 'the republican axiomatization develops even shared intuitions in a highly distinctive yet compelling way. … It offers an attractive way of justifying egalitarian and even communitarian intuitions'.[29]

It should not be a surprise that Postema would align his thought with Pettit's. His notion of mutual accountability is not distant from Pettit's conception of freedom as non-domination applied to the rule of law. After all, we cannot lose sight that his core idea of the rule of law implies that 'when law rules, it provides protection and recourse against the arbitrary exercise of power through the distinctive offices – ie, instrumentalities, powers and capacities of – law'.[30] Furthermore, Postema directly quoted Pettit to illustrate his approach to arbitrary power:

> The rule of law sets its face against 'arbitrary' power and its exercise. … An exercise of power is arbitrary in the rule-of-law relevant sense when it is the expression of the *liberum arbitrium*, the free decision or choice, of its agent.[5] … 'An act is perpetrated on an arbitrary basis … if it is subject just to the *arbitrium*, the decision or judgment of the agent; the agent was in a position to choose it or not choose it, at their pleasure'.[31]

Nonetheless, it is one thing to adhere to Pettit's conception of arbitrary power, and another quite different thing to maintain that the ground of Postema's conception of the ideal of the rule of law lies on those neo-republican bases. In other words, to borrow Pettit's notion, arbitrary power does not entail the need to assign to the concept of freedom as non-domination the status of a fundamental principle. And this is exactly what I suggest here. It is undeniable that Postema and Pettit have some important similarities. But it is also clear that Pettit himself advocates that many of his conclusions are quite similar to those defended from a leftist liberal perspective, as already mentioned above.[32] In this sense, I want to suggest a more promising dialogue between Postema and one of these leftist liberals: Ronald Dworkin.

On my view, the fundamental principle underlying Postema's view of the ethos of the rule of law is more fundamentally connected to equality than to the value of freedom as non-domination. Although the concern here is not with

[28] ibid 8–9.
[29] ibid 12.
[30] See GJ Postema, 'Fidelity, Accountability and Trust: Tensions at the Heart of the Rule of Law', ch 1 of this volume.
[31] Postema (n 2) 18. The quotation at the end of the extract from Postema is from Pettit (n 25) 55.
[32] Pettit (n 25) 12.

substantive equality, I believe that, in order to ensure the mutual accountability that lies at the core of Postema's account of the rule of law, there must be some sort of redistributive background institutions.[33] Without these institutions, social and economic inequalities would create a second class of citizens, and this would undermine the direct link between citizens through 'interpersonal structured normative relationships'. In other words, it would undermine one of the major conditions for the law to rule, which is mutual accountability to the law. Instead, only the few who concentrate economic and political power would actually have the capacity to rule.

To sketch a parallel, Rawls presents a very similar reasoning to dismiss the claim that welfare-state capitalism encompasses his principles of distributive justice,[34] for this system does not grant fair value to the political liberties.[35] To be clear, Rawls believes that failure to surmount social and economic inequalities typical of welfare-state capitalism enables the concentration of political power only in the hands of the economic elite. In other words, this system creates a second class of citizens, who do not feel part of the public political culture since they inherently depend on social welfare.

> It [welfare-state capitalism] permits very large inequalities in the ownership of real property (productive assets and natural resources) so that the control of the economy and much of political life rests in few hands. And although … welfare provisions may be quite generous and guarantee a decent social minimum covering the basic needs (§38), a principle of reciprocity to regulate economic and social inequalities is not recognized.[36]

On the other hand, when I claim that Postema's theory is fundamentally based on the principle of equality, I do not assume a raw notion of material equality. Rather, I mean a broader and more abstract egalitarian ideal: Dworkin's requirement of treating every member of the political community 'as an equal'.[37] In other words, the bridge I want to build connects Postema's rule of law and Dworkin's demand for equal concern and respect. This egalitarian demand, as coined by Dworkin, is something like a second-order value, which he identified

[33] In the Q&A of his keynote lecture given at the 3rd International Conference on Constitutional Law and Political Philosophy, Curitiba, Brazil, 25 October 2017, Postema already reckoned that severe inequalities might prevent law's rule. He also mentioned that he would like to address this question specifically in future works.

[34] In a nutshell, his principles of distributive justice are, in this order, equal basic liberties, fair equality of opportunities and difference. See Rawls (n 11) 266–67.

[35] In sum, Rawls' first principle of justice encompasses the following basic liberties: 'freedom of thought and liberty of conscience; political liberties (for example, the right to vote and to participate in politics) and freedom of association, as well as the rights and liberties specified by the liberty and integrity (physical and psychological) of the person; and finally, the rights and liberties covered by the rule of law'. Rawls and Kelly (n 17) 44.

[36] ibid 137–38.

[37] Dworkin (n 10) 227.

as the ultimate foundation of Rawls' works. This value implies a right that all men and women have to equality of concern and respect, which is possessed 'not by virtue of birth or characteristic or merit but simply as human beings with the capacity to make plans and give justice':[38]

> We may describe a right to equality of the second kind, which Rawls says is fundamental, in this way. We might say that individuals have a right to equal concern and respect in the design and administration of the political institutions that govern them. This is a highly abstract right.[39]

This interpretation of equality as a foundational value is also endorsed by Will Kymlicka. In this regard, he follows Dworkin's claim that 'every plausible political theory has the same ultimate value, which is equality'.[40] Kymlicka adopts this position in order to make possible the dialogue between conflicting philosophical approaches to politics, such as utilitarianism, libertarianism, communitarianism, feminism and egalitarian liberalism. Of course, he acknowledges that not every political theory is egalitarian in the broad sense Dworkin suggested. However, he believes that any philosopher who avoided this egalitarian premise – and claims that there are some citizens who are not entitled to equal consideration from the government – would be immediately rejected: 'Dworkin's suggestion is that the idea that each person matters equally is at the heart of all plausible political theories.'[41]

It is this simple yet powerful value that I maintain is underlying Postema's account of the rule of law. Equal consideration is the fundamental principle of such conception, bringing Postema closer to Ronald Dworkin than to Pettit or any other source in his insight about the concept of the rule of law. On this subject, I must clarify that this value of equal concern and respect sustains the whole work of Ronald Dworkin. As Stephen Guest puts it, it is Dworkin's major concern in moral and political philosophy, his fundamental principle.[42] According to Dworkin:

> [Law as integrity] supposes that law's constraints benefit society not just by providing predictability or procedural fairness, or in some other instrumental way, but by securing a kind of equality among citizens that makes their community more genuine and improves its moral justification for exercising the political power it does.[43]

Postema himself is aware of the role equal concern and respect play in Dworkin's thought. He acknowledges that, for Dworkin, legal reasoning has an inescapable argumentative character, because law serves a purpose that is an essential part of

[38] ibid 182.
[39] ibid 179.
[40] W Kymlicka, *Contemporary Political Philosophy: An Introduction* (2nd edn, Oxford University Press 2002) 3.
[41] ibid 4.
[42] S Guest, *Ronald Dworkin* (3rd edn, Stanford University Press 2012) 19.
[43] R Dworkin, *Law's Empire* (Harvard University Press 1986) 93–95.

the concept of law itself.[44] In this regard, integrity is the purpose Dworkin attributes to legal practice as the one that best fits and justifies it. And this purpose, as Postema argues, underpins equality as its second-order value:

> The fundamental requirement of society and its agents in positions of political power is to treat each citizen *as an equal*. ... A community of principle demonstrates its commitment to the treatment of each member as an equal by *striving* for justice, but *insisting* always on integrity in this striving.[45]

Not only does Postema perfectly understands what Dworkin means with his defence of integrity, but he also seems to have subscribed to it (at least to his understanding of what integrity means), due to the relationship he establishes between fidelity and integrity. According to Postema, in the circumstances of integrity,[46] legal institutions, political decisions from the past and judicial tradition substantiate the claim that the quest for justice takes an oblique turn:

> When people committed to justice in their community recognize that there is a sincere, reasonable, and principled disagreement about what justice requires, the pursuit of justice changes direction. In the circumstances of integrity, justice is pursued obliquely: integrity replaces justice as the primary target.[47]

Moreover, Postema claims that the very idea of fidelity to the law in a community in those circumstances takes the form of integrity. In other words, he advocates that communities – whose members aim at justice – display a set of legal institutions as the suitable *locus* for that quest:

> *Integrity is the form fidelity takes in the circumstances of integrity, that is, in a community committed to justice but divided over what justice requires.* Integrity is the way members of such a community keep faith with each other and with their collective commitment to justice as the fundamental mode of their relationships.[48]

Having said that, it seems clear to me that Postema's conception of the rule of law would find itself in a position very difficult to sustain if it were detached from the model of a community of citizens where the pursuit of justice is oblique – as integrity demands. Due to its shared egalitarian basis, it seems reasonable to hold that Postema's approach presents an adequate application of the demands of equal concern and respect to the rule of law. This claim gains strength when we realise that, although Dworkin did not write many lines specifically on the rule of law, the conclusion of one of his few writings about it connects the rule

[44] GJ Postema, *A Treatise of Legal Philosophy and General Jurisprudence*, vol 11: *Legal Philosophy in the Twentieth Century: The Common Law World* (Springer 2011) 446.

[45] ibid 445.

[46] Jeremy Waldron coined this expression in his seminal essay 'The Circumstances of Integrity' (1997) 3 *Legal Theory* 1. According to Postema, these circumstances establish the conditions when the pursuit of integrity becomes significant, 'among people who want justice, but disagree about what justice requires'. GJ Postema, 'Integrity: Justice in Workclothes' in Justice Barley (ed), *Dworkin and His Critics with Replies by Dworkin* (Blackwell 2004) 291.

[47] Postema (n 46) 300.

[48] ibid 311 (emphasis added).

of law with democracy through his egalitarian demands of equal concern and respect:

> I may have made it seem as if democracy and the rule of law were at war. That is not so; on the contrary, both of these important political values are rooted in a more fundamental ideal, that any acceptable government must treat people as equals.[49]

Another point of contact between the authors is Postema's chain of 'normatively structured interpersonal relationships' and Dworkin's notion of associative obligations. For Dworkin, these special kinds of obligations are the foundation of the political community, where law as integrity is possible. Dworkin describes associative obligations as

> a repeated feedback loop between a special responsibility we have to people in certain relationships with us, just in the nature of the case, and a set of social practices that progressively reduces the uncertainties inherent in that kind of responsibility. … Social practices create genuine obligations only when they respect the two principles of dignity: only when they are consistent with an equal appreciation of the importance of all human lives and only when they do not license the kind of harm to others that is forbidden by that assumption.[50]

The point that I would like to emphasise here is that both Postema and Dworkin show how important it is to establish a direct relationship among citizens. This is what makes it possible for citizens to see each other as equals when they think about the imposition of political obligations on one another.

Moreover, Dworkin understands his notion of equal concern and respect as a condition of his theory of substantive legitimacy. It is important not to lose sight that, for him, legitimacy has two dimensions: 'it depends on both how a purported government has acquired its power and how it uses that power'.[51] According to Dworkin, equality lies at the root of any plausible conception of legitimacy, for 'equal concern is the sovereign virtue of political community', and 'without it government is only tyranny'.[52]

I believe that with a closer look, Postema's account of the rule of law embraces this special type of equality – equal concern and respect – as a fundamental principle on which his notion of the rule of law (based on legality and fidelity) is founded. Furthermore, as explained above, there seems to be textual evidence in Professor Postema's work to ground this interpretation, given that he offers an elegant relation between integrity and fidelity: 'fidelity takes the shape of integrity in a community bound to pursue justice in the circumstances of integrity'.[53]

[49] R Dworkin, *A Matter of Principle* (Harvard University Press 1985) 32.

[50] R Dworkin, *Justice for Hedgehogs* (Harvard University Press 2011) 312–15.

[51] ibid 321.

[52] R Dworkin, *Sovereign Virtue: The Theory and Practice of Equality* (Harvard University Press 2000) 1.

[53] Postema (n 46) 311.

If this is correct, it is important to shed some light on this fundamental principle, in order to realise the bridge that Postema builds between justice, integrity (as a political value that represents the practice of justice), fidelity (as the collective shape of integrity) and equality:

> Fidelity calls for keeping faith with the past as a way of keeping faith with each other. … The arrangements must be recognizable as expressions of just and *proper regard for each member as an equal member of the community*, or at least as bona fide attempts to give concrete shape to that fundamental attitude. Respect for past practice, then, must always be in the service of the aspiration for justice, and hence never uncritical.
>
> In communities aimed at justice, where not only the reality falls short of the standard, but the standard itself is in dispute, *fidelity is integrity*.[54]

When all those pieces are brought together, it becomes clear that there is a crucial relationship between the works of Postema and Dworkin. On the one hand, to recognise that equal concern and respect is Postema's fundamental principle makes perfect sense when we contrast what he wrote on the rule of law and on the relationship between integrity and fidelity. On the other hand, Postema presents substantive gains on what an egalitarian rule of law would look like.

IV. CONCLUDING REMARKS

In this chapter, I have put forward an egalitarian interpretation of Postema's account of the rule of law. Nevertheless, the focus here is not on the distributional consequences required to warrant that the law rules. The point was to make explicit the role of the idea of equal treatment as one of the main conditions for the law to rule, as explained by Postema.

In order to show the reasonableness of this claim, I presented the gist of Professor Postema's conception of the rule of law: the combination of legality with fidelity through 'normatively structured interpersonal relationships' of mutual accountability. In this conception, the rule of law demands an ethos. I hope to have showed that it makes sense to claim that Postema's ethos implies a monist account of the rule of law, based on principles that are equally applied to citizens and institutions.

Ronald Dworkin's principle of equality of concern and respect can, if I am right, constitute such fundamental principle. Although Pettit is an important influence in Postema's thought, it is not the case that freedom as non-domination is apt to this foundational task.

[54] ibid 311 (emphasis added).

Part II

Legal Reasoning, Integrity and Protestant Interpretation

3

Postema's Account of Integrity

BARBARA BAUM LEVENBOOK

I. INTRODUCTION

THIS CHAPTER FOCUSES on Postema's conception of integrity and its relation to common law adjudication, as presented in his 'Integrity: Justice in Work Clothes'.[1] Although in this article, Postema assumes the essentials of an integrity theory of law, he tells us that he is not interested in defending such a theory.[2] Instead, he is interested in defending a moral thesis in the service of a theory of adjudication. He introduces the idea that there can be what he calls an 'internal justification' for following precedent, even when it is morally incorrect; and he wants to defend this idea by arguing that there is a genuine and distinct moral value for political communities that morally binds legal officials to precedent. Borrowing from Dworkin, Postema calls this value *integrity*.[3] The practice of integrity provides the requisite internal justification.

I have said that Postema assumes the outlines of an integrity theory – a broadly Dworkinian interpretive theory – of law. This appears in his insistence that law contains principles 'drawn from past political decisions of the community', his 'broad' characterisation of law as providing a 'framework of practical reasoning' for 'justifying actions' by appealing to legal 'principles',[4] and his claim that 'law seems by its nature to be committed to the discipline that

[1] GJ Postema, 'Integrity: Justice in Work Clothes' (1997) 82 *Iowa Law Review* 821, reprinted in J Burley (ed), *Dworkin and his Critics: with replies by Dworkin* (Blackwell 2004) 291. All page references are to the reprinted edition.

[2] ibid 298.

[3] ibid 293.

[4] ibid 294. See also the claim at 312: 'Law is a framework of practical reasoning that anchors the public justification of decisions and actions to past communal decisions and actions.' The claim that law 'defines a ... framework for practical reasoning' goes back to Postema's seminal 'Coordination and Convention at the Foundations of Law' (1982) 11 *Journal of Legal Studies* 165. There, Postema assumes without argument two things that have guided his methodology: (i) laws provide reasons for action; and (ii) 'any adequate theory of law must give a satisfactory account of the normative (reason-giving) character of law' (ibid 165).

integrity imposes'.[5] Any system of social norms, including conventional morality and conventional religion, is a framework of practical reasoning based on past communal actions, since social norms are so based. Moreover, any system of social norms (even the norms of a game) is one to which the members of that community will appeal in an attempt to justify their actions, demands and so on. Doing so is part of what Hart called the 'internal aspect' of social rules. In other works, as I understand them, Postema characterises law's framework as having, one might say, a more abstract level than conventional religion, games or etiquette.[6] However, for the purpose of the work under discussion, it is the idea that certain past actions – in particular, certain past political actions – establish legal *principles* that is important.[7] This idea found its most influential articulation in the early works of Dworkin, as many readers are aware.

If law contains principles drawn from past political decisions, and if judges are pro tanto morally obligated to apply the law (because, for instance, they promised to do so), then they are pro tanto morally obligated to apply legal principles from past legal decisions, *ceteris paribus*. (There may be other parts of law that outweigh or exclude the principles.) If past judicial decisions are one of the generators of legal principles, then judges are pro tanto morally obligated to apply principles from past legal decisions – even if they are morally incorrect. So Postema would have a case for following precedent based on the assumptions about law he makes *without* relying on the idea of integrity as a distinct value. Indeed, if past judicial decisions establish principles broader than them, and principles are part of law, what Dworkin called 'the gravitational force' of precedent is accounted for.

But in his article, Postema attempts to justify the practice of precedent by a new and different route. That route does rely on holding that past judicial decisions are generators of legal principles; so, his answer to why, if at all, judges should follow morally incorrect precedent is founded on assumptions about the nature of law. However, Postema's ideas about the nature of law have little to do with his main task, that of showing that integrity, understood a certain way, is a genuine moral value. It is this task that I shall examine.

II. OUTLINE OF THE ARGUMENT FOR INTEGRITY

To repeat, Postema's declared interest in defending integrity is to provide a moral justification for following precedent in a common law system, even when

[5] Postema (n 1) 312.

[6] Its framework extends to reflective criticism of forms of legal argument offered in subordinate legal practices. In an earlier work, Postema seems to be saying that conventional morality has a certain self-critical aspect as well. GJ Postema, 'Morality in the First Person Plural' (1995) 14 *Law and Philosophy* 35.

[7] See also Postema (n 1) 293: 'The distinctive feature of this framework is that official and citizens alike seek to justify their actions by appeal to rules or principles drawn from past political decisions of the community …'. He adds, 'as recorded in the books and reflected in the practices of its law'. This, of course, is circular as a theory of what law is.

the precedent is mistaken (morally and, perhaps, legally as well).[8] This justification is to be 'internal', rather than 'external'. To give an internal justification, Postema says, is to 'find a sound reason *for the rule* of the precedent case, not merely a sound reason for acting in *accord with* the rule'.[9] In service of this, Postema announces his intention to make a case for the value of integrity. Postema attempts to show that it is a *distinct* value, to be 'placed alongside values like justice, fairness, liberty, equality, community, benevolence, and desert'.[10] (He will later argue that integrity is not independent of justice under certain conditions.)

Postema tells us that his argument that integrity is 'an important value governing law' rests on three theses: (i) 'justice is public and political'; (ii) the past is normative for communities meeting certain 'conditions of unity'; and (iii) 'law is governed by integrity'.[11] I shall examine his argument for the first two and explain the way in which he means the second claim. (He does not attempt to justify all types of traditionalism, no matter what the past practice happens to be.) Success in this argument would be an important contribution to legal theory, since it would show that an interpretive conception of the nature of law also provides moral legitimacy to the resulting laws so conceived. Along with a stout defence of an interpretive theory of law – in particular, an integrity theory of law – which Postema does not attempt, success would be the key to defending the widespread intuition that legal claims are not just formally normative, or normative in some special legal sense, but robustly – and so, morally – normative. Reasons for complying with law, properly understood, and for applying and enforcing it would be shown to transcend the realm of the merely prudential and the contingent.

Accounting in a satisfactory way for the normativity of law, or at least the strong intuition that there is normativity, has been a challenge for the hitherto dominant theory of law, legal positivism. Dworkin's interpretivism was thought to offer such an account. But, as Postema notes, there is an important gap in Dworkin's attempt – the lack of a 'compelling case for integrity' as a genuine value.[12] Postema hopes to offer one.

So Postema is undertaking an important endeavour in legal philosophy. One honours such an endeavour by engaging deeply with it – hailing the sound or plausible, identifying assumptions for further work, reconstructing a line of reasoning, clarifying terminology where this is helpful, exposing the doubtful and challenging what seems false. All that I claim to do in this chapter. The conclusion of deep engagement with the details of Postema's argument,

[8] I am oversimplifying. Common law reasoning treats precedent as binding, *ceteris paribus*, and Postema is aware of this. As I shall say later, sometimes in common law cases, precedential decisions appear to be narrowed, other times extended and, finally, sometimes flatly overruled.

[9] Postema (n 1) 292 (original emphasis).

[10] ibid 293.

[11] ibid 298.

[12] ibid 293.

unfortunately, reveals that it fails in its objective. In particular, as I shall argue, Postema does not succeed in establishing that integrity is a distinct moral value of political communities.

III. TERMINOLOGY

I start by clarifying terminology left unclarified in the work under discussion. The chief term Postema uses, in a way somewhat divergent both from the dictionary and from Dworkin, is 'integrity'. Clarification of Postema's meaning will receive its own section. But there are other terms Postema uses that might be misleading to those who are not familiar with his work, and which I will clarify to some extent in this section.

The first of these is 'justice'. Postema uses some descriptions compatible with what philosophers call 'distributive justice': 'Justice is essentially comparative: it calls for a balancing of benefits or burdens – a proper … distribution of advantages and disadvantages'.[13] But Postema's claims get broader: justice is 'right order', 'a kind of ordering of human communities'.[14] He also says, '[Although] justice presupposes a common stock of goods or bads that are the products of their life together which must be allocated individually, … [i]t also defines a structure of duties, rights, and responsibilities that governs interactions of individual members of the community'.[15] (He will later refer to this as a 'framework of public justification'.[16]) Given what he says about benevolence being atomistic, it follows that not any principle for distributing resources in a society is a principle of justice, even though, as I said, any moral idea defines a framework *for* public justification. (If I understand him correctly, 'To all according to their needs' is not, in his opinion, a principle of justice; it is a principle of 'benevolence or humanitarian concern'.[17])

The foregoing passages suggest that by 'justice', Postema does not mean to include what philosophers call 'retributive justice', though distributive and procedural justice seem to be included. So Postema's realm of justice is narrower than the realm of justice envisaged by many philosophers. Yet he says it is 'the same justice we hope for and demand from law'.[18] His realm of justice may

[13] ibid 300. See also the contention that justice applies to '[t]he way we arrange our communal affairs, and distribute the benefits and burdens of common life …' ibid 311.

[14] ibid 303.

[15] ibid.

[16] ibid 302.

[17] ibid 307. Postema initially tells us he means by 'justice' to include fairness and due process on a political scale (ibid 295). He claims he is using 'justice' the way that Dworkin did in *Law's Empire* (Belknap Press 1986). However, this cannot be true; there (at 404), Dworkin claims that justice, fairness and due process can conflict.

[18] Postema (n 1) 302.

also be broader. Postema says that justice is *the* fundamental ideal of law;[19] also *the* 'rule by which we measure' law.[20] There are other contenders, such as civil peace, personal security, the common good, whatever welfare can be created or distributed by law and so on. Postema may think that attaining them all is encompassed by attaining justice.

In the foregoing discussion, there are already two possible referents for the term 'justice', and so two senses of 'justice'. One is a set of principles, or the content of an ideal. The principles will be general, free of application to specific cases. Call this *justice in the theoretical sense.* The other is the outcome of applying these principles correctly – a just society – to a particular political community under the contingent circumstances in which that community exists, as when Postema claims that justice is right order. The latter is the result of *casuistry*, in the original, philosophical meaning of the term. Call this *justice in the casuistic sense.*[21] I will, when it is helpful, clarify the sense of 'justice' at issue at different stages of Postema's argument.

Note that justice in the outcome sense does not require a grasp of complete principles, and that to agree on casuistry, people need not agree on general principles. Cass Sunstein pointed out that there can be 'incompletely theorized agreements', which he finds typical in law.[22] John Arras has suggested that agreement on paradigms and what I have called reasoning from example, which does not involve principles, can be sufficient.[23] Postema, however, assumes that his moral agents do grasp complete and general principles.

The second term is 'manifest'. Postema does not mean evident by 'manifest', as the dictionary would have it. What is evident – at least, to reason – cannot be the subject of rational disagreement. Postema will claim (i) that justice is manifest right order, and (ii) that disagreements about its nature and requirements can be rational. Postema's meaning of 'manifest' will be taken up further in the course of examining his arguments, in section V.

The third term is 'fidelity'. What he means by this will be examined in section VI, of this chapter.

[19] ibid 313.

[20] ibid 302.

[21] It is not always clear when Postema is switching senses, which he will sometimes do in a single paragraph. For example, 'Justice is not merely a result, an ordering that obtains in or among social elements; it is also a structure of principles that can be understood and applied to behavior.' Also, 'Justice, then, is right order of communities of rational, moral persons. It is also a framework of principles for public justification [general principles, part of a moral theory] … Justice is not only normative, it is expressive.' [Outcome, result of casuistry.] Both ibid 304.

[22] CR Sunstein, 'Incompletely Theorized Agreements' (1995) 108 *Harvard Law Review* 1733.

[23] B Baum Levenbook, 'The Meaning of a Precedent' (2000) 6 *Legal Theory* 185. See also JD Arras, 'Getting Down to Cases: The Revival of Casuistry in Bioethics' (1991) 16 *The Journal of Medicine and Philosophy* 29.

IV. WHAT IS INTEGRITY?

What Postema means by 'integrity' is closely allied with Dworkin's idea. It is a kind of fidelity in laws ('practical directives') and policies to principles arising from what Dworkin called 'past political decisions of the community'.[24] But it is fidelity to a conception of justice that fits and unifies, in some rather loose way that is not clearly specified, these past decisions (and present ones), a conception the community can be viewed as forming. Postema describes it this way: 'Integrity demands that, through its officials, the community act on a coherent set of principles of justice even when its citizens disagree about what the correct principles of justice are.'[25] '[T]he community achieves integrity only when its members seek *as a community* to act from a coherent vision of justice.'[26] Postema emphasises that integrity's project is communal,[27] historical,[28] and that its goal is a 'vision of justice' abstracted from 'past public decisions and actions of the community'.[29] Moreover, that vision must be 'common'.[30]

The big difference Postema sees between his notion of integrity and Dworkin's is that his integrity is complex, incorporating both 'respect' and what he calls 'regret'. '[I]ntegrity, as I understand it, is a complex moral standard calling for a proper and defensible balance of respect and regret regarding past rules and decisions of a polity ... Regret ... accepts ... compromises of coherence – pockets of incoherence in a body of law,'[31] he says. Regret is consistent with preserving some currency for a morally incorrect decision, but limiting its force.

The reader will note that in this account, Postema has made a number of assumptions. Two of them are: (i) there is a determinate set of principles created by past political decisions; (ii) such principles are determinate enough in content (and weight, perhaps) to have implications for new cases. This is unsurprising, given the influence Dworkin has had on Postema's thinking. It is not my purpose to challenge these assumptions here, though at one point I indicate why they are dubious. There is also this assumption: there can be an ongoing political community responsible for past and present political decisions, including settled rules of law. Postema admits that he has not worked out the metaphysics of an ongoing political community with 'sufficient unity' of action to make integrity applicable, but he thinks it does not much matter to his defence of integrity as a political value, and especially as a justification of the practice of precedent.[32]

[24] Postema (n 1) 294.
[25] ibid 294, following Dworkin; note omitted.
[26] ibid 296 (original emphasis).
[27] ibid 298.
[28] ibid 295.
[29] ibid.
[30] ibid.
[31] ibid 314.
[32] ibid 298.

The ultimate justification for viewing integrity as a virtue of law, Postema argues, is that it serves justice and fidelity, which he conceives of as other, more fundamental, values.[33] The idea of justice thus enters both in the argument that integrity is a virtue and in the explanation of what integrity is. But the service claim has a proviso – only under certain conditions. Postema accepts Dworkin's idea that there must be a kind of coherence of principles that expresses a certain conception of political justice – but it must be a 'morally meaningful' one.[34] If the principles are from the political community, this vision of justice is the community's.[35]

The parameters of moral meaningfulness for a conception of justice are left unclear, except for this: If the political decisions and standards are 'deeply and irremediably corrupt and [objectively?] unjust', the case lies outside of these parameters. The political community does not satisfy the 'essential circumstances of integrity'.[36] So morally egregious states, like apartheid or Nazi states, will not have a morally meaningful vision of justice created by their past decisions.

At one point, Postema switches from talking about principles 'drawn from' past political decisions,[37] 'generate[d]' by them[38] and 'embedded' in them,[39] to talking about historically 'professed' principles.[40] There is a large difference between the two categories. A community may profess ideals it practises but rarely, if at all, and practise quite another vision of justice altogether quite often. Postema thinks that with regard to the ideal of justice, in order for integrity to have value, it must be reasonable for members of the political community to believe their community 'aspir[es]' to justice.[41] For that, presumably, merely being professed as an ideal or only slightly practised is insufficient. We might say that just ideals must be acted on *significantly* in order for this idea about community aspiration to be reasonable.

V. DEEPER LINKS BETWEEN JUSTICE AND INTEGRITY

Recall that Postema's case that integrity is a moral value depends on linking it in service to justice and fidelity. The greater of these in his opinion is justice; hence the title of Postema's work. His main thesis is that integrity is 'justice in political

[33] ibid 298; see also ibid 294.
[34] ibid 295.
[35] ibid 294; Dworkin (n 17) 134.
[36] Postema (n 1) 300.
[37] ibid 293.
[38] ibid 294.
[39] ibid 297.
[40] ibid.
[41] ibid 313.

workclothes'. 'Integrity … simply is justice properly situated in politics …'[42] (But Postema adds that integrity 'displac[es] it in the real world of politics'.[43])

Postema locates an additional connection between integrity and justice in the prerequisites for integrity's having moral value. Pursuing integrity 'makes [moral] sense only among people who want justice, but disagree about what justice requires'.[44] Some of the 'circumstances of integrity', as Postema calls them, include:

(1) the community has 'some degree of unity,' so that past political decisions are actions of a single community. (This is collective responsibility.) Moreover, the decisions and actions of the community, synchronically and diachronically, affect each other's 'meaning' and 'practical force';[45]
(2) people want and demand justice in their institutions and believe it to be feasible. (Hence, they do not find their community, as Postema puts it, 'deeply and irremediably corrupt');[46]
(3) people disagree about what justice requires;
(4) institutions are criticized as unjust on the basis of disputed principles of justice. (Hence, people accept that justice is an ideal or at least worth having. This also follows from (2).);
(5) most citizens[47] regard the society as worth preserving and improving;
(6) citizens do not regard the standards – rules and principles – of the social institutions as 'irremediably chaotic'.[48] (Hence, the people do not think the principles are incapable of being tidied – without too much loss of these standards, I presume – into a coherent system.)

Postema thinks it follows from the circumstances of integrity that it is reasonable for members of the political community to believe that their community 'aspires' to justice. He also adds this condition: 'social and political arrangements are not irremediably unjust'.[49]

Notice that these circumstances impose a significant restriction on the claim that integrity is a moral value of political communities, because they define a narrow set of circumstances. The United States is a common law country for the most part,[50] and has a long history of common law reasoning in its law. There have been and continue to be wide-ranging debates in that country on whether

[42] ibid 306.
[43] ibid 300.
[44] ibid.
[45] ibid 294.
[46] ibid 300.
[47] Postema refers to members of the political community as 'comembers' and also as 'citizens'. The latter suggests he is thinking only of certain types of governments, not monarchies where everyone but the monarch is a subject.
[48] ibid 300 and 298.
[49] ibid 313.
[50] The State of Louisiana is an exception.

the political community is and has been – at least, through its law – 'pervasively unjust'.[51] The charge that the US has been pervasively unjust has been raised, for example, by Marxist-Leninists on economic grounds, and by those painfully aware of the lingering racial stigma of slavery and all its consequences.[52] There are also, significantly, debates on whether the idea of justice is worth pursuing. The charge that justice is not worth pursuing has been raised by those who reject the idea of justice as infected with the wrong moral perspective (eg, irremediably patriarchal). (People believing this will not demand justice of their institutions.) It seems as if Postema is conceding that in this situation, that is the US as it actually is and has been, integrity has no moral value. But perhaps he would emphasise the difference between thinking that political and social arrangements have been pervasively unjust and thinking they are irremediably unjust. Perhaps, too, Postema would say that the persons who must regard their community as aspiring to justice (and think that is a good thing) need not be everyone, nor every reasonable person, nor every reasonable moral agent, in order for integrity to have moral value.

A more significant restriction on the claim that integrity is a moral value of political communities stems from Postema's assumption that the persons in the circumstances of justice criticise social arrangements on the basis of disparate principles, and so commit themselves to principles of justice (and endorse them). Recall some points made in section III about casuistry. That a way of distributing wealth, opportunities for education, opportunities to participate in political life and so on are just, is a conclusion of casuistry. One can publicly justify an institution under some real-world conditions by publicly proclaiming that it is just (that is, if it is just), as opposed to being benevolent, for instance. One can publicly justify a social arrangement by making an empirical point – for example, that a particular redistribution of wealth does not take all that much from the rich, and enables mothers earning minimum wage to buy both food and medicine for their children. Ordinary people justify incompletely, sometimes by labelling something as fitting a moral category, sometimes by giving empirical facts, rarely by reaching to provide some principle which it satisfies, and almost never by defending such a principle. Postema's communities in which he will argue that integrity is a genuine value consist instead of idealised moral reasoners who adopt a general principle and then apply it. They are ideal also because they use critical reflection, that is, deliberation, to assess the principles they and others endorse and to apply their principles.

[51] Postema's phrase in Postema (n 1) 312.

[52] Postema, ibid 297, takes an address by Frederick Douglass in 1852 to be an example of a call for what Postema calls 'regret', which is an aspect of integrity. (See discussion of regret, to follow.) I take it as a claim that the political community in which Douglass finds himself is pervasively unjust and does not, in fact, aspire to justice, whatever its rhetoric suggests. Alternatively, Douglass might be taken to claim that the standards of his society are normatively inconsistent to the level of being 'irremediably chaotic'.

I have mentioned some connections Postema draws between integrity and justice. But by far the most important connection between integrity and justice lies elsewhere. Postema provides an argument that there is both an 'ideal' and a 'consensual' aspect to justice, then admits that these are in 'tension'. If I understand him rightly, he thinks integrity strikes just the right middle point between the ideal and the 'mere[ly] convention[al] or consensus[ual]'.[53] Integrity, he thinks, feeds the need to 'approximate [ideal] justice in the political circumstances in which we find ourselves'.[54] That, apparently, is the best one can do, given the tension in justice; so, Postema concludes, 'We are bound to the complex discipline of integrity whenever we have reason to seek justice in the circumstances of integrity'.[55]

All of this depends, of course, on his case for the 'consensual' facet of justice, which is part of what he calls a 'communal' aspect.[56] That case begins with two premises, designed to show that 'justice is public':

(a) It is a public good.[57]
(b) It 'provides a scheme of public justification, and so is deliberated about publicly'.[58]

To evaluate this argument, it is important to consider some metaethical assumptions about justice. On the first assumption, there is a correct vision of a just society. There are correct general principles about justice, ordered in a certain way, and there is a correct method of doing the casuistry. On this assumption, when Postema is writing about principles approximating justice,[59] he means principles approximating the right answer. The 'fundamental concerns' of justice Postema will refer to are parts of, or implications of, this correct theory. On the second assumption, there is no single correct vision of a just society. Instead, there are competing defensible theories of justice, which are either equally morally defensible or incommensurable. On this assumption, when Postema is writing about principles approximating justice, he means principles approximating one (or more) of these alternatives. The 'fundamental concerns' of justice on this assumption will be something that all of these theories have in common.

Postema does not commit himself to the first assumption, but he does not reject it either. It matters to the nature of the argument which assumption he is making. I propose to go through his argument in two stages – with the first assumption, and then with the second.

[53] ibid 306.
[54] ibid.
[55] ibid.
[56] See, on the communal project aspect, Postema (n 1) 298.
[57] ibid 305.
[58] ibid.
[59] Integrity, Postema claims, is a search for the 'justice-approximating principles' to which a community is 'committed in virtue of [its] … past collective decisions': ibid 300–01.

A. The Argument, on the Assumption that there is a Right Answer to the Question of What Justice Requires

I start by noting that Postema seems to be drawing on an earlier work, in which he assumes that moral agency requires one to do moral reasoning through deliberation.[60] The reader will recall that Postema is considering only communities consisting of moral agents who fulfill that requirement. Note, second, that premise (b) is itself an argument, and that it is invalid. It is uncontroversial that principles of justice provide a scheme of public justification in that they are available and appropriate to use in public for this purpose. So, as I noted in the Introduction, do other moral ideals such as benevolence or perfectionism when applied to states. But it does not follow – and it would be equivocation on 'public justification' to conclude – that the principles of justice must provide such a scheme in the sense that they are actually used as justification by the public (or anyone else) in public.

But I doubt that (b) is meant as an argument. Postema contended in that earlier work that morality requires thinking from a collective, or plural, point of view in which one considers the best collective plan for discharging 'our' obligations, adopts, along with others, 'plural intentions' for us, and tries to do one's part in this collective plan by meshing one's sub-plans with others. Perhaps Postema assumes that if we are all deliberating and we are all adopting this plural point of view, in order to mesh our sub-plans we must be publicly deliberating.

On the other hand, Postema seems to provide quite a different argument for (b) on page 304. There he claims that justice brings right relationships to members of the same community and that 'it is important' for rational, moral persons 'who are members of the same community' to recognise that their relationships are right. His reasons start with the idea that recognition – as a social and moral equal, I assume – is 'a critical need' of individuals; he also says there is a 'hunger' for it that 'sometimes even outstrips in importance, the needs addressed by the specific goods that justice distributes'. He claims that social arrangements have expressive capability – apparently expressing a judgment about relative value or status.[61] So social orders send messages, and just social orders send the message people hunger for. He seems to assume the same about the proffering of principles for justifying them.[62] People have a 'critical need' for

[60] Postema (n 6) 35.

[61] '[M]oral persons,' Postema tells us, 'are concerned not only with the benefits of just arrangements, but with what those arrangements say publicly about the moral status of each member': Postema (n 1) 304.

[62] All of the above from ibid 304. See also ibid 311: justice applies to '[t]he way we arrange our communal affairs and distribute the benefits and burdens of common life'; but it is also concerned with 'the messages we send to each other regarding our respective places in the community'.

'recognition of each other as rational moral persons'. He adds that this recognition 'takes the form of endorsement of a set of principles by which they justify their individual actions and common institutions'. He concludes from this that the justification must be 'a matter of offering reasons *to each other*'.[63]

If I understand him rightly, being the appropriate addressee of my justificatory principles is morally insufficient, because of the 'critical need' for recognition as a moral peer. Being the intended addressee of my justificatory principles is insufficient, as well. I must actually address you – that is, attempt a communication – and since the 'you' in this case is every other moral agent in my political community, I must, given the contingencies and practicalities of actual political life, communicate in some forum that is sufficiently public. (Going about to every other individual to deliver this message privately is usually unfeasible.) Since this requirement is on you as well, there is a moral requirement for mutual address in a public forum. It does not follow, however, that this has to be the same forum in both cases.

There is a good of social recognition as a peer.[64] As Postema may agree, mere endorsement of principles for justifying institutions and individual actions communicated publicly is insufficient for it. The good in question depends, in part, on those institutions and the larger culture – for example, on whether the larger culture identifies you as a member of a sub-group and on how members of that group are portrayed in art, literature, myth, history, on public monuments, in humour and so on. Then there is what and who gets memorialised, and whether the shared epistemic life of the community discounts or ignores or appropriates concepts from your group. In addition, social recognition as a peer depends on the existence of structural injustices (injustices in those social arrangements and institutions), some of them created or protected by laws, and whether criticism of them as unjust is discounted, silenced or blocked from general circulation. (For example, is there a dominant and privileged group with a virtual monopoly in what Mill called the 'marketplace of ideas'?) All of this carries messages relevant to justice, regard and recognition as a peer. This recognition depends, too, on what empirical facts are generally assumed about you; because factual claims are part of justifying individual actions.

Postema's point may be that this endorsement of principles in a public forum is a necessary condition for the social good in question. The justification of political actions ideally would be public, addressed to the public, because doing so both helps to satisfy an important psychological need and thereby helps to confer a social good. If the justification were successful and the institutions just, principles of justice would be used as a justification of them, publicly.

If Postema's argument rests on the good of social recognition as a peer, it is in tension with his later claim that justice is 'temporally extended,' which will be

[63] ibid 304 (original emphasis).

[64] Postema would insist it is *mutual* recognition (ibid 317 at note 55).

examined in section VI. The psychological needs of most past generations will be unaffected by the social arrangements we change or institute now, because those psychological needs no longer exist. The only generations' psychological needs for recognition of their moral status that can be met by perceiving a message from social arrangements or principles publicly alluded to are the ones wholly or partially still in existence.

Postema then adds, by way of supporting the claim that justice is essentially public: 'justice is *manifest* right order'.[65] By calling justice 'manifest', Postema wants, in part, to claim that it is knowable by the public. Justice is 'not some transcendent matter accessible only to a few'.[66] Presumably, discovering its nature and requirements is feasible by the path of public discussion, argumentation and deliberation. (Because they are so discoverable, correct principles of justice can be used for public justification.) So 'manifest' is something like *recognisable*.

One can ask why we should believe that it is a requirement of justice that people recognise a just social institution or society when it exists. On the current metaethical assumption, it is unclear what reason Postema would provide. Perhaps he could argue: (i) justice requires not only that a just society exist but that it be stable; and (ii) a just society will not be stable once it exists unless everyone (or every reasonable moral agent) recognises its justice. Assumption (ii) is an empirical claim for which, to the best of my knowledge, we have no evidence, as a just society has never existed among humans.

There is no obvious connection between public deliberation, however, and achieving the recognition. Public deliberation is not guaranteed, and perhaps not very likely, to carry a society toward convergence on a moral truth. The history of western political (and moral) philosophy seems to confirm this notion. Moreover, the public is not, in general, very good at deliberation. Postema might claim that, in order to attain a just society, they ought to become good. It may be another circumstance of integrity that the moral agents in question are good deliberators; I shall assume so in all that follows. (Perhaps I should say in this section that the moral agents are capable of being very good deliberators, in order to account for disagreement at the theoretical level about justice on the twin assumptions that justice is manifest and that there is one right answer to theoretical questions about justice.)

My discussion reveals that Postema has at least three (major) premises: (i) justice is a public good; (ii) justice provides a scheme of public justification; and (iii) justice is deliberated about publicly. Using the further premise that in the circumstances of integrity, people disagree about what justice requires and this disagreement is reasonable, he draws the conclusion that 'justice is by its

[65] ibid 305.

[66] Gerald Postema, private correspondence, 31 July 2018. (Thus, the manifest nature is consistent with divergence of opinions, even reasonable opinions, about justice.)

very nature *political*'. He adds, 'By this I mean that it is essential to justice that it be achieved only through the group efforts of members of political society *working out its basic terms*.'[67] At first glance, it may seem he means to make a purely empirical claim: 'In the world in which we live, we can secure the public good of justice only if we work in concert with others …'[68] Although I will shortly suggest a scenario that challenges the breadth of this claim, it is true to some extent – perhaps a great extent – about justice in the casuistic sense. However, it does not follow from the major premises alone. Moreover, this characteristic does not distinguish justice – in the casuistic sense – from other public goods like peace on earth or climate change mitigation. But I doubt that the conclusion is meant to be purely empirical.

Recall that we are making the metaethical assumption of a right answer. Let us now, for the sake of argument, grant that we need to discover what justice is at the general principles level in order to (i) create just institutions and (ii) have their justice be recognised by the public; and that we need to have their justice be recognised by the public. The who and how of participation in the cooperative and deliberative process is vitally important. One plausible assumption is that, as a decision procedure, public discussion and deliberation requires for its success (or, rather, the probability of its success) the broadest possible range of participants, representing all of the divergent views. Moreover, it requires shared epistemic resources rich enough to express all divergent views and ensure equal uptake, and willingness on the part of participants to credit each other and to comprehend divergent views respectfully.

All of these additional provisos look like demands of justice: justice in the conditions for public deliberation about justice.

Postema's argument here ends with the contention that when the requirements of justice are in dispute and there are various reasonable beliefs circulating about it, justice not only requires 'right order' but 'equally' requires a certain procedure. That procedure is as follows: the move toward a vision of justice in a society (and toward a just society) must be 'established … through reasonable members of political society working together to forge a conception all can recognize as reasonable'.[69] This is the 'consensual' aspect of justice, according to Postema. (Recall that he also thinks there's an 'ideal' aspect.) Notice that if people recognise the conception as reasonable, it must be reasonable. And Postema has claimed that 'all can' recognise it as reasonable. One must suppose

[67] Postema (n 1) 305 (emphasis added). Compare with ibid 302, 'justice is essentially political'.

[68] ibid.

[69] ibid 306. So ibid 301, 'in the circumstances of integrity, justice itself demands that we seek some common understanding of the requirements of justice'. This is why he says (ibid 301), 'Justice … is a … product of deliberation and common action … [T]his is true … in virtue of the very structure and point of justice itself'. On the same page he says, 'integrity comes into play as a significant moral value … when there is reason to forge or at least work to approximate a common conception of justice'.

this is all who are affected – all such moral agents, at any rate. The 'reasonable' subset of them may be the class of persons he envisages as 'working together'.

Note, too, that 'reasonable' does not mean correct. So Postema would be claiming that justice requires that the society produce, from a procedure with near-universal participation, a vision of justice that is reasonable but may be nonetheless off the mark. On the assumption about a right answer, justice requires a society to produce a vision of justice that is correct and on the mark. Merely reasonable does not fit the demands of justice. Note that Postema needs reasonable approximations to justice, or morally meaningful conceptions of justice, to hope to connect integrity to serving justice, let alone to produce an 'internal justification' for following morally incorrect precedential decisions.

At this point, it might seem obvious that by assuming that there is a right answer about justice, I have doomed Postema's argument at the start. There is reason to think I have not, however. Postema claims that there is a 'dynamic' aspect to justice, which applies to progress toward a just society. He might respond that on the way to a just society, justice permits us – actually, requires us – to aim at the merely reasonable. This is to assume that there is a set of requirements set by justice for social progress in its direction, and also to suppose that set lowers the bar for the kind of collective vision of justice to be achieved. However, it is as plausible to assume that set lowers the bar for the procedure for achieving this collective vision of justice. Maybe it is permissible, en route to a just society, for a conception to be forged by a few working together, and it is promising if these people represent all the divergent views and meet some other conditions of rationality. If there are just compromises on the ideal aspect of justice, required by progress toward justice, we can expect that there are just compromises on the consensual. Asserting the former and denying the latter appears *ad hoc*.

I think that Postema has another argument for his contention on procedure in the circumstances of integrity: this procedure respects 'fundamental concerns' of justice. He does not explicitly state those fundamental concerns of justice, but it is clear that he thinks one of them is some kind of moral equality. He talks about a 'proper regard for each member as an equal member of the community'.[70]

Postema does not explicitly connect this premise to a procedure. Filling in some of the gap will be instructive in assessing Postema's case for integrity. It seems clear that procedural justice for choosing substantive justice principles to shape social institutions of one's society requires giving every affected person (or those who qualify as moral agents, anyway) an equal voice and equal influence. So, a consensus procedure serves justice *only* under some important conditions. We might call them *peer participation conditions*. The opportunity

[70] ibid 311.

to participate in the consensus must be fairly distributed. No one with reasonable views must be silenced or unheard. That is the who of participation. I am assuming Postema means to convey all of this by the 'reasonable members of political society working together' language (ie he may mean *all* reasonable persons …).

In addition, the how of 'working together' is important, as I remarked earlier. Peer participation conditions also include the conditions for successful communication among those with divergent views. The interlocutors must understand each other and accord a proper level of credibility to each other. This requires, as Davis puts it, that the 'set of interpretive epistemic resources (eg, concepts, meanings …) … is shared between interlocutors'.[71] Roughly, the participants must share the conceptions of moral concepts, or the concepts themselves, that they use to articulate the principles they think are principles of justice, so that their thoughts are or can be made thoroughly intelligible to others. The shared set of conceptual tools must be rich enough and broad enough for this kind of interchange, particularly if there are attempts to defend the views. Finally, and at least equally important, no one's views must meet with prejudice that interferes with uptake, that automatically discounts.[72] There must be no unfair 'blockages in the circulation' of their ideas to others;[73] ideas must have equality of access to the public domain. Obviously, if the society is not ideal to begin with – the interlocutors are arguing about justice in a society that historically has been, to some extent, unjust – one or more of these conditions will not be met. Usually, several will not be.

When some of the peer participation conditions are not met, the 'critical need' for recognition of their proper moral status held by members whose views have been marginalised is inconsistent with preserving the views arrived at unjustly, even with a limited scope, in social arrangements. This is what narrowing, but not overruling, a morally incorrect precedent does. Doing that magnifies the insult. It is, then, somewhat puzzling that Postema should appeal to needs for recognition of moral status and proper regard for 'rational, moral persons' in an attempt to justify precedential following of morally incorrect judicial decisions in a society that can at best claim to only approximate justice, and so is, and has been, at least somewhat unjust.

Let us now suppose that the peer participation conditions are satisfied and also that the political community is in the circumstances of integrity. We are now confining the defence of integrity to a political situation that is in many respects ideal. In this situation, does justice require a consensual procedure? Suppose, for the sake of argument, that it does. Recall that justice, according to Postema, has two facets: the consensual and the ideal. Postema claims that the two are of

[71] E Davis, 'On Epistemic Appropriation,' (2018) 128 *Ethics* 703.
[72] Note that some of these conditions improve the ability of interlocutors to deliberate together.
[73] Davis (n 71) 721–22.

equal importance. This claim is important to his argument for integrity, which, the reader will recall, he thinks strikes just the right compromise between the two facets. But *contra* Postema,[74] it does not follow from his arguments that the consensual aspect of justice is as important as the ideal aspect in justice, even under these ideal participation conditions.

I have already argued that consensus – moving toward general agreement – is not *more* important than justice in the participation conditions for it. Otherwise, one might get general agreement but the movement toward it consists of some – the marginalised – adjusting their sense of justice much more towards that of others, the privileged. Consensus and peer participation are not equally important for the same reason. Equally important values are such that a gain in one may compensate for a loss in another. But we get the same problem – a skewed movement toward the views of the dominant or privileged – in a gain in consensus that is a loss in peer participation; and there is no compensation on grounds of justice for that loss (unless, of course, the views of the dominant happen to be more morally defensible or even objectively correct). With all of this, I should emphasise, Postema may well agree.

Now I will argue that this consensual aspect is not as important as the ideal aspect in justice. That is, it is not if some conceptions of justice are either mistaken or less defensible than others; *a fortiori*, if there is only one correct conception of justice. First, the claim of equality requires that the two aspects be commensurable. Let us assume that they are. Next, consider a conception of justice that would be formed in the process of public deliberation where everyone has equal input but the emerging conception is off the mark, though not egregiously off the mark. A less-than-truly-just society or decision means that a set of persons will be cheated of something that they should have, and sometimes the price they pay in this situation is high. For instance, suppose that the evolving conception of justice gets the economic principles about wealth distribution a little wrong. That can cost a number of persons enough of a loss of income that they have to choose between food and medicine, cannot find an affordable place to live or a secure one, cannot keep all their children well fed or properly educated, and so on. Some of this leads to perpetuating an underclass in society; some of it is life-threatening. Health, security and other core goods can be seriously affected by the mistakes of the coalescing conception, or by the absence of the proper social distribution mechanisms while society waits for a consensus. When these goods are at stake, avoiding the kind of injustice to individuals who lose big under the non-ideal *status quo* seems to me to be a far more pressing demand of justice than anything else Postema has mentioned: viz, avoiding having a non-ideal process in choosing the conception of justice to apply, closing persons out of deliberations, precluding the formation of consensus about what is just, sending messages about relative standing that people understand.

[74] Postema (n 1) 306.

From the point of view of justice, I maintain that it is sometimes, and perhaps often, *less* important to allow individuals to slowly coalesce on a conception of justice that is off the mark than it is to make one's society as on the mark as is feasible. It certainly can be from the point of view of other moral values, such as welfare.

Postema would respond that, under the conditions I envisage, the only way to correct the distributions is to impose them; and he argues that, given the public (and political) nature of justice, such imposition is precluded by the very idea of justice.[75] He admits that this contention is not 'immediately evident',[76] so he produces an argument. His argument relies on his claim that justice is manifest right order in a situation in which, nonetheless, 'what justice requires is itself reasonably in dispute'.[77] He may be referring to disagreements in casuistry, not necessarily at the theoretical level. Different theories can concur on an outcome, and persons with the same theory can differ on an outcome if they hold different empirical beliefs. The only other premise he produces is the one about justice (at the theoretical level) requiring fundamental concerns be respected in the process. One does not get support for his conclusion from these two without adding a premise that results in circularity. One example is the premise that respecting these fundamental concerns in procedure is more important than respecting the concerns (are they not fundamental?) of just distributions of material conditions necessary for human health and personal security. Another is the premise that being 'manifest' means that justice is, by definition, the thing that is only discoverable by public deliberation in a consensual procedure among all reasonable affected persons.

I conclude that Postema has not shown the equality of the consensual and ideal aspects of justice; and he must, for his purposes, or he must restrict the argument for integrity to those situations in which they are equal. But it follows from the latter move that integrity need not serve justice, even in the circumstances of integrity, even when the peer participation conditions are and have been met, even when a society has a 'morally meaningful' vision of justice drawn from past political decisions. Recall that Postema wants to say that integrity serves justice. Another way to summarise my point is this: The way to serve justice is to satisfy its processes and make the distributions in the order in which

[75] Postema wants to show that his consensus process is required by 'the very structure and point of justice itself' (ibid 301). Postema asserts (ibid 306) that 'in the circumstances of integrity, justice cannot be [ie must not be] imposed'. In a later work, Postema presents an argument that supports a similar conclusion. Roughly, he argues that because of the conditions that must be met for a state in which law functions to coordinate behaviour (when there are deep divisions on moral matters), for the compliance of law subjects to be morally justified, a vision of justice cannot be imposed on them by an authority. See GJ Postema, 'Law's Autonomy and Public Practical Reasoning' in RP George (ed.), *The Autonomy of Law: Essays on Legal Positivism* (Clarendon Press 1996) 79. Examining this argument is beyond the scope of this chapter.

[76] Postema (n 1) 305.

[77] ibid.

justice ranks them. Integrity, as Postema understands it, sometimes reverses that order.

But perhaps Postema wants to argue that integrity serves justice to some extent, or pro tanto – procedurally. There is a core of good sense to Postema's strategy of tying consensus on political principles for governing a society with a fundamental concern of justice. If a non-ideal society were to implement a set of principles in political actions, and it had a choice between imposing a set of principles selected by one or a few and implementing a set of principles on which there was consensus among all reasonable persons in the society under peer participation conditions, it would be better to choose the latter, *ceteris paribus*. The latter is more respectful of persons as rational and autonomous choosers and moral agents; or perhaps the latter treats all reasonable persons as political equals, and they have moral rights to be so treated. (Consensus to some extent serves equality and respect and is a *pro tanto* reason for certain procedures.) This shows that there is some moral value in consensus, *ceteris paribus*. Perhaps what Postema wants to say is that, under certain conditions, consensus satisfies procedural justice; and this seems to be true. But the *ceteris paribus* clause does significant work here. If consensus must emerge slowly while real substantive injustices persist but the imposed principles will end them, if consensus will emerge on something that maintains real substantive injustices but the imposed principles will not, it is *not* better to wait for principles on which there is consensus. It is not more just, all things considered.

Though I do not want to press the point, one could go further. In cases in which life and health for some depend upon immediately curing distributive injustices, it is arguable that procedural justice is what Rawls in *A Theory of Justice* called 'imperfect'.[78] Imperfect procedural justice has an independent criterion for a fair outcome (eg, everyone has an income sufficient to meet both food and medical needs) but no procedure that guarantees this outcome. If procedural justice is imperfect under these non-ideal conditions, and if consensus leads toward or perpetrates real justices, consensus will not be procedurally just at all. So perhaps sometimes there is no extent to which justice requires a consensus procedure. At any rate, the circumstances in which that procedure is pro tanto just may be more limited than Postema allows. This has implications for the kind of theory of adjudication he is contributing to; but that point will be postponed for the conclusion.

B. The Argument, Assuming No Right Answer on Justice

Now let us assume that there is no right answer to the question of what justice requires but, rather, several morally defensible, reasonable, 'morally significant' ones.

[78] J Rawls, *A Theory of Justice* (Belknap Press 1971).

It does not much matter to morality which conception of justice a society ends up with from the set of morally defensible ones, but it does matter to morality how the society ends up with implementing a conception of justice from the list – that is, does the casuistry. It matters, for instance, that the society ends up with general agreement arrived at under what I have called 'peer participation conditions'. The argument for this is that part of what it is to be a reasonable (morally defensible, morally significant) conception of justice is to recognise this procedure for settling issues of justice when there are reasonable disagreements about justice. It is to recognise, and draw the correct implications from, fundamental concerns of justice.

This set of assumptions looks much more promising for Postema's argument. The set is in line with his interest in public reasoning, the moral point of view and his earlier characterisation of a 'plural perspective'.[79] The set of assumptions fits nicely with his language, cited in section V.A, about 'forg[ing] or at least work[ing] to approximate a common conception of justice'. But appearances can be deceiving. Though the current set of metaethical assumptions renders some of the previous criticisms inappropriate, it does not render all of them inappropriate. In this section, I will argue that the metaethical assumptions cannot support some of Postema's argument.

Recall that Postema is assuming that there are disputes among reasonable members of society about justice (at the level of general principles, in addition to casuistry). That is one of the circumstances of integrity. The first immediate problem for Postema is that it does not follow on assumptions now being made that society must aim for any particular permissible conception of justice. Justice requires that society implement a conception of justice, that is, have the institutions and social arrangements that would be the outcome of a permitted (ie reasonable) conception of justice. This is not the same as fastening on a particular conception, since the same outcome could be arrived at through different conceptions. The social arrangements and institutions must be *as if* they were selected on the basis of a permitted conception, but they need not be actually selected on that basis.

Society needs a fair procedure to settle the question of casuistry – is this new social arrangement or that institutional rule or structure just? If the empirical facts are both settled and widely accepted (and so are the economic theories), we have come to the limits of argumentation in the sense of reason-giving. If the peer participation conditions are met, given that the idealised moral agents engage in public justification by way of proffering principles to each other, proper respect for the interlocutors as rational agents has been paid. What the proffering of justificatory principles in public can do for their recognition as social peers has been done. Why, in such a situation, is it not fair and appropriate, consistent

[79] See Postema (n 6).

with justice, to cast a fair lottery for the winning theoretical view? Why insist on a consensual procedure aiming at general agreement?

As I understand him, Postema would rely at this point on a claim about coherence. If we now cast a lottery and decide in accordance with reasonable conception 1, and later cast another lottery (when another dispute arises in casuistry) and decide in accordance with reasonable conception 2, our decisions are not coherent, because the principles on which they are based are not coherent. But justice requires coherence, Postema contends.[80]

Now, under these conditions, the society will not be approximating any particular conception of justice. But by hypothesis, under these conditions, each decision is just in its outcome. The social arrangement chosen in each case is a correct result of casuistry from a permitted conception of justice. So the society ends up with two just social arrangements. If the mandate of justice is to implement just social arrangements from a fair procedure respecting the fundamental concerns of justice, the society has fulfilled that mandate twice.

Justice requires coherence in this respect: coherence is a necessary condition of the moral defensibility of a theory or conception of justice – that is, a theory containing general principles. If Postema were to claim that justice in casuistry requires that the outcomes all be defensible on the same coherent theory, he would beg the question. It is not obvious, given the considerations adduced in the previous paragraph. (I will later, in section VI.B, mention an exception for reasonable reliance by those who manage to discern the principles in the outcomes from the past.) Moreover, since the case for integrity in casuistry is in large part that it approximates coherence (in the principles applied), this case requires that coherence in casuistry have moral value. If you assume that integrity has moral value then of course you assume that a large piece of it – a polity acting on coherent principles – has moral value. But when the question is whether integrity (either understood as Dworkin does or as Postema does) has moral value, the question extends to all of its features. We need some argument for this same piece having moral value. Under the metaethical assumption we are now making, the value of integrity will be challenged precisely by persons who do not see why it is morally better to have a polity act from a set of coherent principles than to act each time on reasonable principles, whether or not they belong to the same set of coherent principles. Postema cannot, then, assume in the premises that coherence in casuistry has moral value, let alone that societies are morally required to attain it.

I have issued what Postema anticipates as 'a fundamental challenge to the claims' of his essay.[81] Postema's response is to say it 'strikes me as utterly implausible' that it is 'no matter for concern' if 'principles underlying one part of the

[80] '[I]ncoherence undermines any attempt to do justice in a community': Postema (n 1) 313.
[81] ibid.

law do not fit intelligibly with those underlying a different part'.[82] Unfortunately, this is an appeal to intuitions, not an argument.

Finally, Postema might refer to the circumstances of integrity and claim that decisions based on principles that are not coherent are 'irremediably chaotic'. As the reader will recall, a circumstance of integrity is that citizens believe these principles are not so chaotic. If the lottery were implemented, Postema might claim, after a while the citizens will not hold that belief. If they started with this belief, abandoning it in response to successive lotteries would require that citizens engage in enough philosophical deliberation to check that the outcomes chosen are not all defensible on a coherent set of principles. If the people are real, most of them will be either incapable of doing so or unwilling to do so.

Since, however, we are imagining idealised moral agents, we can imagine that they are so capable and so willing. Yet the envisaged response contains a concession that undermines it. The concession is implied by the phrase 'after a while'. Before that point, the society is in the circumstances of integrity. The case for the value of integrity in this interval cannot be made if and to the extent that it depends on coalescing on a particular permissible conception of justice.

So if such coalescing is the goal of the consensual aspect of justice, on the present metaethical assumption, Postema has not provided a compelling argument that the alleged consensual aspect of justice is of equal importance with the ideal aspect (which, on this metaethical assumption, consists of more than one ideal).

Integrity is not confined to consensus on principles among the current population, as Postema makes clear. Integrity is tied to past legal and political decisions in non-ideal societies so tightly that its outcome in any particular judicial case may be very different not only from what justice in an ideal society demands, but from what the conception of justice that the community would coalesce upon now demands. The main task of arguing that the consensus extends diachronically into the past Postema defers to his discussion of fidelity and its connection to justice.

VI. THE PAST: LINK BETWEEN INTEGRITY, FIDELITY AND JUSTICE

Recall that initially, Postema says that integrity serves fidelity. He does not mean by 'fidelity' mere faithfulness to something in the past – say, observances. That would not make for a very plausible argument, as this kind of fidelity has, at best, only extrinsic value. That is to say, its value comes from the value of the thing one is faithful to or from another value that being faithful is related to or serves in some way.[83] (By 'extrinsic value' I do not mean merely instrumental

[82] ibid.

[83] Postema chooses the latter only: 'fidelity … has its value only in service of other values': ibid 307 (emphasis omitted).

value.[84]) There seems nothing good in the paedophile or rapist's being faithful to his sexual pattern, for instance (save instrumentally – it may make it possible for the police to catch him); nor, to use a more innocuous example,[85] does there seem anything good in Rawls' ritualistic grass-blade counter continuing his pattern.[86] Fidelity to patterns, observances or practices is not automatically worth serving.

Postema means by 'fidelity' a kind of 'keeping faith' with other persons;[87] and in the case of a political community, with other members of that community. But 'keeping faith with' someone normally means being loyal to that person or supporting that person. That is the sense in which it is plausible that in friendship, as Postema claims, friends keep faith with each other.[88] The past enters epistemically to provide information on which one can decide if one wants to keep faith, what is the likely reaction by the other to loyalty or support, what kind of support is appreciated by this person and the like.[89] It may also enter to ground obligations of gratitude, compensation and so on.

That will not do for Postema's purposes. Instead, he applies an idea by Thomas Hill, at first to the relationship of friendship, and then to the relationship of co-membership in a political community: some moral values are 'temporally extended' wholes. A value is temporally extended when it is 'tied up with its mode of coming to be or its manifestation to others'.[90] This coming to be or manifestation extends across time. Postema claims that the value of friendship is 'temporally extended'. The truth in this is that important human relationships like friendship are diachronic for their very existence, and when judging the value of a friendship, we (almost) always look diachronically.

The value of a community, Postema contends, is also a temporally extended whole. Now Postema is looking only at communities that 'mak[e] justice a fundamental aim'.[91] He adds that 'in [a] … way' the value of justice is also temporally extended. Now, it is clear that a realised and good plan to achieve a just society would be temporally extended, in part because such plans take much time to execute. A just society takes generations to build (is unattainable within a single generation), especially when one starts with a society that is not (perfectly) just. Moreover, just social arrangements may endure from the past, and so would be temporally extended. But this is not all that Postema has in mind. He alludes once more to the expressive character of just institutions,

[84] Postema is clear that the value of fidelity is not instrumental: ibid.

[85] A common objection to examples like this is that if the example is particularly morally egregious, our intuitive response may be so blunted that it is blind to the subtle difference some factor does make.

[86] Rawls (n 78) 423.

[87] Postema (n 1) 308. He also says it is 'a matter of keeping faith with a common past': ibid 307.

[88] ibid 309.

[89] This is to hold the past as, Postema says, 'merely the source of causal traces that we must now take into account in our practical or moral reasoning': ibid 310.

[90] ibid 309.

[91] ibid 310.

presumably those structures that have been created in the past and are preserved and maintained now. 'Through it [justice],' he claims, 'we give expression to our regard for each other *across generations* …'[92]

From considerations of justice Postema switches to fidelity, namely 'keeping faith with the past'. He writes about a certain '[r]espect for past practice',[93] which is a kind of fidelity. Postema thinks it is fidelity to past persons. The 'collective commitment to justice as the fundamental mode of … relationships,' which is shared by the past and the present members of the society in the circumstances of integrity, requires, he explains, viewing past political decisions 'as committed to and directed towards establishing and maintaining justice'.[94] So a kind of fidelity to past political decisions is required as well. Postema describes all of this as a partnership over time among the generations.[95]

The argument summarised above is both vital and importantly compressed. It is compressed not only in my presentation but in Postema's. I propose to unpack it by asking, and then exploring the answers to, two questions.

We approach the first question by considering the terms of this partnership. It is clear that the current population in the circumstances envisaged is a partner with past populations in the general quest for justice in at least the following way: they share that goal in common. There is another partnership Postema may assume: every person, or every reasonable person, or every reasonable moral agent, from the past of the community with a view about substantive principles of justice (or perhaps, a reasonable view) counts as much as the present population in a consensus on principles that should shape the current and future social institutions. Indeed, Postema might argue that regard for past persons and procedural justice in an ongoing community require this. The result would be the consensual aspect of justice, inter-generationally.

But partnership in and faithfulness to a general goal is not faithfulness to particulars, including *the way* the past generations went about pursuing that goal. Faithfulness to a goal does not automatically require faithfulness to the content of previous conceptions of the goal, or to the casuistic outcomes of those views.

So what are the reasons to think that a current population in these circumstances pro tanto ought to 'respect' 'past practices' as they show up in past political decisions in the way that integrity, or for that matter, any robust notion of fidelity, demands? That is the first question. And the second is, would doing so have moral value? (That is, is this kind of fidelity extrinsically valuable?) As before, let us examine these questions by adopting alternatively the two metaethical assumptions considered in section V.

[92] ibid 311 (emphasis added).
[93] ibid.
[94] ibid.
[95] ibid 310.

A. On the Assumption that there is a Correct Vision of Justice

'In communities aimed at justice, where not only the reality falls short of the standard, but the standard itself is in dispute, fidelity is integrity,' says Postema.[96] But integrity is not mere fidelity. Postema adds that fidelity has to be 'appropriate'. This entails, he says, criticism of the past, and room for what he calls 'regret'. Now, regret, as developed by Postema, is an interesting idea. For it does not require us to reject an idea (or, in the case of a judicial decision, overrule it, and thus end its legal influence) by way of being critical of it; we can limit its current and future effect, and that will be exercising regret. (We can also compensate for it or do other forms of historical redress, and that will be exercising regret.[97]) The role for appropriate fidelity is why Postema says that integrity requires a balance of respect and regret.

It is important to emphasise that Postema cannot mean by 'appropriate fidelity' faithfulness only to those aspects of a vision of justice that ought to be implemented for independent reasons of correctness. That would make nonsense of his talk of justice-approximating principles; it also eviscerates his case that integrity is a distinct moral virtue, a reason supplanting justice in the search for justice ('in the real world of politics'[98]). So, appropriate fidelity, and integrity, as Postema conceives them, preserve some moral mistakes of the past. On the current metaethical assumption, the moral myopia of the past will, through appropriate fidelity and integrity, drag the emerging 'vision of justice' into, at best, a mere approximation of the real thing.

This discussion is getting closer to a connection with the practice of precedent in common law systems; for in precedent, previous decisions (so the claim goes) are either followed, or overruled, or distinguished and narrowed. So it may seem that, on the one hand, Postema has made philosophical progress. But, on the other hand, it also seems that the progress is at the cost of making it less than plausible that appropriate fidelity is morally good, let alone a moral requirement. Can we construct a counter-argument using Postema's ideas?

Consider whether a due regard procedural justice argument can adequately defend the conclusion that 'appropriate fidelity' has moral value. On this argument, giving past persons their due regard requires taking in the content of their views (the winning views?) on justice and implementing those views partially or completely in present decisions. One problem is that, while regard for past persons does seem to support letting them have an initial say, it does not support leaving what Postema calls 'islands of compromised coherence'[99] in a body of

[96] ibid 311. Again, 'my thesis is that fidelity takes the shape of integrity in a community bound to pursue justice in the circumstances of integrity': ibid 307.

[97] Postema points out that, in addition, reparative justice may require compensation for the injuries done by the mistake.

[98] Postema (n 1) 300.

[99] ibid 297. See also ibid 314, 'pockets of incoherence'.

law 'striv[ing]' for what decades ago I called 'global coherence'.[100] In the islands of compromised coherence, we uphold some past decision representing an old but 'regretted' idea, but limit its influence going forward. However, I will argue that if we think an old idea is a mistake, and that mistake is the only thing that justifies a past judicial decision, then nothing in regard for past persons requires us to preserve it in the legal system, give it any current or future influence. Respect for the goal – a just society – seems, rather, to require that we stop the influence of any mistaken ideas about justice we identify, and reject them in our practical consideration. Faithfulness at this level – to the inter-generational goal – requires rejection, not the limited-influence form of 'regret'.

We show past persons regard, and are procedurally just, when we let them have equal input into the decision-making process under conditions of peer participation. That is a procedure. Why make Postema's further assumption on the outcome of the procedure, namely that giving past persons their due regard requires taking in the content of their views on justice and implementing those views partially or completely in present decisions? On the current metaethical assumption, this is irrational and will not be good – unless, that is, the past persons got the outcomes right or they had more moral expertise than we have. In the latter case, that is due regard to their expertise, not to them.

When we exercise critical faculties to reject past persons' views, we do not thereby disregard them as persons, so long as we apply these same faculties to all views before us. So, regard for past persons alone does not support Postema's idea of exercising 'appropriate' fidelity – that is, fidelity tempered by 'regret' as Postema understands regret. Since integrity also incorporates this conception of regret, regard for past persons alone does not support exercising integrity.

I conclude that, on the current metaethical assumption, due regard for past generations does not require faithfulness to any particular principles that may have been embedded in their past political decisions. Due regard does not require faithfulness to *the way* past generations went about pursuing their goal of a just society, including political decisions they made in a certain way because they had certain ideas about what that goal amounted to. I have already remarked that faithfulness to the general goal of justice does not either. The general idea of fidelity will not help here, because fidelity is not, as I have argued, an independent moral value. When it has (positive moral) value, that value comes from something else good that fidelity serves or is related to. That leaves the idea of justice. Unfortunately, I can discover no further justice argument in Postema's work. The value of being faithful to someone's particular 'vision of justice' is that the vision is correct, there are reliance and fair notice reasons for employing it nonetheless, one is thereby keeping a promise to do so, and so on. None of these reasons is a new reason, and none of them amounts to integrity.

[100] B Baum Levenbook, 'The Role of Coherence in Legal Reasoning' (1984) 3 *Law and Philosophy* 367.

One might assay an argument that when we are uncertain, in the circumstances of integrity, which views are correct and which are incorrect, we must have a fair procedure for adopting the principles of justice on which to base political and social institutions. The procedure of compiling a 'vision of justice' by some refining function of the views of past and present members of a distinct political community (what millennials would describe as a 'crowd sourcing') may, then, be claimed to be fair. But the situation is not one of what Rawls called 'pure' procedural justice, where there are no criteria for an outcome independent of the fairness of the procedure. It is not what Rawls called 'perfect' procedural justice, where we have independent criteria for the outcome and a procedure certain to give that result. The outcome, in this case, is coalescing on a correct vision of justice. Confining the input to only the views of past generations of our particular political community (let alone those views that made it into past political decisions) will not guarantee that result. The procedure rationality requires under uncertainty is one that maximises the probability of the desired outcome. That procedure would require wider 'crowd sourcing' – trying to compile a defensible 'vision of justice' from every reasonable view in history, including views of persons who are not and never will be members of the political community in question. It is a better procedure if the goal is to do our best to approximate the moral truth, rather than to find the principles that have the longest or greatest historical social acceptability in the political community. The wider procedure pays due regard to past members of the political community with reasonable views, because it pays, initially, equal regard to all reasonable persons everywhere and every when with reasonable views on justice. To think otherwise is to beg an important question in this argument; it is to assume that past generations have a special moral right, or a special moral claim, to have their 'vision of justice' for the community – assuming there is a distinct vision of justice – prioritised over others in the future. As I argue in the next section, despite his work on moral reasoning and the plural point of view, Postema provides no compelling reason to believe this.[101]

The metaphysics Postema sets aside may play a part here. If there is a diachronic collective in a political community, it is clear that outsiders are not part of this collective.[102] Postema might make the assumption that there is diachronic collective agency when judges act now in an ongoing political community aiming at justice. But if he does, his insistence on justice requiring

[101] He may have begged this question in his assumption that a political community is – at least in the circumstances of integrity – 'committed' to a vision of justice, or to 'justice-approximating' principles 'in virtue of … past collective decisions': Postema (n 1) 300–01. There are at least two senses of 'commitment' that could be at work here. The first is logical, in the broad sense. In that sense, Kant maintained, roughly, that if I act on a maxim, I am committed to the view that everyone ought to act on that maxim. But the second is 'morally obligated'.

[102] They are not, or may not be, 'comembers of a common enterprise'. Phrase from ibid 304.

due regard for the members of a community will make no sense, because it penetrates the alleged agent. It brings in considerations of inter-generational relations – and, I have pointed out, intragenerational relations as well. Once Postema has opened the door to consider these relations in his attempt to justify precedent, the points I have made are relevant. He cannot then maintain that they are irrelevant because, for example, the judge who carries out the programme of a diachronic ('temporally extended') collective is just acting as a voice of the collective, doing precisely what 'we' have chosen or committed ourselves to. If the law permits him or her, the judge has a choice; and the choice stands in need of moral justification. (If the law does not permit him or her, that, too, stands in need of moral justification.)

B. On the Assumption that there is No Right Answer on Justice

The assumption that there is no right answer to the question of what justice requires but, rather, several morally defensible ones, may, once more, look promising for Postema. One problem is that if the previous generations had a 'morally significant' conception of justice they were acting on but there are better, more morally significant, conceptions, then almost everything in the previous section can be repeated here.

However, if (i) there is some single conception of justice embedded in previous decisions of past generations (or a conception to which the past generations were rationally committed), and (ii) there is no improving on that conception (although there are equally good alternatives), appeals to fidelity as extrinsically valuable (fidelity to this conception) and justice seem to get traction. Note that this set of assumptions would not be consistent with the picture of a community still forming a conception of justice.[103] The role of integrity in this situation would be to elucidate the conception to which the community has already committed itself and to require its accurate application in particular situations.

Does the appeal to (due) regard for past generations do better here? The argument might be that due regard for past generations requires the current generation to pursue the vision most rationally compatible with past political decisions. We are to assume that past generations have, wittingly or unwittingly, set the polity on a particular path to justice; and due regard for them and their project of a just society requires fidelity to the way they have set about aiming at a just society. (In terms made popular by Bratman and Shapiro, it is fidelity to the shared plan – achieve a just society – and the sub-plan – on this particular conception of justice.) That is, the claim is that regard requires this rather than

[103] The set is consistent with the language of justice-approximating principles; such principles approximate one of the permissible conceptions of justice. But why, then, would integrity consist of justice-approximating principles?

allowing the current generation to make decisions compatible only with a new but (on the metaethical assumption being made) nonetheless permissible vision of justice – that is, to change the sub-plan.

A first problem concerns sources. Suppose that a single 'vision of justice' can somehow be abstracted from past political decisions. Assume, too, that when there is widespread disagreement about the content of justice principles, and when the pursuit of a just political community is an inter-generational project, procedural justice requires that the current generation let the previous generations have an initial 'say' on the subject. Postema provides no compelling reasons in the pursuit of faithfulness to the conception of justice held by past generations why this say should be confined to the principles allegedly to be found in past political decisions. On the contrary, there are reasons why it should not be. Reading past generations' pamphlets, editorials, books and diaries, for example, culling all the views – even those that never influenced the past political decisions – of the past members of society may be a fairer procedure. (It will in fact be fairer if the peer participation conditions were not met in the previous generation.) So, the first point is that Postema fails to support his limitation to the views somehow connected to past political decisions.[104]

The second and chief problem with a (due) regard argument is that it packs into the notion of (due) regard what must be proven. Thinking that due regard requires finding a permissible vision of justice to fit past political decisions is in part viewing the decision-makers of those past political decisions as equal partners with the living in the creation of a just society. (This view has plausibility only if the peer participation conditions are met.) But there is a very good reason *not* to regard past generations as equal partners in the creation of a just society. To belabour the obvious, most members of the past generations are dead. Dead members of past generations no longer have welfare interests addressed by principles of substantive justice.[105] That gives them much less of a stake (if any) in the way the justice project is pursued going forward than that of current members of society. This is a reason to regard the past members as less than equal partners now in the creation of a just society.

I conclude that Postema cannot use regard for past persons to justify a mandate giving their views on justice currency.

Postema cannot use the idea of adopting the moral perspective itself to support the claim that the current population is required to be true to the old sub-plan. To be true to the sub-plan (the plan's being to have a just society),

[104] Here is where Postema may elect to use his idea about what law is and that it contains principles. Law, he holds, is drawn from past political decisions, not these other sources. But see n 106.

[105] Even if some welfare interests somehow survive the holders of them, members of past generations who are deceased do not have the full range of relevant welfare interests that members of the current population have. We can inquire what these temporally extended interests might be, and ask for the argument for them. Are there interests surviving death in how a project is carried out? Is the life of any deceased person going to be worse off if society subsequently sets out in a new direction with a new but permissible idea of justice?

the current generation must not consider afresh the question the sub-plan is alleged to answer, namely, 'What would a just society/institution/rule look like?' But simply taking the moral perspective does not demand that you exclude such reasoning and such considerations. Morality requires, and therefore pro tanto obligates, the current population to work toward a just society. But this does not produce the exclusionary factor. Nor does the fact that the current population has committed itself to achieving a just society, as we are assuming it has. There must be an additional factor to produce an exclusionary reason. As I remarked earlier, fair notice and reasonable reliance considerations might generate an obligation to the sub-plan, but only if and to the extent that law subjects can discern the sub-plan (the conception of justice) and accurately apply it. However, recall that fair notice and reasonable reliance are not new considerations for following precedent, and so not ones Postema is allegedly relying on here.

However, Postema may have other arguments – in particular, one from justice. Recall that Postema contends that justice is 'temporally extended'. Let us reconstruct that claim as the conclusion of an argument. Drawing from Postema's discussion, some of which I touched on in section V.B, two of its premises would be as follows:

(a) Justice requires public action on principles.
(b) Justice requires acting on a coherent set of principles.

Now by hypothesis, there is some permissible conception of justice (some sub-plan in the pursuit of a just society) that is embedded in past political decisions. Suppose that the current population does not exercise fidelity to this sub-plan but substitutes one of its own, one that is also a permissible conception of justice. Under these conditions, Postema may assume that subsequent decisions based on the imported conception will be either unprincipled, or drawn from an incoherent set.[106] (Notice that this switch in sub-plans need not be due to the belief that one's polity has been 'irremediably unjust', so one circumstance of integrity is not violated.) But of course such an assumption presupposes the very thing to be proven, namely, the relevance and weight of past conceptions of justice. If a conception of justice must be coherent, and if the present population is accurately applying a conception, albeit an imported one, then its members are acting on a coherent set of principles, and so can be doing justice (in casuistry).

But perhaps the argument can be supplemented with this: If conceptions of justice acted on are altered from what they were in the past (or what fits past decisions), the original sub-plan of justice will never be fully implemented.

[106] Postema would hold, because of his assumptions about the nature of law, that the current population is departing from seeking the antecedently existing law. However, even on an integrity theory of law, where a set of principles fitting, in the appropriate way, past political decisions (of the appropriate sort) are law, disputants about justice need not look to law to find a conception of justice. The current population may have reason to, in Postema's words 'forge … a common conception of justice' that would reform law. The political decisions they draw on, if any, may be outside of the ones that count for law.

If conceptions are switched every so often across time, no sub-plan of justice will be fully implemented. One might conclude that this is an obvious moral problem, one that morality forbids. Its remedy is appropriate fidelity.

This is a better argument. The assumption that justice in process requires that a single conception of justice be (increasingly) implemented diachronically may seem natural or even obvious. But it is not on the current metaethical assumption. There is no guarantee that switching sub-plans delays an overall gain in justice. Perhaps, under the current conditions, a single generation can make more progress towards (and create a greater overall gain in) an imported conception of justice than by continuing an older one. In such circumstances, justice in progress would seem to require the generation to choose the imported conception of justice.

I have argued that appeals to justice cannot require, even with peer participation, fidelity to a conception of justice partly implemented by past political decisions. But this argument does not reckon with all that Postema says about the circumstances of integrity, especially the first one. As I characterised it, it is relatively undemanding. When Postema introduces it, he builds in much more substance. He says that 'integrity assumes there is some compelling moral reason for treating the various actions and decisions [of the polity, "both synchronically and diachronically"] as unified in this way, namely, as … needing unification' 'into a scheme that relates them to a common … set of themes, purposes, or principles'.[107] Characterised this way, no society in which there is a moral option to switch conceptions of justice is in the first circumstance of integrity. And Postema is willing to admit that 'integrity has no place', '[w]here we do not have sufficient reason' to see the society in this way.[108]

Consider, however, the justification of such a strong first circumstance of integrity. Postema contends, 'To legitimate the actions of the community and its members, the principles drawn from past decisions and actions of the community must (in the ideal case) express a unified, common, and relatively comprehensive vision of justice for the community'.[109] The 'compelling moral reason' that integrity assumes may be the following. Acting within the law and under colour of law and obeying the law (and making other political decisions under political or legal authority or with the legal permission to do so?) will not be morally justified unless:

(a) the moral agents are acting on principles;
(b) those principles are drawn from past decisions and actions; and
(c) they are unified into a 'relatively comprehensive vision of justice'.

This argument, however, begs the question. If following integrity is a way to produce this relatively comprehensive vision of justice (and this becomes true

[107] Postema (n 1) 294 (emphasis omitted).
[108] ibid.
[109] ibid.

by definition), and acting on it is either necessary or sufficient to morally justify all sorts of political and legal actions and decisions, and if morality requires such a moral justification, then of course integrity has value. It has extrinsic value because it allows us to meet a moral requirement. No excursion into arguments from justice, regard for persons or fidelity is needed.

However, acting on integrity will not be sufficient to morally justify all sorts of political and legal actions and decisions unless integrity has an independent moral value. One burden of my criticisms so far is that Postema's appeals to justice, regard for persons and fidelity do not establish this claim. They do not, in addition, supply the 'compelling moral reason' for treating the decisions of any polity, 'both synchronically and diachronically', 'as … needing unification' 'into a scheme' of principles appropriate for integrity. Moreover, assuming that acting on integrity is necessary to justify all sorts of political and legal actions begs the question for the reason just rehearsed in the preceding paragraph.

It would seem, then, that my previous criticism is not barred by anything in the circumstances of integrity that does not beg the question. Another way to put the point: Postema's excursion into justice, regard for persons and fidelity does not support the strong moral claims he makes about the first circumstance of integrity.

Much of the previous discussion has been about moral requirement. Let us look again at the case for value without relying on moral requirement. It may seem clear that, where a society has made strides toward a just society in decisions, fidelity has some extrinsic value: it advances or preserves some permissible vision of justice. But there are three major difficulties for Postema if he takes this line.

First, as before, it eviscerates his case that integrity is a distinct moral virtue, a reason *supplanting* justice in the search for justice. The principal reason to exercise fidelity to a permissible conception of justice fitting past decisions is that it is a permissible conception of justice. The past comes in for efficiency reasons, since this conception is partly implemented already in political decisions we have inherited. (There will not be another kind of efficiency unless enough people correctly draw the conception from the past political decisions – that is, recognise it – and can apply it correctly. That may mean the people have to be good moral reasoners and well informed about empirical matters.) The past also comes in because and to the extent that it offers headway toward the goal of having every (continuing) social arrangement and institution be just.[110]

Note that when past political decisions determine a unique conception of justice on the theoretical level, there does not seem to be much about faithfulness to persons involved. The sub-plan could have been implemented by partly

[110] Postema considers a version of the headway appeal (Postema (n 1) 307), and concludes that it is 'too weak to bear the full weight of the case for the historical character of integrity'.

autonomous machines. The fact that it was people who implemented it is irrelevant. So, the analogy with friendship breaks down. The sort of fidelity involved in continuing to implement an embedded conception of justice is not fidelity to persons. We are not showing them special regard, or special respect, except incidentally.

I have been supposing that a unique sub-plan on justice is embedded in past political decisions. Suppose instead that only an inchoate conception of justice is embedded in past political decisions, one that may be part of several different permissible conceptions of justice. There is no unique embedded sub-plan in this case. Past political decisions underdetermine a particular conception of justice. Then Postema's conception of integrity neither serves fidelity nor is an example of it. If the current population were tied to those sub-plans on justice that are compatible with that inchoate conception, *and* if this were a significant restriction of their moral options, there might be a point to talking about fidelity to the past and having more than a general partnership with past generations. But on Postema's schema, the current population is not tied in any significant way, because of the operation of regret. Without limits, regret can be used on any number of past decisions to produce a permissible conception of justice that fits some (but perhaps an insignificant number) of past decisions. Then there is hardly fidelity to anything in this scenario, save to the general idea of having a just society. But one would have an obligation to pursue a just society whether or not that general plan had been adopted in the past.

Perhaps Postema would object that anyone using a permissible conception of justice to regret a significant number of past political decisions does not view his or her society as historically aiming at justice – and so is not in the circumstances of integrity. But this claim cannot be sustained. Casuistry requires that one get the non-moral facts correct; and someone viewing a large number of past political decisions as regrettable may simply credit past deciders with ignorance or some other cognitive error (eg discounting) with regard to the relevant facts. (Indeed, the possibility of cognitive error and its plausibility in many cases is one of the reasons to doubt the existence of a distinct embedded sub-plan. It is also one of the reasons to believe that past political decisions underdetermine a distinct embedded principle.)[111]

Second, there is still the problem of justifying 'islands of compromised coherence', even when there is a distinct embedded sub-plan on justice. Recall that in the islands of compromised coherence, we uphold some past decision representing an old but 'regretted' idea, but limit its influence going forward. Consider on what basis it is to be regretted. Is it because it is not defensible on a permissible conception of justice that seems embedded in past political decisions? Then removing any trace of its current influence – overruling in the

[111] For others, see Levenbook (n 23).

case of judicial precedent – can be thought of as paying high regard to past generations (we are being more faithful to their conception than they managed to be) and cannot be objected to on the grounds of justice or coherence. Alternatively, are the past decisions regretted because they are not defensible on a new permissible conception of justice, one that the present generation finds more attractive? If the balance of reasons supports retaining the old conception, there seems no reason to limit the influence of the past decisions going forward. On the other hand, if the balance of reasons supports using the new conception, then upholding the old decision again seems unjustifiable.

So it appears that on the current metaethical assumption there is still no justification for the following (with or without narrowing) of a regretted past judicial decision. Recall that Postema claims that integrity strikes a balance between respect and regret. My point is that no justification for this balance has been produced by Postema.

Third, although it follows from the discussion in this section that there is an extent to which (and circumstances under which) fidelity to (one of) the domestic vision(s) of justice has some extrinsic value, nothing follows about obligations. One reason is that fidelity can have disvalue too. I have been calling a conception of justice *imported* when it does not fit well (to the proper degree) with past political decisions. Call a conception of justice *domestic* when it does. Suppose that an imported but permissible conception of justice has, compared to the domestic candidate(s), a virtue in present circumstances. For example, suppose that only the distributive principle of the imported conception can be satisfied in an economically efficient way. Alternatively, suppose that the imported conception is the presently popular view, and so it is the one law subjects are likely to think of in judging the justice of their institutions and laws and expecting outcomes.[112] Then using the imported vision going forward gives the members of the community fair notice in an efficient manner. In either set of circumstances, there is disvalue in sticking to a domestic conception. In such a case, there may be no pro tanto obligation to be faithful to the domestic conception.

This leaves open the possibility that even when there are alternative visions that are either equal or incommensurable, being faithful to a morally defensible conception of justice established by the past is *sometimes* a pro tanto obligation. However, the obligation is not grounded on fidelity, and so not on integrity. It is grounded on the same grounds as the value of this fidelity, namely, the permissibility of the conception of justice. In contrast, Postema is aiming for Dworkin's idea that integrity 'grounds binding obligations on moral agents, especially legal officials'.[113]

[112] One must be careful here not to depart from the circumstances of integrity, and so not to assume that it follows that the law subjects think their law to date has been 'irremediably unjust'. Recall that the moral agents in question are not bad at moral reasoning. However, they may be ignorant of empirical facts about the past, and for this reason may suppose that enough of their favourite conception of justice has been implemented in past political decisions.

[113] Postema (n 1) 293.

VII. CONCLUSION

I have contended that Postema's arguments that integrity has moral value are plausible only in special circumstances that he has not described. These are: (i) the political decisions that are decisions of the diachronic community represent a consensus on a conception of justice that meets peer participation conditions, and it is not more important to justice to disregard the consensus and distribute social goods more correctly; or (ii) they are decisions accurately applying the correct conception of justice (or, on another metaethical assumption, a permissible conception of justice that cannot be improved). Even then, it is not integrity that has this value, because integrity allows 'islands of incoherence'. Moreover, in the second situation, the main reason for faithfulness to the principles is the correctness of the principles (or the moral defensibility of the conception of justice). This is pursuing justice 'directly', as Postema puts it, not integrity.[114]

It should be obvious that actual common law systems do not satisfy the first ideal condition and rarely satisfy the second. So Postema is not offering a new justification for following precedent in actual common law systems, in the real world of the common law. The setting he presupposes for his argument for both integrity and a justification for precedent is to some extent ideal. It is not entirely ideal, because it includes the fact that the society only approximates justice, and has made morally incorrect political decisions, including judicial rulings, in the past.

In this setting, I conclude that Postema has not provided a compelling argument that integrity is a genuine moral value. Even assuming that his views about the nature of law are accurate, he has not shown that integrity is 'an important [moral] value governing law',[115] because he has not shown that it is an important moral value.

[114] ibid 314.
[115] ibid 298.

4

Revisiting the Idea of Protestant Interpretation: Towards Reconciliation between Dworkin and Postema

THOMAS BUSTAMANTE*

I. POSTEMA'S WORRY ABOUT PROTESTANT INTERPRETATION

SHORTLY AFTER THE publication of *Law's Empire*, Gerald Postema wrote one of the strongest challenges to have been posed to Ronald Dworkin's theory of law and interpretation. In the article '"Protestant" Interpretation and Social Practices', Postema does not present a direct objection to Dworkin's theory of law, which is based on the fundamental notions of interpretation and integrity; rather, he challenges the theory of interpretation on which Dworkin's theory of law is based.

Postema assumes, at least for the sake of argument, that the concept of law might be an interpretive concept and that jurisprudence might as well be conceived of as a general interpretation of the practice of law. By the same token, he does not counter Dworkin's view that legal reasoning is interpretive, or that 'philosophical interpretations of the practice as a whole' can be 'continuous with, indeed necessarily presupposed by, the more concrete interpretations

* This chapter benefited from very helpful and thoughtful comments by Misabel Derzi, Thiago Decat, David Gomes, Franklin Dutra, Igor Enríquez, Rodrigo Dornas, Thiago Clemente Souza, Ludmila Lacerda and Henrique Noya. It has also received important critical comments from Veronica Rodríguez-Blanco, Paula Gaido, Barbara Levenbook and Gerald Postema, who took part in the Colloquium on Postema's work that I organized at the 3rd International Conference in Constitutional Law and Political Philosophy, in Curitiba, Brazil, in November 2017. Finally, the penultimate version was kindly revised by Dennis Patterson. I am indebted to these brilliant scholars for their input to the argument sketched in this chapter. I am also especially indebted to the National Council for Scientific Development (CNPq), a research agency of the Ministry of Science and Technology in Brazil, who financed part of the research that led to the paper and granted a Research Productivity Scholarship to its author (Grants # 305645/2017-0 and 423696/2018-1).

offered by lay and official practitioners'.[1] Finally, he does not wish to contest Dworkin's assertions that a theory of law must fit legal practice as we know it while providing the best normative justification of that practice.

Postema's target, in the paper, is the theory of interpretation that Dworkin believes one must apply in order to get to the content of the law.

Dworkin's conception of interpretation maintains that the meaning of interpretive social practices, such as law, political morality or courtesy, must be established from within the practice, and not from a second-order or metaphysical point of view. As Postema puts it, 'social practices are not only meaningful human activities, but they are meaningful to those who take part in them'.[2] The participants' understanding of the practice, as a consequence, is at least in part *constitutive* of the practice itself. No one can understand the practice without making an internal statement about the point or purpose of such practice. The distinction between a full-blown 'internal' statement of the participants of the practice and the 'engaged-external' point of view, which Hart claims to be the point of view of legal theorists,[3] disappears under Dworkin's understanding of legal practice.

When lawyers argue about the law, according to Dworkin, questions of fidelity do not arise.[4] Participants in legal argumentation do not disagree about whether or not they should apply a 'law' that is identified according to a neutral

[1] GJ Postema, 'Protestant Interpretation and Social Practices' (1987) 6 *Law and Philosophy* 283, 283–84.

[2] ibid 286.

[3] In *The Concept of Law*, Hart distinguishes between two senses of the 'external point of view'. According to the first, which Stephen Perry has called the 'engaged external point of view', the observer looks at the practice with a hermeneutic eye. Although he wants to describe a practice from the outside, the observer, 'without accepting the rules himself, asserts that the group accepts the rules, and thus may from the outside refer to the way in which *they* are concerned with them from the internal point of view'. HLA Hart, *The Concept of Law* (2nd edn, Oxford University Press 1994) 86–87. According to the second, which can be called an 'extreme' external point of view, the observer simply describes the 'regularities of physical behaviour', without regard to the acceptance of norms or the internal attitudes of the participants of the relevant social practice (ibid 90). According to Perry, Hart's view is that legal theorists must look at law from the 'engaged external' point of view: '[A]lthough Hart is not explicit about this, it is clearly just this kind of statement that jurisprudence requires in order accurately to describe normative practices and, in particular, law. This type of statement takes account of the internal point of view, but it is not made *from* that point of view; since the internal point of view is only referred to, not utilized, such external statements (and the theories of which they are a part) can be characterized as descriptive rather than normative in character.' S Perry, 'Interpretation and Methodology in Legal Theory' in A Marmor (ed), *Law and Interpretation* (Oxford University Press 1995) 97, 103.

[4] To put it in a different way, Dworkin accepts what Mark Greenberg has more recently described as the 'binding hypothesis', which is the view that there is a special relation between legal and moral obligations: 'a legal system is supposed to operate by arranging matters in such a way as to reliably ensure that, for every legal obligation, there is an all-things-considered moral obligation with the same content'. M Greenberg, 'The Standard Picture and its Discontents' in L Green and B Leiter (eds), *Oxford Studies in Philosophy of Law*, vol 1 (Oxford University Press 2011) 36, 84. When Dworkinian interpreters argue about the law, they assume that legally correct answers about the content of the law are morally obligatory, and this is why they must strive to make the law the best it can be in their constructive interpretations.

and second-order metaphysical standard. When they find themselves in theoretical disagreement about the 'grounds' or 'fundamentals' of the law, which go deeper than the empirical question of whether a set of uncontroversial criteria of legal validity are satisfied, they must resolve this disagreement by making evaluative judgments about the point of law. While joining a discourse about the meaning or the best concept of law, participants look neither for a linguistic convention about the meaning of words nor for the 'deep structure' of a natural kind.[5] On Dworkin's view, interpretation is not a process to determine the meaning of words or authoritative pronouncements. It is, instead, an exercise of justificatory reasoning we must engage in when we argue that certain propositions – 'interpretive' propositions – are true or false. According to Dworkin, to establish the truth of an interpretive proposition one requires an attitude that takes into account not only the linguistic content of a given sentence, but also most importantly the *point* of the practice in which such proposition is sustained.

On Dworkin's view of legal philosophy, the 'substantive value judgments' of ordinary people and the 'philosophical analysis' of such judgments are not at 'different levels of discourse'.[6] There is no distinction between questions *of* morality and questions *about* morality, since both of these questions are placed in the same level.[7] When, for instance, liberals and conservatives debate whether progressive taxation is just or unjust, they do not apply common criteria of justice, but this does not mean that they do not share the same concept. They share the concept of justice 'because they participate in a social practice of *judging* acts and institutions just and unjust and because each has opinions, articulate or inarticulate, about what the most basic assumptions of that practice, its *point* or *purpose*, should be taken to be'.[8]

The core of Postema's objection to the theory of interpretation proposed in *Law's Empire* concerns the process of determining the point of law. Dworkin argued, in *Law's Empire*, that in order to understand the law, one must adopt an interpretive attitude that requires assuming that the social practice under consideration 'does not simply exist but has value', in the sense that 'it serves some interest or purpose or enforces some principle – in short, that it has some point – that *can be stated independently of just describing the rules that make up the practice*'.[9] Once the interpreter identifies this point, he must also assume that the interpretive practice is sensitive to this point, so that 'the strict rules must be understood or applied or extended or modified or qualified or limited by that point'.[10] According to this account of interpretation, after identifying

[5] R Dworkin, *Justice in Robes* (Belknap 2006) 225–26.
[6] ibid 142.
[7] R Dworkin, *Justice for Hedgehogs* (Belknap 2011) 10.
[8] Dworkin (n 5) 221.
[9] R Dworkin, *Law's Empire* (Belknap 1986) 47 (emphasis added).
[10] ibid.

the point of a practice one must 'try to impose meaning on the institution', that is, to 'see it in its best light', and then 'to restructure it in the light of that meaning'.[11] Once the point of a practice is established, it might be the case that interpreters press for a change in the practice, for the assumed point 'acquires critical power'. In many cases, 'interpretation folds back into the practice, altering its shape, and the new shape encourages further interpretation, so the practice changes dramatically, though each step in the progress is interpretive of what the last achieved'.[12]

Postema's main objection refers to the process of identifying this point. He believes Dworkin is wrong when he takes a step further and claims that each participant in the practice 'is trying to discover *his own intention* in maintaining and participating in that practice'.[13] On Postema's reading, this appeal to the participant's private understanding of the point of the law is what characterises Dworkin's notion of 'protestant interpretation'. Social interpretation, for Dworkin, would be a 'conversation with oneself',[14] such that each interpreter seeks to determine the point of the practice by herself, without considering the other interpreters' judgments about this point. Although Dworkin recognises that social practice is a 'collectively meaningful activity', his theory of interpretation fails, because 'while he regards the activity of the practice as public and collective, he seems to regard the enterprise of understanding that activity as private and individual'.[15]

Since the point of the practice is identified by the interpreter and can be said to be 'independent of the practice', two other assumptions of Dworkin's interpretive theory of law become implausible. First, one can no longer uphold the view that at the first stage of interpretation – the so-called 'pre-interpretive' stage – participants identify the materials – such as statutes, precedents, custom and so on – that constitute the 'raw data' of an interpretive theory.[16] If these raw materials are going to be given meaning according to a value or point that is independent of the practice, each interpreter becomes the sole architect of the practice and can read it with no concern for the interpretations of her fellow citizens. Second, Dworkin's assumption that jurisprudence is a 'silent prologue to any decision at law' (in the sense that 'any practical argument … assumes the kind of abstract foundation jurisprudence offers')[17] becomes heretical. If, as Postema puts it, 'theory drives practice, for the practice is what the (best) general interpretive/justificatory theory says it is',[18] then it is very dangerous to rely on

[11] ibid.
[12] ibid.
[13] ibid 58.
[14] ibid, also quoted in Postema (n 1) 287.
[15] Postema (n 1) 288–89.
[16] ibid 292.
[17] Dworkin (n 9) 90.
[18] Postema (n 1) 293.

one's own understanding of the point of the practice in order to construct one's interpretive theory of such practice.

If Postema's criticism is right, 'a participant's working theory will be responsive to her background evaluative or normative convictions' and, as a consequence, 'need not, as a general matter, be responsive to the views of other participants in the practice'.[19]

When Dworkin maintains that the attitude of interpreters must be a 'protestant' attitude that makes 'each citizen responsible for imagining what his society's public commitments to principles are, and what these commitments require in new circumstances',[20] Postema infers from this that Dworkin actually advocates that each interpreter is implicitly allowed change the practice, by herself, according to her own private interpretation of the common purpose that makes the practice worthy of allegiance. On Postema's terms, the failure of Dworkin's interpretive theory of law can be summarised as follows:

> The only alternative to unreflective compliance with a practice is critical interpretation focused around a 'purpose' or 'point' defined entirely independently of the agreed-upon rules or recognized activities of the practice. To understand or learn a rule of a practice is to accept a general proposition which accounts for, but always transcends, the accepted instances of the rule. To understand a practice as a whole is to accept a general interpretive theory of that practice. Interpretation is the activity of an individual participant articulating a theory, a structured set of general principles and aims, which in her judgment puts the practice in its best light. The theory is offered as a general justification for the consensus elements of the practice which constitutes its 'raw data'. But while the 'data' is common ground, interpretations are private, and they may conflict widely. Logically speaking, theory precedes and determines practice; that is, interpretive theory at the ideal limit determines what the practice is and requires. That which appears common in the practice is merely the overlap of extensions of the (more or less explicit) interpretive theories of individual participants.[21]

Dworkin's view of interpretation, therefore, is regarded as problematic because it 'makes interpretation of social practices insufficiently practical, insufficiently inter-subjective and, and thus insufficiently political'.[22]

If this is correct, critics would be justified to accuse Dworkin of offering no more than a *monolithic* process of interpretation, in which the interpreter (for instance, a judge) 'must rely only on herself, should her own interpretation happen to deviate from all others'.[23] Once the point of the social practice of

[19] ibid 296.
[20] Dworkin (n 9) 413.
[21] Postema (n 1) 300.
[22] ibid 301.
[23] J Habermas, *Between Facts and Norms*, tr W Rehg (Polity Press 1996) 222. A similar point, probably under the influence of Postema, is made by Nigel Simmonds, who argues that Dworkin's account of constructive interpretation cannot resist the centrifugal forces that drive each interpreter to rely on her own preferences instead of the 'common language' or shared concepts accepted in the

law is 'logically independent of the practice's activities',[24] there is little in the practice that interpreters can really share.

Postema proposes, therefore, an alternative to Dworkin's interpretive theory of social practices. To understand the meaning of a social practice, one should avoid either adopting the protestant attitude suggested by Dworkin or appealing to abstract theories to figure out the principles that define such practices. Rather, to understand a practice involves 'grasping a discipline or mastering a technique'.[25]

According to Dennis Patterson, who adheres to this criticism, Dworkin's interpretive attitude is rare, and Postema rightfully acknowledges this because he rejects 'the Heidegger/Gadamer view that interpretation is a fundamental feature of everyday existence'.[26] Postema would be right, because he subscribes to Wittgenstein's position that 'interpretation is a second-order activity one engages only when understanding breaks down'.[27]

We should avoid, therefore, a 'protestant' or 'constructive' interpretation that purports to impose a purpose on the practice. Although Postema shares many views with Dworkin, including, as one can read in his more recent works, much of what Dworkin says about the value of 'integrity', he believes that the 'protestant' attitude is inadequate to explain what participants do in a social practice because it 'ignores the interactive, public character of the practical reasoning demanded by integrity'.[28] In the circumstances of integrity, which prop up when we have a strong commitment to a community and its political principles while disagreeing about what these principles entail, 'justice cannot be imposed';[29] rather, it must be jointly pursued in a common way. In Postema's words, 'it is not enough that right order be established, it is equally important, from the point of view of justice itself, that right order be established through ordinary politics – through reasonable members of political society working together to forge a conception all can recognize as reasonable'.[30]

How can Dworkin respond to this critique? This is the topic I intend to discuss in the second section of this chapter.

'preinterpretive' agreements of the participants in legal practices. For Simmonds, 'Dworkin simply ignores the fact that the situation he is discussing resembles in its structure the classic "tragedy of the commons" beloved of economists and Hobbesian philosophers: Individual agents would have a strong incentive to proffer interpretations of law that favored their own position and preferences.' NE Simmonds, 'Protestant Jurisprudence and Modern Doctrinal Scholarship' (2001) 60 *Cambridge Law Journal* 271, 294.

[24] Postema (n 1) 304.

[25] ibid.

[26] D Patterson, 'Can We Please Stop Doing This? By the Way, Postema was Right' in P Banas, A Dyrda and T Gizbert-Studinicki (eds), *Metaphilosophy of Law* (Bloomsbury Publishing 2016) 49, 58.

[27] ibid.

[28] G Postema, 'Integrity: Justice in Workclothes' in J Barley (ed), *Dworkin and His Critics: With Replies by Ronald Dworkin* (Blackwell 2004) 291, 295–96.

[29] ibid 306.

[30] ibid 306.

II. A DWORKINIAN RESPONSE TO POSTEMA'S CRITICISM

Notwithstanding the importance of Postema's criticism, which has been praised by Patterson as the 'single best work devoted to the mature thought of Ronald Dworkin',[31] Dworkin never offered a fully-articulated response to Postema's critique of his theory of interpretation. He never answered in print Postema's paper '"Protestant" Interpretation and Social Practices', although he did give a short answer to a later paper, where he wrote the following paragraph:

> I also agree that the pursuit of integrity is in essence a collective enterprise. He [Postema] worries, however, that my endorsement of a 'protestant' attitude towards the law, 'while rightly highlighting individual responsibility, ignores the interactive, public character of the practical reasoning demanded by integrity'. I meant that description not to deny the public character, however, but to deny one way in which people might suppose that the public character must be realized. I do not believe that citizens must accept either that they must all hold the same beliefs about what their law requires, or that they must accept any person's or institution's statement of what it requires as automatically correct. Integrity requires that people reason about law together, and also that each aim at an understanding that states principles to which he believes all are committed through a shared history. But it does not require consensus or cognitive as distinct from political deference to the conclusions of any group or institution.[32]

This is probably the only published response that Dworkin offered to Postema's critique. Further from this response, Postema has kindly shared with me a private response that Dworkin gave him in person at another time, which I think deserves a literal quote:

> What I remember of it [Dworkin's response in person] is that he thought my criticism was based on a misreading of his view of interpretation at one point. I suggested that, on his view, interpretation starts with raw data as it were, but he denied this. It starts with materials which may already be given some sort of social meaning, it is uninterpreted relative to the specific context of interpretation (some portion of the law, or the entire law of a jurisdiction).[33]

How can we make sense of these fragments? Can we read them in a manner that makes Dworkin's theory survive the critique? I will try to answer these questions in the following paragraphs.

The core of the first citation, as I see it, lies in the concession that interpreters indeed reason together in political communities. When they argue about the best interpretation of the law, they must do it publicly, and each must 'aim at an understanding that states principles to which he believes all are committed through a shared history'.[34] But this concession is accompanied by a critical

[31] Patterson (n 26) 56.
[32] R Dworkin, 'Ronald Dworkin Replies' in Burley (ed) (n 28) 386 (notes omitted).
[33] Gerald Postema, private communication with the author.
[34] Dworkin (n 32) 386.

epistemic attitude: it does not require '*cognitive* as distinct from *political*' deference to the group.[35] Does this protestant attitude undermine the social character of the law?

I am inclined to think that Dworkin can find a way out of this criticism if he manages to show us that even though the 'point' of the social practice of law can be stated 'independently of just describing the rules that make up the practice',[36] this point is not, as Postema thinks, logically independent of the practice.[37] Hence, when two people disagree about the point of a social practice, they do not appeal to a metaphysical explanation of the practice. Although they are asked to produce a theory to uphold the propositions they assert about the requirements of the practice, this theory itself is *internal* to the practice, given that Dworkin refuses to admit the possibility of a second-order theory that can be stated from an Archimedean point of view. When participants engage in philosophical reasoning about the abstract considerations that constitute the purpose of the practice, they do not leave the practice, given that Dworkin believes that theories, just like principles, are drawn from within the practice. A theory of a social practice is just an abstract description of the practice, and when one makes a (theoretical) claim about the meaning of this practice, one's statements are also internal to the practice at stake. When one makes interpretive claims about morality, for instance, 'the practices of interpretation and morality give these claims all the meaning they need or could have'.[38]

Although Dworkin's conception of interpretation is 'constructive', the 'history' or 'shape' of the social practice, for Dworkin, 'constrains the available interpretations of it'.[39] In this sense, I think that Postema might have overstated the importance of Dworkin's assertions that the 'point' or purpose of a practice can be stated 'independently' of its rules, and that at the pre-interpretive stage of legal interpretation we merely identify the raw materials that constitute the object of interpretation. If this is correct, the problem is that Postema's critique of 'protestant interpretation' underestimated the role played by history in Dworkin's constructive account of interpretation.

It is partly because of the importance of history for interpretation that Dworkin makes reference to Gadamer's hermeneutics. Dworkin's theory of interpretation endorses Gadamer's recognition of the importance of *tradition* and, in the case of law, holds that *institutional history* plays a crucial part in any sensible effort to interpret a given norm. As Dworkin puts it while explaining the importance of 'intention' in artistic interpretation, he does not intend to 'deny what is obvious, that interpreters think within a tradition of interpretation from which they cannot wholly escape'.[40] To judge with integrity is, for Dworkin,

[35] ibid.
[36] Dworkin (n 9) 47.
[37] Postema (n 1) 306.
[38] Dworkin (n 9) 83.
[39] ibid 52.
[40] ibid 61–62.

to engage with historical decisions of the political community, to find out the rights and duties that 'flow from past collective decisions and for that reason license or require coercion'. History matters in interpretation, because to argue with integrity is to commit to a scheme of principles that justify 'the standing as well as the content of past political decisions'.[41]

But there are also some differences between Dworkin and Gadamer, which must be considered if one wants an accurate description of his theory of law and interpretive concepts. First, Dworkin does not subscribe to Gadamer's general thesis that all knowledge is interpretive.[42] Interpretivism, for Dworkin, is not a general ontology. The interpretive attitude, for Dworkin, is not adopted in every type of intellectual challenge. Instead, it is appropriate only when we consider an interpretive concept, or when a concept that can be used differently in different contexts is employed in a justificatory argument – as it is in the case, for instance, of the *doctrinal* concept of law.[43] In other words, Dworkin thinks that we must adopt an interpretive attitude towards law not because he accepts a general theory of meaning (that we could use to explain each and every aspect of the world), but because there is something in the law (or more properly in the doctrinal concept of law) that requires the interpretive attitude.[44]

[41] ibid 227.

[42] As Gadamer explains in the Preface to the 2nd edn of his most influential book, Kant 'asked a philosophical question: what are the conditions of our knowledge, by virtue of which modern science is possible, and how far does it extend?' Gadamer's hermeneutics, in the same vein, 'also asks a philosophic question in the same sense. But it does not ask it only of the so-called human sciences (which would give precedence to certain traditional disciplines). Neither does it ask it only of science and its modes of experience, but of all human experience of the world and human living. It asks (to put it in Kantian terms): how is understanding possible? This is a question which precedes any action of understanding on the part of subjectivity, including the methodical activity of the "interpretive sciences" and their norms and rules.' According to Gadamer, 'Heidegger's temporal analytics of *Dasein* has … shown convincingly that understanding is not just one of the various possible behaviors of the subject but the mode of being of *Dasein* itself. It is in this sense that the term "hermeneutics" has been used here [in Gadamer's book]. It denotes the basic being-in-motion of *Dasein* that constitutes its finitude and historicity, and hence embraces the whole of its experience of the world. Not caprice, or even an elaboration of a single aspect, but the nature of the thing itself makes the movement of understanding comprehensive and universal.' H-G Gadamer, *Truth and Method*, trs J Weinsheimer and D Marshall (Continuum 2004) xxvii.

[43] But not, as Dworkin makes it plain, of the sociological concept of law, which might be used in a historical or anthropological argument, or with the taxonomical concept of law, which might be employed in certain types of analytic philosophical discourse. The interpretive concept of law, for Dworkin, is that which we deploy in *doctrinal* debates in which we 'explore the concept of "the law" of some place or entity being to a particular effect': Dworkin (n 5) 2. Our interest is practical, since we are considering the law that is understood as having a practical point: the point of justifying the exercise of coercion in a political community. See also T Bustamante and TL Decat, 'Introduction', section II, in this volume.

[44] It is because of the failure to understand this point that some critics argue that Dworkin's interpretive theory of law is based on a 'fallacy' of deriving a concept of law from a general meta-semantic theory of meaning. See esp MS Green, '"Dworkin's Fallacy", or What the Philosophy of Language Can't Teach Us About the Law' (2003) 89 *Virginia Law Review* 1897. According to Michael Green, a meta-semantic theory is a second-order theory that 'concerns how concepts get their content': MS Green, 'Does Dworkin Commit Dworkin's Fallacy? A Reply to Justice in Robes' (2008) 28 *Oxford*

Second, and perhaps more importantly, Dworkin parts ways with Gadamer when he proposes to understand the 'point' or purpose that gives value to interpretive concepts in an explicitly moral sense.

Gadamer and Dworkin share the view that the interpreter plays an *active role* in interpretation, inasmuch as Gadamer does not adopt the 'conversational' model of interpretation that Dworkin rejects.[45] In effect, an important assumption of Gadamerian hermeneutics is the *integration* between understanding and applying a concept or a text:

> Understanding always involves something like applying the text to be understood to the interpreter's present situation. Thus we are forced to go one step beyond romantic hermeneutics, as it were, by regarding not only understanding and interpretation, but also application as comprising one unified process. This is not to return to the pietist tradition of the three separate 'subtleties', for, on the contrary, we consider application to be just as integral a part of the hermeneutic process as are understanding and interpretation.[46]

The idea that 'interpretation must *apply* intentions', which lies at the core of Gadamer's interpretation, is described by Dworkin as a 'crucial point'.[47] As Dworkin explicitly acknowledges, *applying* a purpose to our situation 'is very far from a neutral, historical exercise in reconstructing a past mental state'.[48] But despite this important convergence between Dworkin and Gadamer, one

Journal of Legal Studies 33, 52. Green is assuming in this objection that Dworkinian interpretivism is an Archimedean theory of how the meaning of *words in general* is constructed, including the meaning of criterial concepts (like the concept of 'bachelor') and natural-kind concepts (like the concepts of 'gold' or 'tiger'). But this is a mischaracterisation of Dworkin's account of interpretive concepts and incurs another fallacy, which Dworkin has described as the 'semantic sting'. The semantic sting, in its revised version that appears in *Justice in Robes*, is precisely the mistake of assuming that value concepts and political concepts can be explained with the same kind of theories that we use for other concepts like 'criterial' and 'natural kind' concepts (Dworkin (n 5) 225–26). Perhaps Dworkin's position would be silly if he claimed that law is interpretive because of some set of commitments that the interpreter accepts at a meta-theoretical level. But he does not make this mistake. In fact, this description misrepresents the direction of the inference. Correctly construed, Dworkin's view is that 'it follows from the fact that moral concepts are interpretive that they can't be analyzed neutrally. Engaging in what the best sense is of a particular moral concept rules out a non-committed, detached and neutral account': S Guest, *Ronald Dworkin* (3rd edn, Stanford University Press 2013) 76. Green fails to see that the gist of Dworkin's argument about interpretation is to show that interpretive practices are special because their purpose plays a distinctive role in the determination of their content. In the realm of interpretation, the 'point' or 'justifying purpose' is 'at the heart of success': Dworkin (n 7) 153. When we interpret, 'our standards for success in an interpretive genre' depend 'on what we take to be the best understanding of the point of interpreting that genre'. We give a right answer to a question whether an interpretive proposition is true only if we grasp the point of the interpretive genre to which it belongs and we construct the object of our interpretation in the best possible way.

[45] They agree, thus, that to interpret a concept we use in a social practice, we must consider the concept in its own context; we must seek to find it in the practice, rather than in an intention of a speaker that can adjust its meaning by adding stipulations to clarify what she means.

[46] Gadamer (n 42) 306–07.

[47] Dworkin (n 9) 55.

[48] ibid 56.

relevant disagreement between these authors remains: what guides the interpretive attitude of a Dworkinian interpreter is a *moral purpose*, a *value* that is capable of providing a justification of the practice being interpreted. What establishes the meaning of a practice is not only a tradition or a historical appreciation of the practice. Important as this aspect may be, there will always be an additional component: the relation between the object of an interpretation (for instance the social practice of law) and a value that provides the normative justification of such object.[49]

This observation shows a central aspect of Dworkinian interpretation: Dworkinian constructive interpretation seems to place a burden on interpreters that might be harder than that which Gadamer would be willing to admit, since the 'purpose' under consideration is conceived of as the *value* that can make the practice the best species of its kind. A Dworkinian interpreter will always need to make a moral judgement about the purpose of the law. Nonetheless, what generates this burden is a crucial aspect of any Dworkinian interpretive practice: the fact that these values are embedded in the practice implies that it is the practice itself that establishes the interpreter's *personal responsibility* to understand it critically, making it the best it can be. We have a special responsibility when we interpret the practice because of a special property of the practice, which is the ability to justify coercion. The idea that we must proceed with this interpretive responsibility is part of the grammar of the practice, part of a set of norms implicit therein (I hope that it is not difficult to spot some form of Wittgensteinean influence here).[50]

For these reasons, I am sceptical of Patterson's idea that the core difference between Postema and Dworkin in their conceptions of interpretation is that the former adopts Wittgenstein's account of social practice while the latter dismisses it in exchange for Gadamer's philosophical hermeneutics, since Dworkin is influenced equally by Gadamer and Wittgenstein. Although neither of these influential philosophers agrees with Dworkin when he claims that the

[49] According to André Coelho, 'Dworkin sees the articulation between meaning and intention as a central component of the conversational method and as one of the reasons of its mistakes and limits. He argues, in response to this method, that the meaning of an object should be regarded as inhabiting not the relation between object and author but rather the relation between object and value. The interpreter should seek not for the sense intended by the author but for that which is capable to attribute to the object the greatest possible value as a species of its genre.' ALS Coelho, 'Dworkin e Gadamer: Qual é a Conexão?' (2014) 6 *Peri – Revista de Filosofia* 19, 23–24.

[50] Dworkin can be read as endorsing some of Wittgenstein's main ideas about the nature of social practices. Even though Patterson may be right to contend that Dworkin would never argue either that interpretation is a second-order activity that is needed only occasionally (Patterson (n 26) 58), Dworkin accepts that in different language games we can use different concepts. Dworkin does not argue that it is logically impossible to try to describe the law with a second-order theory that uses criterial concepts, but only that such theories are unfit to provide a full understanding of the law because legal practice is interpretive. To put it in Wittgenstein's terms, Dworkin's point seems to be that *interpretive* practices have their *own grammar*, and this is why criterial concepts fail to explain them.

appropriate attitude towards an interpretive practice commits one to assigning a fundamental role to moral purpose, Dworkin borrows something from both. He borrows from Gadamer the idea of a historical consciousness and from Wittgenstein the idea that each interpretive practice can be regarded as a distinctive language game.

Dworkin seems to be committed both to the Gadamerian point that history, tradition and the interpreter's 'pre-interpretive' views are crucial for a sound interpretation, and to Wittgenstein's idea that 'concepts are tools and … we have different kinds of tools in our conceptual toolbox'.[51] According to Dworkin, there is something special about evaluative or interpretive concepts.[52] We need to understand interpretation as a *special* type of linguistic practice. This idea, in fact, underlies Dworkin's claim that one cannot adequately understand an interpretive practice with a non-interpretive theory, given that interpretive practices have their own grammar and their own standards of successful interpretation.[53]

It is in their different descriptions of this grammar that we can find the explanation for a relevant aspect of Dworkin's disagreement with legal positivists, which concerns the importance of consensus and convention for determining the content of the law. In Dworkin's view, one of the structural elements of the practice of law is that it is an *argumentative* social practice, and 'it is a feature of such practices that an interpretive claim is not just a claim about what other interpreters think'.[54] When one participates in an interpretive social practice such as law, one must make a judgment about this point, inasmuch as without this personal judgment one cannot be morally responsible for such practice. When Dworkin says interpreters must 'impose' a point upon the practice, he must be taken to mean that he is merely requiring that interpreters assume an individual responsibility for their own judgments about the practice's point. As a consequence, when citizens join the practice, they must agree about many things, but only up to the point when they do not refrain from making their own judgment about what this collective practice entails. According to Dworkin:

> They must, to be sure, agree a great deal in order to share a social practice. They must share a vocabulary … They must understand the world in sufficiently similar ways

[51] Dworkin (n 7) 160.

[52] As Joseph Raz also recognised, alongside Dworkin, evaluative properties and social practices have a 'special character' and special 'ontological properties' that make them unintelligible without evaluative considerations. J Raz, *Value, Respect and Attachment* (Cambridge University Press 2001) 49. Values need to be 'interpreted' because we can make them intelligible to us with 'non-reductive evaluative explanations' of their 'evaluative qualities' (ibid). There seems to be a very interesting similarity between the way Raz thinks we interpret values and the way Dworkin thinks we interpret the law.

[53] For this reading of Dworkin, see R Porto Macedo Jr, 'On How Law is Not Like Chess: Dworkin and the Theory of Conceptual Types' in T Bustamante and B Fernandes (eds), *Democratizing Constitutional Law – Perspectives on Legal Theory and the Legitimacy of Constitutionalism* (Springer 2016) 293, 305–14.

[54] Dworkin (n 9) 63.

> and have interests and convictions sufficiently similar to recognize the sense in each other's claims, to treat these as claims rather than just noises. That means not just using the same dictionary, but sharing what Wittgenstein called a form of life sufficiently concrete so that one can recognize sense and purpose in what the other says and does, to see what sort of beliefs and motives would make sense of his diction, gesture, tone and so forth. They must 'speak the same language' in both senses of that phrase. But this similarity of interests and convictions need hold only to a point: it must be sufficiently dense to permit genuine disagreement, but not so dense that disagreement cannot break out.[55]

As we can see, Dworkin does not say that when speakers use interpretive concepts they lack any background agreement on the general features of the concepts that they interpret. 'Sharing an interpretive concept *does depend*, as sharing criterial and natural-kind concepts do, *on agreement*.'[56] Participants must share, for instance, entrenched interpretations that constitute a *paradigm* from which they can argue in order to ground further interpretations of the legal practice.[57]

We should stress, here, that paradigms are *not* conventions but rather entrenched interpretations that are generally regarded as justified for the time being. Although most people share a paradigm and use it as a starting point for further interpretations, no paradigm – for Dworkin – can be said to be arbitrary in the sense that conventions usually are. The problem, for Dworkin, is that the background agreement of participants of interpretive practices is a distinctive kind of agreement, for it is 'not an agreement on a decision procedure as a test for instances'.[58] What users of concepts in interpretive practices share is more than a clear-cut semantic test for determining the meaning of these concepts. Even in the so-called 'easy cases', in which we can reach an agreement about the content of a legal proposition, the basis of such agreement 'lies in a shared consensus of conviction rather than convention; its basis lies in a shared sense of what political morality requires'.[59]

There are at least two features that distinguish Dworkinian interpretativism from conventionalism: the ideas that the point of an interpretive practice is a value (and therefore that it cannot be an arbitrary point) and that this point is embedded in concrete aspects of this practice.

Interpretation is a distinct 'mode of knowledge' that entails, for interpreters, a special type of *responsibility* to the practice in which they participate. In short, as Dworkin famously said, an interpretation 'must both fit that practice

[55] ibid 63–64.
[56] Dworkin (n 7) 161.
[57] Dworkin (n 9) 72.
[58] Dworkin (n 7) 161.
[59] TRS Allan 'Justice, Integrity and the Common Law' in S Khurshid, L Malik and V Rodriguez-Blanco (eds), *Dignity in the Legal and Political Philosophy of Ronald Dworkin* (Oxford University Press 2018) 81, 94.

and show its point or value'.[60] If, as Dworkin argues, the correct interpretation depends on an interaction between the concepts used in a practice and that practice's purpose, then the truth of an interpretive proposition depends not only on the application of some linguistic criteria or scientific test, but rather, at least in an important part, on a normative judgment of the interpreter. One cannot interpret a concept correctly without assuming the political and moral responsibilities involved in that judgment.

In *Law's Empire*, Dworkin stresses (for several pages) that his conception of interpretation is *constructive*, and that it is 'essentially concerned with purpose and not cause'.[61] This idea of constructive interpretation leaves us with two important questions, the answer to which is crucial to offer a Dworkinian response to Postema's criticism. *First*: how should an interpreter proceed to engage in constructive interpretation? Or what are her basic interpretive commitments? *Second*: why does Dworkin think that the interpreter must 'impose' the purpose upon the practice and resort to her own view about such purpose?

Let us begin with the *first* question. If we look at Postema's account of legal analogy, we can notice an important methodological perspective that is also present in Dworkin's conception of constructive interpretation. Although the face-value of Dworkin's assertion that an interpreter must resort to 'her own view' on the point of a social practice does not encourage this hypothesis, I think that a systematic reading of Dworkinian interpretivism supports a closer connection between this theory and Postema's works on analogical reasoning. Postema's theory of analogical reasoning rejects both the 'particularist' comparison of cases, which reflects a reasoning based only on feeling, intuition or perception, and the abstract justification of analogical rules offered by 'rule-rationalism', which insists on the question-begging idea that the only way to offer an analogical argument is to show that the two cases under comparison fall within the scope of a single rule.[62] For rule-rationalists, analogical reasoning requires that a prior and independent rule 'justifies the inference from the source analogue to the target analogue', in the sense that it has '*normative* priority' and '*grounds* the judgment of the analogy and the inference based on it'.[63]

What matters, here, are both Postema's objection to rule-rationalism and the solution that he finds for this problem in Robert Brandom's inferentialism. The problem of rule-rationalists, according to Postema, lies in their inability to provide a rule for connecting analogous cases without an infinite regress:

> No application of an explicit rule to a particular case, no application of a concept, is possible without the exercise of what Kant called the power of judgment, a power

[60] R Dworkin, *A Matter of Principle* (Harvard University Press 1985) 160.
[61] Dworkin (n 9) 52.
[62] GJ Postema, '*A Simulibus ad Similia*: Analogical Thinking in Law' in D Edlin (ed), *Common Law Theory* (Cambridge University Press 2007) 102, 108–16.
[63] ibid 111–12.

> which defies explicit articulation. If we insist that judgment is legitimate (rationally guided) only in virtue of one's grasp of a bridging rule, then we face the same problem with respect to the application of the bridging rule. It requires in turn the exercise of a judgment, which, if the judgment's legitimacy depends solely on a rule to guide it, posits another rule that in turn requires a further exercise of judgment, and so forth.[64]

There must be a point, therefore, where the inference from a source-analogue to a target-analogue is not driven by any rule. It is here that Postema resorts to Brandom's inferentialism[65] in order to solve the riddle of the possibility of analogical thought:

> Strictly speaking, there is no such a thing as *argument from* analogy, but only *reasoning with* analogy, or rather *analogical reasoning*. (Of course ... while analogical reasoning is not a *form of argument*, it is a *mode of argumentation*.) Analogical reasoning is not a linear process but rather a dynamic one of locating a new case in a network of inferences; reasoning – tracing compatibilities and incompatibilities or reasons and inferences – occurs throughout the process. If we understand it in this way, we can resist the temptation to reduce it either to a form of intuition or to a mere rule application ... A thinker making use of any explicit formulation of a rule to decide a new issue must rely on the mastery of the same inferential network that the rule was meant to make explicit. The content and normative significance of rules, as the content of examples, is fixed by this network.[66]

Part of a judge's responsibility in this analogical method, therefore, is to make explicit the norms that remained implicit in the network of inferences. As an insightful commentator observed, the philosophy of language underlying Postema's solution to the problem of analogy – developed by Brandom in a long series of studies – is based on a set of pragmatic commitments and responsibilities of the participants of social practices, which can be found, among other theories of concepts, in the philosophy of the second Wittgenstein:

> One of the central subjects of [Wittgenstein's] *Philosophical Investigations* is the existence of norms implicit in practices. That is why ... to take a linguistic performance to have certain meaning is committing oneself to the correctness and incorrectness of some uses of the expression. To grasp a concept or intention is to commit to norms implicit in practice that define the correct use of the first and the fulfillment of the second.[67]

[64] ibid 114.

[65] For a succinct and informative summary of Brandom's inferentialism (a sophisticated and comprehensive theory of concepts according to which to employ a concept is to commit to a set of norms implicit in practices, which must be made explicit), see R Brandom, *Articulating Reasons: An Introduction to Inferentialism* (Harvard University Press 2000) 1–35.

[66] Postema (n 62) 121.

[67] TL Decat, 'Inferentialist Pragmatism and Dworkin's "Law as Integrity"' (2015) 1 *Erasmus Law Review* 14, 17.

But how does Dworkin relate to this inferential network of justification? Why should we assume that his views that 'analogy without theory is blind'[68] and that we need to construct an interpretive theory based on abstract principles to bridge analogical conclusions are not the kind of rule-rationalism that Postema is at pains to avoid? Why should we ignore Postema's explicit characterisation of Dworkin as an example of rule rationalism?[69]

Once we take Dworkin's Anti-Archimedeanism seriously, we can relax about our worries with the thought that one must appeal to 'principles' or construct 'theories' to build analogies and justify inferences from cases to cases:

> On Dworkin's view, any legal theory must be interpretive because there is no second-order and non-evaluative theory that can provide an adequate understanding of an interpretive concept. … If Dworkin is right about the nature of legal argument, there is no external standpoint to which one can resort in order to apply a second-order test to determine the status of a legal fact.[70]

The principles to which one appeals to extract a rule that can bridge the cases in analogical inferences are *not* extracted from some second-level metaphysical realm. They do not transcend the practice. What we got, rather, is a historical series of statutes, precedents and other materials, whose impact is to be measured by the interpreter according to the standards of fit and justification. Dworkin's theory of legal interpretation seems, in fact, to commit to a form of normative pragmatism of the same kind that Postema accepts, as 'can be clearly seen in the pride of place Dworkin affords to the idea of norms implicit in practices'.[71] This inferentialist idea – it is argued – 'is in the core of his concept of legal principles and of the distinctive rational process of simultaneously applying the law and developing the law that he calls constructive interpretation'.[72] Dworkin's 'law as integrity', as he puts it, 'argues that rights and responsibilities flow from past decisions and so count as legal not just when they are explicit in these decisions, but also when they follow from the principles of personal and political morality the explicit decisions presuppose by way of justification'.[73]

That brings us to the *second* question: Why must Dworkin believe that interpreting a social practice is 'a matter of imposing purpose' on such practice to 'make it the best possible example of the form or genre to which it is taken to belong'?[74] Why does he not say that we can simply retrieve or extract a purpose that is already defined by the practice itself? In other words, why must the interpreter resort to her *own view* about the purpose at stake?

[68] Dworkin (n 5) 69.

[69] See Postema (n 62) 107.

[70] T Bustamante, 'Law, Moral Facts and Interpretation: A Dworkinian Response to Mark Greenberg's Moral Impact Theory of Law' (2019) 32 *Canadian Journal of Law and Jurisprudence* 5, 16.

[71] Decat (n 67) 24.

[72] ibid.

[73] Dworkin (n 9) 96.

[74] ibid 52.

I think that the Dworkinian answer to this question must stress the fact that law is an *argumentative* social practice. 'Every actor in the practice understands that what it permits or requires depends on the truth of certain propositions that are given sense only *by and within the practice*: the practice consists in large part in deploying and arguing about these propositions.'[75] This explains why Dworkin argued that in spite of sharing a concrete form of life, 'each of the participants must distinguish between trying to decide what other members of his community think the practice requires and trying to decide, for himself, what it really requires'.[76] According to Dworkin, an interpreter must try 'for himself' to establish what the practice requires not because he has authority to make others abide by his personal interpretation, but only because he is personally responsible for his constructive interpretation, that is, because he knows the propositions he sustains can have serious implications about one's rights and duties in a political community. Our interest, when we construct such a jurisprudential theory, is *practical* rather than historical, since we 'do not want predictions of the legal claims they [lawyers] will make' but responsible '*arguments*' about which of the claims made by participants in the social practice are sound.[77]

Dworkin's idea of protestant interpretation can be read, therefore, as an aspect of the thought that interpreters of the law – whether they are judges, lawyers, jurisprudence scholars or citizens – must frame their legal arguments as claims in the 'space of reasons', in the sense that Brandom uses the term. To be in the space of reasons is to bind oneself by conceptual norms, that is, to 'undertake discursive commitments and responsibilities, and so make [oneself] liable to distinctive kinds of normative *assessment*'.[78] Dworkin's account of interpretation is partly based on the Kantian notion of *freedom* as a kind of *authority*, not in the sense of imposing a judgment upon others, but in the sense of having authority to 'make ourselves *rationally* responsible by *taking* ourselves to be responsible'.[79] To engage on a protestant interpretation is, thus, to accept a normative commitment, and to place oneself under a norm.

Brandom explains, however, that this commitment is only part of the story of how we enter the space of reasons, for it is equally important that we accept the Hegelian point that 'all authority and responsibility are ultimately *social* phenomena',[80] because 'what institutes normative statuses is *reciprocal* recognition'.[81] When I commit myself to the norms of rationality that

[75] ibid 13.
[76] ibid 64.
[77] ibid 13.
[78] R Brandom, *Reason in Philosophy: Animating Ideas* (Belknap 2009) 60.
[79] ibid. 63.
[80] ibid 68.
[81] ibid 70.

define the content of concepts in the space of reasons, part of what makes my commitment intelligible is the recognition of other agents in the same discursive environment.[82]

This seems to be coherent with Dworkin's interpretivism, and it brings this theory close to what Postema says about the nature of jurisprudence. The argumentative aspect of the practice of law has important consequences for Dworkin's jurisprudence. Philosophical theories of law must be abstract because they 'aim to interpret the main point and structure of legal practice'.[83] But since this practice is argumentative and sensitive to the arguments about the grounds of the practice itself, legal philosophers cannot step out of this practice. The arguments they make are also part of this practice, no matter how abstract they are. This is the core of Dworkin's famous assertions that 'no firm line divides jurisprudence from adjudication or any other aspect of legal practice' and that jurisprudence is a 'silent prologue to any decision at law'.[84] A judge's practical argument, in turn, 'no matter how detailed and limited, assumes the kind of abstract foundation jurisprudence offers'.[85] Interpretation, for Dworkin, is a way to make sense of a social practice from within that same practice, and not from an independent metaphysical point of view. Hence, although each interpreter must resort to her own sense of what makes the practice the best it can be, each interpreter must also submit her own sense of the matter to all other participants in a practical argument. Each interpreter must try to find the meaning of social practices by herself, but no interpreter is allowed to trust only in herself, since she knows her interpretation will not settle the case. A Dworkinian interpreter knows that the outcome of her reasoning has a sort of provisional character, since she knows her constructive interpretations will be assimilated by the participants of the practice as a fallible claim. Perhaps more importantly, she knows that in several cases disagreement will persist, and future interpreters will retain this responsibility to continuingly engage with arguments, principles and purposes while interpreting the social practice. Every Dworkinian interpreter will know that her own interpretation may, despite all these efforts, fail; but she knows also that there is nothing in the interpretation of the majority that can assure us that it is right, even when it is final for the time being.

The crucial aspect of Dworkin's account of interpretive responsibility is that interpreters must adopt the *correct attitude* towards an interpretive issue. Interpretation provides the way to *make a case* for the truth of any given moral proposition, and involves a special *discipline* or *responsibility* to pursue moral

[82] ibid 73. Brandom's endorsement of this idea is, however, more radical than both Dworkin and Postema, for he claims that it explains not only how we make practical inferences and interpret moral or legal norms, but also that it can be used as a general semantic theory, applicable both to practical and theoretical inferences. We do not need, however, to engage in this argument here.

[83] Dworkin (n 9) 90.

[84] ibid.

[85] ibid.

truths by an integrative reasoning process: 'the nerve of responsibility is integrity and the epistemology of a moral responsible person is interpretive'.[86]

Something similar can be said about law. Dworkinian judges are subject to the 'doctrine of political responsibility', which Postema would have little reason to reject. In its 'most general form', according to Dworkin, this doctrine states that 'political officials must make only such political decisions as they can justify within a political theory that also justifies the other decisions they propose to make'.[87] This is important to understand the relation between 'fit' and 'justification' in Dworkin's theory of law. The dimension of 'fit' is added when we move from morality to law, because the law has an institutional aspect that is absent in ordinary morality. The historical political decisions of the community always matter in legal argument. Because of the mutual dependence between 'fit' and 'justification', which are regarded as two equally important aspects of legal integrity, legal justification is not free-standing; it is not independent from the practice of law. The theories we employ to justify a legal proposition are integrated in legal practices.[88] As Waluchow recently acknowledged, Dworkin's requirement of fit implies that historical legal materials such as statutes and precedents 'include elements the interpreter might well wish, for first-order moral and political reasons, were not there to constrain her interpretations'. Nevertheless, 'they *are* there and they *will* inevitably restrict her interpretive efforts in highly significant ways'.[89] If a moral argument does not fit the law practices it purports to justify, any justification based on this argument will be flawed. What makes the ideas of 'fit' and 'justification' mutually supportive in Dworkin's account of law is the fact that both are required for the success of any legal interpretation.[90] Interpretation, for Dworkin, is not anything external

[86] Dworkin (n 7) 101.

[87] R Dworkin, *Taking Rights Seriously* (2nd printing, Harvard University Press 1978) 87.

[88] Dworkin (n 5) 50–53.

[89] WJ Waluchow, 'Normative Reasoning from a Point of View' in KE Himma, M Jovanovíc and B Spaíc (eds), *Unpacking Normativity: Conceptual, Normative and Descriptive Issues* (Hart Publishing 2018) 119, 127.

[90] Although Dworkin's account of integrity might be open to different interpretations of the requirements of 'fit' and 'justification', it seems to me clear that the exigency of fit should be read not as a simple threshold that constrains an interpretation before the interpreter is allowed to make a judgment about the justification of the proposition under consideration. As Mark Greenberg ('The Moral Impact Theory of Law' (2014) 123 *Yale Law Journal* 1288, 1300, fn 29) argued, these requirements should not be read as 'two unrelated dimensions, one non-normative and other normative', given that the requirement of fit is better described as also an 'aspect of justification'. Fit and justification seem to be, indeed, two aspects of the value of integrity. 'Fit' is an aspect of 'justification just as much as 'justification' is an aspect of 'fit'. I think Trevor Allan explains this connection very well, in the following fragment (Allan (n 59) 92): '[C]ontrary to the initial impression given by Dworkin's talk of threshold requirements of fit, the interpreter's moral judgment is engaged throughout. If a specific account of statute or precedent (or of legislative or judicial authority) is rejected, it will be because moral judgment excludes it. Easy cases are only those whose solution most of us readily agree on it in the light of our shared convictions about the relevant political values.' As I argued elsewhere, 'because justification is something made *within* the practice of law, *by participants* of this practice and with the *arguments* that these participants employ when they succeed in establishing the truth of their legal propositions, justification must be also an aspect of fit': Bustamante (n 70) 23–24.

to the practice or the realm that constitutes its object. The content of principles does not precede interpretation, and the same goes for the point of law.

But still, why do interpreters need to appeal to their own sense of the point of that practice? We might try a proceduralist answer to this question. We might read 'integrity', for instance, as a process of argumentation through which citizens constantly keep open the possibility of further argumentative activity about the content of the law. As Jeremy Waldron puts it, law as integrity is incompatible with authoritative settlement of legal issues:

> To the extent that legality depends on moral argument, there is always a basis for refusing to accept any particular determination as final: 'a citizen's allegiance is to the law, not to any particular person's view of what the law is'. In fact, Dworkin's insistence on the existence of objective right answers to constitutional and legal questions (not just to moral questions) has exactly this effect of undermining settlement. 'No judicial decision', he says, 'is necessarily the right decision'. True, a determination by a court may make a difference to what the law is, as a matter of precedent. But the difference it is supposed to make is itself a matter of moral argument … and that too is an argument about an objective issue, an argument that any particular fallible human decision maker may get it wrong. So citizens who believe a court has made a legal or moral mistake … are not morally required to accept its determination as conclusive. Particularly where they conceive the matter to be one of moral importance, they must be allowed to persevere with their challenge.[91]

The point of a 'protestant' interpretation, for Dworkin, is to ignite this argumentative process that undermines authoritative settlement and turns the law into an argumentative social practice.[92] When people argue about the law, they must make a judgment about the *point* of the practice of law, but there is nothing in the nature of this judgment that precludes interpreters from arguing that

[91] J Waldron, 'The Rule of Law as a Theatre of Debate' in Burley (ed) (n 28) 319, 326.

[92] The idea that law is not entirely fixed by authoritative settlement is not new. As Postema argues in a well-articulated restatement of classical common law, this thought was deeply entrenched in the jurisprudence of jurists like Coke and Hale, who also advocated that the law is essentially argumentative. In the practice of precedent, for instance, judicial decisions were respected not merely because of having been posited, but rather because a later court recognised that they 'found a place within the body of [legal] experience'. A past case contributes to the determination of the content of the law neither because it is 'regarded as establishing authoritative rules' nor because it 'precludes deliberation and reasoning in subsequence cases'. It was always open for a later court, instead, 'to test any precedent court's formulation of the rule of its decision in light of the legal community's shared sense of reasonableness': GJ Postema, 'Classical Common Law Jurisprudence (Part II)' (2003) 3 *Oxford University Commonwealth Law Journal* 1, 17. I believe, however, that Postema would reject the comparison between Dworkin and classical common lawyers. Even though Dworkin and these classical lawyers would agree that judges should not appeal to 'the reason of broad, universal principles *external* to the ordinary sources of law' (GJ Postema, 'Classical Common Law Jurisprudence (Part I)' (2002) 2 *Oxford University Commonwealth Law Journal* 155, 178), Postema believes, given his interpretation of Dworkin's theory of law, that the model of law as integrity is distinct from the 'artificial reason' of common law because only the latter presupposed a conception of reasoning that is regarded as *common* or *shared* among the practice's participants. See Postema, 'Classical Common Law … (Part II)', 8; and Postema (n 28) 295.

this point is a 'common point', and that although this point is distinct from the specific rules that figure inside the practice, it is still the case that this purpose must be found in an integrative reading of the practice. Rather than a purpose that is logically independent from the practice, the point of the law is extracted from the same practice that it purports to explain and justify.

I think that this argumentative character of law is an important feature of every legitimate legal system, and that it is one of the constitutive elements of the ideal of the rule of law. As Neil MacCormick explains, the rule of law as a political ideal implies the recognition of 'law's domain as a locus of argumentation'.[93] Law must be argumentative, and in this sense incapable of authoritative settlement in the sense of Joseph Raz, Scott Shapiro or Frederick Schauer, for otherwise a citizen, an official or any other individual interpreter will not be able to take up his or her own individual responsibility to interpret the law.

It is thus not surprising that Postema himself made sound and severe criticisms on Raz's conception of legal authority, which revolves around the so-called 'Autonomy Thesis'. The Autonomy Thesis comprises not only the idea that the law is a limited domain of reasons, but also: (i) the thought that authorities utter directives that constitute a pre-emptive reason for action, that is, 'a reason for its performance which is not to be added to all other relevant reasons when assessing what to do, but should exclude and take the place of some of them';[94] and (ii) the thought that all laws are source-based, in the sense that legal content 'can be identified by reference to social facts alone, without resort to any evaluative argument'.[95] *Contra* Raz, Postema persuasively makes a case for a jurisprudence that integrates legal theory, practical reason and adjudication. On this view, 'when they distinguish or overrule established precedents, or creatively interpret statutes, courts typically appeal to principles and values just of the kind that the argument for the Autonomy Thesis would lead us to expect to be excluded'.[96] 'Legal reasoning in its public manifestation in legal practice,' Postema says, 'is continuous with and inseparable from moral reasoning.'[97] Legal theory should therefore get rid of two Razian separations: first, the separation between theory of law and theory of adjudication; and, second, the pretension to isolate legal reasons from moral reasons, which lies at the core of the Autonomy Thesis. In place of such thesis, we should 'look for a model which *integrates* arguments of political morality into proper legal argument and justification, starting from recognition of the reflectively self-critical character of legal practice'.[98]

[93] N MacCormick, *Rhetoric and the Rule of Law* (Oxford University Press 2005) 13.

[94] J Raz, *The Morality of Freedom* (Oxford University Press 1986) 46.

[95] J Raz, *Ethics in the Public Domain* (Oxford University Press 1994) 211.

[96] GJ Postema, 'Law's Autonomy and Public Practical Reason' in RP George (ed), *The Autonomy of Law: Essays on Legal Positivism* (Oxford University Press 1996) 79, 102.

[97] ibid 104.

[98] At some point, Postema's criticism against Raz assumes a typically Dworkinian tone, when he claims to integrate legal practice and moral justification. The 'reflectively self-critical

I believe that Postema's contribution to the philosophy of law is just as concerned with this integration between arguments of political morality and proper legal arguments as is Dworkin's *law as integrity*. Perhaps Postema's objection to HLA Hart's theory of the normativity of law can further illustrate this point. According to Postema, one of the reasons why Hart's conventionalist account of the rule of recognition fails to provide an adequate explanation of the normativity of law is that it does not succeed in its attempt to establish a stable distinction between *legal* and *moral* obligations. According to Postema, Hart's attempt to separate these two types of obligations depends on the possibility that the rule of recognition binds legal officials just because other officials have accepted this rule. Furthermore, it depends on the possibility of giving them reasons for action while implying 'nothing about the reasons the subjects may have to obey'.[99] Legal officials would have reasons to apply a law even in those cases in which citizens lack any reasons to follow it. Postema argues that this assumption is problematic, inasmuch as it prevents the law from complying with its task of directing social behaviour. 'If the law is to succeed even minimally in this distinctive task (of guiding human behaviour)' then 'there must be a shared context of interpretation of the rules in which law-makers, law-appliers, *and* law-followers participate'.[100]

But how can law-makers, law-appliers and law-followers share a context of interpretation of legal reasons if the law is understood only in terms of strict conventions? In response to this question, Postema makes an important concession to a mild form of natural law jurisprudence, since he does not believe that mere agreement is enough to provide practical guidance: 'if appeals to existing law are to justify judicial decisions and exercise of coercive power, they must rest on something morally more substantial than the mere fact that others follow the rules'.[101] Legal rules cannot guide the action of judges, citizens and institutions in the way that a game guides the action of its players:

> Law is different from most games and etiquette in this respect. With regards to the latter, it is usually enough to say (and normally all that can be said is) that there is a general acceptance of the rules one proposes to follow and they constitute the rules of the game, or simply that 'it's done'. But this is not enough in the case of appeals to law, because, both as a matter of fact, and a matter of design, law much more directly touches matters of public moral significance. Arguments adequate for games or etiquette are unsuited to this task.[102]

character' of legal practice seems to be very similar to Dworkin's integrity-based legal reasoning, for it is 'not shared with many other rule-governed activities, like games'. The 'rules which govern deliberation … themselves can be made objects of practical deliberation and critical assessment *within the practice* itself': Postema (n 96) 111.

[99] GJ Postema, 'The Normativity of Law' in R Gavison (ed), *Issues in Contemporary Legal Philosophy: The Influence of HLA Hart* (Oxford University 1987) 90.

[100] ibid 92.

[101] ibid 101.

[102] ibid.

Although Postema does not think that this reasoning should lead us to abandon a conventionalist explanation for the normativity of law, he believes that it does provide an argument to reject a *strict* form of conventional explanation. He argues that strict conventionalism should be replaced by a 'constructive' version of conventionalism, in which officials must recognise both a moral point for the practice of law and a principled process of argumentation for determining their legal authority. Under this 'constructive' conventionalism,

> officials recognize, and are committed by their actions and arguments to recognize, that their joint acceptance of the criteria of validity must be linked to more general moral-political concerns. Only in this way can their appeal to those criteria, and the practice on which they rest, provide the right sort of justification for their exercise of power in particular cases. But they also realize that *an essential part* of the case to be made for the criteria rests on the fact that they jointly accept the criteria, or *could come to accept* them after reflection and participation in a forum in which reasoned and principled arguments are exchanged among equals. That is, officials recognize that the law they identified and administer is a collective product, and the process of determining its main outlines is essentially a collective and public process.[103]

Postema's account of the normativity of law seems to me very attractive, and I do not see any reason why Dworkin should reject it. The problem of this 'constructive' version of conventionalism, which Dworkin would describe as 'soft conventionalism', is not that it is wrong but rather that it is 'not really a form of conventionalism'.[104] It appears to be, instead, in the same camp as the 'weak conventionalism' that Dworkin discussed in *Law's Empire*.[105]

[103] ibid 104.

[104] Dworkin (n 9) 127.

[105] According to Dworkin, weak conventionalism is 'a very abstract, underdeveloped form of law as integrity': ibid 128. This criticism, however, does not apply to Postema. As a matter of fact, in certain aspects Postema's theory of law is even more detailed and sophisticated than Dworkin's *law as integrity*. One of these aspects is the way that Postema explains the mindfulness of time in legal deliberation. According to Postema, an important aspect of legal normativity can be explained with the metaphor of a melody, which is designed to highlight the 'temporal dimensions of law's normativity': GJ Postema, 'Melody and Law's Mindfulness of Time' (2004) 17 *Ratio Juris* 203, 207. Consider the following description of how time provides a structure for musical melodies (ibid): 'A performance of Bach's *Erbarme dich* is a temporal sequence of pitches each of a specific duration. The pitches in their respective durations are heard not just in sequence, nor merely as a sequence, but as a melodic sequence, a temporally unfolding, musically meaningful whole. The melodic pattern relates the notes sounding over time according to a sense of musical significance. For this meaningful musical pattern to take shape, it must sound over time – the notes represented in the score or played all at once do not constitute a melody – yet the object of the hearer's awareness is the melodic whole, not just the individual notes.' The melody metaphor can explain, better than any other of which I am aware, the necessary mindfulness of time in intentional action and in particular in legal action as one of its special cases: 'Bratman helpfully suggests that we view intentions as relatively stable, partial plans for present and future action. They are *partial* in the sense of being *indeterminate*, needing to be filled out as time goes by. With this in mind, we can look at the role of mindfulness of time in intended action from two points in the process: *ex ante* and *in medias res*. The place for us to start is *in medias res*. The agent in mid-course typically faces new problems for deliberation. This deliberation is framed by three parameters: the intention-plan, current circumstances, and the

Although Postema used a conventionalist vocabulary in his critique of Hart, he left conventionalism behind when he made this argument. 'Constructive' conventionalism is analogous to Dworkinian interpretivism, both in the claim that legal interpretations are sensitive to a moral point – the moral-political concern to justify coercive application of norms by political institutions – and in the claim that the process of interpretation is one in which participants can come to accept common norms 'after reflection and participation in a forum in which reasoned and principled arguments are exchanged among equals'.

Nonetheless, there is nothing that can make sure that in actual argumentative processes participants will in fact accept these common norms, since there will always remain a possibility of disagreement about the best interpretation of the practice's value. What should we do when this kind of disagreement emerges? According to Dworkin, the possibility of disagreement changes nothing in one's interpretive responsibilities, and I do not see how Postema could disagree with this. In fact, when we consider Postema's criticism of Hart's methodology, his approximation to Dworkin becomes clear. Philosophical jurisprudence, for Postema, 'is in the first instance a *practical*, not a *theoretical*, study'. In other words, it is a 'branch of practical philosophy'.[106] According to Postema, jurisprudence's practical concern persists 'even when questions are asked about its foundational rules'.[107] Even when officials or citizens disagree about the grounds of law or the rule of recognition, 'there is no reason to assume that reflection on the practical normative force of law requires that we step outside the practice entirely'.[108] So just like Dworkin, Postema seems to imply that we need to make evaluative judgments about the law *all the way down*, and some of these judgments are not only judgments about epistemic values, but moral, practical judgments.

Although Postema employs a conventionalist vocabulary when he uses words like 'criteria' and 'consensus', he does *not* advocate a criterial theory about how legal concepts are constructed, and neither does he assume a consensus at the outset of the process of argumentation. The consensus to which Postema

initial installments in the execution of the plan. Deliberation with respect to these parameters is governed by norms of coherence (taking this term in a very broad sense). … Rational execution of one's intention depends on integrating these three parameters into deliberation. So, the agent *in medias res* cannot limit her attention to the past installments and current circumstances, ignoring the intention-plan, for, as she sees it, the practical deliberative problem she faces now is shaped by her intention, and not merely by the causal antecedents of her situation and the current state of play in the world. Her past conduct is related to present options not primarily as cause to effect but as constitutive parts of a temporally extended project – the already sounded notes of the melody, as it were. The practical, normative significance of the relevant range of past conduct for the present depends directly on this fact' (ibid 209–10). Postema is, in my opinion, very insightful when he proposes to describe the temporal aspect of legal normativity in this way.

[106] GJ Postema, 'Jurisprudence as Practical Philosophy' (1998) 4 *Law and Philosophy* 329, 330.

[107] ibid 337.

[108] ibid 330.

appeals in order to vindicate a convention is presented as the appropriate result of an interpretive process, which is driven by principles found in a social practice that regards argumentation among equals as the correct attitude for interpreting the rules that give the practice its shape and content. The kind of social practice that Postema has in mind is very similar to the practice that Dworkin describes as *law as integrity*.

If we read Dworkin's interpretive theory of law in light of his own assumptions about the nature of moral argument – and especially in light of the claim that we need not to appeal to transcendental arguments in order to make a case for an interpretive proposition – I believe that Postema's own work is not only coherent with Dworkin's account of protestant interpretation but also depends on it. This claim is particularly strong with regard to his views on the principle of the rule of law. Postema's conception of the rule of law requires that the people themselves, and not only courts, legislatures or other officials, become both legally accountable and accountability-holders in the political community. According to Postema,

> The law can rule only when those who are subject to it, the prince and officials of government and citizens alike, are bound together in a thick network of mutual accountability with respect to that law. The rule of law is robust in a polity only when the members of that polity undertake and carry out commitments of mutual faithfulness to a set of differentiated and interconnected responsibilities, core among them being the responsibility to hold each other accountable under law.[109]

Postema's account of the rule of law, in which each member of the community is both accountable and an accountability-holder, provides a very powerful interpretation of the political ideal of the rule of law. Although one of the central aspects of the rule of law is that it repeals any sort of *arbitrary* power, this notion alone is not sufficient to capture all the aspects of the rule of law. For Postema, the rule of law only flourishes if the members of the polity 'embrace and practice a distinctive ethos', which comprises the values of legality – constituted of formal, procedural aspects of the rule of law – and fidelity – constituted by 'a robust practice of holding each other accountable under the law'.[110]

The proper way to understand the practice of law, for Postema, is through a revision of Hobbes' thesis that 'to be bound by the law is to be subject of the judgment of another'[111] in light of Kant's thesis that 'no one can bind another to do something without also being subject to a law which he in turn can be bound in

[109] GJ Postema, 'Law's Rule: Reflexivity, Mutual Accountability and the Rule of Law' in Xiaobo Zhai and M Quinn (eds), *Bentham's Theory of Law and Public Opinion* (Cambridge University Press 2014) 7, 25.

[110] GJ Postema, 'Fidelity in Law's Commonwealth' in LM Austin and D Klimchuck (eds), *Private Law and the Rule of Law* (Oxford University Press 2014) 17, 20.

[111] ibid 31.

the same way by the other'.[112] In the network of mutual accountability relations created by the law, every citizen is therefore considered and qualified *as equal*, in the same sense as Dworkin supposed in his 'community of principles'.[113]

This horizontal accountability, which seems to be central in Postema's conception of the rule of law, is not satisfied when a person obeys a law authoritatively settled by a superior authority. For the emergence of the ethos of fidelity to law, no one can have the right to make a preemptive authoritative settlement of the law. This raises a question that places Postema in the same camp as Dworkin: How can a citizen be an accountability-holder and share the mutual faithfulness and responsibility towards the law if such citizen is denied the opportunity to interpret by herself (before trying to convince others) the purpose that she believes is capable of providing a moral justification to our existing legal practices? In my view, without something analogous to Dworkin's protestant interpretation, Postema will not be able to answer this question: each citizen must have a personal and non-delegable responsibility to make an interpretive appreciation of the point and purpose of law.

Even under Dworkin's conception of interpretation, the point of law, in every interpretive exercise, must be a common purpose; it must be shared by the members of the community, and our arguments deployed to retrieve it must be constructed from within the practice in which we participate. And the same can be said about the theories we use to describe this point at a more abstract level. These theories are not separated from the practice. Instead of preceding the practice, they are deeply embedded in them. They are *part* of the practice, and every participant of the practice needs them to understand the principles she lives by. Participants in civil societies must not accept the rules of the social practice as if they were conventions that have some sort of arbitrary content and are normative because of the mere fact of agreement among the members of a relevant social group. Rather, they accept the general norms of the practice as interpretive paradigms that will stand only as long as they are proved in argument to be generally justified. Although we need tradition and history to interpret a practice, tradition, history and convention alone will not do the interpretive work. Each participant of the practice has to make a case for her interpretation of the point of the practice and to make a judgment about the norms that she claims to extract from the practice in her constructive interpretation. Each participant has an individual responsibility to interpret the practice in order to raise public claims about the meaning of the practice and to hold other members of the practice accountable. It is precisely this responsibility that makes the practice argumentative and that explains why we can share the practice even when we disagree about the best interpretation of the practice's core principles.

[112] I Kant, 'Toward Perpetual Peace' in *Practical Philosophy* ed and trs MJ Gregor (Cambridge University Press 1996) 311, 323; Postema (n 110) 33.

[113] Dworkin (n 9) 200.

III. CONCLUSION

I hope to have shown in the previous section not only that Postema's objection to protestant interpretation is ungrounded, but also that Postema's more recent work on the rule of law has important affinities with the interpretive attitude that Dworkin advocates in his theory of law. Fidelity to the rule of law, for Postema, requires the same kind of moral responsibility in the interpretation of law that Dworkin demands when he argues that citizens and officials should seek for integrity in their legal arguments. Postema's account of the rule of law, if I am correct, should be read as a reconciliation with Dworkin. Interpretation must be protestant, if my argument is sound, because there is no interpreter with authority to settle legal questions, and every member of the community enjoys both the right and the responsibility to make a judgment about the integrity of the community to which she belongs.

We should abandon, therefore, the three basic assumptions that led Postema to reject Dworkin's idea of 'protestant' interpretation: first, that the point of law is logically independent from legal practice; second, that theory precedes practice and is imposed upon such practice; and, third, that pre-interpretive materials are 'raw data' that lack any social meaning before they are interpreted by legal participants.

We should attempt, instead, a more generous reading of Dworkin that upholds the following three alternative claims. First, the point of the law is extracted from legal practice itself; it is *given* by legal practice even though we are capable of identifying it as distinct from the practice it justifies. Second, once we take seriously Dworkin's idea that the content of the law is dependent on interpretation, we should think that theory is continuous with practice. Rather than being 'imposed upon the practice', jurisprudence is a more general part of the practice, since there is no qualitative distinction between arguments *of* the practice and arguments *about* the practice. Legal practice is made up (partly) of arguments, even when such arguments are arguments about the nature of law. Third, given the reflective and interpretive character of the legal practice, pre-interpretive materials are not 'raw data'; they are 'pre-interpretive' relative to our current interpretive effort, but they are historically constructed in previous interpretive efforts. Interpretation is dynamic and revisable, and any participant (citizens and officials alike) can reinterpret an authoritative pronouncement. It is precisely this feature that makes interpretation *protestant* in Dworkin's theory of law.

If these claims are sound, as I believe they are, we can reconcile Postema's brilliant conception of the rule of law with Dworkin's insightful method of legal interpretation. Postema's advocacy of fidelity to the practice of law requires the protestant attitude that makes interpreters personally responsible for their arguments and opinions about the content of the law.

5

Postema, Dworkin, and the Question of Meaning

DENNIS PATTERSON

I AM IMMENSELY grateful for the opportunity to participate in a tribute to Jerry Postema. Postema is one of the most important philosophers of my generation. In addition to his wide-ranging philosophical talent, he is one of the most incisive minds I have met in my 30 plus years in academic life. I have learned so much from him over the years, I cannot begin to quantify the depth and breadth of his insights. For me, he represents the pinnacle of the philosophical profession.

My contribution to this volume is a comment on Professor Bustamante's effort to forge a rapprochement between Postema and Dworkin.[1] Bustamante mounts an attractive position when it comes to the question of common ground between Postema and Dworkin. At the end of the day, I remain unconvinced by Bustamante's attempt at reconciliation. Interestingly, our disagreement can be rather tightly focused: in fact, I think the debate really comes down to one fundamental point. Before turning to Bustamante's chapter, let me say a few things by way of background.

The fundamental philosophical issue in the debate between Dworkin and Postema is how to understand and characterise the move from signs to meaning. I shall call this 'the question of meaning'. Of course, this is a huge topic. It implicates many different theories from a wide variety of fields. Everything from literary theory, philosophy of language, to social science data is potentially

[1] The frame of 'Postema v Dworkin' arises out of Postema's article '"Protestant" Interpretation and Social Practices' (1987) 6 *Law and Philosophy* 283. The article is an extended review and commentary on R Dworkin, *Law's Empire* (Belknap 1986). In my estimation, Postema's article is the most incisive commentary in the literature on Dworkin's legal philosophy. The importance of the article lies in the fact that Postema identifies the core philosophical contention of Dworkin (ie, the centrality of interpretation to legal practice) and demonstrates why it is implausible. For a critique of Dworkin's theory of law as interpretation with a view to a positivist account of interpretation, see D Patterson, 'Theoretical Disagreement, Legal Positivism and Interpretation' (2018) 31 *Ratio Juris* 260.

relevant. In previous work, I have detailed some of the intricacies of the depth and breadth of the notion that meaning is the product of interpretation.[2] I will not rehearse that here.

I follow Vincent Descombes[3] in locating the source of the question of meaning in Nietzsche. In *The Will to Power*,[4] Nietzsche articulates his 'perspectivism'[5] in clear and bold terms. He writes:

> 'Everything is subjective,' you say; but even this is interpretation. The 'subject' is not something given, it is something added and invented and projected behind what there is. – Finally, is it necessary to posit an interpreter behind the interpretation? Even this is invention, hypothesis.
>
> In so far as the word 'knowledge' has any meaning, the world is knowable; but it is interpretable otherwise, it has no meaning behind it, but countless meanings. – 'Perspectivism'.
>
> It is our needs that interpret the world; our drives and their For and Against. Every drive is a kind of lust to rule; each one has its perspective that it would like to compel all the other drives and accept as a norm.[6]

As I see it, there are two paths out of Nietzsche on the question of meaning. The first starts with Heidegger and runs through Foucault and Derrida.[7] This is the 'wild' path, the gravamen of which is the idea that meaning is produced by the individual subject through an act of interpretation. The same idea, expressed in a lower key, is found in the thought of Gadamer[8] and Charles Taylor.[9] The radical version of this point of view yokes politics onto the metaphysical account of meaning. That dimension is absent in the more nuanced views of Gadamer, Taylor and their fellow-travellers.

In both the radical and sober hermeneutical accounts of meaning, the same basic idea prevails. This is the notion that what lies between signs and meaning is interpretation. In other words, understanding – grasping the meaning of a sign – is impossible without an intellectual operation. That operation is interpretation.

[2] eg D Patterson, *Law and Truth* (Oxford University Press 1996).

[3] V Descombes, 'Nietzsche's French Moment' in L Ferry and A Renault (eds), *Why We Are Not Nietzscheans* tr R de Loaiza (University of Chicago Press 1997).

[4] FW Nietzsche and A M Ludovici, *The Will To Power*, trs W Kaufmann and RJ Hollingdale (Random House 1967).

[5] For discussion of this topic, see R Lanier Anderson, 'Friedrich Nietzsche' in EN Zalta (ed), *The Stanford Encyclopedia of Philosophy* (Summer 2017 edn), available at plato.stanford.edu/archives/sum2017/entries/nietzsche/.

[6] Nietzsche (n 4) 267.

[7] There are others, of course, like Paul Ricoeur. And we could also locate Freud and perhaps Marx as well.

[8] eg H-G Gadamer, *Truth and Method* (2nd edn, trans J Weinsheimer and DG Marshall, Crossroad 1992).

[9] The best expression of Taylor's view is found in C Taylor, 'Interpretation and the Sciences of Man' in C Taylor *Philosophical Papers*, vol 1: *Human Agency and Language* (Cambridge University Press 1985) 15.

As Descombes reminds us, what is lost in the hermeneutical point of view is a crucial distinction, that between understanding and interpretation. This is the difference between directly accessible meaning (understanding) and meaning that is accessible only by way of inference (interpretation).[10] Understanding 'is not a mental episode parallel to the reading of the printed signs'.[11] Rather, it is the demonstration of a capacity: 'we can, if we are asked to, summarize the article, react to its contents, comment on it, etc'.[12]

The philosophical opposition to the hermeneutical approach to meaning is best represented by the later Wittgenstein. As I have detailed elsewhere,[13] Wittgenstein famously argued that the idea of understanding grounded in interpretation is a non-starter. Although he gave two arguments for this in *Philosophical Investigations*,[14] the best-known argument is the infinite regress argument. He wrote:

> This was our paradox: no course of action could be determined by a rule, because any course of action can be made out to accord with the rule. The answer was: if any action can be made out to accord with the rule, then it can also be made out to conflict with it. And so there would be neither accord nor conflict here.
>
> It can be seen that there is a misunderstanding here from the mere fact that in the course of our argument we give one interpretation after another; as if each one contented us at least for a moment, until we thought of yet another standing behind it. What this shews is that there is a way of grasping a rule which is not an interpretation, but which is exhibited in what we call 'obeying the rule' and 'going against it' in actual cases.
>
> Hence, there is an inclination to say: any action according to the rule is an interpretation. But we ought to restrict the term 'interpretation' to the substitution of one expression of the rule for another.[15]

For Wittgenstein, the linguistic sense of signs is found in practices. Meaning arises out of the intersubjective use of linguistic symbols the sense of which is a function of their shared use in practices. Everything from texts, signposts and numbers all have meaning in virtue of their use in practices. The key to learning meaning is acquiring the repertoire of behaviours that accompany the use of signs in practices. Meaning is, at bottom, a social phenomenon and not the product of interpretation, individual or otherwise.

Wittgenstein and the hermeneutical philosophers are metaphysically at odds: as I see it, there can be no reconciliation. Wittgenstein does not rule out interpretation: far from it. What he does rule out is a *foundational* place for

[10] Descombes (n 3) 80.
[11] ibid 81.
[12] ibid.
[13] Patterson (n 2).
[14] For superb explication of these two arguments, see M Williams, *Wittgenstein, Mind and Meaning* (Routledge 1999) 157–87.
[15] Wittgenstein, *Philosophical Investigations*, revised tr GE Anscombe (Blackwell 2001) Sec 201.

interpretation in a proper account of linguistic meaning. The point cannot be made any clearer than the way Descombes articulates it. Hermeneutics puts the operation of interpretation between signs and meaning. The difference between the wild and sober dimensions of hermeneutics is a function of what is built into 'interpretation'. It can be 'politics' (Foucault and Derrida) or 'prejudice' (Gadamer). What unites both dimensions of the hermeneutic perspective is the foundational or constitutive role of interpretation in the production of meaning.

Now let us turn to legal philosophy. We start with Dworkin. Everything we need to know about Dworkin's views of interpretation occurs on one page of *Law's Empire*.[16] For Dworkin, law is an interpretive concept. Dworkin says two things about this that are critical for a proper understanding of his view. First, that '[a]ny jurisprudence worth having must be built on some view of what interpretation is'.[17] The second point is the question of how important is this view of interpretation? Dworkin says 'the analysis of interpretation I construct and defend in this chapter is the foundation of the rest of the book'.[18] It is difficult to overestimate just how important interpretation is to the Dworkinian project.

And what is Dworkin's view of interpretation? He starts with this example: 'The most familiar occasion of interpretation – so familiar that we hardly recognize it as such – is conversation. We interpret the sounds or marks another person makes in order to decide what he has said'.[19] With this sentence, Dworkin plants his flag firmly in the hermeneutic camp. Everything that follows in the development of his theory of interpretation is grounded in the view that it is through an individual act of interpretation that an agent produces the meaning of signs.[20] The text – be it a road sign or a statute – has meaning only in so far as an individual agent engages in an act of interpretation that breathes life into the sign, the object of interpretation.

How does Postema contrast with Dworkin on the meaning of signs? Postema consistently employs the Wittgensteinian trope of understanding as embedded in social practices. Understanding a practice is 'mastery of a discipline'.[21] Ability is a matter of 'shared capacity'.[22] Disagreement – especially interpretive disagreement – takes place against the background of a world of 'common meanings'.[23] 'Conflict always presupposes consensus',[24] as Postema rightly puts it.

Bustamante writes that 'Dworkin does not subscribe to Gadamer's general thesis that all knowledge is interpretive'.[25] He goes on to say that 'Interpretivism,

[16] Dworkin (n 1) 50.
[17] ibid.
[18] ibid.
[19] ibid.
[20] This is why Postema was right to describe Dworkin's view as 'Protestant'.
[21] Postema (n 1) 313.
[22] ibid.
[23] ibid 316.
[24] ibid 318.
[25] T Bustamante, 'Revisiting the Idea of Protestant Interpretation: Towards Reconciliation between Dworkin and Postema', ch 4 of this volume, section II.

for Dworkin, is not a general ontology. The interpretive attitude, for Dworkin, is not adopted in every type of intellectual challenge.'[26] I think these statements are mistaken. First, Gadamer is not doing epistemology (knowledge): he is advancing a metaphysical account of the nature of linguistic meaning. Second, *contra* Bustamante, Dworkin is advancing a general theory of understanding, one that is employed in every kind of legal case.[27]

Bustamante writes:

> I am sceptical of Patterson's idea that the core difference between Postema and Dworkin in their conceptions of interpretation is that the former adopts Wittgenstein's account of social practice while the latter dismisses it in exchange for Gadamer's philosophical hermeneutics, since Dworkin is influenced equally by Gadamer and Wittgenstein.[28]

As we have seen, it is precisely because Dworkin advocates the hermeneutical/interpretivist position that his view of meaning, law and interpretation is irreconcilable with the view so cogently advanced by Postema.

It has sometimes been suggested that Wittgenstein's account of the nature of linguistic meaning has little to contribute to debates in legal philosophy.[29] Of course, this is a view profoundly at odds with some of the central problems of legal philosophy. Postema's work confirms that this view is profoundly mistaken. When it comes to meaning, there is no clearer choice than that between Wittgenstein and the interpretivists. Every legal theory depends on a choice – conscious or not – between these two irreconcilable perspectives. From my perch, Postema got all of this just right.[30]

[26] ibid.

[27] Importantly, Dworkin says there is no difference between easy and hard cases when it comes to the role of interpretation. 'Hercules does not need one method for hard cases and another for easy cases. His method is equally at work in easy cases, but since the answers to the questions it puts are then obvious, or at least seem to be so, we are not aware that any theory is at work at all': Dworkin (n 1) 354.

[28] Bustamante (n 25).

[29] For discussion and refutation of these claims, see D Patterson, 'Wittgenstein, Ludwig,' in M Sellars and S Kirste (eds), *Encyclopedia of the Philosophy of Law and Social Philosophy*, (Springer 2021).

[30] eg D Patterson, 'Can We Stop Doing This? And by the Way, Postema Was Right' in T Gizbert-Studnicki (ed), *Metaphilosophy of Law* (Hart Publishing 2016) 49.

6

Protestant Interpretation, Conventions, and Legal Truth

BRIAN H BIX

I. INTRODUCTION

GERALD POSTEMA HAS made influential contributions to many parts of legal philosophy (as well as moral philosophy, political philosophy and the history of philosophy). This chapter will focus on the intersection of just two of those points of influence – his critique of Ronald Dworkin's work and his equally important discussion of the role of conventions at the foundation of legal practice and legal theory – to consider some implications for the difficult question of truth in law.

Postema's work, supplemented by the works of other scholars along similar lines, directs us towards important interlocking insights regarding the nature of law and the nature of legal truth. The emphasis on the shared, social and institutional nature of law both raises and helps us to begin to respond to issues about how to understand what makes propositions about law true or false.

In what follows, section II introduces Dworkin's 'Protestant approach' and the critique it evoked from Postema (supplemented by points raised by Robert Cover and Sanford Levinson). Section III looks at Postema's discussions about the conventional groundings of law, and explores how they offer both answers and further questions regarding the nature of legal truth.

II. DWORKIN'S 'PROTESTANT INTERPRETATION'

In 1986, Ronald Dworkin published *Law's Empire*,[1] his only monograph on the nature of law and legal theory.[2] In that book, Dworkin presented his

[1] R Dworkin, *Law's Empire* (Harvard University Press 1986).

[2] Dworkin's other works on the topic, both earlier and later, were collections of articles: *Taking Rights Seriously* (Harvard University Press 1976), *A Matter of Principle* (Harvard University

most careful and comprehensive picture of his interpretive approach to law. In a 1987 review of that work, Gerald Postema focused on what he described as '"Protestant" interpretation' in Dworkin's theory.[3] The description is based on the basic structure of Dworkin's approach, but is reinforced by some language near the end of *Law's Empire*:

> Law's empire is defined by attitude, not territory or power or process. We studied that attitude mainly in appellate courts, where it is dressed for inspection, but it must be pervasive in our ordinary lives if it is to serve us well even in court. It is an interpretive, self-reflective attitude addressed to politics in the broadest sense. It is a protestant attitude that makes each citizen responsible for imagining what these commitments require in new circumstances. The protestant character of law is confirmed, and the creative role of private decisions acknowledged, by the backward-looking, judgmental nature of judicial decisions, and also by the regulative assumption that though judges must have the last word, their word is not for that reason the best word.[4]

One can find comparable language elsewhere in Dworkin's text as well. For instance, in the example of a social practice of courtesy (which Dworkin offers as an analogy to legal practice), the text states:

> Each citizen … is trying to discover his own intention in maintaining and participating in that practice – not in the sense of retrieving his mental state when last he took off his cap to a lady but in the sense of finding a purposeful account of his behavior he is comfortable in ascribing to himself.[5]

The idea of 'Protestant interpretation' within the relevant religious tradition is not any sort of extreme relativism: it is *not* the assertion that the Bible means whatever each of us *thinks* it means. The point is not relativism but equality (or anti-hierarchy), that we should not think that the clergy have any greater access to biblical or religious truth than the rest of us. There is an initial equality among interpreters. However, this initial presumption of equality could be overcome through the evidence of actual interpretations, that some might have better or more persuasive reasoning, etc.

What of legal interpretation? Could an average citizen state that her claim to interpret the law was as good as anyone else's? Consider lawyers: lawyers arguably occupy a role similar to the clergy. If a lawyer has a greater claim to have her interpretation preferred to that of an average citizen, it is grounded on the merits, on the expertise that does (or at least should) come from years of education, training and practice in the profession. (And, doubtless, clergy might make comparable claims based on *their* training and practice in biblical interpretation.)

Press 1985), *Justice in Robes* (Harvard University Press 2006) and *Justice for Hedgehogs* (Harvard University Press 2011).

[3] GJ Postema, '"Protestant" Interpretation and Social Practices' (1987) 6 *Law and Philosophy* 283.

[4] Dworkin (n 1) 413.

[5] ibid 58.

Ultimately, though, there is no reason *automatically and conclusively* to prefer the interpretations of lawyers over non-lawyers (or clergy over non-clergy): in all cases, the interpretations of legal texts (and religious texts) can be judged on the quality of the interpretive arguments offered, independent of the role or status of the interpreter.

In legal interpretation, however, the category of judicial interpreters raises a different set of issues. It is not that we think that judges, just by being judges (or based on their training, experience or selection), have some greater access to legal truth than do people who are not judges (though it is true that we may be inclined to defer to the views of *some* judges, for the same reasons that we would be inclined to defer to the views of *some* lawyers: that we know from past experience that their views tend to be well-reasoned and persuasive). However, with judges, especially in common law countries, there is an additional and significant difference. Judges do not merely *describe* the law, they help to *make and change it*. While many judges purport only to be stating 'what the law is', the fact remains that their having announced 'X is the law' makes it so, even it had not been so beforehand. The focus here is not on expertise but on power (authority).

Of course, this claim is only partly, and complexly, true, and the complexity is something we need to examine more closely. Among the complications to note is that the decision of a lower court might be overturned on appeal, a court might change its mind on the legal issue in a later decision, and an earlier decision can be 'clarified' or reinterpreted by the decision of a later court (which purports to be affirming, not reversing, that earlier decision). So what a judge declares to be law might, not long thereafter, be modified or declared not (or 'no longer') to be law by other judges, exercising their power (authority).

Returning to Dworkin and Postema's critique: there is an obvious tension between the social nature of law – law as a social practice (with emphasis both on 'social' and on 'practice')[6] – and the individualistic emphasis described in *Law's Empire* of each person interpreting the law for herself. The tension runs deep in Dworkin's analysis: law is a *shared* activity, but a shared activity for which *disagreement* is pervasive, even as to essential matters.[7] For Dworkin, this leads to the conclusion that law should be understood as data that every legal official – indeed, every person – can interpret differently. However, as Postema points out, this is incorrect: if it is a common (social, shared) practice, its meaning is necessarily common as well.[8] 'Interpretive activity of common practices is

[6] As Dennis Patterson points out, there are obvious Wittgensteinian elements to Postema's analyses. D Patterson, 'Postema, Dworkin and the Question of Meaning', ch 5 of this volume; cf D Patterson, 'Can We Please Stop Doing This? By the Way, Postema was Right' in P Banaś, A Dyrda and T Gizbert-Studnicki (eds), *Metaphilosophy of Law* (Bloomsbury 2016) 49.

[7] eg Dworkin (n 1) 11; cf Dworkin, *A Matter of Principle* (n 2) 171; Postema (n 3) 289–90, 297–99.

[8] Postema (n 3) 306–08.

collective, and, while it is always carried on by individual participants (and not by some collective mind), it is nevertheless essentially interactive.'[9]

Robert Cover, along with Postema, emphasises the extent to which law is a *collective* enterprise – including the way that the actions of judges and legislators, to be effective, must take into account how later officials will understand those prior decisions.[10] While Dworkin presents a hypothetical super-judge, Hercules, who heroically brings in all of the legal system in an interpretation of what the law requires in a case, no American judge can similarly impose her individual view, even if her intellectual abilities were super-human. Trial court decisions are subject to appellate review, and appellate review is by a panel of at least three judges. Therefore, the trial court judge must obtain the assent of the appellate court, and any appellate court judge must obtain the assent of at least one other judge on the panel to constitute a majority. Additionally, courts require other legal officials (sheriffs, wardens, prosecutors, etc) to bring their directions into effect.

Cover's discussion is part of a larger argument, that aspects of legal practice and legal interpretation are best understood in connection with law's purpose (in criminal law cases) of imposing violence on criminals.[11] To overcome our natural or learned reluctance to coerce other people,[12] the law uses hierarchy and ritual. Another, more obvious part of the practical operation of legal coercion is that those enforcing a judgment (eg sheriffs and jail wardens) must be able to understand the 'interpretation' the courts are offering. The need to write opinions with which other judges (co-panellists and/or appellate court judges) and other legal officials can understand sufficiently to implement limits the ability of heroic/superhuman individual judges to promulgate their own idiosyncratic interpretations of the law.

Sanford Levinson argues against a Dworkinian 'Protestant' approach to law by emphasising that the American legal system is, in fact, clearly 'Catholic' in its approach to legal interpretation. In the United States (and in many, and likely most, legal systems) there is an entity that is the equivalent, in some ways, of the Pope within the Catholic Church: a figure or institution whose views are the final word on what the law is, just as the Pope is infallible in certain pronouncements about Catholic doctrine.[13] That entity in the United States is the United States Supreme Court. Whatever the Supreme Court (or, perhaps more precisely, a five-Justice majority on that nine-member court) declares the law to be, that

[9] ibid 308 (footnote omitted).

[10] R Cover, 'Violence and the Word' (1986) 95 *Yale Law Journal* 1601, 1612–13, 1625–28; Postema (n 3) 308–13.

[11] The other (connected) general point of the article is that the focus on interpretation by some scholars of the law and literature school is mistaken, because it underestimates the effect on legal reasoning and legal practice of law's necessary focus on coercion.

[12] Cover constructs his arguments around Stanley Milgram's well-known experiments about the imposition of violence. Cover (n 10) 1610–17.

[13] S Levinson, 'Law as Literature' (1982) 60 *Texas Law Review* 373, 392–402.

is what that law is ... at least until the Court changes its mind.[14] As Supreme Court Justice Robert Jackson famously observed, 'We are not final because we are infallible, but we are infallible only because we are final.'[15] And the Court emphasised 'the basic principle that the federal judiciary is supreme in the exposition of the law of the Constitution'.[16] (Of course, it would not be sufficient simply for the courts to proclaim their supremacy in declaring what the law is for it to be the case; it must be added that in the United States, with rare exceptions, other legal officials and the general public act in a way that shows their acceptance of this supremacy.)

Levinson offered his observation about 'Catholic' interpretation in the course of making a broad criticism of American law professors (including himself). Most of us – now, as well as at the time Levinson wrote that article – are critical of many of the United States Supreme Court's interpretations of the United States Constitution. The Court, then as now, took positions more 'conservative' ideologically than those favoured by the vast majority of American law professors. However, there is a deep problem in the criticisms we make in our writings and our teaching: what does it mean to say that our Supreme Court is regularly and consistently wrong in its interpretations? It may be one thing to criticise a particular decision – it might be poorly reasoned or out of line with precedent, or the like. However, when one moves to more general or more methodological questions, the difficulty becomes clearer. For example, one's complaint might be that the Court gives too much (or too little) attention to the original understanding of constitutional provisions in determining its present meaning and application, or that it very frequently under-values certain individual rights. However, if a consistent majority of the Court has prescribed a particular methodological approach, where does one derive a source of correctness from which this methodological approach could be criticised as wrong? The 'correct' methodology for interpreting the United States Constitution is simply whatever the Supreme Court says it is, for on this matter the Court establishes *what counts as right* (at least within the court system).

Perhaps it is not quite a self-contradiction or category mistake to say that (a majority of) the Supreme Court was wrong about some case. The tie between what courts decide and what is right is complicated. HLA Hart, in his work, *The Concept of Law*, introduces the imaginary game of 'scorer's discretion'. Hart points out that in games where there is an official scoring judge, there is a sense in which 'a score occurs when the scoring judge says that it has'; however, in these games, the scoring judge purports to be applying a scoring rule.

[14] Which does not happen often but does happen from time to time (eg on being required to salute the flag, *West Virginia State Board of Education v Barnette*, 319 US 624 (1943), on the right to own guns, *District of Columbia v Heller*, 554 US 570 (2008), and on same-sex marriage, *Obergefell v Hodges*, 135 S Ct 2071 (2015).).

[15] *Brown v Allen*, 344 US 443, 540 (1953) (Jackson, J, concurring in the result).

[16] *Cooper v Aaron*, 358 US 1, 18 (1958).

Hart asks us to imagine a game without a scoring rule, where the only rule is 'a score occurs when the scoring judge says that it has'.[17] The point is that there are significant differences between this imagined game of 'scorer's discretion' and the conventional games with which we are familiar, even if in both cases one might equate outcomes with the decisions of officials. Still, as noted, when we move from single cases to general approaches and persistent views taken by stable majorities of the Supreme Court over a significant period of time, to declare that the consistent view of the majority of the court is wrong seems to lie somewhere between paradox and self-contradiction.

And yet this also does not seem entirely correct. It might be that part of our resistance to Levinson's insight is just a defence against despair – that those who are inclined towards a different political or ideological view than that of the current Court do not want to admit that they have not only lost the (political, legal, judicial) contest, but also that they have no grounds even to cry from the margins that those in power are wrong and they, the dissenters, are right. Those who dissent, those who resist, point out that it could all change one day. In some near or not so near future, a different set of political leaders could appoint judges of a different inclination than the current judges, and those judges could endorse the interpretations of the Constitution, and the methodological approaches, currently advocated by dissenters.

And it is not merely that this is a possible future, and that we have seen comparable political/legal/judicial reversals in the past. Courts can and do sometimes change their views, not merely on particular legal questions, but also on more general matters, like approaches to interpretation. As important, when such changes do happen, the judges defend the change in terms of the overall practice, and these defences (though controversial) are generally accepted. In the meantime, the dissenting view is just 'the Constitution in exile'[18] or perhaps a competing normative system.[19] Law is not – or not *only* – what the judges (or a majority of judges on the highest court) say it is, because one cannot erase or ignore the legal sources the judges purport to be interpreting and applying. And those texts and decisions can occasionally be the offered justification for significant changes in legal rules, principles and methodologies.

To come back to where we started: Postema argued that Dworkin's 'Protestant Interpretation' approach 'is problematic because it makes interpretation of social practices insufficiently practical, insufficiently intersubjective and thus (at least in the case of law) insufficiently political'.[20] In later works,

[17] HLA Hart, *The Concept of Law* (3rd edn, Oxford University Press 2012) 142.

[18] cf RE Barnett, *Restoring the Lost Constitution* (rev edn, Princeton University Press 2013).

[19] See RM Cover, 'Nomos and Narrative' (1983) 97 *Harvard Law Review* 4.

[20] Postema (n 3) 301. For an intriguing argument that Dworkin's work(s), charitably read, are not subject to Postema's critique, see T Bustamante, 'Revisiting the Idea of Protestant Interpretation: Towards Reconciliation between Dworkin and Postema', ch 4 of this volume.

Postema went on to emphasise the 'public character of law'[21] and the way that in conventions and customs 'the standards of correctness [are] implicit in the practice'.[22] It is thus helpful to tie Postema's critique of 'Protestant Interpretation' to his work on the role of conventions in law, which will be the topic of the next section.

III. CONVENTIONS, REASONS FOR ACTION AND LEGAL TRUTH

In an important article written some years before his critique of Dworkin's 'Protestant Interpretation', Postema introduced the idea of conventions as a tool to resolve a central problem for legal positivism in particular, and legal theory in general.[23] The general problem is that under legal positivism, law is determined by social sources, yet we speak of law's creating obligations. How can obligations arise from a mere collection of social facts?

Postema used as his starting point HLA Hart's influential legal positivist theory of law. In Hart's theory, the criteria for legal validity within a legal system are set by a 'rule of recognition', which, in turn, derives from (is read off of) the convergent behaviour of legal officials.[24] It is this rule, grounded on shared behaviour, that determines which norms are valid legal rules. Postema's important argument was that Hart's rule of recognition was best understood as a coordinating convention.[25]

A convention (in David Lewis's understanding of conventions) is a rule that is followed in large part because one expects others to follow that same rule; it is arbitrary in the sense that there are alternative rules that also would have served the same purpose comparably well.[26] Postema argued that the rule of recognition is a 'coordination convention', because it is or reflects a 'regularity of behavior in recurring situations calling for coordination'.[27] Coordination conventions occur when it is more important that the parties agree on some

[21] GJ Postema, *Legal Philosophy in the Twentieth Century: The Common Law World* (Springer 2011) 453.

[22] GJ Postema, 'Custom, Normative Practice, and the Law' (2012) 62 *Duke Law Journal* 707, 728.

[23] GJ Postema, 'Coordination and Convention at the Foundations of Law' (1982) 11(1) *Journal of Legal Studies* 165.

[24] Hart (n 17) 94–110.

[25] Hart did not refer to the rule of recognition as a convention in the original text of *The Concept of Law*, but he did use that label in his later, posthumously-published 'Postscript': ibid 94–110, 256–59; see also A Marmor, *Social Conventions* (Princeton University Press 2009) 160–62.

[26] See generally D Lewis, *Convention: A Philosophical Study* (Blackwell 1969); M Rescorla, 'Convention' in EN Zalta (ed), *The Stanford Encyclopedia of Philosophy* (2019), available at plato.stanford.edu/entries/convention/; see also Marmor (n 25) 1–30. Lewis's approach to conventions derives in part from work done much earlier by David Hume. Postema (n 21) 486–500.

[27] Postema (n 23) 201; see also Postema (n 21) 483–545; Postema (n 22); see also JL Coleman, 'Incorporationism, Conventionality, and the Practical Difference Thesis' (1998) 4 *Legal Theory* 381, 398.

behaviour or choice and less important upon what it is they have agreed. A well-known example is road travel: it matters little whether all cars drive on the left side of the road (as in Britain) or on the right side (as in the United States); what *is* important is that all drivers make the same choice. Coordination of behaviour is important, expected and mutually relied upon. The relevant parties – in the case of law and the rule of recognition, judges – prefer conforming to the agreed solution (following a particular shared set of standards regarding the identification and application of legal rules) to any other path. In Postema's words, through coordination conventions one can '[construct] a bridge linking social facts of judicial practice to bona fide normative considerations, indeed, to a species of genuine official obligation'.[28]

While Postema's analyses in this area were focused on the extent to which the actions of legal officials could give other legal officials – and perhaps also citizens – reasons for action (beyond purely prudential reasons),[29] we can also look at implications for legal truth. There is one sense in which truth by convention is roughly analogous to truth by authority: X is true by authority because it correctly reflects the view or decision of the person or entity who is the authority; X is true by convention because that is what practice or opinion is shared by the relevant group. In each case, the truth-making fact is a choice or declaration, without regard to the merits of that selection. There are, at the same time, two significant differences. First, authorities can sometimes be individuals (though they can also, of course, be groups), while conventions are by their nature

[28] Postema (n 23) 199. Andrei Marmor argued that the rule of recognition was not a coordination convention but rather a 'constitutive convention' – a convention whose primary purpose is not solving a coordination problem but rather constituting social practices. Such conventions 'determine what the practice is, and how one goes about engaging in it'. A Marmor, 'Exclusive Legal Positivism' in J Coleman and S Shapiro (eds), *The Oxford Handbook of Jurisprudence and Philosophy of Law* (Oxford University Press 2002) 104, 106. For example, the rules of chess do not solve a coordination problem among players; they create the rules that constitute what it means to play chess. Marmor (n 25) 22–24. Marmor argues that the rule of recognition is a constitutive convention that primarily constitutes the practice of law for a particular community, and the normativity of establishing and maintaining this practice must be 'determined on moral-political grounds': ibid 169; see also A Marmor, 'Conventions, Reasons, and the Law' in L Ramírez-Ludeña and JM Vilajosana (eds), *Legal Conventionalism* (Springer 2019) 47. For Postema's argument that Marmor's analysis is in part mistaken or ungrounded and that it in part converges with other approaches, see Postema (n 21) 528–33.

[29] There is a fairly strong argument that the rule of recognition, as a convention, creates reasons for judges (and other officials) to obey the rule. There are straightforward reasons for judges to want to be in at least rough agreement on the legal standards they are applying, and this will depend, in turn, on their being in at least general agreement on the criteria of legal validity and the hierarchy of legal sources. Additionally, it is probably more important that the judges be in agreement on such ultimate standards than that the standards be this set of criteria rather than that set, at least where there is not a sharp moral or policy disadvantage to the set of criteria chosen. However, it is far less clear that there is a convention-based argument for the view that the rule of recognition, or rules validated by the rule of recognition, create reasons for citizens. Certainly, citizens have an interest in the consistent and predictable application of law, but it is less obvious that citizens have a general moral obligation to obey whatever rules have been authorised by the rule of recognition.

always the practice of a group. Second, the ideal for an authority is choice or declaration based on the truth or the right reason. A theoretical authority is someone likely to know the right answer on some theoretical question. Even with practical authorities, something may be the law because the sovereign has so commanded, but for the law to give us a reason to do as it prescribes (beyond the prudential reasons created by threatened punishments for non-compliance), the sovereign's orders must be a reasonable estimate of what is required of us as a moral matter. By contrast, the paradigmatic examples of coordinating conventions involve choices among alternatives where none of them is significantly preferable to the others.

An intriguing variation of the conventional understanding of legal truth and the rule of recognition has been offered recently by Leslie Green. Green points out that if the rule of recognition reflects convergence of opinion, this is a process that takes time, and one might reasonably wonder about the intermediate stages. In particular, when a view is given about the legal/authoritative status of some source, but there is not yet sufficiently broad assent to that view for it to be considered part of the rule of recognition, how should we understand its status?[30] (As Green points out, we can also think of actions that are habitual among many members of a group, but which have not yet attained the status of '[legally binding] custom'.[31]) In such intermediate stages, 'there will be gray areas in which something may, or may not, be a source; or may be a source-to-be; or, I will now suggest, a source of a permissive kind'.[32]

As Hans Kelsen pointed out, what is distinctive about law, compared to other normative systems, is that it is dynamic – it is in flux and it (largely) controls its own modifications.[33] Whatever is settled is settled only for the moment. And truths by convention are always subject to being unsettled by officials or institutions that claim authoritative status, or legal texts claimed to be authoritative. This is the ongoing tension: on one hand, the law may be whatever (a majority on) the highest court says it is; it may also be that this could change if the convergent criteria endorsed (expressly or implicitly) by legal officials placed ultimate authority elsewhere, or in more than one place.[34] And even where the highest court has the final word, it can change its mind, claiming that this change is required by (the proper understanding of) an authoritative text (eg the proper understanding of the constitution).

[30] L Green, 'Positivism, Realism and Sources of Law' in P Mindus and T Spaak (eds), *The Cambridge Companion to Legal Positivism* (Cambridge, forthcoming 2020), also available at papers.ssrn.com/sol3/papers.cfm?abstract_id=3443743.

[31] ibid; cf Postema (n 22).

[32] Green (n 30).

[33] See, eg, H Kelsen, 'The Pure Theory of Law and Analytical Jurisprudence' (1941) 55 *Harvard Law Review* 44, 61–63.

[34] See, eg, MS Paulsen, 'The Most Dangerous Branch: Executive Power to Say What the Law Is' (1994) 83 *Georgetown Law Journal* 217 (arguing that the Executive Branch has, or should have, the final word on constitutional interpretation, and need not defer to the Supreme Court, at least in regard to the powers of the Executive Branch).

IV. CONCLUSION

Gerald Postema has for decades reminded us of the social nature of legal practice, with all that entails for the proper understanding of legal interpretation and legal truth. His critique of Dworkin's 'Protestant Interpretation' shows how the social nature of law is not rebutted by the deliberative and argumentative nature of law, but is in fact integral to those characteristics.[35] At the same time, if law in general, and the American legal system in particular, is not best understood as 'Protestant', there is a sense in which it is 'Catholic' – in a hierarchical structure, in which one institution is (treated as), in at least in one sense, infallible (as in Justice Jackson's quotation about finality and infallibility of the United States Supreme Court).

Another aspect of the social nature of legal reasoning and legal truth is displayed in Postema's important discussions of the role of conventions at the foundation of legal theory and legal practice. Part of what grounds legal truth are criteria and standards agreed upon by legal officials. However, there remains a tension in discussions within and about legal practice, where the existing consensus might be questioned or altered by an institution (for the moment) treated as the ultimate arbiter of legal truth, or by reference to legal texts treated (for the moment) as the ultimate authority.

[35] As Postema puts it, legal regimes can be described as 'public, discursive, and argumentative': (n 22) 732.

Part III

Analogical Reasoning in Law

7

Some Inferentialist Remarks on Postema's Conception of Analogical Thinking in Law

THIAGO LOPES DECAT

I. TRACES OF AN INFERENTIALIST THEORETICAL FRAMEWORK IN POSTEMA'S TWO-LEVEL CONCEPTION OF ANALOGICAL REASONING IN LAW

POSTEMA'S CONCEPTION OF analogical thinking in law purports to be both an improvement on and a defence of the classical common law conception of analogy against sceptical views on the matter that take analogical reasoning to be void of content.[1] According to this conception, analogical reasoning 'focuses primarily on local, case by case judicial reasoning', and is used 'both to extend and to distinguish precedent judgments'.[2] In the second part of his paper, Postema offers what he calls a rough characterisation of the classical understanding of analogical reasoning:

> First, proceeding by way of analogy is an intellectual process, a form of reasoning, with a legitimate (if possibly limited) claim to practical force. Second, it takes the general form of an inference from observed similarities among precedent and novel cases to the appropriateness of, or warrant for, deciding the novel case in the same way as its analogues. Third, this form of reasoning does not necessarily involve applying a general rule to a particular case. Rather, it proceeds *a similibus ad similia* – 'from part to part and like to like', as Aristotle put it.[3]

His defence of the classical view on analogy adopts three complementary argumentative strategies. First, it dissociates the classical conception from the

[1] GJ Postema, '*A Similibus ad Similia*: Analogical Thinking in Law' in ED Edlin (ed), *Common Law Theory: Cambridge Studies in Philosophy of Law* (Cambridge University Press 2008) 103.

[2] ibid 104.

[3] ibid 106.

particularism frequently associated with it. The rejected particularism is the sum of two theses: the substantive thesis according to which only particular practical situations can function as reasons for decisions reached by analogy; and the epistemological thesis that sustains that relevant similarities between source and target cases are grasped through some form of direct, immediate and ineffable insight. In Postema's version of this conception, however, the fact that it is up to the relation between two particulars (the facts of the novel case and the facts of earlier cases) to justify decisions reached by analogy does not mean that the articulation of a rule plays no role in the process. It does mean, however, that 'such general rule will be a product of the identified analogy, not its precondition. In the order of intellection, identification of the 'likeness' precedes and provides basis for the articulation of a rule'.[4]

In order to ground this claim, Postema needs to deal with criticism that takes analogical reasoning in law as a merely heuristic technique or an optional manner of stating a conclusion, instead of a rational way of getting to one. The rationale of these criticisms is the same: the sharing of properties between the source analogue case(s) and the target analogue case does not suffice to provide reasons for a conclusion or decision. There must also be reasons to consider the shared properties relevant to the legal purposes in play, and such reasons take the form of a rule, principle or theory.

According to these objections, the problem of the classical conception of analogy boils down to the stark particularism that emerges from it and manifests itself in the absence of rational or normative criteria of relevance for the selection of the similarities structuring analogies.[5] Postema is aware that any suitable reformulation of the classical conception will have to address the problem of relevance, since the similarities holding between a source case and the target case – that are taken to provide reasons for deciding the target case – must be distinguished and selected from a wide set of similarities by their relevance.

The second strategy consists in criticising and eschewing what he calls the rule-rationalist conception of analogical reasoning. Such a conception, espoused by, among others, Dworkin and Posner, objects to the classical conception arguing that the problem of relevance requires that all legal analogies be guided by explicit rules, principles or theories. In this view,

> two cases are analogous just when they are similar *in relevant respects* and their relevant similarities are greater or more important than differences between them. Second, it is argued that, necessarily, relevance is determined by the norm or rule that supplies criteria of relevance.[6]

Postema's purpose of taking analogy seriously as a form of practical reasoning requires rejecting particularism since, in analogical reasoning, the cases

[4] ibid 106.
[5] ibid 107.
[6] ibid 111.

and examples function as reasons, and to do so they must be able to guide action in other circumstances as well, that is, be logically repeatable and, in this sense, universalizable.[7] Therefore, he concedes to rule-rationalists that acknowledging this fact means that judging two cases as relevantly similar may be described as grasping a rule that treats them as members of a wider class.[8]

That does not imply, however, that taking two cases as analogues requires the antecedent grasping or formulating of a rule, as rule-rationalists claim. In order to back the rejection of this inference it has been necessary to develop an argument that showed this last claim as a *non sequitur*.

The last strategy used to sustain a version of the classical understanding of analogy consists in elaborating a two-level conception of analogical reasoning in law. At the first level, named 'base-level analogical thinking', tentative analogies are formed independently of the explicit base-ruled evaluations that happen in the second one named 'reflexive assessment level'.

This two-level conception was conceived to accommodate, in the first one, Postema's rejection of the rule-rationalist requirement that all forms of practical reasoning be guided by explicit rules or principles. At this level, where 'credible [and relevant] analogies are identified and inferences are made based on them', what happens is a special form of pattern recognition.[9] This process is thought to have rational credentials, since holist considerations of contextual consistence restrain and guide the selection of relevant similarities between source analogue and target analogue cases. At this stage, 'while rules are not necessary, context is. Analogy formation is not a matter of applying a rule to an instance but rather of fitting something into its place into a sense-making context.'[10]

The assessment level, on the other hand, recognises, against particularism, 'the influence of broader principled constraints on analogical reasoning'.[11] It is the level of analogical reasoning at which critical assessment and reflexive thinking occur. At this level, to which reasoners may or may not feel the need to move, already formed analogies and judgments are evaluated by explicit principles. The pressure to move to this level comes from dissatisfaction with base-level results. The decision reached may have systemic coherence problems on account of the difficulty in integrating it with precedent on a broader scale, despite its local soundness and consistency. Decisions reached by analogies formed at the base level may also be unacceptable for reasons of political morality. If it happens, norm-based explicit assessment will demand new analogies are formulated at base level.[12]

Postema's conception of analogical reasoning in law also takes the whole process (comprising the two levels) to be normatively structured, discursive and

[7] ibid 109.
[8] ibid 109.
[9] ibid 117.
[10] ibid 117.
[11] ibid 116.
[12] ibid 130–31.

contextually constrained by its institutional character. This last feature imposes on analogical reasoning certain requirements: it is a practically intelligible, historical, public, collaborative activity that is guided by a sense of concrete justice and takes place initially (although this is defeasible) in limited disciplinary domains of law.

Following this three-stage strategy, Postema presents and defends a plausible version of the classical conception of analogical legal reasoning. He is diligent in acknowledging the restraints imposed on analogical reasoning by the institutional character of legal practices, and the argumentation advanced is clear, well-reasoned and convincing. Furthermore, the variety of sources used in making the case for his conception ranges from German idealism to cognitive science, with special consideration for authors and theories specialised in legal theory. These features expand the relevance, interest and application of this version of legal analogical reasoning beyond the restricted domain of specialised discussions concerning common law systems.

Interestingly, if the reader shifts her focus from the criticisms and concrete proposals Postema made in the paper to the nature and substance of the arguments used to ground them, she may notice a pattern emerging. Both his criticism of particularist and rule-rationalist conceptions of analogical reasoning and his revised two-level version of the traditional conception point to the same understanding of the doings of rational beings. There seems to be a recognisable theory of reasoning in the background that has not been rendered completely explicit. Adopting the Dworkinian conception of constructive interpretation,[13] according to which social practices (and theoretical accounts of social practices) incorporate the reasons that better explain and justify them, this paper argues that this partially unarticulated framework is noticeably the Brandomian version of inferentialism.

In addition to explicit references to Brandom, we can see its trail in Postema's adoption of an interpretation of Kant that stresses the normative nature of judgments, since he takes judgments to be something for which judgers are responsible.[14] It is also visible in the emphasis afforded to Hegel's view of the role of negation in conferring meaningful content to propositional attitudes and linguistic expressions.[15] Another central inferentialist theoretical commitment structures Postema's criticism of Dworkin and Posner's regulism. It takes the activity of following a rule (that is, applying an explicit norm) as ultimately resting on a form of know-how: the practical ability to master the rational (because inferential) relations between normative statuses implicit in social practices.[16] Furthermore, the inferentialist (and pragmatist) distinction between norms

[13] R Dworkin, *Law's Empire* (Harvard University Press 1986).
[14] Postema (n 1) 119.
[15] ibid 118.
[16] ibid 121.

implicit in practices and explicit in the form of rules or principles provides the criteria Postema uses to distinguish the two levels of analogical reasoning.

The questions orienting this paper stem from these findings. Had Postema explicitly adopted inferentialism as his theoretical framework for understanding analogical reasoning (and reasoning in general), would he have reasons to alter some features of his conception? Had he extracted even more elements from Brandom's inferentialism so as to explain the legal use of analogies, would he still be justified in claiming a two-level structure to analogical reasoning as a necessary means to navigate between particularism and rule-rationalism (regulism)? The remainder of the chapter will address these questions and justify answering the first question positively and the second negatively.

II. REGULISM, INFINITE REGRESS AND FUNDAMENTAL PRAGMATISM

The argument Postema used to criticise and set aside rule-rationalist conceptions of analogical reasoning is a cherished commitment of inferentialism. It concerns rule-based activities in general, therefore is also operative in understanding linguistic meaning and reasoning. It states that following or applying a rule is itself something that can be done correctly and incorrectly. If, the argument continues, we codify the conditions of correct rule employment in a second-level rule, since this new rule can also be applied correctly or incorrectly, we would be faced with infinite regress in case we wanted to codify – in the form of an explicit rule – the conditions for following every rule in a normative practice.

As Wittgenstein remarked, somewhere along the sequence of norms, interpretations[17] must end: 'What this shows is that there is a way of grasping a rule which is *not an interpretation*, but which is exhibited in what we call "obeying the rule" and "going against it" in actual cases.'[18]

Postema's version of this argument, which denies the need for a rule to ground the inferential transition from source analogue case to target analogue case, can be seen in the following:

> If we insist that judgment is legitimate (rationally guided) only in virtue of one's grasp of a bridging rule, then we face the same problem with respect to application of the bridging rule. It requires in turn an exercise of judgment, which, if the judgment's legitimacy depends solely on a rule to guide it, posits another rule that in turn requires a further exercise of judgment, and so forth. If every exercise of judgment requires a rule, then not only is judgment impossible, but so are rules and reasoning.[19]

[17] 'Interpretation' is meant here, in Wittgenstein's sense, as a rule providing the criteria of correctness for applying another rule or, in short, a rule for applying a rule. See L Wittgenstein, *Philosophical Investigations*, tr GEM Anscombe (Basil Blackwell, 1986) 80–81.

[18] ibid 81.

[19] Postema (n 1) 114.

One could say, correctly, that undertaking a commitment to this understanding of normatively structured activities, however, does not necessarily make someone an inferentialist, since we can find instances of it in the writings of other philosophers who had previously rejected regulism, such as Kant, Lewis Carrol, Frege, Wittgenstein and others. Adopting this understanding would make someone, at most, a fundamental pragmatist in Brandom's sense:[20]

> It is characteristic of pragmatism in the broad sense to see knowing *how* as having a certain kind of explanatory priority over knowing *that*. This is one influential form taken by an insistence on the explanatory primacy of the practical over the theoretical. Explicit theoretical beliefs can be made intelligible only against a background of implicit practical abilities. Pragmatism in this sense – call it 'fundamental pragmatism' – is opposed to the kind of platonistic intellectualism that seeks to explain practical abilities in terms of some sort of grasp of *principles*: some sort of knowing that is behind each bit of know-how.[21]

That is precisely the point of Postema's rejection of an emthymematic structure in analogical reasoning. According to the author,

> There cannot be a *rule*, a genuine guide for thought and action, unless at some point there is a *nonrulish*, albeit normative responsible, exercise of judgment. But the same capacity relied on for applying rules and concepts is involved in following examples – that is, in identifying something as an example and recognizing another case as its analogue.[22]

[20] Brandom distinguishes philosophical pragmatism in a narrow sense from pragmatism understood in a broad sense. The first names a 'philosophical school of thought centered on evaluating beliefs by their tendency to promote success at the satisfaction of wants. Its paradigmatic practitioners were the classical American triumvirate of Charles Peirce, William James and John Dewey.' In a broad sense, pragmatism may be described 'as a movement centered on the primacy of the practical, initiated already by Kant, whose twentieth-century avatars include not only Peirce, James and Dewey, but also the early Heidegger, the latter Wittgenstein, and such figures as Quine, Sellars, Davidson, Rorty and Putnam'. See RB Brandom, *Reason in Philosophy: Animating Ideas* (Harvard University Press 2011) 56. He also understands inferentialism as a kind of conceptual pragmatism, since it 'seeks to explain how the use of linguistic expressions confers conceptual content on them'. See RB Brandom, *Articulating Reasons: An Introduction to Inferentialism* (Harvard University Press, 2003) 4. In order to disambiguate the meaning of the term 'Pragmatism' in this broad sense, Brandom distinguishes four theoretical commitments that describe different ways one can afford primacy to the practical: methodological, semantic, fundamental and normative pragmatism. He then goes on to explain the adoption of instrumentalism in classical American pragmatism – the idea that the norms implicit in practices have instrumental character. Instrumentalism, the argument continues, is the strategy Peirce, James and Dewy found to reconcile their fundamental and normative pragmatism (their normative specification of the implicit practical abilities conditioning belief formation and judgment) with their Darwinian project of explaining the rational ability of men and women as located on a continuum, which also includes the instrumental capacities of other animals. (See Brandom, *Reason in Philosophy*, 56–82.) For an argument that applies these classifications and distinctions in understanding Dworkin's theory of Law as Integrity as an example of a non-instrumentalist pragmatist theory, see TL Decat, 'Inferentialist Pragmatism and Dworkin's Law as Integrity' (2015) 1 *Erasmus Law Review* 14.

[21] Brandom, *Reason in Philosophy* (n 20) 65.

[22] Postema (n 1) 114.

Postema's conception, however, did not restrict itself to these negative remarks concerning the rejection of regulism in the context of analogical reasoning. He relied on these findings to make substantive claims about what this kind of implicit know-how – involved in applying rules and following examples – consists in. And the resulting explanation, the next section argues, is explicitly inferentialist.

III. MAKING POSTEMA'S INFERENTIALISM EXPLICIT

Postema's version of the classical conception of analogical reasoning in law explains the implicit know-how involved in applying rules and following examples as a matter of being able to master, in a holistic way, an inferential network of reasons. In his account of base-level analogical reasoning, he claims that

> Analogical reasoning is not a linear process, but rather a dynamic one of locating a new case in a network of inferences; reasoning – tracing compatibilities and incompatibilities of reasons and inferences – occurs throughout the process.[23]

It is this account of the implicit practical abilities conditioning analogical reasoning that provides the criteria demanded by rule-rationalists to distinguish relevant similarities between source and target analogue cases:

> To judge the (robust) relevance of certain features of a case is not to report the deliverance of some kind of special or ineffable insight, intuition, or perception. It is, rather, to endorse a judgment the content of which is given by its location in a web of reasons that support it and that it supports. To articulate the content of a judgment of robust relevance is to show its place in a network of reasons.[24]

This understanding of the implicit know-how involved in applying or following a rule – being able to practically distinguish reasons from things that are inappropriate for playing the roles of premise or conclusion within inferences – already points beyond mere fundamental pragmatism. When one also takes into consideration Postema's understanding of the practical mastery of the web of inferential relations as normatively structured, his conception of analogical reasoning seems not only to be compatible with, but also to instantiate the inferentialist model of rationality theorised by Brandom.

According to Brandom's inferentialist conception of rationality, to be rational is to be able to play the language game of giving and asking for reasons. This language game is not understood, however, as having the same status as other existing and possible language games. The ability to participate in this specific game is a precondition to taking part in other linguistic activities, given the inferentialist understanding of conceptual content: 'Utterances and states are propositionally contentful just insofar as they stand in inferential relations

[23] ibid 121.
[24] ibid.

to one another: only insofar as they can both serve as and stand in need of reasons.'[25]

To be rational, then, is to be able to produce and consume reasons in the sense of being capable of operating with structures that can play the role both of premises (reasons) and of conclusions in a network of inferentially articulated linguistic expressions and intentional attitudes.[26] More specifically, inferentialism takes the conceptual content possessed by intentional states and linguistic expressions to be articulated by the set of concrete normative statuses – commitments and entitlements – that license inferences from and to what is asserted, meant, thought or claimed in other bearers of propositional content (whose very own conceptual content is determined in the same inferential holistic manner). In short, Brandom argues, 'Conceptual contents are functional inferential roles.'[27]

This conception of rationality also incorporates normative pragmatics in inferential semantics, since it explains contentfullness in terms of inferential relations and specifies inferential relations (being a reason or standing in need of a reason) in terms of normative statuses committing or entitling someone to inferential transitions:

> Nothing is recognizable as a practice of giving and asking for *reasons*, I claim, unless it involves undertaking and attributing *commitments*. And those commitments must stand in *consequential* relations: making one move, undertaking one commitment must carry with it further commitments … commitments whose contents follow from the contents of the first commitment. Further, a practice of giving and asking for reasons must be one in which the issue of one's *entitlement* to a commitment one has undertaken (or that others attribute) can arise. And those entitlements, too, must stand in consequential relations: entitlements to one move can carry with it entitlement to others.[28]

In Brandom's philosophy of language, those normative statuses are indirectly instituted by the social practical attitudes of taking and treating someone as committed or entitled to other claims or actions.[29]

In a very similar vein, the normative spelling out of content conferring inferential relations is also visible in Postema's understanding of base-level reasoning:

> The reasoning process by which judgments are formed is necessarily normative. The root thought here is the fundamental Kantian idea that judging is an activity for which judgers are, and take themselves to be, responsible. When they engage in

[25] RB Brandom, *Tales of the Mighty Dead: Historical Essays in the Metaphysics of Intentionality* (Harvard University Press 2002) 6.

[26] Brandom, *Articulating Reasons* (n 20) 45–77.

[27] Brandom (n 25) 6.

[28] ibid 7.

[29] RB Brandom, *Making it Explicit: Reasoning, Representing and Discursive Commitment* (Harvard University Press 1998) 30–55.

> analogical reasoning, judgers do not merely respond … to their environment, but rather their responses manifest proprieties in their practice. … In making judgments, judgers vouch for the correctness of their judgments. Of course, the correctness of their judgments cannot be constituted by their commitment to them; for then no distinction between their seeming to be correct and their being so could be made, and without that no mistakes could be possible, and without the possibility of mistake, the normative idea of correctness loses its content.[30]

The improved version of the classical conception of analogical thinking in law sees the pragmatic commitment every judger must acknowledge, concerning the correctness and grounding of her judgments, as an opening to argument and liability to challenge. Reasoners and judgers take part in a *discursive* social practice that includes being regarded, and regarding themselves, as capable of justifying their judgments and decisions. Their judgments are not only in need of reasons, but must also be able to function as reasons for other judgments, in a non-contingent, constitutive manner: 'Analogical formation is a process of fitting responses into a network of reasons used to justify beliefs, claims and decisions.'[31]

This dovetails nicely with Brandom's own understanding of the discursive structure of linguistic and inferentially articulated social practices. He follows Kant in taking judgments as things rational creatures are responsible for, and in this sense as possessing *normative status*.[32] However, in Brandom's interpretation of Kant as a proto-pragmatist, the responsibility someone undertakes in making a judgment should be understood as a task responsibility, that is, a responsibility to do something, namely, to integrate the new judgment into a unity of apperception. To do that, the judger must integrate the endorsement of the new judgment with her previous endorsements. This activity demands she accepts the critical responsibility of rejecting commitments that are incompatible with her previous commitments and entitlements. In addition, integrating the new judgment requires accepting the ampliative responsibility to extract inferential consequences of each commitment, including new ones undertaken to accommodate the judgment recently endorsed to previous commitments and entitlements. According to Brandom, 'Each commitment gives one reason to accept others, which one ought to accept in the sense that one has already implicitly committed oneself to them by acknowledging the commitment from which they follow.'[33]

Finally, making a judgment involves assuming the justificatory responsibility to be willing to provide reasons for one's acknowledged theoretical and practical commitments. It is not difficult to see, in Kant's justificatory dimension

[30] Postema (n 1) 118–19.

[31] ibid.

[32] Brandom, *Articulating Reasons* (n 20) 8; RB Brandom, *Perspectives on Pragmatism: Classical, Recent and Contemporary* (Harvard University Press 2009).

[33] Brandom, *Reason in Philosophy* (n 20) 36.

of integrative task responsibilities – as interpreted by Brandom – a discursive structure similar to the one Postema assigns to analogical reasoning.

Postema credits the cognitive resources or competences of 'contrast' and 'consilience'[34] with the power of locating a target analogue in a context of comparables. However, he also claims that

> the context within which analogical reasoning works is not merely a set of objects or instances, but a network of instances linked by inferential relations, of reasons supporting, refining, elaborating other reasons, and being supported, restricted or elaborated by yet others.[35]

Thus, if the assignment of fundamental pragmatism to Postema's conception of analogy is correct, 'contrast' and 'consilience' are to be seen as part of the implicit ability or know-how required to perform the '*nonrulish*, albeit normative responsible, exercise of judgment' he sees going on in legal analogical reasoning. These competences have a significant role in his account of base-level analogical reasoning, since

> [t]hey trace compatibilities and incompatibilities of judgments and reasons for them, drawing connections that make sense and distinguishing cases that are incompatible; they work out implications and determine whether they can stand together with other commitments in the network.[36]

Interestingly enough, this tracing of compatibilities and incompatibilities between judgments and reasons for them, as well as the working out of implications to and from such judgments, were all, on Brandom's account of Kant, made possible by the practical capacities corresponding to critical and ampliative task responsibilities. In his philosophy of language, Brandom's fundamental pragmatism explains these abilities in terms of different kinds of material inferences language-speaking beings are able to make.

The concept of material inferences and its relevance in understanding analogical reasoning will be explained in the next section. It will also be argued, then, that the use of the full conceptual resources of inferentialism would have provided Postema with the theoretical tools to offer a more judicious explanation of how implicit practical abilities make the kind of context-fitting reasoning he has in mind possible. For now, it suffices to stress the convergence of Brandom's and Postema's conception of the know-how behind linguistic and conceptual practices.

The conclusion of this section is straightforward. The rejection of regulism, the acknowledgement of implicit practical abilities (know-how) behind rule

[34] Postema defines 'contrast' and 'consilience' (along with 'focus' and 'frame') as cognitive competences. Regarding 'consilience' and 'contrast', he offers a complementary definition of them as tools for refining the grasp of objects in analogical reasoning. See Postema (n 1) 118.

[35] ibid 120.

[36] ibid.

following, the inferential nature assigned to this know-how, the normative specification of inferential abilities implicit in practices, and understanding reasoning as the holist allocation of particulars in a network of commitments through incompatibility and implication relations are common to both authors. Since these philosophical commitments appear, in a more restricted domain, in Postema's conception of analogical legal reasoning and in Brandom's broader dimension of his fourth model of rationality, this correspondence provides enough reason to claim that Postema's conception of analogy instantiates Brandom's inferentialist conception of rationality.

IV. MATERIAL INFERENCES AND THE EXPRESSIVE FUNCTION OF LOGICAL VOCABULARY: EXPLAINING 'CONTRAST', 'CONSILIENCE', 'FRAME' AND THE ARGUMENTATIVE NATURE OF ANALOGICAL REASONING

Postema's rejection of rule-rationalist accounts of analogical legal reasoning is not incompatible with the acknowledgement that rules play an important role in analogical reasoning. In fact, the main criteria for distinguishing two levels in analogical reasoning is the use of explicit rules, at the second level, to assess, and eventually review, tentative judgments of relevant similarities between target analogue cases and source analogue cases. After claiming that, at base level, analogies are identified and inferences drawn from them, he goes on to say that, at the reflexive level of analogy assessment, 'analogical inferences and judgments are evaluated in light of wider legal (and possibly moral) principles'.[37]

Distinguishing between two levels of analogical reasoning is thought of as a way to accommodate apparently irreconcilable claims. It makes it possible to recognise, in one domain, the existence of forms of reasoning that do not rely on rules or principles, while acknowledging, in the other, the role and influence of principled constraints in this form of reasoning.

Postema sees these levels as interdependent, since the possible revision of candidate analogies required in the reflexive analogy level must work with materials 'retrieved' and 'encoded' at the base level. Conversely, analogy formation in base-level reasoning requires a specific context of comparables that is built, in part, from the deliverances of the reflexive assessment level, since they underwrite structural constraints on the former level.[38] However, in concrete circumstances, reasoners may not feel the need to move to the second level when deciding cases analogically.[39]

In this section and the next, it will be argued that inferentialist central concepts of material inference and the expressive function of logical and

[37] ibid 116.
[38] ibid 117.
[39] ibid 116.

normative vocabulary may provide tools to reconcile those apparently contradictory claims regarding the role of explicit norms (rules or principles) in reasoning. In this sense, this section prepares the argument put forth in the final section that claims no such distinction of levels of analogical reasoning is required to reach an adequate understanding of legal analogical reasoning, and that there are theoretical gains in acknowledging a unitary structure in analogical reasoning in law.

The inferentialist model of rationality, as understood by Brandom, reserves a central place for inferential relations in the explanation of the rational activities of knowers and agents. In this conception of rationality, however, the set of inferences relevant to articulating the conceptual content of claims and beliefs, are *material* and not *logical* (formal) inferences. These inferences are thought of as *material* inferences because what makes them acceptable, good, inferential transitions, in the eyes of the participants of linguistic social practices, is the content and not the form of the assertions involved.

The theoretical inferences from 'A is to the west of B' to 'B is to the east of A' and from 'It rained' to 'the streets will be wet'; and the practical inference from 'it rained' to 'I shall bring my umbrella' are typical examples of this kind of inference. For those who reject the interpretation of those inferences as enthymemes, the lack of conditional premises – namely, 'If X is to the west of Y, then Y is to the east of X', 'If it rains, then streets get wet' or 'One ought, when it rains, to take an umbrella' – makes no real difference. There is nothing in these complementary premises that can license inferential transitions in a way that the mastery of the concepts involved in them does not already do. In short, 'Endorsing these inferences is part of grasping or mastering those concepts, quite apart from any *logical* competence.'[40]

Since meaning and, therefore, interpersonal communication are dependent on inferential licences based on commitments and entitlements that follow from claims and actions in general, inferentialism must provide an explanation for the public administration of those normative statuses. Brandom calls this activity of attributing inferentially articulated commitments and entitlements to oneself and others 'deontic scorekeeping'. Explained succinctly,

> deontic scorekeeping requires keeping two sets of books, one on the consequences and antecedents of the other interlocutor's commitments when they are conjoined with other commitments one attributes to her, and the other on the consequents and antecedents of those commitments when they are conjoined with the commitments one undertakes or endorses oneself.[41]

Brandom identifies three possible combinations between the two kinds of normative statuses – commitments and entitlements – that constitute the modes of scorekeeping relations he calls material theoretical inferences. The first is

[40] Brandom, *Articulating Reasons* (n 20) 52.
[41] Brandom (n 25) 6.

an inferential relation that preserves commitments, and is a generalisation of deductive relations. One example: If John is the son of Mary, anyone committed to John being a great painter is also committed to the son of Mary being a great painter, whether he knows this or not. The second mode of scorekeeping relation consists of transitions that preserve entitlements, and is a generalisation of inductive relations. For example, supposing the drop of temperature in some specific place is a common cause both of the migration of some bird species and of the increase in rain, a person who is both entitled and committed to the fact that bird migration has already started, has reasons entitling him to believe that the rainy days are coming. The third and final mode consists of incompatibility entailments. It blocks inferential transitions between two claims when commitment to one precludes commitment to the other. The example Brandom gives is the relation between two claims about the same patch of cloth, one saying it is wholly red, and the other saying it is wholly blue.[42]

It is not hard to see how this conceptual frame is capable of accounting for many features of Postema's version of the classical conception of legal analogical reasoning. When describing the process that goes on at base-level analogical reasoning, he assigns an important role to the *nonrulish* implicit competence of 'contrast':

> Contrast is essential to cognition. … To grasp something meaningful is to recognize its boundaries and determinacy. This presupposes a context in which it can be distinguished. The context cannot just be some background of indeterminate light; it must be populated by other relatively determinate and constraining elements … Integration requires finding a basis for distinguishing those elements in the frame that are truly different, and accounting for that difference, and uniting those elements that can be woven into a fabric of consonance.[43]

Although there are no theoretical problems or improprieties in describing this process by reference to the competences of frame, focus, contrast and consilience, the three kinds of material inferences Brandom distinguished explain in a more detailed and conceptual manner the rational (because inferential) operations behind contrast and consilience. The unveiling of relevant similarities and differences between source analogue cases and target analogue cases is explainable in terms of the commitments and entitlements involved in acknowledging the facts of both cases simultaneously. The intellectual resource referred to as 'frame', meaning 'the cognizer's sense of the point of seeking out the pattern of analogy',[44] also becomes clearer when explained in explicitly inferentialist terms. One sees the point in drawing analogical inferences when one is able to distinguish what one commits and entitles oneself to in acknowledging the tentative inferential transition in question. This is easily understood in terms of

[42] ibid 8.
[43] Postema (n 1) 118.
[44] ibid.

the inferential licences and prohibitions implied by material inferences. In addition, inferential relations that preserve commitments, inferential relations that preserve entitlements, and incompatibility entailments provide a more nuanced and conceptual account of the activity of 'fitting something into its place in an intelligible, sense-making context'.[45]

The pride of place inferentialism confers on material inferences in understanding linguistic practices, does not imply it reserves no place for formal inferences and for the kind of formal coding of reasoning that logical vocabulary enables. But the role it affords logical vocabulary is quite different. In using material inferential articulation to explain both semantic content *and* what rationality consists in, and in understanding material inferential licensing in terms of the implicit and socially instituted normative statuses of commitments and entitlements, inferentialism has made it possible to see the rational function of logical vocabulary as an *expressive* one.

The expressive view of the function of logic shows that 'Instead of seeing conformity with logical truths as what rationality consists in, one can see logical vocabulary as making possible the explicit codification of meaning-constitutive inferential relations.'[46] This expressive understanding of logical locutions sees their characteristic task in providing linguistic tools that 'let us *say*, in the form of explicit claims, what otherwise we could only *do* – namely, endorse some material inferential relations and reject others'.[47]

Brandom follows Frege in considering conditional locutions as having a special role in expressing the rational pattern of inferences behind the things we do (claim and act).[48] Before the introduction of conditional locutions in a natural language, Brandom argues, people could *do* things, that is, *treat* a judgment as having certain content. Since, for inferentialism, conceptual contents *consist in* inferential roles, treating some judgments as good or bad by practically (with actions) endorsing or rejecting them amounts to grasping their meaning, but not yet to expressing this meaning. Once conditionals are in place, one can also *say that* an inference is acceptable or correct.[49] Thus, one can also explicitly express the judgment's conceptual contents. In Brandom's terms:

> Prior to the introduction of the conditional, for instance, one can implicitly take or treat the material inference … from *p* to *q* as a good or bad one, endorsing or rejecting it in practice. Once a suitable conditional is available, though, one can explicitly *claim that p entails q*.[50]

In short, conditionals enable speakers 'to make inferential commitments explicit as the content of judgments'.[51]

[45] ibid 117.
[46] Brandom (n 25) 9.
[47] ibid 9.
[48] Brandom, *Articulating Reasons* (n 20) 59.
[49] ibid 60.
[50] Brandom (n 25) 9.
[51] Brandom, *Articulating Reasons* (n 20) 60.

Postema himself recognises that some of the constraints imposed on legal analogical reasoning by its context are better understood in terms of the expressivist conception of logical vocabulary. It is especially true of the 'public and collaborative nature of analogical reasoning in law', in the sense of being 'institutionalized as the *modus operandi* of a public forum'.[52] It is precisely the expressive function of logical vocabulary that makes placing analogical judgments in a 'public forum' possible. That forum should be understood as an institutionalised version of the language game of giving and asking for reasons, and only explicit claims are the sort of things for which reasons can be asked and given.[53]

The expressive function of logical expressions can also explain why, according to Postema, assessment of analogies should restrict itself to materials gathered in base-level analogical reasoning. The content of judgments of relevant similarities between cases can only be subject to rational criticism and rational defence once material inferences that articulate their content are made explicit in the form of claims. It is not true, however, that before logical expression made them explicit, those judgments and the operations that led to them were irrational. The inferential structure articulating their content – the inferential articulation of commitments and entitlements – grants such judgments rationality. But although in this view logic does not define rationality, it promotes a higher level of rationality as a tool for exploring consequences and discordances among commitments.[54] In this sense, being logical is subsequent to being rational: 'Logic is the organ of semantic self-consciousness.'[55] Postema's agreement with the idea is straightforward: 'As Brandom puts it, to articulate such rules is to try to *say* what it is we are *doing*, but it is the doing, the mastery of the inferential network, that is constitutively prior.'[56]

The next section of this chapter will discuss how this last notion seems to provide the criteria for distinguishing Postema's two levels of analogical reasoning.

V. NORMS IMPLICIT IN PRACTICES AND NORMS EXPLICIT AS RULES: DISTINGUISHING TWO LEVELS OF ANALOGICAL REASONING

Throughout his paper, Postema acknowledges the normative character of analogical reasoning without accepting, however, its reduction to explicit rules or principles.

He makes this point when he criticises Westen for the *non sequitur* in trying to derive from the universality of example-giving practices a supposed

[52] Postema (n 1) 125.
[53] Brandom (n 25) 9; Postema (n 1) 121.
[54] Brandom (n 25) 10.
[55] ibid.
[56] Postema (n 1) 121.

need to 'first ... appeal to a rule that marks the cases as alike'.[57] Exercising epistemic charity, he acknowledges that 'the conclusion might just be an awkward way of putting the point that *in* grasping that two cases are relevantly similar one grasps a rule – that is, one grasps that they properly go together'.[58]

Postema not only accepts that the relation among particulars established in analogical reasoning is subject to normative proprieties, but also acknowledges that grasping these normative relations is at least a part of what the activity of analogical reasoning consists of. The problem would be the supposition of a previous explicit articulation of these normative constraints in the form of an explicit rule:

> Of course, if the claim is that someone seeking to follow the example must have ready to hand an explicitly formulated rule, it is manifestly false. Much of our lives, from a very early age, are rule-guided, but rarely do we appeal to explicit rules. Indeed, we would be hard pressed to make explicit the rules that allegedly guided us.[59]

Postema agrees with inferentialists in considering the expressive powers of logic as responsible for rendering social practices discursive activities. In the account of legal inferential reasoning he offers, however, the distinction between norms implicit in practices and norms explicit in the form of rules provides criteria for demarcating the boundaries of his two levels of analogical reasoning. And here, again, inferentialist theses are capable of supplying the theoretical background for that claim.

Brandom assigns the same expressive role he connects with logical expressions to normative practical vocabulary. According to this view, practical normative vocabulary makes explicit those inferential relations that govern transitions from doxastic to practical commitment, 'that is, from the commitments acknowledged in assertions to commitments to *do* something'.[60] From this perspective, expressions of preference or desire, institutional obligations and moral duties are seen as 'codifying commitment to the propriety of patterns of practical inference'.[61]

The expressive understanding of practical normative vocabulary sees the *instrumental ought* expressed, for example, in one's preference to stay fit as an explicit acknowledgement of one's commitment to the correction of the practical material inference from 'only doing X will keep me fit' to 'I shall do X'.

The functional correspondence with logical vocabulary is clear. This 'instrumental ought' expresses acknowledgement of implicit commitments

> in much the same way that the conditional $p \rightarrow q$ expresses a commitment to the correctness of inferences from p to q. In both cases it is a mistake to confuse

[57] ibid 110.
[58] ibid.
[59] ibid 114.
[60] Brandom (n 25) 10.
[61] ibid.

> the statements that make inference licenses explicit with the *premises* required for the inference to be licit in the first place.[62]

Besides preferences and desires, Brandom acknowledges two other kinds of practical inference licence, that is, two kinds of 'oughts' that make one's commitment to the correctness of patterns of practical material inferences explicit. He calls them *institutional ought* and *unconditional ought*. The first, as the name suggests, concerns obligations associated with some institutional *status*. Thus, the following statement of obligation, 'public agents have the obligation to be respectful to the public', makes explicit the commitment to the correction of the transition from 'doing X would be disrespecting the public' to 'I shall not do X'. The distinction between these two kinds of oughts is that the instrumental ought is binding only for those who endorse the preference, while the institutional ought is binding only for those who share the relevant institutional *status*.

The third kind of '*ought*' is called unconditional because the pattern of practical reasoning it renders explicit in its normative claim is not conditioned by preferences, desires or institutional status. For example, the statement of obligation saying that 'it is wrong (one ought not to) to lie to others' makes explicit the commitment to the correction of the transition from 'doing X would be lying to others' to 'I shall not do X'.[63] In Brandom's understanding, all these oughts 'are in the most basic sense *rational* oughts. For they codify commitments to patterns of practical *reasoning*.'[64]

Although Postema had not explicitly mentioned the expressive role of normative practical vocabulary in his paper, the idea is not only coherent with his acknowledgement of the expressive role of logical vocabulary, but also provides him with the tools to ground an important distinction. This is the distinction between norms implicit in practices (the web of implicitly acknowledged commitments and status) and norms explicit in the form of rules and principles, and it constitutes the criteria used to differentiate the base level from the assessment level of analogical reasoning:

> This is not to deny that trying to make the products of our analogical reasoning explicit is an important task. Doing so subjects them to critical reflection from a different quarter that can correct and refine our analogical reasoning. In law, this is the task of analogy-assessment, second level analogical thinking.[65]

Postema conceives the passage to this reflexive level of analogical reasoning as not necessarily occurring in every case but as always possible, and believes the pressure to do so to come from failure to ground satisfactory results in the analogy construed at the base level. This failure may be caused by systemic

[62] ibid.
[63] ibid.
[64] ibid 11.
[65] Postema (n 1) 121.

coherence reasons or reasons of political morality. Given this understanding, one could ask – once one accepts that the explicit oughts taken as parameters of valuation at the assessment level are but the explicit form of commitments to the correction of practical material inferences – if the constraints imposed on reasoning by explicit norms are not already operative in a different, implicit manner, at base level. A positive answer to this question becomes possible if one broadens the focus of one's understanding of analogical reasoning to a scale that encompasses the rational social process by which the base-level rational parameters of judgment integration are instituted. But then questions about the absence of reasons for a two-level account of analogical reasoning in law become pressing.

VI. THE HISTORIC-EXPRESSIVE RATIONALITY OF SOCIAL PRACTICES AS THE RATIONALE FOR A ONE-LEVEL CONCEPTION OF ANALOGICAL REASONING

The inferential model of rationality, applied in the analysis of Postema's conception of legal analogical reasoning in sections III, IV and V of this chapter has, however, its own limitations. It is useful to explain theoretical and practical reasoning and the role implicit normative statuses play in them. But, since it takes – uncritically, in Kant's sense – the set of inferentially articulated conceptual norms as a given, it falls short of the crucial critical question: How are conceptual norms possible? Or, in Brandom's phrasing, 'What do we have to *do* to establish or connect with, subject ourselves to, such determinate norms?'[66]

This line of questioning may seem excessively abstract, but the answer Brandom gives to this question has consequences for the justification of the two-level version of analogical reasoning discussed.

Brandom accepts Kant's understanding of concepts as norms for judgments. They determine the correctness of the application of terms that express universals to particulars. But he also accepts the Hegelian idea that the only thing available to linguistic practitioners with which they can determine the propriety of a tentative determinate judgment – the claim that the particular word falls under a certain universal – 'is the way that word – and others linked to it inferentially – has actually been applied in *prior judgments*'.[67]

This raises the question of how previous applications of universals to particulars are able to establish the correctness of applying the universal to a particular that has not yet been under this universal. It is all about understanding how previous uses of terms in judgments may settle how we should use them in new cases. It is interesting to see the resemblance between this question and the questions raised by Postema, concerning legal analogical reasoning, about how a

[66] Brandom (n 25) 13.
[67] ibid.

context of comparable particulars can muster rational authority to propose a prospective solution to a case without appeal to previous explicit rules.

The social practices we call judging, applying concepts or assigning universals to particulars, must have a specific historical structure to be able to determine the proprieties in question. In this sense, this widening of view also honours Postema's historicity constraint on analogical reasoning, but does it by extending the demand to every linguistic social practice. Social, linguistic practices must, if they are to determine correction of application of concepts in judgments, instantiate a reconstruction of a tradition.

This reconstruction, however, must exhibit the tradition 'as having the expressively progressive form of the gradual, cumulative unfolding into explicitness of what shows up retrospectively as having been all along implicit in that tradition'.[68]

Since Brandom understand concepts and conceptual norms as involved in theoretical as well as in practical reasoning, social practices having such historical reconstructive structure can ground both novel judgments and novel practical duties. In the context of analogical legal reasoning, this kind of practice may be said to establish either proprieties of judgments of relevant similarities between source and target analogue cases, or new concrete norms to the case at hand.

The excess of abstraction dissipates when one uses a historically known social practice to help understanding what it is to retrospectively pick out an expressively progressive trajectory from past judgments. The important thing is that the example enables us to see what it is to engage oneself in such reconstruction in a way that those judgments determine a norm that can be seen, then, to have been implicitly governing the process all along. The example Brandom gives is especially illuminating here, for it consists of the activities of judges in common law tradition.

Brandom finds the common law decision process especially illustrative, because he takes it to differ from statutory law in an important way. Common law restricts the possible determinants of the propriety of the application of legal concepts (and norms) to cases that serve as precedents. In a (slightly idealised) common law system, 'There is no explicit initial statement of principle governing the application of legal universals to particular sets of facts – only a practice of applying them in novel circumstances.'[69]

This means not only that the contents of those concepts are provided by the history of their previous use, but also that judges justify their decisions rationalising them in light of a reading of the set of decisions *as* a tradition. It means they make a norm emerge as an 'implicit lesson' through selecting and stressing some of the prior decisions.

To be able to find such norm, 'the judge must make the tradition cohere, must exhibit the decisions that have actually been made as rational and correct,

[68] ibid 12.
[69] ibid 13.

given that the norm she finds is what has implicitly governed the process all along'.[70] Each decision selected from the set of previous applications helps make explicit some aspect of the implicit norm or legal concept. Social practices that instantiate this kind of historical-expressive rationality justify the current decision as correct application by reconstructing the tradition of its application. It involves offering a progressive and expressive account of it, as well as adopting a performative attitude towards it: 'It is insofar as one *takes* the tradition to be rational … by a Whiggish rewriting of its history, that one *makes* the tradition be and have been rational.'[71]

Interpreted through these lenses, the reasoning involved in typical processes of decision in common law systems – whether they are described as deciding based on precedents, based on examples or deciding analogically – presents both features Postema's two-level conception of analogical reasoning was designed to accommodate. First, it incorporates the authority of particulars (cases) over universals (rules), since it acknowledges the individual contribution of cases, chosen from the set of previous cases, in making the implicit rule emerge and in shaping its boundaries. Second, it requires the possibility of making justified judgments, concerning the existence of relevant similarities between cases, in the absence of explicit rules defining relevance. After all, inferentialism understands the correctness of inferential transitions as determined by the articulations of implicit normative statuses of commitment and entitlement.

It may, however, be objected that if a slightly different and general description of common law is all that explicitly adopting inferentialism as theoretical framework amounts to, there is no reason to consider the invitation to think of analogy on inferentialist terms. But appearances are deceiving. Not only is the difference in understanding common law through these lenses not superficial, but it also makes the inferentialist model stronger.

Accepting historic-expressive rationality as instantiated by legal social practices grants, in the context of the acceptance of the inferential theoretical commitments assigned here to Postema, a better understanding of implicit normative statuses. It allows one to see not only how explicit rules are instituted by the same acts that consist of their application, but how implicit commitments and entitlements are conferred as well. If one accepts the expressive function of practical normative vocabulary, prior to the first explicit application of a legal principle in court, the commitments and entitlements that constitute its content are already in inferential articulation with normative statuses constituting the conceptual content of yet other norms, explicit or otherwise. Moreover, in this condition they still can exert pressure, and are still affected by the history of the social practices (legal or otherwise) of the community. Inferentialism is a holist conception through and through.

[70] ibid 14.
[71] ibid.

Understanding this has a liberating effect. It renders it unnecessary to create a level of reasoning protected against the use of explicit rules, since judgments may have rule-independent standings and may always exert pressure over universals.

There are many convergence points between this historical-expressive conception of common law and Dworkin's concept of constructive interpretation guided by integrity.[72] Although his explicit rejection of theoretical-independent bases for justified judgments in analogical reasoning is quite contrary to Postema's view, they make a symmetrical exaggeration. Postema thinks that if one does not provide a space for analogy formation from which explicit rules are banned, there cannot be acknowledgement of independent pressure exerted by cases and we are left with an infinite regress of rules. Dworkin, on the contrary, seems to think that once we recognise the independent force of cases, we are immunising decision making against the grasp of theory.[73]

None of these alternatives are inevitable. The association of inferential and historical-expressive rationality allows one to understand the fundamental historical and expressive nature of the social practices that constitute the privileged game of giving and asking for reasons. The institutional character of legal social practices should encourage awareness of the distinctive features of those practices. But it remains an open question if it establishes a different structure for reasoning in law. Nonetheless, if this approximation between Brandom's historical-expressivist interpretation of common law practices and Dworkin's interpretivism is warranted, it is possible to take Postema's positive attitude towards Dworkin's method – as 'an account of an important part of common law reasoning' – as an indication that the argument developed in this section is at least plausible.[74]

A one-level account of analogical reasoning, understood in inferentialist terms, would still provide middle ground between rule rationalism and particularism. It would allow for analogies to be grounded in explicit rules, principles or theories, but it would also admit that they may be independently grounded in implicit practical abilities of distinguishing reasons from non reasons on the basis of commitments and entitlements. In fact, this distinction between norms implicit in practices and norms explicit in rules or principles may not be as sharp as one should expect. When talking about the inferential consequences of applying concepts as partly constitutive of their conceptual content and meaning, Brandom claims that grasping those consequences

[72] In a previous work, I tried to show that the same inferentialist and historical-expressive models of rationality are instantiated in Dworkin's Interpretive Theory of Law as Integrity, and its consequences for Dworkin's cognitivism on values. See TL Decat, *Racionalidade, valor e teorias do direito* (D'Plácido 2015).

[73] This idea seems to go against the spirit of Dworkin's understanding of principles in *Law's Empire*: as norms implicit in practices that are not merely discovered nor fabricated by the interpreter but discursively established in a practice, and by interpreters who are sensitive to historical reconstructions of legal practice. See Dworkin (n 13).

[74] Postema (n 1) 132.

> is not an all-or-none affair; the metallurgist understands the concept of tellurium better than I do, for training has made her master of the inferential intricacies of its employment in a way that I can only crudely approximate.[75]

If one considers this possible partial failure in grasping inferential connections that articulate the meaning of linguistic expressions may also happen in grasping practical material inferences, one will also have to consider the possibility that these implicit material inferential relations will license practical transitions with various degrees of explicitness, and therefore practical intelligibility. The discursive nature of legal practices may set a minimum standard of explicitness needed for legal discussions, but that does not mean rational implicit inferential connections below this standard will not also be at work guiding decisions.

A one-level inferentialist account of analogical reasoning could also account for the distinct ways in which justice concerns shape analogical reasoning according to Postema. What he calls a 'sense of justice' – a cautionary practical force that operates in the absence of explicit principles, in a mostly local manner, rejecting some unfair solutions but not necessarily pointing to a conclusive decision – may be seen as the implicit practical force of normative considerations not yet made explicit in the form of principles. Until something like Dworkinian constructive interpretation makes explicit the implicit commitments and entitlements that constitute the sense of justice operating on a case, the sense of justice may share practical guidance with other explicit principles of political morality bearing on a certain case.

The arguments presented in this chapter, and the criticism it directs at the two-level version of the classical conception of analogical reasoning, were not designed to preclude someone from adopting it. In this sense, they do not show that Postema should, let alone that he must, think of legal analogical reasoning on the terms presented in this chapter. The line of thought developed has been intended to show, however, that once one accepts theoretical developments that are compatible with, if not implied by, some inferentialist commitments Postema had already undertaken, one might be able to build a different model of analogical reasoning. A model that is simpler, structurally similar to other linguistic social practices, more equipped to make rational operations behind analogical reasoning explicit, and also able to address the concerns that have given rise to Postema's model of legal analogical reasoning.

[75] Brandom, *Articulating Reasons* (n 20) 64.

8

Postema on Analogies in Law

FÁBIO PERIN SHECAIRA*

THIS CHAPTER DISCUSSES Professor Postema's account of analogy in law. It takes issue with Professor Postema's contention that 'strictly speaking, there is no such thing as *argument from* analogy, but only *reasoning with* analogy, or rather *analogical reasoning*'.[1] Professor Postema holds the view that analogies appear in ordinary judicial discourse in a simplified form that does not reveal the underlying complexities of analogical reasoning. He contends that analogical reasoning must be uncovered and understood if we are to assess ordinary analogies properly. Professor Postema's views are evaluated in section III after some preliminary remarks in sections I and II.

I. CLAIMS AND REASONS

A person, P, believes claim C. Two different questions may be asked about the relation between P and C:

(1) How did P come to believe C?
(2) What considerations (if any) is P prepared to adduce as reasons to believe C?

A third question, which does not pertain to the relation between P and C but to the truth of C, is the following:

(3) What considerations (if any) would in fact give evidential support for C?

In some circumstances all three questions will have the same answer. 'Red paint on a certain submerged rock is reason to think it's what damaged the

* A draft of this chapter was read by Katharina Stevens, to whom I am grateful for many valuable suggestions. I also had the pleasure of discussing the contribution with Professor Postema himself in October 2017 in Curitiba, Brazil. At the time he gave a thoughtful reply to my objections, which I am eager to be able to see in writing.

[1] GJ Postema, '*A Similibus ad Similia*: Analogical Thinking in Law' in DE Edlin (ed), *Common Law Theory* (Cambridge University Press 2007) 121.

QE II's hull.'[2] First, red paint on a rock may be what causes a person to believe that the rock damaged the ship. Second, it may be something that the person is willing to give as a reason to believe that the rock damaged the ship. Finally, it is a good (even if not conclusive) reason to believe that the rock damaged the ship. In other circumstances, however, the answers to the three questions will *not* coincide. Beliefs are sometimes induced by social and psychological factors that a person would not use for the purpose of argumentation. Also, since human beings are fallible, the mere fact that a person is ready to adduce certain considerations in support of a claim does not mean that those considerations genuinely support that claim.

One may be tempted to explain the difference between questions 1 and 2 or between questions 1 and 3 in terms of the famous distinction between the 'context of discovery' and the 'context of justification'. I will resist the temptation here, however, because the context distinction is a slippery one that is subject to different interpretations. To use that distinction in an essay with a limited scope is to risk getting involved in inapposite controversies related to different chapters in the history of epistemology.[3] For the sake of clarity, it seems wiser to take the more long-winded route of referring to the three-fold distinction underlying questions 1, 2 and 3.

II. THINKING, ARGUMENT AND JUSTIFICATION

There is no consensus about how to use the terms that make up the title of the current section. Since the choice of terms is less important than keeping clear the concepts that the terms are meant to express, let us make some stipulations. Let 'thinking' refer to the psychological process through which one forms beliefs, often by inferring new beliefs from previously acquired beliefs. 'Argument' can be understood as referring to any set of claims put forward by a speaker or writer who holds that some of the claims in the set (the premises) provide support for one particular claim in the set (the conclusion). 'Justification' refers to the capacity of the premises of a given argument to provide evidential support for the conclusion of the argument. If we realise that the premises fail to support the conclusion, we can still understand the relevant set of claims as an argument, although we have to admit that it is a flawed argument in the sense that it does not justify belief in the conclusion.

[2] L Wright, 'Justification, Discovery, Reason & Argument' (2001) 15 *Argumentation* 98.

[3] See P Hoyningen-Huene, 'Context of Discovery Versus Context of Justification and Thomas Kuhn' in J Schickore and F Steinle (eds), *Revisiting Discovery and Justification* (Springer 2006) 119 (identifying several different, though often conflated, versions of the context distinction).

With these definitions in mind, it should be clear that question 1 (section I) is a question concerned with P's *thinking*, that is to say, with how P acquired a belief in C, possibly by inferring it from previously held beliefs. Question 2 pertains to P's willingness to *argue* in support of C. Question 3 is about whether there is anything that can be said in defence of C that will actually *justify* belief in it.

In some cases an argument advanced by P may be a good argument, and thus an argument that justifies belief in C. At the same time, P's public argument may be a reflection of P's private thinking process. In such cases, thinking, argument and justification will coincide. But there is no guarantee that this will always happen. Sometimes our processes of thought are complicated and non-linear, while our arguments are attempts to render our thinking more systematic and persuasive. But even thoughtful arguments may fail to justify belief in their conclusions. In such cases, thinking, argument and justification come apart.

These seemingly banal remarks have important consequences for the understanding of analogies (in law and elsewhere). Indeed, these remarks have important consequences for the theoretical analysis of many different types of argument. Before we get to analogies, let us consider the case of inference to the best explanation (IBE). Giovanni Tuzet explores IBE by means of an example taken from Edgar Allen Poe's tale, *The Murders in the Rue Morgue*.[4] In Poe's story, a detective investigates the murder of two women, one of whom was brutally strangled and forced up a chimney. The abnormal strength of the perpetrator and other bizarre aspects of the case (eg the events took place in a fourth-story apartment locked from the inside) lead the detective to suppose that the killer might not be human. The hypothesis is unusual, and the detective decides to test it by falsely announcing in the local newspaper the capture of an orangutan. A man responds to the newspaper announcement, and eventually admits that he is the owner of an orangutan who had recently escaped and climbed the victims' building.

According to Tuzet, the detective's thinking is complex, and involves more than one inference. It begins with the abduction of a hypothesis on the basis of partial evidence about who the killer might be. The hypothesis is then tested by means of an inferential process that involves both induction and deduction. Tuzet's account is quite illuminating as an explanation of how the detective *thinks*. It might not fare so well, however, as an attempt to characterise the way in which the detective would *argue* if he were to try to persuade a judge or

[4] G Tuzet, 'Usos Jurídicos de la Abducción' in JA García Amado and P Bonorino (eds), *Prueba e Razonamiento Probatorio en Derecho* (Editorial Colmares 2014) 121, 129–36. I also discuss this example in FB Shecaira, 'How to Disagree about Argument Schemes' (2016) 36 *Informal Logic* 500.

anyone else that the killer was an orangutan. Here is a representation of how the detective would probably argue if his goal was to *persuade*, not to explain the details of his method:

1. There is a set of facts in need of explanation, namely, two women were killed by an agent of abnormal strength in an inaccessible apartment locked from the inside, the building being in an area where an orangutan had been let loose.
2. The hypothesis that the aforementioned orangutan killed the victims explains all the foregoing facts.
3. No other hypothesis (eg that the victims were killed by a thief) does a better job of explaining those facts.
4. Therefore, probably, the hypothesis that the orangutan killed the victims is true.

The argument represented above contains just one logical step (from premises 1, 2 and 3 to conclusion 4), not two or more. This is so because no attempt is made to represent the way in which the orangutan hypothesis was originally formed in the detective's mind and later ingeniously tested. The fact that there was orangutan in the area where the events took place is part of the evidence that could be given *in argument* by the detective in support of his conclusion. Never mind that this fact was only established after the detective first envisaged the hypothesis that the killer might be an ape. This chronological fact, important as it is for understanding the detective's method, has no clear significance from the point of view of argument.

The detective's thinking and the detective's argument do not coincide. That is why it would be misleading to represent them by means of the same argument scheme. An additional question that might be posed is whether the detective's argument is probative as formulated, whether it truly justifies belief in the conclusion that the killer is an orangutan. This question would lead us into broader philosophical debate about whether IBE (as represented above) is a cogent form of argument.[5] The representation above is meant only as an explanation of how the detective would probably argue, given our knowledge of typical instances of IBE.

These points can be generalised to other forms of argument. In the same way that typical arguments about the best hypothesis for explaining certain facts may be significantly different from typical *thinking* about the best hypothesis for explaining certain facts, typical arguments by analogy may be different from typical analogical thinking. Indeed, there is no consensus in the argumentation literature about what abstract scheme best represents the structure of analogies. Here are just some of the possibilities (where 'A' and 'B' refer to acts or facts; 'x',

[5] Arguments of that form are clearly not deductively valid but they could still be inductively strong.

'y', 'z' are specific features of those acts or facts; and 'W' refers to ways in which the acts or facts are to be treated – eg as morally or legally (im)permissible):

(a)	(b)
A is W;	A has x, y, z;
B is just like A;	B has x, y, z;
therefore, B is W.	A is W;
	therefore, B is W.
(c)	(d)
A has x, y, z;	A has x, y, z;
B has x, y, z;	B has x, y, z;
A is W;	A is W;
it is in virtue of x, y, z, that A is W;	all things which have x, y, z are W;
therefore, B is W.	therefore, B is W.[6]

One plausible reason for the lack of consensus about which scheme is best is that different authors who write about analogies often have different phenomena in mind. Scheme *a* might be thought to be an accurate representation of the way in which we intuitively approximate analogous facts or acts in everyday thinking.[7] Schemes *b* and *c*, on the other hand, give perhaps a better idea of how philosophers and jurists tend to argue when they hope to establish that certain acts or facts are similar because they share morally or legally relevant features that can be specified. Finally, a formal logician might contend that only scheme *d*, albeit infrequently instantiated in ordinary argumentation, would give rise to undeniably cogent (because deductively valid) arguments. Again, the point is to show that analogical thinking, analogical argument and analogical justification may come apart in the sense that they may be structured differently and therefore require different explanations or theoretical representations. In the following section, I consider how this thought relates to Professor Postema's account of analogy in law.

III. POSTEMA ON ANALOGICAL THINKING IN LAW

Professor Postema does not reject the general distinction between thinking and argument. However, he minimises its relevance to the study of analogical

[6] These schemes are borrowed from T Govier, 'Analogies and Missing Premises' (1989) 11 *Informal Logic* 143.

[7] Professor Postema would disagree. He rejects the view that analogies are based on rules, but he also rejects what may be conceived as the natural alternative, namely, that analogies involve simple, intuitive leaps from case to case. He writes, 'Analogical reasoning is not a linear process but rather a dynamic one of locating a new case in a network of inferences … If we understand it in this way, we can resist the temptation to reduce it either to a form of intuition or of mere rule application'. Postema (n 1) 121.

reasoning when stating that analogy is not 'a form of argument, like *modus ponens* or *reductio ad absurdum*, but rather it is a dynamic mode of reasoning that relies on, and builds on, competencies and protocols of thought basic to cognition'.[8] The idea is apparently that one cannot understand (and properly assess) analogies by attending only to their visible form, to the way in which they are typically structured and adduced in ordinary argument. One must attend also to the underlying process of thought that underwrites the visible form of analogies.

By denying that analogy is a 'form of argument', Professor Postema does not seem to be making the uncontroversial point that ordinary analogical arguments are not deductively valid. For he suggests that analogical reasoning is too elaborate to fit into *any* scheme as simple and linear as the schemes discussed in the previous section. It is of little relevance whether those schemes represent deductively valid forms of argument (as only *d* does) or not. At best, those schemes may be able to represent the ways in which analogies are advanced in ordinary judicial opinions, which, due to the 'conventions of their genre,' only provide a 'greatly truncated' and 'formulaic'[9] representation of the reasoning process that actually takes place in the mind of the analogy-making judge. That reasoning process is supposed to be too complex and non-linear to be represented by any standard argument scheme.

It might also be thought that Professor Postema is not putting forward a very contentious view insofar as he is simply making clear that he is not in the business of assessing analogies *as they appear* in judicial opinions. Although argument analysis of that kind is a worthwhile project, Professor Postema is entitled to make the decision to focus his attention on the complexities of analogical thinking, a different (though equally important) subject. If that were the case, I would find little to disagree with in Professor Postema's account of analogy. However, Professor Postema's text suggests otherwise. As noted above, he makes the significant claim that analogical reasoning *is not* a form of argument, like *modus ponens*, but rather a dynamic mode of reasoning, a non-linear process that involves 'locating a new case in a network of inferences'. This could mean that there is something distinctive about analogical reasoning, something that is essential for understanding and assessing analogies but which is typically left unstated in judicial opinions that compare cases, past and present. Arguments of other kinds (like *modus ponens*) do not face the same problem, presumably because there is not, hidden behind the way in which they are typically presented, a complex reasoning process that deserves to be explored.

This interpretation of Professor Postema's position is confirmed by passages such as the following, where he writes that analogy assessment depends upon

[8] ibid 117.
[9] ibid 124.

a complex network of inferences that takes place at the level of analogical thinking:

> The first step toward a more adequate account is to distinguish two levels of analogical thinking in law and to recognize their interdependence. I call the base level *analogical reasoning*. At this level, credible analogies are identified and inferences are made based on them. Beyond this is a reflective level involving *analogy assessment*. At this level, analogical inferences and judgments are evaluated in light of wider legal (and possibly moral) principles. Although analogical thinking in law *may* proceed sequentially through these levels, we should not think of these as stages through which all analogical thinking must pass but as different yet interdependent kinds of reasoning that can, sometimes, go on nearly simultaneously.[10]

This position faces two objections. The first objection has to do with whether Professor Postema is engaged in real disagreement with the authors whose views on analogies he purports to oppose. The second objection pertains to the problematic implications (for other kinds of argument) of what Professor Postema has to say about analogies:

Objection 1: Professor Postema and his opponents (eg Richard Posner and Ronald Dworkin) are interested in different phenomena – analogical thinking vs analogical argument – and are therefore speaking at cross-purposes.

Discussions of analogy in law often begin with examples of real analogies advanced by judges in significant decisions. In fact, authors who are interested in legal argumentation often do the same in respect of various types of argument: the legal syllogism, proportionality tests, *a fortiori* arguments, slippery slopes, etc. The goal is to interpret arguments as given by legal actors (especially judges) and to consider their cogency. Are they deductively valid? Are they inductively strong? Could they be improved by the addition of specific premises? If new premises were added to an argument, might that entail its transformation into an argument of a different kind?[11] These are some of the questions that authors working on analogy and other kinds of argument may bring to the fore. Are they the wrong questions? Are they questions that can only be answered if one goes beyond the face value of legal argumentation and theorises about legal thinking in a deeper sense?

I think the right answer to the last two questions is 'no'. The purpose of much legal argumentation theory is to assess how judges fare in the modern culture of justification, a culture in which the legitimacy of our legal institutions depends upon 'the cogency of the case offered in defence of [their] decisions'.[12]

[10] ibid 116.

[11] For instance, if we add a premise expressing a general rule to an analogy, does that argument cease to be an analogy – ie a comparison between particular cases – and become something akin to a legal syllogism?

[12] E Mureinik, 'A Bridge to Where? Introducing the Interim Bill of Rights' (1994) 10 *South African Journal on Human Rights* 32.

Theorists want to know if judges base their rulings on reasons that will be found persuasive by rational and inquisitive citizens.[13] Paying attention to argument is not just a philosophical pastime; it is motivated by a deep concern for the cogency of the judicial opinion.

Consider what Richard Posner, one of Professor Postema's intellectual targets, says about analogies in recent writing. Referring to the famous case of *Adams v New Jersey Steamboat Co*, where a court 'analogized the steamboat company to the innkeeper … rather than the railroad',[14] Posner claims that analogies such as this 'cannot resolve legal disputes intelligently. To say that something is in some respects like something else is to pose questions rather than answer them.'[15] To be sure, I do not agree with Posner's dismissive attitude. As opposed to simply posing rhetorical questions, judges often go through great pains in order to explain why they consider the similarities between analogues to be legally relevant. But the point is not whether Posner makes a fair critique of judicial arguments by analogy. The point is that Posner is concerned – and understandably so – with how analogies are *given* in judicial opinions. He questions their justificatory potential, and argues that they are underdeveloped, unsatisfactory forms of argument that serve as bad substitutes for frank and explicit consideration of policy.

The cogency of analogical arguments *as they appear in judicial opinions* is an important subject in its own right. Professor Postema has not made it clear why he thinks one is obligated to explore the intricacies of legal thinking when one's main concern is to assess the grounds officially given for judicial rulings. In fact, in other work Professor Postema has put forward a broad standard of rationality for legal reasoning that might clash with his view about how analogies are to be assessed:

> Broadly speaking, a judgment is correct … if it is backed by sound reasons that are or can be articulated and assessed publicly. More precisely, a judgment is correct if but only if it is maximally supported by the arguments and the balance of reasons available for articulation and assessment by reasonable and competent persons in a fully public deliberative process. On this view, correctness of judgments is a direct function of the arguments that can be offered publicly in support of them.[16]

The publicity standard requires judges and other authorities to articulate reasons that can be understood and assessed by reasonable persons. But how can analogies in judicial decisions live up to this general standard if to assess them one must have access to a non-public, undisclosed and quite complex dimension of judicial thinking?

[13] Not to speak of the fact that the reasons actually given in a judicial opinion are the reasons that litigants will refer to if they appeal the case to a higher instance. This is an additional reason why the face value of arguments matters so much in law and legal theory.

[14] R Posner, *How Judges Think* (Harvard University Press 2008) 180.

[15] ibid 181.

[16] GJ Postema, 'Objectivity Fit for Law' in B Leiter (ed), *Objectivity in Law and Morals* (Cambridge University Press 2001) 117.

Objection 2: If Professor Postema's view about analogies were generalised (and there is no reason to think that it could not be generalised), then that could mean the end of argument analysis as formal and informal logic understand it.

My second concern is that if we were to accept what Professor Postema says about analogies, we might also have to revisit our conception of many other kinds of argument – including *modus ponens* – which Professor Postema does not classify as 'dynamic modes of reasoning'. Every argument that is put on paper (especially if represented in standard form, with numbered premises, etc) is a *model*, that is, a simplified reconstruction of some possibly very intricate reasoning process. Is that not true of *modus ponens* itself? When giving an argument of that form, an individual puts forward certain premises and a conclusion. Those premises and conclusion (at least if the arguer is sincere) correspond to beliefs that the arguer holds. In addition to that, the arguer applies an unstated rule of inference that permits the derivation of the conclusion from the premises. Without a grasp of the rule, the arguer would not be able to move confidently from premises to conclusion – so, the rule must in some sense be part of his reasoning process. But to suggest that the reasoner has a general *modus ponens* rule in mind that he applies from case to case is to ignore the role likely played in his reasoning by memory of past examples of *modus ponens*. The reasoner does not just subsume every new case under the rule; his grasp and application of the rule are dependent on his capacity to relate the argument currently advanced with similar arguments from the past. He poses to himself – perhaps in a flash – the following questions: Is this a case of *modus ponens* in the same way as other arguments whose validity I endorsed in the past? Is it different from arguments that I have encountered before that resemble *modus ponens* but are in fact fallacious?

Professor Postema would probably agree with this picture, as he makes a general point about rule-application to similar effect:

> The rule-rationalist argues that it is not possible to judge one case relevantly similar to another without the guidance of a rule that brings them under some category or description: We can judge them relevantly similar just in case they are instances of the same rule or concept. However, in fact the opposite is true. *It is possible to identify something as an instance of the rule or concept only if one judges that it is relevantly similar to cases already falling under the rule, and that is possible only if at some point it is possible to judge cases as relevantly similar without appeal to a mediating rule.* ... No application of an explicit rule to a particular case, no application of a concept, is possible without the exercise of what Kant called the power of judgement, a power that defies explicit articulation.[17]

In this passage, Professor Postema is not discussing *modus ponens*. He is discussing analogies and whether *they* depend on rules. Yet he seems to hold that every judgment concerning the application of a rule (whether it be a moral

[17] Postema (n 1) 114 (emphasis added).

rule, a legal rule, or a rule of inference) requires 'unruly' analogical judgment. So, there may be much more to *modus ponens* than meets the eye. The formula 'If p then q; p; therefore q' is a truncated representation of a complex reasoning process that involves the application of an unstated rule of inference and perhaps comparisons to other inferences from the past. But if this is true, must all argumentation theorists be concerned with it? How might this information about the thinking underlying *modus ponens* impact one's judgment about the soundness of a particular instance of *modus ponens*? Is an argument of that form better or worse depending (inter alia) on the comparisons to unstated cases that were made by the author of the argument in the course of his thinking?

The point of the second objection is that we need an explanation of why and when arguments appearing in public discourse should be regarded as truncated reports of complex reasoning processes that deserve to be uncovered and understood. Professor Postema's contention about analogies, if I interpret him correctly, is that the process of analogical reasoning should be explored, not only for the sake of acquiring a deeper understanding of reasoners' psychology (which is a legitimate enterprise), but also for the purpose of assessing analogical arguments *as they are adduced* in ordinary argument. But if there is no principled way to explain how analogies are different from *modus ponens* in that respect, then *modus ponens* and perhaps all other arguments that we currently analyse by formal and informal logical methods would have to be submitted to the same kind of philosophical-cum-psychological study that Professor Postema has developed in respect of analogies. I wonder if Professor Postema realises the possible implications of his view, and whether he would be willing to accept them.

Part IV

Methodology and the Nature of Jurisprudence

9

Postema on Hart: The Illusion of Value-Neutrality

MARGARET MARTIN*

THE RALLYING CRY of the legal positivists is found in HLA Hart's account of the nature of his project in the Postscript to his *Concept of Law*, where he insists that he is offering a 'descriptive' theory that is 'morally neutral and has no justificatory aims' insofar as 'it does not seek to justify or commend on moral or other grounds the forms and structures which appear in [the] general account of law'.[1] Hart assumes that law can be understood in non-normative terms. Legal philosophers, according to this account, do not need to turn to controversial moral claims to grasp the content of the concept of law. Rather, an understanding of law is available to anyone who is willing to make careful observations about legal systems as experienced by those who live under law's sway. In particular, Hart places great emphasis on the perspective of the participant: the legal philosopher, Hart insists, must 'put himself in the place of an insider'.[2]

Gerald Postema is not convinced. In 'Jurisprudence as Practical Philosophy', he bemoans the fact that Hart has 'convinced a whole generation of legal philosophers that philosophical jurisprudence is a kind of descriptive sociology, the key to which is the notion of the 'internal point of view'.[3] His point is not simply that Hart and his fellow travellers should have taken a different path if the promise of jurisprudential insight is to be realised. Rather, Postema's point is that there is only one path: 'If we accept Hart's insight that the central task of jurisprudence is to give a philosophically illuminating account of the distinctive normative character of law, we must also accept that this is a task of practical philosophy.'[4] The philosopher, insofar as she is committed to exploring and

*I am very grateful to Thomas Bustamante, Nigel Simmonds and Dan Priel for their excellent comments on an earlier draft. Any errors, of course, are my own.

[1] Hart, *Concept of Law* (2nd edn, Oxford University Press 1994) 240.

[2] ibid 2.

[3] Postema, 'Jurisprudence as Practical Philosophy' (1998) 4 *Legal Theory* 329, 335.

[4] ibid 330.

explaining law's normativity, must inevitably explain if and when law carries with it normative authority. To be clear, Postema is not suggesting that the legal philosopher occupies the same position as the 'participant': the participant is always determining how to act. The legal philosopher's task is to illuminate one dimension of the participant's practical landscape – the normative dimension of law. Legal philosophy, Postema argues, is fundamentally and inescapably practical; this also means that it is fundamentally and inescapably normative.

In order to demonstrate this point, Postema carefully uncovers the numerous ambiguities, instabilities and logical fallacies that mar Hart's canonical work. By canvassing Postema's arguments in detail, readers can begin to see the need to re-think a host of Hart's central claims, including, but not limited to, his professed methodology. Postema reveals that 'neutrality' has more than one possible meaning. Once this is clear, it becomes more difficult for Hart and his followers to shore up their positivist account. Their easiest manoeuvre – to insist that one is describing values – is taken away by Postema. And, as we shall see, so too is the possibility of turning to meta-theoretical values. Once these popular escape routes are closed down, the tenability of Postema's central claim comes into increasingly sharper focus.

Postema then turns his careful philosophical gaze to a fundamental distinction that is at the centre of Hart's *Concept of Law*: the distinction between the internal perspective (which his famed committed participant adopts) and the external perspective (which Hart argues is the perspective of the legal philosopher when she is doing her job properly).[5] Hart does not reserve the external perspective for the philosopher alone. According to Hart, the external perspective is also occupied by the proverbial 'bad man', the 'malefactor' and the 'victim'. Postema is, once again, deeply suspicious: it is not clear that these characters occupy the 'external' perspective. At the very least, this is a claim that must be defended. Postema rightly argues that Hart's use of the internal/external divide is misleading: it hides from view the nature of Hart's normative commitments, and, as a result, the nature of the jurisprudential project more generally.[6]

I will argue that Postema's assessment of Hart's position is correct. I will then build upon a central insight that Postema offers: once we see that Hart's cast of characters, listed above, are not occupying a perspective that is clearly external to the practice, we begin to see that Hart is not offering descriptive empirical observations about what participants actually do or how they actually think. Rather, I will maintain that Hart is constructing a typology that serves his particular philosophical purposes. Through an exploration of

[5] Hart (n 1) 242.

[6] The distinction between the internal/external divide is not saved by the introduction of additional distinctions that are parasitic on this initial one (ie the distinction between an extreme or moderate external point of view, or the introduction of the 'detached perspective'). This point will become clear in the course of the argument.

these various character types, it is revealed that a deep moral judgement runs through Hart's work. The 'bad man' is bad because he does not behave as he should. Conversely, the committed participant, who has 'accepted' law's requirements, behaves correctly: he has recognised law's reason-giving potential and proceeds to treat legal norms as (authoritative) reasons for action. These judgments, which are not made explicit by Hart, only make sense if Hart presupposes that the bad man and the committed participant live in a relatively good society that has relatively good laws (or, at least, not morally problematic ones). These moral assumptions, which are latent in *The Concept of Law*, come to the surface in Hart's discussion of the 'victim.'

Hart's 'victim' appears in chapter 9 of the *Concept of Law*, which is also the chapter where Hart introduces us to the idea of the minimum moral content of natural law. Hart defines the latter as 'simple truisms', or 'universally recognized principles of conduct', that are found in all legal systems.[7] All legal systems include legal norms that prohibit murder and theft, for instance. Law offers us basic protections but Hart recognises not all of laws' subjects enjoy such protections: some classes of individuals are law's victims.[8] We meet Hart's victim long after we have already become acquainted with Hart's 'committed participant', and his version of Holmes's 'bad man'. The victim is significant because, unlike the other characters, legal norms *do not* offer her reasons for action. The legal system, Hart makes clear, has not secured basic protections for the victim class, and hence the victim complies with law's demands for prudential reasons. Not only does the law fail to protect the victim from her fellow citizens; officials use the law to target her. The law reaches the victim, as Postema perceptively notes, in the form of arbitrary power.[9]

Once we have the victim in our sights, not only is it clear that the *Concept of Law* is built upon a series of moral judgments, but it is also clear that Hart has the resources to explain law's normativity. It is here where Hart sows the seeds of a plausible account of the source and scope of law's moral authority, or so I will argue. In other words, Hart has the resources to explain what distinguishes a legal system from the proverbial gunman writ large. However, the account on offer undercuts both the method and the substance of Hart's legal positivist account. If we take seriously his discussion of the victim, and the minimum moral content of natural law more generally, then Hart's positivist account proves untenable. While Hartians may be tempted to jettison chapter 9 in the hopes of preserving Hart's project, this is not possible: the discussion of the victim does not introduce the relevant moral judgments, it simply exposes them. Postema is right: there is only one path towards jurisprudential insights, and it is the well-trodden one.[10] *The Concept of Law* is an exercise in practical philosophy.

[7] Hart (n 1) 193.
[8] ibid 201.
[9] Postema (n 3) 340.
[10] ibid 330.

I. THE ILLUSION OF VALUE-NEUTRALITY

What, precisely, does Hart mean when he declares that his account is 'morally neutral'? Postema's answer points us toward the complexities that lie just beneath the surface of Hart's account. By disentangling three possible definitions of 'neutral,' it becomes clear this word is, itself, riddled with ambiguity. Postema begins with what appears to be Hart's starting point: if one hopes to offer a morally neutral account then one can adopt (or attempt to adopt) an approach to the study of law that is 'neutral'. That is, a legal philosopher who is writing in the Hartian tradition can rely on 'principles and techniques' that are identified as 'neutral'.[11] Alternatively, the *result* of the investigation into the nature of law may be presented as a value-neutral concept.[12] However, Postema is right to point out that the decision to rely on a neutral set of resources at the outset does not guarantee that the result of the inquiry will itself be neutral.[13] Hartians will, no doubt, be tempted to limit the nature of the output of their investigation given their goal of value-neutral account. While the possibility of begging the questions remains live, this is not Postema's central worry. Instead, Postema introduces us to a third possible definition of 'neutrality', one that seems to provide positivists with the perfect escape route from all possible arguments that could be raised against them: the adoption of the *detached* perspective.[14]

Legal positivists, after all, tend to be untroubled by the possibility that certain values may accompany legality.[15] Hartians often claim that a theorist is able to *describe* value-laden practices without endorsing the values found in the practice.[16] Hart himself insists that 'Description may still be description, even when what is described is an evaluation.'[17] While this point seems unassailable, Postema spies the weakness at the heart of this claim: the ability of a theorist to remain uncommitted is not a property of a theory but of the *individual theorist*.[18] Postema rightly points out that 'nothing prevents a theorist from maintaining a "detached" attitude toward a justificatory theory'.[19] For instance, one can insist that law is a morally robust concept, as Ronald Dworkin proclaims,[20] without endorsing the values that are implicated in

[11] ibid 331.
[12] ibid 330.
[13] ibid.
[14] ibid.
[15] One version of this claim that I will not explore here is that of Joseph Raz. Raz endorses the sources thesis, which is the claim that the identification of the content of law involves ascertaining certain social facts – evaluative arguments are not needed. Raz then claims that any values that accompany the sources thesis (if such values exist) do not undermine his positivist claims. For a detailed defence of the sources thesis, see J Raz, *The Authority of Law* (Clarendon Press 1979) ch 3. I criticise this position elsewhere. See M Martin, *Judging Positivism* (Hart Publishing 2014) ch 2.
[16] WJ Waluchow, *Inclusive Legal Positivism* (Oxford University Press 1994) 19–30.
[17] Hart (n 1) 244.
[18] Postema (n 3) 331.
[19] ibid.
[20] See R Dworkin, *Law's Empire* (Harvard University Press 1986).

Dworkin's account.[21] If all natural law theories can be treated in this detached manner, the possibility of adopting this posture fails to tell us anything about the viability of legal positivism. Postema has cleverly closed off this popular escape route. This brings Postema's key question back into focus: does the legal philosopher necessarily make normative judgments when trying to elucidate the nature of law?

Postema's point, which has also been made by philosophers like John Finnis, is that judgments of importance – judgments about what should be included in one's account of law – are inherently evaluative. After all, empirical observations, without judgments of importance, lead to the creation of an undifferentiated list. Finnis rightly draws attention to the fact that 'even a list requires some principle of selection'.[22] Of course, many positivists are happy to admit that judgments of importance are value-laden; they simply insist that the values that are being appealed to are not moral in nature. The Hartian philosopher maintains that she is appealing *not* to human goods but to meta-theoretical values, like 'simplicity' and 'comprehensiveness.' Postema judges this to be a 'mistake':[23]

> First, the kinds of values lying behind judgments of the relative importance or centrality of features of law (for example, the relative importance of coercion and of private arranging in the debate over the analysis of legal powers (see *Concept*, 33–42)) are not typical meta-theoretical, epistemic values like simplicity, comprehensiveness, theoretical fecundity, and the like. They are substantive, human goods, practical values. Moreover, the 'explanatory power' of an analysis is not itself one of the values, but rather the *result* of judgments of importance that depend on these practical values. That is to say, an account has greater explanatory power because it gives priority to features judged more important by appeal to such values.[24]

Arguably, John Austin's account of law is simpler than Hart's, but this does not mean that it is correct. After all, if Hart is correct, Austin's account of the participant's perspective is *too simple*: citizens are not merely obeying the law out of habit, they also internalise law's demands.[25] In addition, what counts as a 'comprehensive' theory is itself theory-dependent – some will argue that Hart's decision to exclude coercion from his concept of law means that his account is not 'comprehensive'. Others, of course, will agree with Hart and insist that a complete account of the concept of law need not include coercion. Whether a theory is considered comprehensive or not will turn on a prior judgment about what ought to be included in one's concept. And, of course, it is the nature of this prior judgment that interests Postema. In order to bring the nature of the judgment of importance into focus, consider, once again, Hart's claim that

[21] Postema (n 3) 331.
[22] J Finnis, *Natural Law and Natural Rights* (2nd edn, Oxford University Press 2011) 4.
[23] Postema (n 3) 334.
[24] ibid.
[25] See Hart (n 1) 18–25.

philosophers must attend to the participant's perspective in order to grasp the nature of law.

Postema's point is that it is far from obvious that legal philosophers should follow Hart's lead. At the very least, Postema explains that Hart has not discharged his argumentative burden: Hart's core claim rests on a *non sequitur*. Hart, Postema argues, begins with the premise that any complete legal theory must account for law's normativity. He then 'concludes that the framework from within which inquiry regarding law or other social practices should alone proceed is theoretical, in the hermeneutic mode'.[26] Postema is right to point out that, 'from the observation that behavior is normative or rule-governed it does not follow that the regularities of behavior are consciously available to those who engage in it'.[27] Participants may only be dimly aware of the way in which law is shaping their behaviour, or their judgments about law's normative authority may be altogether mistaken. Postema is helping us see that the adoption of the participant's perspective is unlikely to be clear or univocal; rather, turning to this perspective will reproduce some of the uncertainties that are at the centre of jurisprudential disputes.

Hart assumes, without argument, that the hermeneutic framework is the *only* framework a legal philosopher can adopt:

> It does not follow that the only appropriate, or even the most natural, approach to explanation and understanding of this social practice is through interpreting the beliefs and attitudes of its participants. We are likely to get no closer to an adequate explanation of law's normativity – its agent-guiding, reason-giving character – by reporting the beliefs and attitudes of participants than by reporting regularities of their behavior. If facts about the regularities of participant behavior won't do the trick, adding psychological facts about them will not be the answer either.[28]

Again, the self-understanding of participants is not a self-evident source of philosophical insight. Philosophers have a long history of casting doubt on participants' views.[29] Hart must explain why the participant has it right. More precisely, he must defend his decision to place *his account* of the committed participant at the centre of his theory.

Even if one agrees with Hart that the committed participant is the natural starting point for a proper jurisprudential analysis, the question now becomes: Which committed participant should we turn to and what characteristics should we endow him with? What Hart offers us is not a mere observation about what participants in fact do; rather, it is a careful construction of a particular

[26] Postema (n 3) 354.

[27] ibid. Postema explains (footnote omitted): 'It is possible to account for the normativity and rule-governed character of behavior of hoverflies, for example, without assuming that the hoverflies have any particular take on their behavior or the rules that it seems to follow. For all we know, and for all the theory explaining their behavior is committed to, hoverflies are entirely incapable of having any beliefs or attitudes regarding those rules.'

[28] ibid 355.

[29] D Priel, 'Toward Classical Legal Positivism' (2015) 101 *Virginia Law Review* 987, 996.

perspective that he believes is important. In order to begin to see that Hart is not offering a set of simple facts about the practice, we only have to attend to the kinds of choices that he is making – choices that Hart neither identifies nor defends. Again, if a defence of these decisions was offered, the account would no longer appear to be descriptive – it would quickly become a straightforward normative theory about law's authority, which, as we shall see, is precisely what Hart ultimately provides us with.[30]

Postema underscores the controversial nature of the choice Hart is making when he lays bare the panoply of possibilities open to Hart: 'Judges and high governmental officials, petty functionaries, lawyers, and conscientious citizens will all qualify as participants.'[31] It is not self-evident that one should be focused on the perspective of the committed participant rather than the judge, for instance. And of course, the choice that Hart makes will have a significant impact on the content of his theory, '[b]ecause the nature of their participation and the stakes involved will be different'.[32] In other words, the choice of what to prioritise will, in turn, shape the content of one's concept.

To see this point, consider the kind of judgment a legal sceptic would likely make if she believed, like Hart does, that the perspective of the committed participant is central. If she believes that law can never enjoy moral legitimacy, she might then give priority to the perspective of the bad man: one should *always* be critical of law's demands given that law is but the gunman writ large. But of course, the bad man would not be bad, just sceptical in this case. While Hart might reply that the sceptic would be unable to account for the coming into being of a legal system, it is not clear that the sceptic must account for this; nor is it clear that Hart himself can do so without making additional assumptions – assumptions that are moral in nature. And of course, Hart should make this point explicit, and he should defend it in full. I will return to this point below. My present aim is to underscore the salience of Postema's point: Hart is making choices that shape his account, and these choices are not adequately acknowledged or defended.

Once the need to make a choice about which perspective should be prioritised is acknowledged, it becomes clear that Hart is straddling the horns of yet another dilemma. Insofar as he is committed to observer theory, he must decide whether to defer to participants and their judgments of importance, or, alternatively, whether he should make an independent judgment. Postema explains why both options are problematic:

> Either [observer theorists] make the determination without regard to the points of view of participants ('external' to their concerns), or they make it with the internal

[30] Also see S Perry, 'Hart's Methodological Positivism' (1998) 4 *Legal Theory* 427.

[31] Postema (n 3) 337.

[32] This point becomes clear if we compare Hart's account to Raz's account in *Practical Reasons and Norms*: Raz places the judge who has a duty to apply the law at the centre. See J Raz, *Practical Reason and Norms* (Oxford University Press 1999) 137. While Raz no longer defends this view, the point at issue becomes clear if one revisits his early work.

> point of view in mind. But the latter course appears to lead in a circle, and the former threatens to be irrelevant or inadmissible. It would be irrelevant if it only explains the functional or causal role of certain participants rather than explaining their role in determining the normativity of the practice; it would be inadmissible if it is purely behaviorist, failing again to explain its normativity. Of course, observer theorists might give priority to one (or a subset) over the others on practical, normative grounds, but that seems inconsistent with the non-committal and self-consciously nonpractical dimension of the external viewpoint. It would involve taking a stand on the practical value of the practice.[33]

Deference for deference's sake is circular and inadequate. But if an additional justification is offered then the argument is normative. And recall, since there is not a single 'participant's perspective', the choice to rely on a particular version of this perspective already involves judgments about what is important. Postema's point is that such judgments are unavoidable and they take us beyond Hart's world of 'descriptive sociology'. And even if there is a single participant's perspective available to us, we can still wonder why the participant would make better judgments than the philosopher. In short, all paths point to the need for normative arguments, and once offered, Hart's professed value neutrality is sacrificed.

Once it is clear that choices must be made, it is useful to explore in greater detail the precise nature of the choices Hart has made. Hart opts to prioritise the perspective of a particular kind of participant, (the committed participant); he is also choosing the defining characteristics of this particular participant. Postema explains that participants 'may be conscientious, and still be vigorous dissenters; others may be mere conformists', adding that 'Some will be very reflective, others utterly unreflective, and many will be more or less reflective at different points in their participation.'[34] How does a legal philosopher choose between these options?

Hart, of course, makes a choice. However, as mentioned, his choice remains unacknowledged and undefended, which makes his account *seem* like it is grounded in a set of uncontroversial observations about legal practice. Postema draws our attention to the fact that Hart's quintessential committed participant is not particularly reflective.[35] Hart's participant internalises the norms, holding them up as standards by which to judge her own behaviour and that of others.[36] Hart's participant does not ask whether the norms in question are morally binding on him: he simply *assumes* that they are and behaves accordingly. This point appears to be of little moment given that elsewhere in the *Concept of Law*, Hart insists that law's subjects can obey for *any* reason: fear, habit or 'acceptance'.[37]

[33] Postema (n 3) 338.
[34] ibid 337–38.
[35] ibid 336.
[36] Hart (n 1) 56.
[37] ibid 116.

It is not clear, however, that this particular claim can co-exist with his decision to prioritise the perspective of the committed participant who 'accepts' the law. I will return to this point momentarily. The point at this juncture is that Postema is, once again, correct: Hart has *constructed* a particular version of the committed participant – one that perfectly suits his needs.

To begin to see the implications of this point, it is helpful to follow Postema and focus on another sharp distinction that runs through Hart's *Concept of Law* – the distinction between the *internal* perspective and the *external* perspective. Hart, Postema argues, assumes that the theorist occupies the external perspective:

> The descriptive legal theorist takes up a distinctive point of view. This is not the perspective of the judge who must decide what the law requires in a particular case, but that of an 'external observer of a form of social institution with a normative aspect' ... Unlike the judge, legal theorists do not seek to commend or justify the practice. They do not participate in the practice and are not committed to it or bound by it. *Qua* theorists, they are not concerned with its practical demands on themselves. It presents itself as a complex social fact, related in complex ways to other social practices and institutions. Their project is to describe and explain this social fact and its relations.[38]

As mentioned at the outset, Hart also insists that, in order to illuminate the nature of law, a theorist must pay attention to the perspective of the participant. Again, if we see the world through these distinctions, one either adopts the theoretical perspective of the external observer, *or* one adopts the practical perspective of the committed participant. Postema argues that this sharp dichotomy veils the normative nature of the assumptions that Hart is relying on.

Unlike the theorist, the participant does not inquire into the source of the validity of the norm. If she did embark on such an inquiry, Hart insists she would be asking questions that are out of bounds.[39] Postema explains:

> To inquire after the authority of the rule of recognition is to shift perspective from within the practice to a perspective outside it. It is to ask whether there is such a (social) rule, and that question is answered fully by pointing to the facts of the practice. The inquirer shifts from the perspective of a committed participant to that of an external observer.[40]

This means that once the participant inquires into the status of the rule of recognition, or into the normative authority of any of the rules it validates, the participant then occupies the 'external' perspective.[41] The participant is asking, much like the philosopher, 'whether there is such a (social) rule, and

[38] Postema (n 3) 331 (citation to Hart omitted).
[39] Hart (n 1) 109.
[40] Postema (n 3) 337.
[41] ibid.

that question is answered fully by pointing to the facts of the practice'.[42] Many of Hart's critics are adamant that the facts of the practice alone do not generate the authoritative reasons for action.[43] Or at the very least, Hart has not adequately defended this claim. In section II, I will suggest that Hart does have the resources needed to defend an account of law's moral authority. However, the account he offers is inconsistent with his positivist commitments.

At this stage in the argument it is imperative to see that Hart's insistence that the participant moves from the internal to the external perspective when questions about law's normative authority is raised, is not self-evident. As Postema notes, even Hart concedes that it is natural for the participant to ask such questions.[44] It is highly doubtful that participants would themselves be cognisant of this shift in perspective. Significantly, Hart has quietly conceded the point that he is not tracking the actual beliefs of actual participants. Again, it is unlikely that any participant would *believe* that she is moving from the internal perspective to the external perspective if she inquires into the bindingness of a given legal norm (or the system in general). Hart has quietly left behind any attempt to accurately portray the participant's perspective.

Postema's point is that this is the quintessential question that should interest the participant. Why, after all, would a participant refrain from asking such questions if she is interested in what she ought to do? Why should the participant simply assume that the law is giving her good reasons for action?[45] Again, it makes sense for a participant to inquire into whether a given norm, or the legal system as a whole, is legitimate. Because Hart's participant does not directly raise the question of law's normative force, Hart does not appear to see the need to address it directly. Once it becomes clear that Hart is making intentional choices about the participant's perspective that he relies upon, choices that he neither identifies nor justifies, it makes sense to inquire further into the nature of the assumptions underpinning his *Concept of Law*.

Postema wants readers to see that this question – the question about normative standing of the rule of recognition (and the rules it validates) – is *precisely* the question that the participant should ask. After all, insofar as the participant wants to know what she ought to do, she should not simply obey the law because the law is technically 'valid'. That is, she should not *assume* that a legal norm is authoritative. Moreover, the status of the rule of recognition is also the question that the legal philosopher should seek to explain: is law capable of enjoying morally justified authority? If so, what are the conditions that must hold for law to enjoy moral authority? In other words, both the philosopher

[42] ibid.

[43] See, for instance, NE Simmonds, 'The Nature of Law: Three Problems with One Solution' (2011) 12 *German Law Journal* 610.

[44] Postema (n 3) 337.

[45] As we shall see in section II, Hart does not consistently make this assumption. I will argue that the shifts in Hart's positions become intelligible once we see that they track a set of moral judgments that are implicit in his discussion.

and the participant are interested in making sense of the same set of questions – questions that are both normative and practical.[46] Hart inadvertently answers these questions in chapter 9 of his canonical work, and the arguments he offers are normative and they cast light on the nature and scope of laws moral authority.

To see this point, we must follow Postema's lead and explore the cast of characters Hart introduces throughout *The Concept of Law*. According to Hart, the 'bad man', the 'malefactor' and the 'victim' all occupy the 'external perspective'. Again, Postema is correct to claim that Hart is using the idea of an 'external' perspective in an inconsistent manner: unlike the theorist who is thought to occupy the external perspective, all three characters are interested in determining how to act, which is a practical concern. Again, by treating the bad man, for instance, as someone who has adopted the external perspective to the law, Hart is able to give priority to his chosen version of the participant's perspective, while simultaneously hiding from view the argumentative burden that accompanies this choice. Postema works to unearth the assumptions underpinning this argument. Once these assumptions come into focus, so does the untenability of Hart's descriptive project.

Once Hart's three characters – the 'bad man', the 'malefactor' and the 'victim' – are placed alongside Hart's committed participant, the moral judgments that underpin Hart's account become visible. Hart assumes that the 'bad man' and the 'malefactor' are bad, but the 'committed participant' and the 'victim' are good, or so I shall argue. Hart's discussion of the victim also contains the foundational elements of an account of the source and scope of law's normative authority. These arguments, once developed, can be seen to inform the entirety of *The Concept of Law*. Nonetheless, their development makes clear that Hart's comments about the victim are incompatible with the method and substance of his positivism. Hart cannot distance himself from the moral judgments that quietly inform his work. Postema is right: Hart, in the course of explaining law's normativity, is offering an answer to the citizens' practical inquiry into law's normative authority.

II. FROM THE 'BAD MAN' TO THE 'VICTIM': LOCATING LAW'S NORMATIVE AUTHORITY

According to Hart, the bad man is only interested in circumventing sanctions; he is not interested in the reason-giving nature of law.[47] It is for this reason that Hart insists that the bad man occupies the external perspective: he wants to avoid punishment but otherwise cares little for the law.[48] Postema explains

[46] This is, of course, Dworkin's point. See Dworkin (n 20) 11–35.
[47] Hart (n 1) 8.
[48] Postema (n 3) 339.

that the bad man's point of view is that 'of one who, while disinterested in its normative demands, nevertheless may find it useful to make his predictions, in part, on the basis of the reasoning of those who administer the law'.[49] Postema is likely right that the bad man does not have to be 'bad',[50] however, I will suggest that it is not a coincidence that Hart assumes that he is. And, as mentioned, Postema is also right that the use of the label 'external' to characterise the bad man's point of view is misleading.

In order to illustrate the power of Postema's position, it is useful to see the assumptions that Hart and Holmes share, before looking at the differences between the two thinkers. Hart and Holmes both seek to identify reasons for action that are quintessentially legal, and both assume that legal reasons for action will motivate action *in isolation* from other reasons. Hart, for instance, insists that the 'committed participant' treats the legal 'ought' as distinct from the moral 'ought'.[51] Holmes rejects this suggestion. Instead, he argues that the legal and the moral are only cleanly separated in the case of the 'bad man', because most people find 'reasons for conduct, whether inside the law or outside of it, in the vaguer sanctions of conscience'.[52] If we are concerned primarily with descriptive accuracy, Holmes is likely going to win this battle. People tend to have complex motivations; it is far from clear that they typically treat legal norms as discrete reasons for action as Hart supposes. At the very least, Hart has a difficult argumentative burden to discharge if he is going to demonstrate that people typically treat legal norms as reasons for action in the precise manner that he assumes.[53]

Again, why should we follow Hart and favour the perspective of the committed participant over that of the bad man? Legal theorists should not marginalise the perspective of the bad man simply because Hart has labelled it 'external'. Again, Postema is correct that the perspective of the bad man is 'eminently practical' and 'internal' to the practice of law.[54] Hart must offer readers more than a label he hopes people will prefer his account to Holmes's. And of course, Postema's point is that any argument offered to justify this decision will be normative. In order to see that Postema is right, it is imperative that we become acquainted with Hart's 'victim'.

Hart introduces us to the victim during his discussion about the minimum moral content of natural law. He observes that all existing legal systems share some basic content. Hart then offers what he sees as a 'simple truism': the law must prohibit acts like murder, theft and assault.[55] The law must ensure our

[49] ibid 341.
[50] ibid 339.
[51] Hart (n 1) 203.
[52] OW Holmes, 'The Path of Law' (1897) 10 *Harvard Law Review* 457, 459.
[53] I discuss this point at length in the context of Raz's account. See Martin (n 15) 10–16.
[54] Also see S Perry, 'Interpretation and Methodology in Legal Theory' in A Marmor (ed), *Law and Interpretation: Essays in Legal Philosophy* (Oxford University Press 1998) 97.
[55] Hart (n 1) 199.

mutual survival, otherwise 'men as they are would have no reason for obeying voluntarily any rules'.[56] Humans are fundamentally interested in survival and the law aims to protect our physical integrity – we are protected from each other, which, in turn, makes the pursuit of other goods possible. Notice that Hart is not suggesting that people will always choose the path of action that will enable them to survive (people often take risks, of course); the claim is that law must secure the pre-conditions for the pursuit of other goods, and it does so by prohibiting interpersonal violence.

Hart insists that this argument is not a devastating concession to his natural law opponents because the minimum moral content of natural law may exist alongside great inequity.[57] Notice that Postema's earlier argument is relevant here, albeit in a different form. The fact that moral problems can be identified does not negate the judgments of 'importance' that are required to construct any concept of law. Moreover, in this particular chapter of *The Concept of Law*, Hart concedes that the judgments he is making are moral in nature.[58] The more we explore the implications of Hart's argument at this juncture, the more difficult it becomes for him to maintain his claim that *The Concept of Law* is an exercise in 'descriptive sociology' that is 'neutral' and has 'no justificatory aims'.[59] Rather, his justificatory aims are revealed in full in his discussion of the victim.

After introducing readers to the minimum moral content of natural law, Hart proceeds to canvass certain 'painful facts' about human history in order to arrive at the conclusion that a viable society must 'offer *some* of its members a system of mutual forbearances, it need not, unfortunately, offer them to all'.[60] Evidence of the existence of a victim class is easily found: Hart points to slavery, apartheid and Nazism.[61] These are law's victims. The victim, like the bad man, fails to 'accept' law's demands. Unlike Hart's committed participant, the victim does not hold up a given legal norm as a standard that ought to be observed by himself and others. However, unlike the bad man, Hart does not suggest that the victim is 'bad' as a result of this failure. Rather, the victim sees her situation clearly when she rejects law's normative authority.

Postema explains that, like the bad man, 'victims ignore the law at their peril'.[62] Postema argues that Hart's victim represents a class of 'persons to whom

[56] ibid 193.
[57] ibid.
[58] ibid.
[59] ibid 240.
[60] ibid 201.
[61] ibid 200. There are many additional examples of law's victims. For a discussion of the way in which racism pervades the American legal system, see A Karakastanis, 'The Punishment Bureaucracy: How to Think about Criminal Justice Reform' (2019) *Yale Law Journal Forum* 857. For a discussion of the pressing problems that Brasil's legal system, see T Bustamante, RMR Queiroz and EPN Meyer, 'Illiberalism in Brazil: from Antiestablishmentarianism to Bolsonarism' in A Sajo, S Holmes and R Uitz (eds), *The Routledge Handbook on Illiberalism* (Routledge, forthcoming).
[62] Postema (n 3) 330.

law does not extend even minimal protections against force and fraud and the exploitation of universal human vulnerabilities, but who, nevertheless, are fully subject to law's demands and burdens'.[63] Legal norms do not present themselves as intelligible reasons for actions to the victim, but as a set of unjustified acts of arbitrary power. The victim's tragic situation forces her to navigate the world in a strategic fashion. Postema is correct to state that 'If the "victims" have even the vaguest sense of the realities they face, they will find it extraordinarily difficult to regard the forces arrayed against them as anything other than utterly and irredeemably arbitrary.'[64] This does not mean that the use of state power is unpredictable; it simply means that the law meets the victim in the form of illegitimate power. From the victim's perspective, law is the gunman writ large.

A Hartian might object: Why does this matter? After all, Hart is interested in identifying the existence conditions for legality. Why does it matter *why* people obey, as long as enough people obey for a system to exist. Notice, however, that when we are focused on the existence conditions of legality as Hart presents them, the perspective of the committed participant is marginalised (if not wholly irrelevant). It is not clear that the existence conditions of legality can co-exist with Hart's account of the importance of the committed participant: the two claims seem to fit together with ease insofar as we assume that Hart is able to merely describe the features of legality as he claims. One sign that the Hartian puzzle does not cohere is the fact that here in chapter 9, the reader is offered an account of law's normativity – an account that legal philosophers appear to have wholly overlooked.

A clear but underdeveloped account of law's authority emerges from this discussion of the victim class: law offers authoritative reasons for action for participants *only if* the legal system secures basic protections for its subjects. Hart has identified the pre-conditions that must be secured if law's ability to give us authoritative reasons for action is to be realised: the source of law's authority derives, at least in part, from its ability to protect us from each other; the scope of law's authority extends only as far as these protections. Again, legal norms are not authoritative reasons for action for the victim, because the victim is not living within the system of 'mutual forbearances' that law is supposed to secure for its subjects.[65] While there may be other additional requirements for law to enjoy authority (I identify one more below), Hart's discussion of the victim makes it clear that the law sacrifices its authority if it fails in its ability to offer minimum protections.

Notice, also, that implicit in Hart's comments about the victim is a version of a social contract: the law offers authoritative reasons for action if and only

[63] ibid 340.
[64] ibid.
[65] I recognise that this is not language Hart would use, but it is what is implied by Hart's discussion of the 'victim'.

if it secures fundamental protections; an individual should accord legal norms authority in practical deliberations if the individual has received these particular benefits of the system. This, of course, is a Hobbesian take on authority. This is not a coincidence since Hart nods in the direction of Hobbes in this chapter of *The Concept of Law*.[66] The point, of course, is not that Hart's account is radically new, but that it is an account that is antithetical to Hart's stated methodological and substantive commitments. The fact that the victim might label the norms in question 'law' means little once we recognise that, if the victim's perspective was universalised, one would be hard-pressed to see law as a potentially legitimate enterprise that is different from the gunman writ large. Near the outset of *The Concept of Law*, Hart insists that legal systems are fundamentally different from the gunman writ large.[67] While Hart does not defend this claim in this early chapter (and has been criticised for this failure),[68] he does offer an answer at this juncture. Hart is offering readers a normative claim about what the law quintessentially *is*.

Notice that Hart's account of law's authority assumes that law's normative authority is piecemeal: the *same* norms may provide authoritative reasons for action for some participants but not others. It is not the content of the law that is in focus at this juncture, but the failure of the law to secure basic protections for *all* citizens. The laws in question may have morally acceptable content, but the norms will still reach the victim as a set of arbitrary dictates. Consequently, the very same norms will have normative authority in reference to some classes of individuals but not others. Put differently, law's fundamental function is to establish a system of mutual forbearances, and only when law fulfils this fundamental function will it offer its subjects reasons for action. Hart's account of law's moral authority, found in chapter 9, is grounded in a particular vision of what law does and how it does it.[69]

Now we are in a position to identify the moral judgment that runs through Hart's *Concept of Law*. Consider Hart's victim, once again. Hart is not telling us how actual victims always respond to the law – he has not carried out an empirical investigation. Hart is telling us how victims *ought* to respond to legal norms (actual victims may or may not respond in this way). Again, the point is that Hart is making a moral judgment: victims are not granted basic protections, hence they should not recognise law's authority. In contradistinction, Hart is implying that the committed participant *does* enjoy the basic protections that law is uniquely positioned to secure. We know this precisely because his committed participant is *not* a victim.

[66] Hart (n 1) 191.
[67] ibid 20–25.
[68] See Simmonds (n 43) 610.
[69] I defend a similar claim about Raz's account. See Martin (n 15) ch 7. (I, once again, side with Postema.)

This point becomes clearer when Hart offers readers more insight into the thought process of the committed participant following his discussion of the victim. Not only does Hart assume that the committed participant 'accepts' norms in a system that offers her basic protections; Hart also assumes that the content of the laws in question is morally acceptable (or at least not morally unacceptable). Hart explains:

> Those who accept the authority of a legal system look upon it from the internal point of view, and express their sense of its requirements in internal statements couched in the normative language which is common to both law and morals: 'I (You) ought', 'I (he) must', 'I (they) have a legal obligation'. Yet they are not thereby committed to a *moral* judgment that it is morally right to do what the law requires. No doubt if nothing else is said, there is a presumption that any one who speaks in these ways of his or others' legal obligations, does not think that there is any moral or other reason against fulfilling them. This, however, does not show that nothing can be acknowledged as legally obligatory unless it is accepted as morally obligatory.[70]

In this passage, Hart insists on the separation of legal and moral judgment on the part of the citizen: when the committed citizen tells us what, legally, ought to be done, she is not also telling us what, morally, ought to be done. It is not clear, however, that citizens use 'ought' in a strictly legal sense (Holmes, as I have suggested, may offer a more plausible account of how people tend to reason with rules). But there is a more significant point worth noting. Hart has made an important concession in this passage: he acknowledges that the committed participant does not think that 'there is a moral or other reason against fulfilling' her legal obligations. Hart appears to assume that the content of the law that the committed participant has internalised is *not* morally worrisome. It is now clear that Hart is assuming that there are least two pre-conditions that must be satisfied before citizens should accept law's authority: first, the content must be morally acceptable (or at least not morally reprehensible); second, the law must secure basic protections for its subjects. In other words, both the legal norm in question and the legal system more generally must be relatively good if the law is to furnish its subjects with authoritative reasons for action.

These same assumptions are found elsewhere in Hart's writings. Remember that Hart wholeheartedly and consistently rejects the proposition that citizens are bound to follow the law because it is the law. Rather, Hart worries that citizens will obey morally questionable laws simply because they assume that law enjoys some kind of moral authority:

> What surely is most needed in order to make men clear-sighted in confronting the official abuse of power, is that they should preserve the sense that the certification of something as legally valid is not conclusive of the question of obedience, and that, however great the aura of majesty or authority which the official system may have, its demands must in the end be submitted to moral scrutiny.[71]

[70] Hart (n 1) 203.
[71] ibid 210.

One of the virtues of legal positivism, according to Hart, is its ability to encourage a posture of critical reflection that is necessary if the unjust laws are going to be met with resistance. When faced with morally questionable laws, it is wise to assess the content of the law before deciding how to act. Legal positivism reminds us that laws are made by humans and humans are fallible. On Hart's account, citizens can happily internalise relatively good norms in relatively good systems, but he is warning all of us about the dangers of internalising morally bad norms in any system. It is now clear why Hart's committed participant is not particularly reflective: Hart is not worried about her, because Hart has assumed she is exhibiting the attitude of acceptance in reference to morally acceptable laws in a morally acceptable society. It is crucial to see that this is the same moral judgment that informs Hart's *Concept of Law*.

This point is placed in relief when we once again compare the position of the committed participant to that of the victim. The committed participant is not in the position of the victim; consequently, the law offers her authoritative reasons for action that she is wise to recognise. Unlike the victim, the committed participant enjoys the basic protections that the legal system provides; and unlike the victim, she is not singled out as a potential target for the use of state-sanctioned force. Hence, when the committed participant internalises legal norms, she behaves in exactly the way Hart believes someone in her position ought to behave: she benefits from law's protections and, consequently, she correctly recognises law's reason-giving authority and acts accordingly. In other words, Hart does not worry about the fact that the committed participant has internalised law's demands: he is assuming that this is precisely what she morally ought to do given both the nature of the legal system that she is inhabiting and the nature of the laws that she has internalised. The assumptions are neither identified nor defended, but they nevertheless inform Hart's discussion throughout.

It is now clear why Hart favours the committed participant over all others. First, only the committed participant treats legal norms as Hart believes they *should* be treated: the legal system has secured basic protections for him, so he correctly treats legal norms as authoritative reasons for action.[72] In other words, Hart has a conception of law's proper function operating in the background of the *Concept of Law*, and the committed participant is the embodiment of this function. Second, Hart maintains that the very existence of the legal system requires the voluntary cooperation of many if not most of law's subjects – this is what creates '*authority*'.[73] Hart is not clear whether he means *de facto* authority

[72] This point re-enforces Finnis's well-known criticism of Hart: Finnis argues that the same trajectory of thought that leads Hart to focus upon the internal point of view should lead him to focus upon the viewpoint of the fully reasonable agent who sees the basis of law's moral authority. See Finnis (n 22) 13–16.

[73] Hart (n 1) 201.

or legitimate authority, but it now appears that he is probably referring to both. The key point at this juncture is that the committed participant internalises law's demands and, by doing so, she helps to maintain the system that benefits her. Law is underpinned by reciprocal obligations that must be undertaken by both the state and its citizenry.

We can now see Hart's version of the 'bad man' is a *bad* man: he is bad because he benefits from the system of mutual forbearances, but he fails to treat legal norms as authoritative reasons for action. He is a free-rider. Likewise, Hart's 'malefactor' is a morally problematic figure for a similar reason: instead of accepting law's demands, he chooses to play a disruptive, subversive role. Like the bad man, the malefactor fails to recognise law's authority even though the legal system has furnished him with a set of intelligible, authoritative reasons for action. The failure of both the bad man and the malefactor to act as they should is a moral failure: they live in relatively good legal systems but they choose to behave badly. They are enjoying law's benefits while attempting to escape from its burdens. This matters because the stability of the system depends on sufficient 'buy-in', and they are not buying in even though they are enjoying the many benefits of life under law.

There is another lesson buried in Hart's discussion of the victim. The gunman writ large, as it turns out, can exist *within* a given legal system. Hart has inadvertently located the distinction between the existence of legality and the rule of arbitrary power *within* a given legal system. More importantly still, the ideal of the rule of law threatens to wholly negate Hart's descriptive account of legality. What if most of law's subjects are victims? Is this still a legal system? The answer appears to be 'no'. Again, in order for law to rule, it must secure a minimum set of protections for its subjects; in order for law to rule, it must not be clearly immoral.[74] This account does not cohere with Hart's own concept of law: when Hart lists the elements of his concept of law, he leaves open the possibility that most citizens may obey out of fear.[75] However, if law only offers us reasons for action for subjects outside of the victim class, it is far from clear that an oppressive state would qualify as a full-fledged legal system, even if it has all the institutional trappings of legality. Consequently, it is no longer clear that the citizens living in constant fear and subjugation are themselves ruled by law. If the system is one where fear is the dominant response to authority, the system itself may be best thought of as a gunman writ large (ie its subjects are mostly 'victims'), even if it has the formal trappings of legality as identified by Hart (ie the union of primary and secondary rules, including a rule of recognition). In other words, if we take Hart's discussion of the victim seriously, and I believe

[74] Of course, Hart expressly rejects this position in 'Positivism and the Separation of Law and Morals' (1958) 71 *Harvard Law Review* 593.

[75] Hart (n 1) 116. According to Hart, '[t]here are two minimum conditions necessary and sufficient for the existence of a legal system', which are as follows: (i) the union of primary and secondary rules, including a rule of recognition; (ii) obedience by most of the population. They may obey 'from any motive whatsoever', including fear.

that we must, then the ideal of the rule of law and questions about the nature of law cannot be disentangled, as positivists, including Hart, suppose.

There are other implications for Hart's account of law that are now visible. For instance, it is no longer obvious that coercion can (or should) be excluded from his theory. Hart excludes coercion from his concept of law, presumably, because he has opted to focus on the reason-giving nature of law *in isolation*. In other words, the reason for the exclusion of coercion has to do with a judgment about the way in which law quintessentially guides conduct: law gives reasons for action; only those who adopt the external perspective (ie the bad man) see law through the lens of the threat of coercion.

However, it is now apparent that if law is going to fulfil the reason-giving role that Hart assigns it, the coercive power of the state must be used in the morally right way. This means that the proper use of coercion by the state is *not* conceptually separate from law's ability to give its subjects reasons for action. Coercion must be used by the state to secure a system of mutual forbearances if law's reason-giving potential is to be realised. Indeed, it is now evident that the morally proper use of coercion is a pre-condition for the possibility of having law at all. Coercion is not just needed to keep the 'bad man' in line; it is needed to allow all citizens to realise any goods of their choosing, including, but not limited to, survival. The proper use of coercion is not simply a means to achieving ends like cooperation or coordination; rather, it is constitutive of the realisation of such goods in complex modern societies. In short, coercion is not peripheral; rather, it is at the very centre of the concept of law on offer in Hart's *Concept of Law*. A failure to use force in the right way transforms legal norms into a set of morally illegitimate rules that reach the citizen as a set of arbitrary demands.[76]

The temptation to sever this seemingly marginal discussion from Hart's canonical work should be resisted given that this will hide, but not solve, the problem. The moral judgment that underpins Hart's discussion of the victim also underpins his discussion of the committed participant. There is, so to speak, no exit. Postema is right to claim that Hart has misdirected the discipline; he is also right to direct us back to the well-trodden path of old. Jurisprudence is practical philosophy, after all.

[76] Also see K Himma, 'A Comprehensive Hartian Theory of Legal Obligation: Social Pressure, Coercive Enforcement, and the Legal Obligations of Citizens' in W Waluchow and S Sciaraffa (eds), *The Nature of Law* (Oxford University Press 2013) 152–82.

10

Analytic Jurisprudence in Time

DAN PRIEL

I. INTRODUCTION

Friedrich Nietzsche had this to say about philosophers:

> You ask me which of the philosophers' traits are really idiosyncrasies? For example, their lack of historical sense, their hatred of the very idea of becoming, their Egypticism. They think that they show their *respect* for a subject when they de-historicize it, *sub specie aeterni* – when they turn it into a mummy. All that philosophers have handled for thousands of years have been concept-mummies; nothing real escaped their grasp alive. When these honorable idolators of concepts worship something, they kill it and stuff it; they threaten the life of everything they worship. Death, change, old age, as well as procreation and growth, and to their minds objections – even refutations. Whatever has being does not become; whatever becomes does not have being.[1]

Rather than take offence, many philosophers these days will consider Nietzsche's words a compliment. Bernard Williams reported on a fellow philosopher who had told him that 'the history of philosophy is no more part of philosophy than the history of science is part of science'.[2] In a similar vein, Tom Sorell observed that 'the techniques and predilections of analytic philosophy are not only unhistorical but anti-historical'.[3] The majority of Anglophone legal philosophers

[1] F Nietzsche, 'Twilight of the Idols: Or, How One Philosophizes with a Hammer' in *The Portable Nietzsche*, ed and tr Walter Kaufmann (first pub 1888, Viking 1954) 463, 479–80 (III, §1). Incidentally, one of Nietzsche's illustrations of how concepts 'become' rather than 'are' dealt with a legal example: punishment. See F Nietzsche, *On the Genealogy of Morals*, tr D Smith (first pub 1887, Oxford University Press 1996) 44–53.

[2] B Williams, 'Philosophy as a Humanistic Discipline' (2000) 75 *Philosophy* 477, 486.

[3] T Sorell, 'Introduction' in T Sorell and GAJ Rogers (eds), *Analytic Philosophy and History of Philosophy* (Oxford University Press 2005) 1, 1. Both Williams and Sorell challenged this view. For a moderate endorsement of this ahistoricist conception of philosophy, see T Williamson, *Doing Philosophy: From Common Curiosity and Logical Reasoning* (Oxford University Press 2019) 105. Interestingly, Williamson calls this philosophical practice 'Oxford-style' (ibid 100). This approach fits nicely within what I consider elsewhere the dominant approach to philosophy at Oxford, which has had much influence on legal philosophy in the English speaking world. See D Priel, 'Evidence-Based Jurisprudence: An Essay for Oxford' [2019] 2 *Analisi e Diritto* 87.

are no different. HLA Hart once wrote that '[a]nalytical and historical inquiries provide answers to different questions not different answers to the same questions'.[4] Sixty years later Andrei Marmor expressed a similar sentiment when he wrote, '[t]he motivation for claiming that *P* is one thing, and the truth of *P* is another. The former is the business of intellectual historians. Philosophy should be interested in truth.'[5]

Ignoring history, you might say, is exactly what gives philosophy its raison d'être, it is precisely what distinguishes the philosophical study of social institutions from all others. Indeed, to the extent that legal philosophers should seek to identify the features that all laws necessarily have,[6] history looks like a distraction. This is not meant to denigrate either method or form of inquiry, just to say that they are different and broadly independent of each other. Legal theorists and legal historians (including historians of jurisprudence) should therefore go on pursuing their valuable interests without caring much about the others' work. For quite some time, this has been, I think, the dominant view.[7]

But can philosophers of law really insulate their inquiries from law's history, from the temporal element of law? And should they? Is there any basis for thinking that the philosophy of law may be different on this score from some other areas of philosophy? Despite the dominance of the ahistorical approach, several legal philosophers have been critical of the almost complete separation between the two inquiries.[8] Few have thought about these questions harder than Gerald Postema, who explored this question in different ways both in his work

[4] HLA Hart, 'Introduction' in J Austin, *The Province of Jurisprudence Determined*, ed HLA Hart (first pub 1832, Weidenfeld & Nicolson 1954) vii, xv.

[5] A Marmor, *Philosophy of Law* (Princeton University Press 2011) 118.

[6] A view defended, among others, in J Raz, *The Authority of Law: Essays on Law and Morality* (2nd edn, Oxford University Press 2009) 104; L Green, 'Jurisprudence for Foxes' (2012) 3 *Transnational Legal Theory* 150, 157–58.

[7] See G Samuel, 'Science, Law and History: Historical Jurisprudence and Modern Legal Theory' (1990) 41 *Northern Ireland Legal Quarterly* 1, 2 ('The modern view is, on the whole, that history itself cannot provide a philosophy of law'); AT Kronman, 'Precedent and Tradition' (1990) 99 *Yale Law Journal* 1029, 1058 ('Professional philosophy … grants the past no more authority than chemistry and physics do, and like them insists that its own accomplishments be judged solely in accordance to the timeless criterion of truth.').

[8] Jeremy Waldron, for example, reported that some think the ahistoricity of jurisprudence is 'a good thing: it means we can study the problems of legal philosophy directly, undistracted by a purely antiquarian interest in the history of ideas'. But Waldron criticised such views as leading to discussions that are 'flat and repetitive'. See J Waldron, 'Legal and Political Philosophy' in JL Coleman and SJ Shapiro (eds), *The Oxford Handbook of Jurisprudence and Philosophy of Law* (Oxford University Press 2002) 352, 381 (hereinafter *Oxford Handbook*). Outside the world of analytic jurisprudence, this criticism has been more common. See, eg, B Edgeworth, 'Legal Positivism and the Philosophy of Language: A Critique of HLA Hart's Descriptive Sociology' (1986) 6 *Legal Studies* 115, 125; MJ Horwitz, 'Why Is Anglo-American Jurisprudence Unhistorical?' (1997) 17 *Oxford Journal of Legal Studies* 551, 564–65. For a recent attempt by a socio-legal scholar to revive historical jurisprudence, see BZ Tamanaha, *A Realistic Theory of Law* (Cambridge University Press 2017) chs 1, 4.

on general jurisprudence and in his work explicating the philosophy of the common law and that of the common law's greatest hater, Jeremy Bentham.[9]

I aim to explore some of these questions in this chapter, partly by engaging in Postema's work on this topic. But the chapter pays tribute to his work in another way. Though he sees himself as a philosopher and not a historian of ideas, Postema's work shows more sensitivity than is common in most contemporary legal philosophy to the historically-situated nature of philosophical work. What he did in relation to Matthew Hale and Jeremy Bentham, I aspire to do in this chapter with respect to aspects of twentieth-century jurisprudence. Because contemporary legal philosophy is written in a self-consciously ahistorical style, it invites an ahistorical assessment of its products. This chapter seeks to contribute to a better historical understanding of analytic jurisprudence itself by tying its emergence to a particular intellectual climate. Finally, this chapter also turns to the history of philosophy to trace the origins of some popular jurisprudential ideas. Just as Postema has shown that, contrary to prevailing belief among legal philosophers, the idea of law as command was not invented by Thomas Hobbes,[10] I want to show that some well-known jurisprudential ideas have a long history outside of jurisprudence. To that end, I show (with the aid of what may be an unseemly large number of block quotations) just how similar are some of the views expressed within analytic jurisprudence to ideas we encounter, sometimes centuries earlier, in other areas of philosophy. This serves yet another goal, one reflected in the title of this volume, that of seeing the connections between legal philosophy and some of the central questions in other areas of philosophy.[11]

II. JURISPRUDENCE AS A PROGRESSIVE SCIENCE

To some of Hart's admirers, his most important contribution to jurisprudence has not been any of his central substantive ideas but the way he oriented jurisprudence towards analytic philosophy and (for lack of a better term) its ethos.[12]

[9] I express my appreciation for Postema's contribution to the study of Bentham in D Priel, 'Bentham's Public Utilitarianism and Its Jurisprudential Significance' (forthcoming).

[10] See GJ Postema, 'Law as Command: The Model of Command in Modern Jurisprudence' (2001) 11 *Philosophical Issues* 470, 470–75.

[11] Showing that serves an additional purpose. I have complained elsewhere about the isolationism of contemporary legal philosophy. See Priel (n 3) 98–109. One way of demonstrating this isolation is by showing how unaware are legal philosophers of the origins of jurisprudential ideas they treat as path breaking.

[12] See, eg, LJ Green and B Leiter, Letter to the Editor, 'H.L.A. Hart and "The Concept of Law"' *Times Literary Supplement* (London, 11 March 2005) 15, 15 ('[Hart] … transformed the discipline of jurisprudence. What had been a dilettantish pastime for law teachers and retired judges, an undisciplined jumble of history, speculative sociology, legal doctrine and party politics, became technical and rigorous branch of philosophy.'); J Murphy and JL Coleman, *Philosophy of Law: An Introduction* (rev edn, Westview 1990) 26–27.

Hilary Putnam captured well that ethos, especially around the middle of the twentieth century, the time Hart was making his most influential contributions:

> (1) Analytical philosophy is nonideological, which means above all that it is nonpolitical and nonmoralizing. (2) Analytical philosophy consists of piecemeal problem solving. … (3) Analytical philosophy for a long time regarded value theory as second-class philosophy, and a concern with literature, the arts, culture, and the history of culture as at best optional for an analytical philosopher (although this has begun to change as a result of the publication of John Rawls's *A Theory of Justice* …).[13]

There can be little doubt that at least in the English-speaking world, it was Hart's work more than anyone else's that gave the impetus for aligning jurisprudence with developments in twentieth-century philosophy, making jurisprudence almost synonymous with legal *philosophy*. And indeed, the central features of analytic philosophy that Putnam identified are also an excellent summary of Hart's conception of jurisprudence: Hart stated that his inquiry is 'general and descriptive',[14] which he took to be morally and politically neutral. Hart also embraced the idea of piecemeal progress: In an interview he gave late in his life, he was explicit that analytic philosophy 'is suspicious of grand theory if it comes along too soon and obscures valuable distinctions',[15] and that he himself 'had no part in that sort of thing'.[16] Putnam's third point is also prominent in Hart's work. His most important work appeared in the two decades prior to the publication of *A Theory of Justice* and it generally avoided questions of value. Hart later stated that he thought that analysing law and politics using 'so far as possible a morally neutral vocabulary … [to be] the sane and healthy centre' of legal positivism.[17]

It may be a measure of Hart's enormous impact on the field that Putnam's three characteristics remain dominant in contemporary jurisprudence, often presupposed rather than defended. So understood, legal philosophy (like much of philosophy more generally) is in *one* important sense modelled after the natural sciences: in terms of its aims, it seeks to provide an accurate description of what law is; in terms of its methodological aspirations, it is to be as value neutral as good science is.[18] Scientific inquiry, specifically about the nature of chemical substances, provides a good analogy for this approach to jurisprudence.

[13] H Putnam, 'Convention: A Theme in Philosophy' (1981) 13 *New Literary History* 1, 10–11.

[14] See HLA Hart, *The Concept of Law* (3rd edn, Oxford University Press 2012) 239.

[15] See 'Hart Interviewed: HLA Hart in Conversation with David Sugarman' (2005) 32 *Journal of Law and Society* 267, 290.

[16] ibid 292; *contra* L Green, 'Introduction' in Hart (n 14) xv, xlvii.

[17] See HLA Hart, *Essays on Bentham: Studies in Jurisprudence and Political Theory* (Clarendon Press 1982) 28; D Priel, 'The Place of Legitimacy in Legal Theory' (2011) 57 *McGill Law Journal* 1, 14–18.

[18] It is important to stress that jurisprudence is modelled after science only in these specific senses. In other senses, much contemporary jurisprudence remains staunchly resistant to the influence of the natural sciences. See D Priel, 'Jurisprudence Between Science and the Humanities' (2012) 4 *Washington University Jurisprudence Review* 269, 301–07. The present chapter aims to make sharper the tension within this ambivalent attitude toward science.

Gold can be shaped in different ways (coins, rings, bullion); the cultural significance of gold has also changed throughout history. But underneath these differences there remains the essence of gold, unchanging throughout history, and completely independent of human knowledge of it.

The progressive-science model of jurisprudence adopts the same view with respect to law. Underneath the superficial differences that distinguish one law or legal system from others, there is a fundamental, unchanging core; and this unchanging core is unaffected by misconceptions, no matter how commonly held. If there is, for example, a necessary connection between law and morality, that remains the case even if all humans think otherwise. By the same token, biographical data on Hobbes or Bentham, or contextual information about debates they had with their contemporaries, bear as much relevance to jurisprudence as the question whether an apple fell on Newton's head or whether Galileo dropped two cannon balls from a tower in Pisa has to the truth of gravity.

This approach has a similar response to legal change. It is not that laws, or even that prevailing ideas about law, do not change. Rather, the thought is that underneath these changes, there is a single, unchanging nature that law in all times and places possesses, one that exists, as it were, outside of time and space. On this view, the most significant sense in which time figures in jurisprudential inquiry is that different scholars work to discover the nature of one object by exploring some questions pursued by their predecessors, on whose answers they hope to build. Thus, John Austin and Jeremy Bentham pointed out errors in then-prevailing natural law theories, Hart improved on Austin and Bentham by correcting their errors and so on. Progress in this kind of inquiry is attained by adopting a problem-solving, knowledge-accumulating inquiry, one in which the bigger picture about law is generated out of solutions to smaller questions such as what an obligation, a right or a duty are.

This model of inquiry explains why legal philosophers are generally uninterested in the history of law: They focus on the timeless, whereas historians are interested in change. It also explain legal philosophers' lack of interest in the history of jurisprudence. No one denies the genius of Newton or Darwin or their epoch-making contributions to physics and biology, but these days scientists do not turn to them for answers to open questions in physics or biology, because physical and biological knowledge has progressed far beyond them. Their insights have been accepted and added to the store of knowledge, built upon, and in important respects also superseded and corrected. Similarly, on the model of philosophy as a progressive science, philosophers today know more and have advanced far beyond Hobbes, Hume, Bentham or Kant, so there is relatively little to learn from them that could assist in addressing contemporary debates.[19]

[19] See LD d'Almeida, 'Book Review' (2015) 78 *Modern Law Review* 699, 707 ('What matters is whether there is philosophical progress to be made by working on [the ideas of earlier thinkers] … [Legal philosophers] are concerned with the same thing Raz is concerned with. They are concerned with getting things right.'). See also text to n 5.

Thus, in the course of defending such a conception of legal philosophy, John Gardner rhetorically asked, 'Why tackle today's problems, the possibly transient concerns of the early twenty-first century, at the expense of the timeless problems that were also of interest to Plato, Confucius, and Maimonides?'[20] But if one wonders why the writings of Confucius, Maimonides (and even Plato) are so rarely discussed in contemporary jurisprudence, the progressive-science approach has a ready response. On the 'timeless questions' that legal philosophy deals with, there has been so much advance since the days of ancient philosophers that there is not much to gain from reading them. Looking at their work may serve a pedagogical purpose, it may help in avoiding some pitfalls,[21] but not much else.

To be sure, one still finds occasional references to historical figures, but there is little interest in reading them in the context of the intellectual debates of their day. To the extent that we should care about what they wrote, it is for their ability to contribute to contemporary debates.[22] As a result, to the extent that we encounter jurisprudential history in most contemporary work, it is a simplistic history in which whole centuries are reduced to a few sentences.[23]

To proponents of this view, the only minor concession to history seems to be the acknowledgement that the *practice* of jurisprudence (and philosophy more generally) is the product of changes in the interests of their audiences. This means some questions will be explored in certain times but not in others, and may make what counts as a good explanation of law relative to a time and a place, but 'there is nothing in the relativity of good explanations to their public to threaten the non-relativity of truth'.[24]

[20] J Gardner, *Law as a Leap of Faith: Essays on Law in General* (Oxford University Press 2012) 297, fn 75.

[21] It is common to find contemporary scholars discussing the works of John Austin in order to learn from his mistakes. See SJ Shapiro, *Legality* (Harvard University Press 2011) 59 (despite its many errors 'Austin's theory of law presents us with a tremendous learning opportunity'). Of course, Hart used Austin's ideas for a similar purpose, and he was not even the first to do so. See HF Jolowicz, *Lectures on Jurisprudence*, ed JA Jolowicz (Cambridge University Press 1963) 15 (based on lectures delivered between 1924 and 1948) ('[Austin's] theories represent a very definite and clear conception which, in outline at least, is easy to grasp … Austin's doctrine forms a very good target – we must set it up and see it clearly in order to throw bricks at it').

[22] Bernard Williams (n 2) 478, described the view as asking us 'to read something by Plato "as though it had come out in *Mind* last month"'. Williams criticised this view, which he associated with the 'heyday of confidence in what has been called the "analytic history of philosophy"'.

[23] cf H Kelsen, 'The Pure Theory of Law: Its Methods and Fundamental Concepts' (1934) 50 *Law Quarterly Review* 474, 483–84 (a brief narrative of jurisprudential progress, in which natural law was replaced with positivist theory, then refined by Kelsen's pure theory of law).

[24] J Raz, *Between Authority and Interpretation* (Oxford University Press 2009) 57–58; see also J Dickson, 'The Central Questions of Legal Philosophy' (2003) 56 *Current Legal Problems* 63, 85–90. Like Raz, Dickson insists that this view does not challenge the enterprise 'understanding the nature of law by identifying and explaining its essential [ie timeless] properties': ibid 90.

III. JURISPRUDENCE AS INTERPRETATION OF A SOCIAL PRACTICE

Not everyone agrees with the view of philosophy as a progressive science. In section II, I quoted Putnam's description of the central features of analytic philosophy in the 1950s and 1960s. A decade or so after Putnam wrote these words, a new understanding of philosophy (re-)emerged:

> There is a consensus, at least among [the] select group of philosophers [who contributed to *Philosophy in History*], that the discipline of philosophy as recently practiced in the Anglo-American context has been much too narrow in scope and outrageously pretentious and anachronistic in its claims. It has focused on obscure linguistic and logical issues tied to the epistemological project of articulating the conditions of certain knowledge, defined these issues as the eternal questions of philosophy, and reconstructed the history of philosophy as successive attempts to answer these questions. The historical perspective is put into operation to reveal the historically contingent nature of this definition of philosophy and philosophical problems, to open up the discipline to a range of new questions (relating to the interpretation of meaning, ethics, and politics) as well as to methods for approaching and writing about such questions. At issue is not simply the revision and enrichment of the history of philosophy through the expansion of its canon of relevant thinkers and questions, but the reformulation of the nature of philosophy as a cultural activity. The conventional analytic distinction between the validity and the historical genesis of truth claims is rejected.[25]

Postema recently endorsed such a view when he wrote that 'philosophy [in general] is constitutionally *historical*'.[26] There is a weak and strong way of understanding this more historically-informed approach to the study of ideas. The weak version asserts that to comprehend what, say, Hobbes wrote, we should not think of him as engaged in debates that were hardly conceived of when he was writing.[27] In this weak version, even philosophers who think they are engaged in timeless questions, even those who think they are writing for the ages, are products of their age, and their works may be far more parochial than they are aware of. Thus, to understand Hobbes, we should pay attention to his actual debates with his contemporaries, not to conjectured debates with ours.

This mildly historicist view is still consistent with the idea that there is a core of fairly stable philosophical questions that philosophers have always been concerned with, as well as that law's nature remains constant. One needs to

[25] JE Toews, 'Intellectual History after the Linguistic Turn: The Autonomy of Meaning and the Irreducibility of Experience' (1987) 92 *American Historical Review* 879, 905. The book referred to in the quote is R Rorty et al (eds), *Philosophy in History: Essays on the Historiography of Philosophy* (Cambridge University Press 1984).

[26] GJ Postema, 'The Data of Jurisprudence' (2018) 95 *Washington University Law Review* 1083, 1088. Postema adds (ibid), 'The long tradition of philosophy is the tradition of engaging continually with its tradition, and this engagement of philosophy in its history is always philosophical, and hence resolutely critical.'

[27] See Q Skinner, *Visions of Politics: Regarding Method* (Cambridge University Press 2002) 59–61.

be better versed in the historical context in which particular theorists wrote to understand how past thinkers sought to answer these questions, but the questions remain enduring. So understood, this critique of timeless philosophy is rather limited. That is why it is better to understand the historicist critique as presenting a stronger challenge. It is not just that the *answers* philosophers offer are contextual, their *questions* and *object* are contextual too. It makes little sense to study Plato as if he is addressing contemporary philosophical concerns, because the questions and problems that past philosophers have addressed were the questions and problems of their time. In a famous critique of the timeless approach to the study of past thinkers, Quentin Skinner attacked the tendency to think of philosophical classics as concerned with 'timeless questions and answers', arguing that there are no 'perennial problems in philosophy'.[28] On the basis of a very similar foundation of Hart's work – the philosophy of language of Wittgenstein and JL Austin – Skinner has doubted the very possibility of 'trying definitely to fix the analysis of key moral terms.'[29] These different contexts and concerns suggest that the subject-matter of inquiry, despite being denoted with the same word, is not the same.

Now comes a surprise. For many of those who have supported the progressive-science conception of jurisprudence have also emphasised its 'hermeneutic' (in plainer English, 'interpretive') nature. This is surprising because a hermeneutic understanding of jurisprudence seems closer to the contextual inquiry considered here, and thus to push against the progressive-science model. To demonstrate this tension, I will make a detour to the philosophy of history, an area of philosophy not frequently discussed together with jurisprudence, but which I think bears important resemblance to some debates in jurisprudence, and one that is particularly pertinent in the context of examining the relationship between jurisprudence and time. This detour will show another benefit of greater familiarity with the history of philosophy, and the philosophy of history. As mentioned, the ahistorical conception of jurisprudence tends to be uninterested in the subject's own history. Consequently, *The Concept of Law* ends up being treated as a book that first mapped an uncharted land, nothing less than 'an authentic "Eureka!" moment in the history of ideas',[30] ignoring its own intellectual history.[31] Examining that reveals a book that is far less original than it is often taken to be. One aim of the ensuing discussion is that ideas treated as philosophical breakthroughs were familiar in other areas of philosophy when Hart wrote them.

[28] ibid 88. Q Skinner, 'Meaning and Understanding in the History of Ideas' (1969) 8 *History and Theory* 3, 5, 50. Skinner here was explicitly following Collingwood. On the significance of this point, see the discussion in text accompanying nn 35–39 below.

[29] See Skinner (n 27) 103, 177.

[30] J Gardner, 'Why Law Might Emerge: Hart's Problematic Fable' in LD d'Almeida et al (eds), *Reading HLA Hart's* The Concept of Law (Hart Publishing 2013) 81, 96.

[31] cf Dan Priel, 'HLA Hart and the Invention of Legal Philosophy' (2011) 5 *Problema* 301.

If one thinks of jurisprudence (as Kelsen did) as the science of norms, one that is in no way dependent on any psychological attitudes or any 'internal point of view', the disregard of the philosophy of history seems to make sense. But if one thinks of law as a social phenomenon, and jurisprudence as part of the effort of explaining it, then the connection with history and its philosophical study becomes more apparent. For history is the attempt to explain human actions, to describe historical processes; against this, the philosophy of history asks what constitutes a good explanation of these 'historical' events. Law involves human action, which jurisprudence tries to organise and explain. Methodological debates in jurisprudence then ask what constitutes a good explanation of these 'legal' events. So understood, jurisprudence and the philosophy of history can be seen as branches of the philosophy of social explanation. One particular question asked in both areas has to do with the applicability of explanatory methods and models derived from the natural sciences to human affairs.

This is the relevant intellectual backdrop for considering Hart's methodological insistence on the importance of accounting for the 'internal aspect' of human action. In the Preface to *The Concept of Law*, Hart wrote that the book could be understood as an essay in 'descriptive sociology'. And the proper way to do *that*, he wrote, requires recognising that 'neither law *nor any other form of social structure* can be understood without an appreciation of certain crucial distinctions between two different kinds of statement, which I have called "internal" and "external" and which can both be made whenever social rules are observed'.[32] As the italicised words make clear, Hart was here making a general claim about the explanation of all social phenomena. It is the inherent inadequacy of external explanations that led Hart to say a few decades later that the methods of the 'empirical sciences are useless' for explaining normative behaviour.[33]

Hart considered the 'internal point of view' the most important idea of *The Concept of Law*. Others concurred: Scott Shapiro, for example, described it as 'perhaps Hart's greatest contribution to jurisprudential theory'.[34] Historical context helps put this idea in its place. Writing some years before Hart, the Oxford philosopher and historian RG Collingwood had this to say of the task of the historian:

> The historian, investigating any event in the past, makes a distinction between what may be called the outside and the inside of an event. By the outside of the even I mean everything belonging to it which can be described in terms of bodies and their

[32] Hart (n 14) vi (emphasis added).

[33] HLA Hart, *Essays in Jurisprudence and Philosophy* (Clarendon Press 1983) 13.

[34] SJ Shapiro, 'The Bad Man and the Internal Point of View' in SJ Burton (ed), The Path of the Law *and Its Influence: The Legacy of Oliver Wendell Holmes, Jr* (Cambridge University Press 2000) 197, 197.

> movements … By the inside of the event I mean that in it which can only be described in terms of thought … [The historian's work] may begin by discovering the outside of an event, but it can never end there; he must always remember that the event was an action, and that his main task is to think himself into this action, to discern the thought of its agent. In the case of nature, this distinction between the outside and the inside of an event does not arise. The events of nature are mere events, not the acts of agents whose thought the scientist endeavours to trace.[35]

To anyone with even a passing familiarity with Anglophone jurisprudence of the last few decades, these words are bound to sound familiar, as will also be the following words:

> In thus penetrating to the inside of events and detecting the thought which they express, the historian is doing something which the scientist need not and cannot do. … [T]he historian need not and cannot (without ceasing to be an historian) emulate the scientist in searching for the causes or laws of events. For science, the event is discovered by perceiving it, and the further search for its cause is conducted by assigning to it its class and determining the relation between that class and others. For history, the object to be discovered is not the mere event, but the thought expressed in it. To discover that thought is already to understand it. After the historian has ascertained the facts, there is no further process of inquiring into their causes. When he knows what happened, he already knows why it happened … The cause of [an] event, for [a historian], means the thought in the mind of the person by whose agency the event came about: and this is not something other than the event, it is the inside of the event itself.[36]

Collingwood, like Hart after him, was trying to articulate the idea that to understand human action is to understand 'the thought in the mind' of the person who made it in terms of reasons for action. That is a classic statement of a humanistic conception of social explanation, concerned not with identifying some general laws of human behaviour, nor with predicting human action, but with 'the inside of events'. In both history and jurisprudence, this view has been the basis for challenges to attempts to align these disciplines with the natural sciences.

It is quite clear that Hart was familiar, at least indirectly, with Collingwood's views.[37] But the origins of the internal point of view are far older than that. The distinction between an internal and an external point of view, and the insistence of the importance of the former for the explanation of purposive human

[35] RG Collingwood, *The Idea of History* (Clarendon Press 1946) 213–14.

[36] ibid 214–15. Compare this to Hart's remarks on the explanation of human action in Hart (n 14) 88–90.

[37] Collingwood's views were further defended in W Dray, *Laws and Explanation in History* (Clarendon Press 1957) 124, 128, 130, 133; and PH Nowell-Smith, 'Are Historical Events Unique?' (1957) 57 *Proceedings of the Aristotelian Society* 107. Both sources are cited approvingly in HLA Hart and AM Honoré, *Causation in the Law* (Clarendon Press 1959) 8, fn 3.

behaviour can be traced to eighteenth-century German philosophy. Here is how a modern commentator summarised the ideas of Johann Gottfried Herder (1744–1803):

> [W]hat distinguishes human agency, so Herder argued, is its capacity for meaning, for which the use of language is crucial and no naturalistic, mechanical account of language is adequate to capture that sense of meaning. What we mean by words depends on an irreducible sense of normativity in their use, and our grasp of such normativity itself depends on our immersion in a way of life (a 'culture'), which functions as a background to all our more concrete uses of language. Since meaning and the expression of meaning is critical to understanding agency, and meaning is irreducibly normative, no third-person, purely objective understanding of agency is possible; one must understand both the agent's culture and the agent himself as an individual from the 'inside,' not from any kind of external, third-person point of view.[38]

Herder was one of the founders of the study of 'hermeneutics', the theory of interpretation of texts and, eventually, of all human action and history. These ideas were then taken up by others. Worthy of a longer discussion than I give him here is Wilhelm Dilthey (1833–1911). Dilthey is significant, because he serves as one possible link between German philosophy and Collingwood, and thus Oxford.[39] Dilthey is especially interesting because in his work he contrasted what he called 'explanatory psychology', whose methods and aspirations were borrowed from the natural sciences, with a different approach, which he called 'descriptive and analytic' psychology, which was the appropriate method for humanistic study.[40] Even if coincidental, the similarity between this and Hart's terminology for his own work as both descriptive sociology and analytic philosophy is noteworthy.

I do not suggest any stronger influence, as demonstrating that is always tricky. To the best of my knowledge, Hart never made any reference in his writings to the work of either Herder or Dilthey; and I am not claiming any unacknowledged borrowing on his part. I doubt that Hart would have found everything Herder or Dilthey wrote congenial. However, it is inescapable that Hart explicitly associated himself with a 'hermeneutic' approach.[41] Though he made the reference only quite late in his career, and possibly after seeing

[38] T Pinkard, *German Philosophy 1760–1860: The Legacy of Idealism* (Cambridge University Press 2002) 133. As Pinkard acknowledges, others have read Herder differently, but it suffices for my argument that others have read Herder in this way. Particularly relevant for my point in the text following is that Wilhelm Dilthey saw Herder as an ancestor. See K Gjesdal, 'Hermeneutics and the Human Sciences' in MN Forster and K Gjesdal (eds), *The Cambridge Companion to Hermeneutics* (Cambridge University Press 2019) 354, 364–66.

[39] Collingwood (n 35) 171–76, offers a short and largely sympathetic discussion of Dilthey.

[40] See W Dilthey, 'Ideas Concerning a Descriptive and Analytic Psychology' in *Descriptive Psychology and Historical Understanding*, trs RM Zaner and KL Heiges (Martinus Nijhoff 1977) 23, 53 ('Contrary to outer perception, inner perception rests on an inner awareness, a lived experience').

[41] See Hart (n 33) 13; see also ibid 162.

it in others' discussion of his work,[42] this was no accidental reference. It fits with ideas that we do know Hart was familiar with coming from the work of Wittgenstein (both directly and via the work of Peter Winch), as well as Max Weber and Collingwood.[43] (In section IV, I suggest another possible source for Hart's method.)

In somewhat different ways, these thinkers have distinguished between 'explanation' (*Erklären*), relevant for accounting for the natural world, and 'understanding' (*Verstehen*) as its equivalent in the domain of human thought.[44] One specific way in which the distinction between the social scientific and the hermeneutic methods of inquiry has been drawn was in terms of a categorical distinction between reasons and causes: the natural world was governed by causes, social reality was governed by reasons.[45] Consequently, many concluded that the attempt to use the methods of the natural sciences to explain human action was misconceived.

Hart made a few short but quite clear references to this distinction in *The Concept of Law*. There is a more elaborate discussion of this point in *Causation in the Law*, co-authored with Tony Honoré and published two years earlier. In that book, drawing explicitly on contemporary writings in the philosophy of history, Hart and Honoré argued that law, like history, is concerned with the explanation of human events, and more specifically with *particular* human events.[46] As such, they argued that human action cannot be explained in terms of general causal laws of the kind that we find in the natural sciences.

[42] See PMS Hacker, 'Hart's Philosophy of Law' in PMS Hacker and J Raz (eds), *Law, Morality, and Society: Essays in Honour of HLA Hart* (Clarendon Press, 1977) 1, 12; N MacCormick, *HLA Hart* (Edward Arnold 1981) 37–38.

[43] On Wittgenstein's links to German hermeneutics, see the brief remarks in PMS Hacker, *Wittgenstein: Connections and Controversies* (Oxford University Press 2001) 37, 57–58, 66 (arguing that Wittgenstein's later philosophy is committed to the 'autonomy of humanistic understanding against the illegitimate encroachment of the natural sciences'). Winch's Wittgenstein-influenced ideas on the social sciences are found in P Winch, *The Idea of a Social Science and Its Relation to Philosophy* (Routledge & Kegan Paul 1958), cited in Hart (n 14) 289, 297. On the connection between Hart and Weber, see H Ross, *Law as a Social Institution* (Hart Publishing 2001); see also BZ Tamanaha, 'The Internal/External Distinction and the Notion of a "Practice" in Legal Theory and Sociolegal Studies' (1995) 30 *Law and Society Review* 163, 186–88 (situating Hart within sociological debates on the internal/external point of view).

[44] See, eg, GH von Wright, *Explanation and Understanding* (Cornell University Press 1971) 4–7; cf Q Skinner, 'Hermeneutics and the Role of History' (1975) 7 *New Literary History* 209, 209–11.

[45] See, eg, AI Melden, *Free Action* (Routledge & Kegan Paul 1961) ch 14; AR Louch, *Explanation and Human Action* (University of California Press 1966); Dray (n 37); R Abelson, '"Because I Want to"' (1965) 73 *Mind* 540, 541, *passim*; JO Urmon, 'Motives and Causes' (1952) 26 *Proceedings of the Aristotelian Society Supplement* 179, 191–94. An exceptionally clear, brief exposition of this view appears in R Abelson, 'Book Review' (1963) 23 *Philosophy and Phenomenological Research* 616; cf Collingwood (n 35) 214 ('words like "cause" are [not] necessarily out of place in reference to history; [but] they are used there in a special sense').

[46] See Hart and Honoré (n 37) 8–9, 48–55.

Hart is not alone in associating jurisprudence with hermeneutics. After a heavily Kelsen-inspired (and quite clearly anti-hermeneutic) stage in his early work, Joseph Raz moved much closer to interpretivism, including drawing a link between jurisprudence and hermeneutics.[47] Raz argued that jurisprudence aimed at illuminating an aspect of human life by trying to 'advance our understanding of society by helping us understand how people understand themselves'.[48] He contrasted this form of explanation with the explanation of electrons, whose nature is independent of what people think about them. Once again, these ideas will sound familiar to those who know Collingwood's views on historical explanation, which he justified by the human desire for self-knowledge. 'Self-knowledge', he explained, does not mean knowledge of humans' 'bodily nature', nor does it mean knowledge of sensation and emotion (as such), but rather it is 'knowledge of [humans'] knowing faculties, [their] thought or understanding or reasons'.[49] This knowledge, Collingwood believed, could not be attained by imitating the methods of the natural sciences.[50]

It is time to return to the problem raised earlier. From a hermeneutic perspective, the separation between legal philosophy and legal history, and with it the search for timeless truths, looks suspect. The hermeneutic, internal approach has been a central plank of Herder's philosophy of history, and served him to argue that different nations and different cultures are fundamentally different, and that therefore they can only be understood by attending to their own self-understandings.[51] Since important social practices like law are bound with

[47] See Raz (n 24) 48, fn 5. Raz has in fact argued that Hart's rejection of the methods of the natural sciences did not go far enough. He attributed Hart's errors to his 'adherence to naturalism and empiricist epistemology, and his rejection of evaluative objectivity': ibid 52.

[48] J Raz, *Ethics in the Public Domain: Essays in the Morality of Law and Politics* (rev edn, Clarendon Press 1995) 237. And see further his remarks in Raz (n 24) 96–97, where he says that 'the way a culture understands its own practices and institutions is not separate from what they are'. See also L Green, 'The Concept of Law Revisited' (1996) 94 *Michigan Law Review* 1687, 1717 (the value of jurisprudential inquiry lies in 'help[ing] us understand our institutions and, through them, our culture'). Add to it that jurisprudential thought is part of that culture and the difficulties with timeless jurisprudence become evident. For comparison, substitute 'art' for 'law'.

[49] Collingwood (n 35) 205.

[50] See ibid.

[51] MN Forster, 'Introduction' in JG von Herder, *Philosophical Writings*, ed and tr MN Forster (Cambridge University Press 2002) vii, xiv–xv, xxv; I Berlin, *Three Critics of the Enlightenment: Vico, Hamann, Herder* (2nd edn, Princeton University Press 2013) 232–37. Consequently, according to Berlin's reading of Herder, '[p]articular words are used in communicating particular experiences as a result of … environmental factors … or of psychological ones; or of mere chance; or of the decisions of human beings, who acquiring some terms by 'natural' means … invent others as they please, arbitrarily. That is why the doctrine of real essences – the … plan of discovering the truth by the analysis of concepts – is a chimera' (ibid 192). Certain aspects of Berlin's interpretation of Herder have come under serious criticism. See, eg, J Israel, 'Foreword', ibid ix, xv; RE Norton, 'The Myth of the Counter-Enlightenment' (2007) 68 *Journal of the History of Ideas* 635, 644–50; but cf FC Beiser, *The German Historicist Tradition* (Oxford University Press 2011) 133 (describing 'Herder's critique of Enlightenment historiography'). But even Berlin's critics acknowledge that later scholars, especially Dilthey, accepted some of the views Berlin attributed to Herder. See Norton ('The Myth of the Counter-Enlightenment') 652.

different groups' culture and history, they are embedded in their particular historical context. And indeed, the central ideas of the German historical school of jurisprudence can be traced to Herder's writings about nation and national spirit.[52] In more modern parlance, we would speak of law as a product of, or at least imbued by, local culture, precisely what hermeneuticists have maintained an 'external', scientific perspective cannot adequately account for.

All this has profound significance for thinking about jurisprudence in time, since it is a central point of historical thinking from the internal point of view that it is wrong to seek law-like universal explanations of historical phenomena and ideas, and that it is wrong to think about concepts, practices, institutions and ideas outside time. Thus, to fully understand Roman law, one has to understand the particular cultural context in which it existed. And this goes beyond understanding the cultural significance of particular legal institutions that Roman law recognised (eg slavery). It goes to the way the Romans understood the idea of law and its place within the universe. If, for example, some form of natural law theory was dominant among Roman lawyers, this is not just a sociological observation, which we can judge as a mistaken belief about the timeless nature of law. Rather, we must try and understand how this fact figured in Romans' understanding and practice of law 'from the internal point of view'.

IV. RECONCILIATION?

The story so far: There is an 'official view' according to which history does not matter to jurisprudence, as the two are largely independent inquiries. But underneath it lurks a different story, where it seems history plays a more significant role. In describing Herder's thought, one commentator wrote that

> he takes relatively little interest in the 'great' political and military deeds and events of history, focusing instead on the 'innerness' of history's participants … Because of it, psychology and interpretation inevitably take center-stage in the discipline of history for Herder.[53]

Turning to our time, Collingwood's ideas served as the inspiration to many in the 'Cambridge school' of history of ideas, an approach that is most associated with the view that political ideas and concepts are embedded in their time.[54]

Given Hart's views on the necessity of adopting a very similar hermeneutic approach to jurisprudence, should the same not be true of jurisprudence? To put it plainly, it is not easy to see a way out of the tension between, on the one hand,

[52] See I Berlin, *Political Ideas in the Romantic Age: Their Rise and Influence on Modern Thought*, ed H Hardy (2nd edn, Princeton University Press 2014) 233–34; Beiser (n 51) 216–17.

[53] Forster (n 51) xxv.

[54] See Q Skinner, 'The Rise of, Challenge to and Prospects for a Collingwoodian Approach to the History of Political Thought' in D Castiglione and I Hampsher-Monk (eds), *The History of Political Thought in National Context* (Cambridge University Press 2001) 175, 175–77.

a commitment to a hermeneutic methodology, justified by the fact that law is a 'self-reflective activity', and, on the other hand, the claim that legal philosophy is fundamentally different from legal sociology, because it seeks to identify the universal and necessary features about law, which exist independently of people's attitudes.

Here is another way of demonstrating the tension. In presenting the progressive-science view of jurisprudence, I wrote in section II that that view is not 'that laws, or even that prevailing ideas about law, do not change. Rather, the thought is that underneath these changes, there is a single, unchanging nature that law in all times and places possesses, one that exists, as it were, outside of time and space.' These words keep the prevailing views about law completely separate from the nature of law itself. But if, as the hermeneutic approach suggests, the nature of law is *constituted* by attitudes about the practice, then the separation breaks down. In that case, it is far more difficult to think, substantively, that law has an unchanging nature; and methodologically, it is far more difficult to keep the philosophical search for law's unchanging nature separate from the sociological inquiry into changing attitudes about it.

Surprisingly, many legal philosophers have adopted these seemingly conflicting positions without acknowledging, let alone trying to resolve, their tension. They in effect hold that the attitudes that happen to be shared by all about law (assuming there are any) are also the ones that constitute the nature of law, even though stating so may require ignoring people's own views on law's essential features (which may change with time and place). One place where this tension comes to light is in the reactions of many legal philosophers to the work of Ronald Dworkin. While sharing with him the commitment to jurisprudence as a hermeneutic (interpretive) enterprise, critics nevertheless dismissed his work as not really jurisprudence. In their judgment, Dworkin's work was too local, too close to actual practice to count as philosophy.[55] And his view that jurisprudence is continuous with legal doctrine[56] was widely criticised as confused. But if legal philosophers take their commitment to a hermeneutic approach and the internal point of view as seriously as they proclaim, then Dworkin seems to have the upper hand. For in essence, Dworkin's critics are saying that legal philosophers should ignore those attitudes that do not fit their working assumption that law has a single nature.

Is there a way of avoiding these problems? In a book published just two years before *The Concept of Law*, Hart's friend and colleague, Peter Strawson, made some methodological remarks that might be read as offering a way of resolving the tension. In the opening pages of his book *Individuals: An Essay in*

[55] See J Dickson, *Evaluation and Legal Theory* (Hart Publishing 2001) 22–23 and fn 31; Gardner (n 20) 184. For similar reasons, one of Postema's essays was also singled out for holding a 'fundamentally anti-philosophical' stance: ibid 24 and fn 6.

[56] R Dworkin, *Law's Empire* (Harvard University Press 1986) 90. Dworkin openly acknowledged his allegiance with the German hermeneuticists: ibid 62, 419–20, note 2.

Descriptive Metaphysics, Strawson explained what he meant by his subtitle by drawing the following contrast: 'Descriptive metaphysics is content to describe the actual structure of our thought about the world, revisionary metaphysics is concerned to produce a better structure.'[57] In explaining how such a 'descriptive' inquiry is to be done, Strawson wrote that it begins with 'a close examination of the actual use of words', as it 'is the best, and indeed the only sure, way in philosophy.'[58] But because of the depth of the inquiry, he added, one must go beyond language. Linguistic practices, 'however revealing at a certain level, are apt to assume, and not to expose, those general elements of structure which the metaphysician wants revealed. The structure he seeks does not readily display itself on the surface of language, but lies submerged.'[59]

This is similar to the distinction legal philosophers draw between what they are doing (conceptual analysis) and linguistics.[60] But this does not resolve a different difficulty this approach faces, that of explaining 'conceptual change'. For even if we go beyond immediate linguistic practices, the possibility of deeper conceptual change remains open. Strawson readily acknowledged that concepts change, 'though mainly, on the specialist periphery'. Nevertheless,

> it would be a great blunder to think of metaphysics only in this historical style. For there is a massive central core of human thinking which has no history – or none recorded in histories of thought; there are categories and concepts which, in their most fundamental character, change not at all. Obviously these are not the specialities of the most refined thinking. They are the commonplaces of the least refined thinking; and are yet the indispensable core of the conceptual equipment of the most sophisticated human beings.[61]

Strawson's claim, if true, accepts that, in general, social phenomena must be understood in their particular context, and that normally that would imply that there are no universal explanations of most concepts referring to social institutions, only culturally-specific ones. At the same time, Strawson maintained that some exceptional concepts have 'no history', and therefore do not change.

[57] PF Strawson, *Individuals: An Essay in Descriptive Metaphysics* (Methuen 1959) 9. It is worth pointing out that Strawson thanked Hart for his comments on the manuscript: ibid 3. Hart, in turn, thanked Strawson in the Preface of *The Concept of Law* for his comments on his text. See Hart (n 14) vii. The connection between Strawson's project and Hart's was first noted in J Mikhail, '"Plucking the Mask of Mystery from Its Face": Jurisprudence and HLA Hart' (2007) 95 *Georgetown Law Journal* 733, 748.

[58] Strawson (n 57) 9; cf Hart (n 33) 2–4.

[59] Strawson (n 57) 10. Again, it is interesting to compare this work to Herder's idea, who wrote that in his conception of philosophy, 'metaphysics become[s] a philosophy of human language'. See JG Herder, 'Selections from *A Metacritique of the Critique of Pure Reason*' in JP Surber (ed), *Metacritique: The Linguistic Assault on German Idealism* (Humanity Books 2001) 89, 90 (emphasis omitted).

[60] See Raz (n 24) 53–6; KE Himma, 'Reconsidering a Dogma: Conceptual Analysis, the Naturalistic Turn, and Legal Philosophy' (2007) 10 *Current Legal Issues* 3, 10–11.

[61] Strawson (n 57) 10.

The argument now to be made on behalf of Hart and others seeking to combine essentialism with hermeneuticism is that law happens to be one of those concepts without history. Though he does not say so explicitly in the original text of *The Concept of Law*, in the posthumous remarks published as the Postscript to the book, Hart said just that: 'in spite of many variations in different cultures and in different times, [law] has taken the same general form and structure'.[62]

Admittedly, this remark is made in a different context, so it takes some interpretive licence to use it as a basis for extending Strawson's view to Hart. The bigger problem is that it is difficult to think of law as one of those concepts that have no history and that do not change. Law seems to fit better within Strawson's other category of concepts, that of the 'specialities' of refined thinking. For instance, the list of beliefs about law that Hart attributes to 'educated people' (so neatly matching the questions his book would later address) is in some ways representative of the law of a modern state, but does not fit other contexts, as Hart himself conceded when he discussed the law of pre-modern societies and international law.[63] This suggests that despite the superficial similarity between Strawson's descriptive metaphysics and Hart's descriptive jurisprudence, the attempt to rely on the former to solve the inherent tension in the latter does not work.

V. THREE CHALLENGES TO TIMELESS JURISPRUDENCE

This failed attempt at reconciliation leaves us where we were before, with what looks like an unresolvable tension at the heart of contemporary jurisprudence. In this section, I consider three possible ways of confronting this tension, three different ways in which time might figure more prominently in jurisprudential inquiry. First, it might be argued that *as a matter of fact* law has a temporal component, and therefore no adequate account of law can fail to acknowledge this fact. A second, stronger, claim is that all law *necessarily* has a temporal component, because law's normative force takes place in time. Finally, one may reject the assumption that law has an unchanging nature. Law is always a product of a particular culture, and like other cultural phenomena, law has a temporal (and geographical) nature. This implies that the proper method for studying law should be the same as the one adopted for the study of other cultural phenomena: historical, situated, contingent. It is here that I come to consider Postema's contributions to the subject, because in different works he made remarks that can be read as supporting all three claims.

[62] Hart (n 14) 240.
[63] See ibid 3, 156, 234–37.

A. The Common Law as a Time-Bound Authority

One path to challenging the ahistoricity of jurisprudence accepts some version of the search for a general, cross-cultural account of law, but insists that, at least in some places, law is a time-constrained phenomenon. This challenge can be gleaned from Postema's pioneering work on what he called 'common law theory'.[64] In this vein Postema can be read as arguing that if we look seriously and carefully at past practices that we call 'law', practices that we treat as ancestors of those phenomena in today's world that we think of as law, we find aspects of them that do not fit with currently-dominant theories of law. Instead, they fit better into a distinct legal theory. These ideas cannot be dismissed (as the progressive-science approach would suggest) as errors of less informed individuals. Rather, they look like a relatively coherent and well-worked out theory of law. Postema identified in the writings of prominent English lawyers like Edward Coke, John Selden and Matthew Hale a distinct theory of law, not reducible to either legal positivism or natural law theory.[65]

At a minimum, this work poses a challenge to those who look at legal positivism and natural law theory as exhausting the theoretical terrain of theories of law, thus showing how a historically-informed philosopher can come to challenge prevailing views. To illustrate the difference, consider the relationship between law and rules. In modern thinking the relationship is axiomatic, indisputable. Scott Shapiro, for example, asked, 'what else does the law consist in if not *rules*?'[66] The answer, common law theorists would have said, is, 'well, not rules': In the words of Postema, in this conception of law, law is 'not a set of rules or laws, but a practised framework of practical reasoning', which 'constitutes a form of social ordering'.[67] Thus, greater familiarity with past legal phenomena can enrich one's thinking about law. But time figures in this challenge in a more substantial way: In common law theory, law develops by a slow process of incremental changes and receives its authority neither from its sources (as positivists have it) nor from its inherent rationality (as natural law theorists argue), but from its historical provenance (and possibly its social acceptance). As Postema put it, '[t]he reason of the Common Law is … historical'.[68] In this conception of law, time and history are inherent to the law's authority.

[64] See generally GJ Postema, *Bentham and the Common Law Tradition* (2nd edn, Oxford University Press 2019) 3–38; GJ Postema, 'Classical Common Law Jurisprudence (Part I)' (2002) 2 *Oxford University Commonwealth Law Journal* 155 (2002); GJ Postema, 'Classical Common Law Jurisprudence (Part II)' (2003) 3 *Oxford University Commonwealth Law Journal* 1.

[65] See GJ Postema, 'The Philosophy of the Common Law' in *Oxford Handbook* (n 8) 588, 599; cf HJ Berman, 'The Origins of Historical Jurisprudence: Coke, Selden, Hale' (1994) 103 *Yale Law Journal* 1651, 1652.

[66] SJ Shapiro, 'The "Hart–Dworkin" Debate: A Short Guide for the Perplexed' in A Ripstein (ed), *Ronald Dworkin* (Cambridge University Press 2007) 22, 26. This, of course, was Hart's view as well.

[67] Postema, 'Classical Common Law (Part II)' (n 64) 14.

[68] Postema, *Bentham and the Common Law Tradition* (n 64) 37.

I think Postema's work here served as an important corrective to so much contemporary legal theory that either ignores the common law altogether or tries to squeeze it into the two more familiar categories.[69] But common law theory describes a practice that, in the words of Holmes, 'did not begin with a theory', and never fully worked out one.[70] The common law, and its theory, remain elusive, because they reflect a never-ending project, a constant chase after decisions, which themselves struggle to catch up with changing reality. It is a theory of a practice that is in an important sense opposed to theorising, at least the timeless theorising of the kind Nietzsche attacked.[71] On this view, the law gets its authority from the environment (and history) in which it exists, but since this keeps changing, the law is in an endless chase with reality.

B. Three Paths to the Normativity of Law

Recognising that the common law reflects a distinct approach to the authority of law is a good starting point for a broader discussion of the significance of time on law's authority. In the last section I invoked the two war horses of legal theory, legal positivism and natural law theory. The standard way of thinking of legal positivism and natural law theory is as competing theories, such that if one is right, the other is necessarily false. A second approach is to try and reconcile them, to suggest that they are complementary in that each contains part of the truth, or that they are ways of looking at the same phenomena from different perspectives.[72] These solutions are in principle possible when we add common law theory to our menu of possible (competing) theories.

[69] For further illustration, in an essay that builds on Postema's work on common law theory, see D Priel, 'Not All Law is an Artifact: Jurisprudence Meets the Common Law' in L Burazin et al (eds), *Law as an Artifact* (Oxford University Press 2018) 239.

[70] OW Holmes, *The Common Law* (Little, Brown 1881) 77. Holmes says this with respect to tort law, but this is a fair statement of the common law in general.

[71] Ideas similar to (and to some extent influenced by) common law theory developed in nineteenth-century Germany. The most important figure in their development was Friedrich Karl von Savigny. Savigny's prominence extended well beyond Germany and even cast some influence on common law jurisdictions, for example in debates in the United States over codification. See M Reimann, 'The Historical School Against Codification: Savigny, Carter, and the Defeat of the New York Civil Code' (1989) 37 *American Journal of Comparative Law* 95. Interestingly, Jhering stated that for Savigny 'laws are not *made*, but rather *become*'. R Berkowitz, 'From Justice to Justification: An Alternative Genealogy of Positive Law' (2011) 1 *University of California at Irvine Law Review* 611, 625 (quoting Rudolf von Jhering, 'Friedrich Karl Von Savigny' (1861) 5 *Jahrbücher für die Dogmatik des heutigen römischen und deutschen Privatrechts* 354, 364–65). This contrast between 'being' and 'becoming' is precisely the one Nietzsche invoked when he criticised philosophers' 'hatred of the very idea of becoming', in the quotation accompanying n 1.

[72] For an example of the first strategy see Gardner (n 20) vii–viii (claiming to borrow from both legal positivism and natural law); for an example of the second strategy, see L Alexander and E Sherwin, *The Rule of Rules: Morality, Rules, and the Dilemmas of Law* (Duke University Press 2001) 196–98.

There is, however, a different way of thinking about these different approaches, the one I want to pursue here. And that is that different theories may not equally fit the law in different times and places. So understood, the word 'law' will refer to several different things that belong to different categories. Some have argued this view is incoherent. John Gardner, for instance, stated that 'If law is not a valid classification, then nor is Cheyenne law, international law, Scots law, shari'a law, or Roman law. If there is no general jurisprudence … then there is also no special jurisprudence.'[73] But this is a mistake. It is perfectly coherent to think that the word 'law' is ambiguous, and that different things we call 'law' belong to different categories and that law (in general) is a disjunctive category. It is also possible to tell a historical, evolutionary story, in which one dominant form of law replaces another.

Where does Postema stand on this debate? Postema associates the insights of the time-based view of law with seventeenth- and eighteenth-century English legal scholars. One may add to them some members of the historical school of jurisprudence, particularly dominant in the middle of nineteenth-century Germany.[74] From the perspective of the progressive-science model of jurisprudence, these theories may be understood as correct or incorrect descriptions of what law is, but descriptions that leave the practice of law largely intact. But if we take seriously the view that different legal philosophies manifest themselves in different understandings or conceptualisations of law and its role in society, different jurisprudential theories will result in somewhat different legal practices. The main proponents of common law theory were lawyers who developed their ideas against the background of a particular legal system. They thus had a role both in shaping the law and theorising it. This would suggest that it would be difficult to see time-based conceptions of law as capturing the essence of law in times and places where other ideas were dominant. Moreover, especially given that appeals to 'tradition' are almost always bound with a certain view of politics as represented in the work of Edmund Burke,[75] it is inviting to think of time-bound authority as reflecting a view that may be true of a particular socio-political tradition, not something that captures necessary features of law true in all political environments.

Between these two possibilities – one where the time-boundedness of law is one possible conception and one where it is part of the essence of law – Postema is not entirely clear. He writes in one place that '[t]he philosophical explanation of law … seeks a general account of a concept deeply embedded in the intellectual and political traditions of our culture and the day-to-day activities and social interactions shaped by them'.[76] At the same time, Postema seems to

[73] See Gardner (n 20) 279.

[74] See Berman (n 65) 1736–37. See also n 71 above.

[75] The link is explicit in Kronman (n 7) 1048–64. It also figures prominently in critiques of Kronman's views. See D Luban, 'Legal Traditionalism' (1991) 43 *Stanford Law Review* 1035, 1055–57; N Duxbury, 'History as Hyperbole' (1995) 15 *Oxford Journal of Legal Studies* 477, 480–82.

[76] GJ Postema, 'Jurisprudence as Practical Philosophy' (1998) 4 *Legal Theory* 329, 357. Similarly, in his writings on common law theory, the claims about time-boundedness seem to be grounded in features of the common law, not all law. See, eg, Postema, 'Classical Common Law (Part II)' (n 64) 21–23.

have embraced the view that the normativity of law is necessarily historical. For example, he has written about '[l]aw's essential temporality … [which] lies in the very nature of law and its distinctive mode of normativity'.[77] Postema has also written about the 'essentially historical' nature of law.[78] It is thus unclear whether Postema thinks that the time-constrained idea of normativity is unique to common law theory, or that this is an idea true of all law even if only common law theory made it explicit.

I want to propose here yet another way of understanding the relationship between natural law theory, legal positivism and common law theory. This view sees these as three models of law.[79] Common law theory is thus one of (at least) three possible accounts of law's normativity, with law in different times and places coming closer to one of the three. On this view, we can distinguish between three pure forms of the authority of law: reason-based, will-based, and time-based. These correspond, roughly, to natural law theory, legal positivism and common law theory.

Real-world instantiations of law rarely if ever exhibit pure cases of these different approaches. Even within a single legal system, some areas may be closer to one type than to another; even within a single legal system some participants will push its law in one direction, others in another. Nevertheless, and despite the fact that ideas travel (which is why all actual legal systems are the product of different and occasionally conflicting influences), arguably there will remain differences among legal systems in how close they are to each of the different pure conceptions. We may think of a 'common law jurisdiction' as a legal system closer to pure time-based authority, which means there are going to be systemic differences between such a legal system and another that is closer to one of the other conceptions. At the same time, the model view acknowledges that labels are always simplifications, and that common law legal systems are complex and diverse. For instance, even in common law jurisdictions, much of the law today is the product of statutes, and statutes are harder to fit within a time-bound conception of law's authority.[80] On the other hand, even the common law element in common law jurisdictions may be subject to interpretation and reconceptualisation in terms of the other theories of law's authority.[81]

These last points help bring in an additional timed aspect into our analysis. To understand it, I borrow the idea of convergent evolution from biological evolutionary theory. In essence, it stands for the possibility that organs

[77] See GJ Postema, 'Melody and Law's Mindfulness of Time' (2004) 17 *Ratio Juris* 203, 207, 219–25 (quotation at 219).

[78] GJ Postema, 'On the Moral Presence of Our Past' (1991) 36 *McGill Law Journal* 1153, 1156–57.

[79] On the idea underlying this sentence, see D Priel, 'Are Jurisprudential Debates Conceptual? Some Lessons from Democratic Theory' (2012) 50 *Osgoode Hall Law Journal* 359, 398–401. It is further elaborated in D Priel, 'Jurisprudential Theories as Models' (unpublished manuscript).

[80] See Luban (n 75) 1047–50.

[81] See generally D Priel, 'Conceptions of Authority and the Anglo-American Common Law Divide' (2017) 65 *American Journal of Comparative Law* 609.

performing similar functions will evolve in different species completely independently. This happens when different species are exposed to similar evolutionary pressures. A well-known example is the eye, which evidence strongly suggests evolved independently several times. Notably, even though different organs of vision perform roughly the same function, they are structured differently and they perform their function somewhat differently.

Similarly, in the context of law, it is possible that institutions we now collectively call 'law' have emerged independently in different societies. The social pressures that led to the emergence of legal structures may have been similar (a society of growing size and complexity, division of social roles and labour), but different background conditions (in existing cultural norms, physical environment, technological development) may have led to the emergence of different bases for legal authority, and consequently to different legal forms that fit those ideas. As a result, something that may count as law under one type of authority may not under another. Unlike the biological case, however, it is easy to conceive of different conceptions of authority existing within a single legal system.

It is a mix of historical ignorance and the philosophical fetish for the unified explanation that explains varied phenomena in terms of one single structure ('all law is necessarily X', where X is a set of structural features) that blinded philosophers to this possibility. What is true, though, is that with time, partly because ideas travel, partly because of convergence in the environmental conditions, partly because even within a single legal system not everyone thinks alike, different ideas of authority got blended together, such that modern legal systems typically exhibit conflicting ideas of authority. Surprisingly, this may have helped make claims to universality seem more plausible, because anyone who sought to explain law's authority in terms of one of three possibilities could find something in any legal system they considered to support their views. However, this is where a historical understanding – one that shows the origins of ideas and their evolution – can explain why ignoring the different conceptions of authority that co-exist within a single legal system, leads to error.

The suggestion made in the last paragraph is, as presented, rather speculative. It clearly requires a lot more than I can do here to substantiate it, but if it is along the right lines then we can make sense of some legal systems' being closer to, say, reason-based ideas of authority (a legal system grounded more in, and thus closer to, natural law theory) while there are others where time-based ideas of authority are more prominent (a legal system closer to common law theory). This approach may explain how different legal systems emerge and evolve in response to particular social pressures, why different theories of law's authority may gain prominence in different places or in different times, and how a legal system that may begin closer to a particular conception of law's authority will drift towards another. It can also makes sense of the fact – very much confirmed by reality – that different legal systems do not just differ in their geographical scope and in the content of their rules; they sometimes differ also in their underlying idea of law. It is this fact that explains why conversation between people in different legal systems is sometimes difficult, and why this difficulty extends to legal theorists.[82]

An important possible implication of this view is that the very idea of law may not be politically neutral. For if there are indeed different conceptions of law's authority, and if those different conceptions are plausibly associated with different political ideologies, and those correspond to somewhat different legal practices, then a legal system more aligned with a particular conception of authority may have a different political hue from law instantiated closer to another conception. It is not a coincidence, I think, that those who have emphasised the time-based conception of law's authority have often found the *political* ideas of Burke and Oakeshott congenial to their account of law. It is also not a coincidence that this brand of conservatism is quite different from the conservatism associated with some versions of reason-based natural law theory.

C. Jurisprudence with Humans

The previous subsection presents a view that could be seen to be in conflict with Postema's. I have argued for (at least) three different possible paths to law's authority, only one of which is time-based; at least in some places, Postema argued that all law's authority is embedded in time. As he put it:

> Time is essential to law's distinctive normativity. Law is capable of offering effective normative guidance to rational self-directing and socially interacting agents only if it is sufficiently congruent with their social lives and the activities and practices that structure them through time.[83]

There are two possible ways of mitigating this apparent disagreement. The first is that while I may have provided a 'sociological' account of people's beliefs about law's authority, Postema's account is philosophical in that it focuses on what *actually* grounds law's authority. The difference is that to show that my view is incorrect takes empirical evidence that will indicate the three different views do not actually exist; to show that Postema's view is incorrect calls for a refutation of a 'philosophical' argument. I will explain below why I reject this attempt of reconciling the two views and the sharp distinction that underlies it. A second response is quite different, and I believe more promising: it asserts that while in theory the three conceptions of law's authority are conceivable, in reality, because of the way humans are, law's authority will always be (albeit to varying degrees) dependent on time.

[82] See D Priel, 'Is There One Right Answer to the Question of the Nature of Law?' in W Waluchow and S Sciaraffa (eds), *Philosophical Foundations of the Nature of Law* (Oxford University Press 2013) 322, 339–40.

[83] Postema (n 77) 225.

Let me begin with the first suggestion. This response is likely to be the more popular one among legal philosophers, reflecting the assumption that a 'theory' of authority (just like a theory of law) should explain all law in one way. This answer strikes me as misguided. In somewhat different formulations I have dealt with it elsewhere, so I will keep my remarks here brief. This view rests on the unstated assumption in much jurisprudential writing that there is one successful account of law's authority. This view also effectively ignores the idea that law is a social construction that humans are free to design as they will. This view assumes that the category *law* (unlike its content) is not a matter of social construction (and as such something whose boundaries are to be learned by empirical inquiry) but a philosophical question to be determined by conceptual analysis.[84]

This argument thus depends on a distinction between attitudes *about* the practice, and attitudes *within* the practice. The latter are the attitudes of those who participate in the practice, while the former are those of the theorists who investigate the practice. In reality, the boundaries between the two types are often blurred. As practices mature they tend to generate self-referential attitudes, and those often influence the practice itself in terms of what it takes to engage in the practice successfully, what makes it worthwhile, what makes it legitimate. Someone who 'erroneously' believes that unjust law is not law (or, if it is any different, that unjust law lacks authority) may practise law differently from someone who rejects this view. Her attitudes about the practice will not be easily separated from how she acts within the practice. If certain views about the 'philosophical' question become dominant, they will change the practice itself. Interestingly, such an influence of attitudes about the practice on the practice itself will sometimes happen even when a scholar seeks to provide an 'external', conceptual account of the practice, one meant to leave the practice as it is. For if a scholar's work is read and influences practitioners, it may affect their understanding of their own practice.[85] Unlike fire, earthquakes or diseases, where we can plausibly say that people in the past were mistaken about them, in the case of law, what people thought about the practice is relevant for understanding the practice itself.[86]

[84] If the category itself is a social construction, why should its features and boundaries not be studied like any other social construction, ie empirically? See D Priel, 'Law as a Social Construction and Conceptual Legal Theory' (2019) 38 *Law and Philosophy* 267.

[85] For one example, consider the adoption, incorporation, and adaptation of Hans Kelsen's ideas in court decisions discussing the legal implications of a revolution. For a survey and discussion of such cases, see T Mahmud, 'Jurisprudence of Successful Treason: Coup d'Etat & Common Law' (1994) 27 *Cornell International Law Journal* 49. Kelsen (along with others) suggested that this may be a mistaken application of his own views (see ibid 110–13), but it is still the case that 'theoretical' ideas purportedly about the practice have become part of the practice.

[86] Even in the case of natural kinds, matters are more complicated. Consider: would the category of *fish* be a matter on which we can declare people in the past to have been wrong? Sometimes, but not always. cf J Dupré, 'Natural Kinds and Biological Taxa' (1981) 90 *Philosophical Review* 66.

The alternative proposed here treats different conceptions of authority as models. It adds to it the idea that even if one can conceive of a purely reason-based conception of authority, real-world specimens of law will not be able to rid themselves of their relation to time, *because humans are time-constrained creatures*.[87] If this is indeed the case, this may be enough to vindicate Postema's idea that all possible *human* law is to going to be related to time.

But why should we think that humans are creatures that necessarily live in time, and 'with' time? Anthony Kronman presented a very strong version of this view, one that he thought posed 'a challenge to the philosophy of law'. The challenge was to explain the fact that '[r]espect for past decisions … is a feature of law in general', something he said 'has no place in philosophy is indeed antithetical to its governing spirit'.[88] The past had this essential role for the law, because in law (but not in philosophy) 'the past is … a repository … of value, with the power to confer legitimacy on actions in the present'.[89] While Postema shares with Kronman the central role he gave to the past in understanding law, and even more the notion of time as the basis for a normative theory for law, he did not accept these rather extravagant claims.[90] The past is not binding upon us for its own sake. Contrary to Kronman's claims that seem to assume that morality is in the domain of timeless ideas, Postema's view is that our entire practical lives (even beyond the law) are deeply embedded in time. Our practical commitments are 'communal' or 'interpersonal' to their core.[91] And since political communities exist over generations, they have a historical dimension. In Postema's view, the basis for law's time-boundedness is that morality, and specifically justice, is time constrained. Law's embeddedness with time is because it plays a role in the communal discourse that is constitutive of morality.[92]

I am sympathetic to this picture, but wish to explain it in a somewhat different way. Where Postema focuses on features of practical reason, I prefer to look to human nature. That makes my approach more overtly naturalistic. It takes

[87] Some have argued that limiting jurisprudence to humans unduly restricts its scope. They have urged us to think about jurisprudence general enough to capture law in alien society. See, eg, Shapiro (n 21) 406–07, note 16. This is an ill-conceived and self-defeating idea. See D Priel, 'Jurisprudence and Necessity' (2007) 20 *Canadian Journal of Law and Jurisprudence* 173, 188–89; Priel (n 17) 23, fn 41.

[88] Kronman (n 7) 1032.

[89] ibid 1033.

[90] Postema (n 78) 1164.

[91] GJ Postema, 'Public Practical Reason: Political Practice' (1995) 37 *Nomos* 345, 357–60, *passim*; GJ Postema, 'Integrity: Justice in Workclothes' (1997) 82 *Iowa Law Review* 821, 840–43, 848–51. A related view is found in M Krygier, 'Law as Tradition' (1986) 5 *Law and Philosophy* 237, 245 ('the past of law, as of every tradition, is not simply part of its history; it is an authoritative significant part of its present'). Krygier insists that law 'must be' understood as a traditional social practice, and that this means that the '"time-free" staples of modern jurisprudence are not enough': ibid 239.

[92] Postema, 'Integrity' (n 91) 854–55; Postema (n 77) 220–21. This is also the essence of Dworkin's view of law and morality.

both morality and law to be human practices, and as such to be human shaped: they are built on foundations of human nature (humans' natural needs, preferences and dispositions), and have been further reshaped by human thought, discourse and action throughout history, as well as the circumstances (social, political, technological) in which they find themselves.[93] To the extent that Postema is correct about the nature of practical reason, it is so, I argue, because of what humans and their living conditions are like. Humans are creatures whose practical lives exist in time, and so are their morality and laws. Thus, even if one can conceive of a purely reason-based (legal) authority, humans may not be able to sustain such a legal system in practice. If there is any necessity here, it is a natural necessity drawn from facts about human nature, not any kind of conceptual necessity.

Perhaps the most basic element of humanity that gives time its normative significance is memory. That memory is crucial for humanity has been the subject of works of art, as well as of psychological case studies of people who lost their memory. Most obviously, without memory, humans lose their ability to form life plans and sustain meaningful relationships; without memory, learning becomes impossible. There is also the fact that humans feel a connection to their ancestors, and see themselves as part of an unbroken historical group (family, clan, tribe, nation) that began before them and will persist after them.

Memory is also significant for some of the most rudimentary aspects of normative thought. To the extent that a legal action is a reaction to a person's past behaviour, it requires memory. Thus, the idea of holding people to account is not possible without memory. Longer-term memory is necessary for one of the most undemanding notion of fairness – treating present actions in the same way we treated similar actions in the past. It is true that human normative thought does not always take this form. In theory, one could always pass judgment 'on the merits' of every case, without regard to past judgments on similar actions. Such a possibility might even suggest that relying on past decisions makes no sense: if we decided wrongly in the past, there is little point in repeating the error; and if we decided correctly, then doing the same now can be justified by appeal to the reasons behind that decision, not to the earlier decision itself. But in reality constraints of time, fairness considerations, and even doubts about the possibility of finding the 'correct' answer may warrant sticking with an earlier decision. These considerations are powerful enough that even in legal systems that do not recognise precedent as a source of law, courts tend to follow past decisions. They also explain why attempts in some legal systems to prohibit the use of precedent have all eventually been abandoned.

[93] For accounts broadly in line with this view, see P Kitcher, *The Ethical Project* (Harvard University Press 2011); K Sterelny, *The Evolved Apprentice: How Evolution Made Humans Unique* (MIT Press 2012) ch 7.

In addition to the psychological pull of norms of fairness ('treating like cases alike'), the past also has a 'sociological' impact on the law, as past normative choices may be constrained by present institutional possibilities. A legal system, unlike a book on moral philosophy, has institutional mechanisms that change in response to past decisions. Enforcement mechanisms, institutionalised knowledge-dissemination devices (courses, books), contracts and other legal documents – all are shaped on the basis of past normative choices, and help enshrine them. They often make maintaining past decisions simpler and cheaper, rather than changing course.[94]

The time-based conception of authority may be thought to derive from these facts and give them normative primacy. Time-based authority in its idealised form does not assume that there is a moral truth out there that law aims to match. Rather, it treats its own past as *constructive* of the relevant legal truth. This is relevant in an underappreciated way to familiar jurisprudence debates: since past decisions change the environment in which present decisions are made, it follows that what constitutes 'the right answer purely on the merits of the case' may be different depending on existing institutional context, which (as explained) is dependent on the past.

The effect of this may be significant: the views described in the previous paragraph are close to those held by Dworkin, and as such are relevant to familiar questions about the relationship between law and morality. They are also relevant when trying to make sense of the way different legal systems differ from each other, and why they have a certain shape and not another. If I am right in my overall view about authority, we can explain some of the substantive differences among legal systems as derived from their historical ties to different conceptions of authority.[95]

All this is significant for the question of the inevitability of some time-based element in an account of law's authority, because it shows how the past may have normative impact even when decision makers do not make any conscious effort to align present decisions with past ones. Can time nevertheless be avoided in the

[94] 'Path dependence' is a general term that has been used for different processes. Some of them are more closely related to the 'psychological' impact of time. For instance, 'mental models' influence the way people interpret the world. See AT Denzau and DC North, 'Shared Mental Models: Ideologies and Institutions' (1994) 47 *Kyklos* 3. This idea is close to what lawyers call 'reasonable expectations'. In the text I talk about the costs of initial institutional choices and subsequent changing course. But the two processes are related, because some of the costs may be in changing (psychological) expectations generated by past institutional choices. All this ties to the work (of Postema and Dworkin, among others) on integrity as a moral ideal of communities, which may be read as broadly in agreement with these ideas. Even if one does not accept these ideas as an account of morality, they make sense in the context of thinking about law. For law is a public institution, whose judgments need to be accepted by those subject to it. It thus has to be mapped against understandings and expectations (the 'mental models') of people. This creates a connection, perhaps surprising, between works that are not overly naturalistic (or even hostile to it) and more empirically-grounded works on morality such as the sources cited in n 93.

[95] For some examples, see Priel (n 81) 645–52.

law, despite all this? In certain domains humans have developed practices that are relatively impervious to time-bound thinking. Perhaps the most notable example is scientific practice. Even where the science in question has a time element built into it (as is the case with evolutionary theory), scientific ethos tends to give little authority to the *discipline's* own past. Admittedly, even here the picture is more complex (scientists are human too), but there is no denying that precedent and tradition have no authority in science in the way they do in the law.

Against this background, we may understand those who argue for law in terms of reason-based ('natural law') or will-based ('positivist') conceptions of authority do not present 'descriptive' or 'conceptual' claims about the nature of law. Rather, their efforts should be understood as idealisations of law based on the model of science, and an attempt to create law whose authority is similarly independent of appeal to the past.

The popularity of the progressive-science model of jurisprudence shows that this ethos has proven attractive in the philosophy of law, so much so that its proponents have put it forward not just at the level of jurisprudential method, but as a foundation for a substantive theory of law as well. But despite centuries of effort, attempts to model human law on science have not proven successful. Perhaps with the advent of legal automation such ideas might finally be more successful. Until this (maybe) happens, it remains an interesting historical and theoretical question why science and law have proven so different on this score. (Here, as elsewhere, law is more like engineering than science, and engineering has a more profound relationship with time.) Until then, a theory of law that aims at descriptive accuracy has to acknowledge the normative role time plays in the law. In saying all this, I have ended up accepting something like Postema's claim about the inevitable connection between law's authority and time.

VI. CONCLUSION

In most jurisprudential thinking time does not play a significant role. This is most evident in the characterisation of the domain as concerned with necessary and, as such, timeless truths. This view, as I suggested at the outset, seems to be based on the assumption that if there are no such timeless truths then there is no room for a philosophy of law, only sociology (broadly conceived): contingent, local, empirical.[96] As I have tried to show, much of contemporary jurisprudence is time-less in other senses as well: uninterested in the history of law, the history of jurisprudence, or the role of time in law. The primary aim of this chapter has

[96] This is the worry that motivates Raz's question (n 24) 17, '[C]an there be a theory of law?' As he defines it, a theory of law is limited to necessary and important truths about law. If there are no necessary truths, then on this view there cannot be a theory (philosophy) of law. One aim of a model-based approach to jurisprudence suggested here (and defended in Priel (n 79)) is to explain why this assumption is not warranted.

been to bring time back in in three different ways. The first and least controversial sense is that jurisprudence, like any learned activity, has a history. This will not be denied by anyone, but it will be deemed insignificant to the subject matter itself as a kind of progressive science with accumulated knowledge. Against this view, I have argued that it is difficult to draw a clear line between legal practice and legal theory, because the latter typically emerges from a more-or-less self-conscious attempt by practitioners to understand their practice. And thus, to the extent that law is tied to time in a more significant sense, so is jurisprudence.

At a second level, jurisprudence is tied to time because law, or at least the kind of law called 'common law', is steeped in time in the sense that the very justification for saying that something is the law now is because it was judged to be the law in the past. The practice of appealing to precedent is one that uses the law's own past as a form of justification. But though familiar to lawyers, to say 'this is what we should do now, *because* we did something similar in the past' is not an obvious statement. Despite the centrality of this kind of reasoning in the common law, it is a feature of law that many jurisprudential theories have neglected.

Finally, at the most philosophical level, there is the fact that jurisprudence is a study of a human practice. Here, I drew on history, both by turning to the philosophy of history and by examining the way that human institutions exist in time. I took Postema's invitation to think of jurisprudence as practical reason as an invitation to think of it in terms of the way humans reason.[97] And it is here that we should look at the way psychologists have improved our understanding of human reasoning. I took ideas that were not developed within a naturalistic framework and have attempted to 'naturalise' them.

It is a testament to the breadth and depth of Postema's body of work that he has made significant contributions to all three levels: to the philosophical study of past jurisprudential thought, to the articulation of common law theory as a distinct theory of law, and to the temporal element in law as an inescapable part of a study of the role of law in practical reasoning.

[97] cf D Priel, 'Action, Politics, and the Normativity of Law' (2017) 8 *Jurisprudence* 118, 121–22.

11

How Postema's Jurisprudence as Sociable Science is Like Dworkin's Interpretivism

On Conceptual Analysis in Legal Theory

SAULO DE MATOS

I. INTRODUCTION: POSTEMA'S JURISPRUDENCE AS SOCIABLE SCIENCE

PROGRAMMATIC ESSAYS ARE a genre of philosophical writing that deals with judging the past and pointing to the future of a realm of scientific knowledge. There are plenty of good examples of this kind of literature. For instance, at the beginning of the nineteenth century, two German professors translated the spirit of the final moments of the *Aufklärung*, through the so-called codification controversy (*Kodifikationsstreit*).[1] Two programmatic essays published in 1812 sought to capture the historic manifestations of their time and to set the borders of the political and constitutional debate, namely, Anton Friedrich Justus Thibaut's 'On the necessity of a general civil law' ('Ueber die Nothwendigkeit eines allgemeinen buergerlichen Rechts') and Friedrich Karl von Savigny's 'On the vocation of our age for legislation and legal science' ('Vom Beruf unsrer Zeit fuer Gesetzgebung und Rechtwissenschaft'). Thibaut maintained that a civil code should be written by the state, and that this should be the only source of valid law within the German territory, whereas Savigny believed that only a systematised science of law (and not a voluntarist legislation) could deliver the necessary legal certainty regarding social relations.

[1] H Hattenhauer (ed), *Thibaut und Savigny: ihre programmatischen Schriften* (Vahlen 2002).

In his recent debate with Professor Jan Wolenski, Professor Gerald Postema admitted that his masterpiece 'Legal Philosophy in the Twentieth Century: the Common Law World'[2] should be read as a '"critical history" of legal philosophy in the century, one that seriously looks at and analyses critically the dialectical movement of arguments and counter-arguments over this period'.[3] Postema's philosophical narrative of analytical legal philosophy in the twentieth century starts with Austin's project and ends with Hart's methodological legal positivism and his legacy. A not so careful reading of his book gives the first impression that it offers a philosophical narrative beginning with the establishment of the limits of the very idea of jurisprudence, then presenting some sceptical views about this project and, finally, announcing the triumph of Hart's concept of law as (even if not consensually) a more fruitful approach to the legal phenomenon.

Nevertheless, a more carefully reading of the last chapter of his book leads to a different conclusion: Postema presents, in some sense, the decadence of Hart's legacy of a descriptive jurisprudence due to its oversight of the social character of legal practice. I will take for granted that Postema's ultimate view on jurisprudence is expressed through these programmatic writings on the social character of jurisprudence, as it is presented in the last chapter of *Legal Philosophy in the Twentieth Century: the Common Law World*.[4]

It is nevertheless hard to grasp the meaning of this social character of jurisprudence. His fundamental thesis consists in the idea that jurisprudence has lost its *social character* or *its capacity to shed light on the practice and experience of law in a larger social and philosophical context*. Hart's legacy to jurisprudence seems to be the fundamental cause for this state of affairs, given that contemporary analytical legal philosophy has become almost exclusively a dispute of method (*Methodenstreit*) between descriptive and normative (evaluative or interpretative) jurisprudence:

> If we are honest with ourselves, we can all recognize that some interests are simply idiosyncratic, leading to explanations that are limited or shallow. We seek explanations that are deep and comprehensive – comprehensive in the sense that they illuminate the connections of the experience and practice of law to other core elements of social and political life. To pursue these explanations, however, requires setting the practice and experience of law in its larger habitat of human social experience, setting the exploration of law in a larger philosophical context, and setting both of these in the context of the history of this philosophical enterprise.[5]

[2] GJ Postema, *Legal Philosophy in the Twentieth Century: The Common Law World*, vol 11 (Springer 2011).

[3] GJ Postema, 'Philosophical Narrative: A Reply to Professor Wolenski' (2013) 26 *Ratio Juris* 139, 140.

[4] That is to say, I will take for granted that Postema's programmatic essays are above all 'Jurisprudence, the sociable science'; GJ Postema, 'Jurisprudence, the Sociable Science' (2015) 101 *Virginia Law Review* 869, and the last chapter ('Concluding Note') of Postema (n 2).

[5] Postema (n 4) 884.

Consequently, one of the main problems of analytical legal philosophy nowadays has to do with its almost exclusive interest in analysing the phenomenon of the identification of the content of the law – that is, legal rights, duties, powers, liberties, etc – from the perspective of the practitioners of law.[6] According to Postema, Hart's, Dworkin's and even Brian Leiter's jurisprudential projects are all good examples of this state of affairs. Finnis's, Waldron's and Bentham's legal philosophies are, in contrast, fine exceptions of the mentioned perspective.

As an alternative to this standard picture of jurisprudence, Postema presents his thesis on jurisprudence as a sociable science. The sociable character has two fundamental dimensions: (i) an external dimension, which consists in the openness of jurisprudence to interaction and partnership with other modes of inquiry, and (ii) an internal dimension based on its synechist methodology.[7]

Thus, considering the external dimension, it is important to explain legal phenomena in a comprehensive perspective that tries to present a picture of the systematic interaction between law and other social practices and institutions, which requires a dialogue between jurisprudence and social sciences. In this regard, sociable jurisprudence expresses an old aspiration of integration of legal science with empirical modes of inquiry in social sciences. The history of legal thought tells us that this has been a fundamental point of critique since the last century. Accordingly, the agenda of jurisprudence should be written *pari passu* with the agenda of social science and political philosophy: 'Jurisprudence gains focus and depth when it self-consciously considers the implications it has for action and institutional design.'[8]

The synechist methodology entails the claim that jurisprudence should focus on continuities of legal phenomenon, exploring the question 'How is law like?' rather than the problem of 'What is law?' Jurisprudential knowledge can shed light on our legal practice if it begins to integrate phenomena, practices and concepts in a systematic framework of a comprehensive account. Synechist methodology has as its counterpart the analytic methodology, which is directed to seek for well-defined limits to the concept of law and for the necessary and sufficient proprieties for classifying a given social fact as law.

> By contrast [to analytical jurisprudence], the synechist, no less interested in probing the nature of law, looks for continuities and illuminating similarities (and differences that build on continuities). The synechist ask: 'What is law like?' and '(How) is this like law?' rather than declaring, 'This isn't like law, so it's not law (properly speaking)'. It seeks understanding by locating, relating, and integrating. It seeks to locate puzzling concepts in a wider network of concepts, integrating them within that network and tracing out relations among them, thereby deepening our understanding of their content.[9]

[6] ibid 899.

[7] ibid 895.

[8] P Nonet and P Selznick, *Law and Society in Transition: Toward Responsive Law* (Transaction Publishers 2009) 3.

[9] Postema (n 4) 894.

In my view, Postema's argument for the future of legal theory runs in the right direction of advocating a systematic approach to law in connection with other social institutions and phenomena, and arguing for a concept of law based on typical features of law rather than its essential properties. I will argue, however, that such a kind of methodology is not in its epistemological essence different from Dworkin's methodology of jurisprudence. I will make a case for the conclusion that the main difference between the two approaches consists in the domain of language that is privileged by each author: whereas Dworkin develops a doctrinal concept of law, Postema sheds light on a sociological concept of law. First, I will reconstruct the dispute of method (*Methodenstreit*) between Hart and Dworkin in analytical jurisprudence as a dispute between descriptive and normative jurisprudence. Second, I will explore a possible understanding of Postema's methodology for legal theory in connection with Schauer's project as stated in his book *The Force of Law*. Finally, I will explain how it is possible to understand Postema's approach in the same direction of Dworkin's project for analytical legal theory.

II. THE DISPUTE OF METHOD IN ANALYTICAL JURISPRUDENCE

A. Analytical Jurisprudence

In 1968, HLA Hart was invited by the legal historian Franz Wieacker to give a talk *in memoriam* of Rudolph von Jhering's 150th birthday at the Academy of Science of Gottingen in Gottingen (Germany).[10] In this opportunity, 10 years after Hart's famous lecture at Harvard,[11] he finally presented his project for an analytical jurisprudence in Continental Europe. The first aspect of Hart's legacy that should be noticed consists in his reformulation of the proper subject of jurisprudence.

In the nineteenth century, jurisprudence was responsible for tracing the boundaries between law and other social sciences, and, consequently, defining the fundamental concepts of legal thought. Hart believed that this was not a fruitful enterprise due to (i) its excessive concern with concepts *in abstracto* and the idea that one can grasp the absolute essence of the concepts, and (ii) its blindness to social conflicts in the background of each legal thought.[12] Jurisprudence should

[10] On this point, I follow Nicos Stavropoulos in taking Hart's essay 'Jhering's Heaven of Concepts and Modern Analytical Jurisprudence' as decisive for his descriptive jurisprudence project. See N Stavropoulos, 'Hart's Semantics' in JL Coleman (ed), *Hart's Postscript: Essays on the Postscript to 'The Concept Of Law'* (Oxford University Press 2005); and HLA Hart, 'Jhering's heaven of concepts and modern analytical jurisprudence' in F Wieacker and C Wollschläger (eds), *Jherings Erbe: Göttinger Symposion zur 150. Wiederkehr des Geburtstags von Rudolph von Jhering* (Vandenhoeck & Ruprecht 1970) 68.

[11] cf HLA Hart, 'Positivism and the Separation of Law and Morals' (1958) 71 *Harvard Law Review* 593.

[12] Hart (n 10) 68–69.

not be seen as a general theory of the fundamental concepts of legal science, that is to say, as a kind of inquiry on the necessary categories – person, property, contract, family, etc – of modern legal thought.[13] The central issue of jurisprudence, for Hart, should not be its relations and boundaries to other sciences.[14] Jurisprudence should be understood as a theory of the content of the law, that is, as an explanation of the modern language of rights.[15] In other words, jurisprudence has to do with an enquiry on the determinants of the concept of the law, whereas the 'concept of the law' means the content of legal thought.[16]

In order to grasp Hart's understanding of jurisprudence, one can compare jurisprudence with theories of mental content. On the one hand, theories of mental content have traditionally had mental contents or thoughts as their object. The fundamental question in this field consists in understanding which proprieties are necessary and sufficient for a thinker to have a concept.[17] A concept or proposition is a statement that affirms or denies the existence of a state of affairs (*Tatsache*) in the world. In this sense, a theory of mental content should answer the question of which facts or proprieties are necessary for having such thoughts. Jurisprudence, on the other hand, has the content of the law as its subject. I assume that Hart's view of law as social practice is based on a kind of deontic language of rights in the Hohfeldian sense of the term.[18] Therefore, the fundamental question in jurisprudence consists in understanding which proprieties are necessary and sufficient for a person having legal thought, which means *having* a right (power, liberty, duty, etc). This shift of the understanding of jurisprudence can be regarded as Hart's answer to the problem of the *Begriffshimmel*, that is, the tendency of legal theorists to look for the essence of the necessary concepts of legal science.[19]

[13] The view that jurisprudence should be regarded as an inquiry into the fundamental concepts of law underlies, for instance, Kelsen's Pure Theory of Law. For a contemporary defence of this kind of enquiry, see R Poscher, 'The Hand of Midas: When Concepts Turn Legal, or Deflating the Hart-Dworkin Debate' in JC Hage and Dietmar von der Pfordten (eds), *Concepts in Law* (Springer 2009) 99; D von der Pfordten, 'About Concepts in Law' in JC Hage and D von der Pfordten (eds), *Concepts in Law* (Springer 2009) 17.

[14] Hart (n 10).

[15] It is important to notice here the influence of Wesley Newcomb Hohfeld on British legal theory through Hart's work, and the possible consequence of his early death for American jurisprudence. See Postema (n 2) 581.

[16] Hart seems to assume this concept of jurisprudence when he criticises the main failure of the legal theoretical tradition before him (Hart (n 10) 71): 'The fundamental error consists in the belief that legal concepts are *fixed* or *closed* in the sense that it is possible to define them exhaustively in terms of a set of necessary and sufficient conditions; so that for any real or imaginary case it is possible to say with certainty whether it falls under the concept or does not; the concept either applies or it does not; it is logically closed (*begrenzt*).'

[17] M Greenberg, 'A New Map of Theories of Mental Content: Constitutive Accounts and Normative Theories' (2005) 15 *Philosophical Issues* 299, 300.

[18] WN Hohfeld, 'Fundamental Legal Conceptions as Applied in Judicial Reasoning' (1917) 26 *The Yale Law Review* 710; C Wellman, *A Theory of Rights: Persons under Laws, Institutions, and Morals* (Rowman & Allanheld 1985); WA Edmundson, *An Introduction to Rights* (Cambridge University Press 2004).

[19] Hart (n 10) 71.

Now, it is necessary to explain the meaning of 'analytical' under this view. There are different methodologies in jurisprudence regarding the identification of legal content. *Analytical jurisprudence* is maybe the most important methodology among American and English lawyers. Bentham called analytical jurisprudence *expository jurisprudence*, whereas Austin classified it as *general jurisprudence*.[20] Analytical jurisprudence is regarded as a *value-free* form of identifying the content of the law, since this form of legal thought implies the so-called *definition in use*: 'instead of attempting to define single words (eg "duty" or "obligation") the analysis takes whole sentences in which the term to be analysed appears'.[21] Analytical jurisprudence is a conceptual enterprise of identifying the necessary and sufficient determinants of the correct use of a term, or, in other words, the conditions for having a concept.

Thus, Hart's first fundamental impact on jurisprudence consists in his understanding of the legal theoretic enterprise. Accordingly, jurisprudence should provide a scientific explanation for the legal proposition 'X has a right to φ', where 'right' means a claim, obligation, power, etc. Law – or the content of the law – is a set of legal propositions of this kind. There are true and false legal propositions in every legal system. Jurisprudence should explain which properties or facts make one proposition true and another false.

B. Stating the Debate between Descriptive and Normative Jurisprudence

Considering that the debate in British and American jurisprudence after Hart became exclusively a discussion on the determinants of the truth of a legal proposition, one can classify legal theories in two different groups: descriptive and normative jurisprudence. Descriptivists claim that a true legal proposition can be identified exclusively with reference to value-free social facts, whereas normativists argue that the identification of content of the law necessarily implies reference to values, although it can make reference to social facts as well.[22]

Perhaps it is important to notice three different concepts of *normative jurisprudence* that existed before Hart, in order to properly understand this debate. First, Kelsen famously argued that jurisprudence as science of law is a normative science, due to the fact that it is, methodological speaking, not subordinated to causal explanation but rather to norms or, more precisely, to legal values derived from legal norms. This is Kelsen's famous first methodological limit to legal science, which regards a 'norm' as a 'scheme of interpretation':

> These external circumstances are always a part of nature, for they are events perceptible to the senses, taking place in time and space; and, as a part of nature, they are

[20] ibid 73–74; R West, *Normative Jurisprudence: An Introduction* (Cambridge University Press 2011) 61.

[21] Hart (n 10) 74.

[22] M Greenberg, 'How Facts Make Law' (2004) 10 *Legal Theory* 157.

> governed by causal laws. As elements of the system of nature, these events as such are not objects of specific legal cognition, and thus are not legal in character at all. What makes such an event a legal (or an illegal) act is not its facticity, not its being natural, that is, governed by causal laws and included in the system of nature. Rather, what makes such an event a legal act is its meaning, the objective sense that attaches to the act. The specifically legal sense of the event in question, its own peculiarity legal meaning, comes by way of a norm whose content refers to the event and confers legal meaning on it; the act can be interpreted, then, according to this norm.[23]

According to Kelsen, jurisprudence is normative due to its object (legal norms) and its methodology for understanding social phenomena (which regards a norm as a scheme of interpretation).[24]

Although one can interpret Kelsen's statement regarding legal interpretation in his famous chapter 8 of *Pure Theory of Law* as part of the debate on the identification of content of the law, it is clear enough that Kelsen's fundamental concern in jurisprudence consists in defining a proper methodology for legal science, and its province regarding other natural and human sciences.

Another important concept of *normative jurisprudence*, on the other hand, refers to Bentham's division of *expository* and *censorial jurisprudence* as a division between two scientific approaches to law: while expository jurisprudence seeks to identify the content of the law, censorial jurisprudence criticises a given content of the law based on references to legal, political or moral goods, that is, to a kind of consequentialist practical thought. Austin divides jurisprudence into *general jurisprudence* as an analytical study of concepts and structure of legal system, and *the art of legislation* as a form of utilitarian criticism of law:[25]

> These questions – the demands of justice, the ideals we have or should have for law, or the nature of the 'good' that a good law exhibits and that a bad law lacks – should be defining questions of jurisprudence. If there is a field of study that could profitably ask questions about our normative framework for evaluating, criticizing, praising or panning law, it should be jurisprudence – both analytic, which might ask what we mean by the justice, or the good, against which we evaluate law, and critical jurisprudence, which might ask how we should, and how we can, sufficiently distance ourselves form the profession in which we participate, so as to better criticize our deepest and most defining legal commitments. They are not, however. … We ask neither ethical questions about a legal regime's or a law's moral goodness nor meta-ethical questions about our own or our fellow lawyer's unexamined practices regarding the legal criticism in which we all nevertheless engage. Jurisprudence has largely turned its back on these normative questions about law's value.[26]

[23] H Kelsen, *Introduction to the Problems of Legal Theory: A Translation of the First Edition of the Reine Rechtslehre or Pure Theory of Law*, trs B Litschewski Paulson and SL Paulson (Clarendon Press 2004) 10.

[24] See SL Paulson, 'Introduction', ibid.

[25] Hart (n 10) 74.

[26] West (n 20) 2.

Thus, *normative jurisprudence* can be regarded in this sense as a scientific inquiry on the goodness or justice of a given content of the law, like, for instance, statutes or court decisions. Although this concept has its historical importance, its meaning corresponds nowadays to the concept of *philosophy of law* in contrast to *legal theory* or *jurisprudence*, if we follow Hart's approach. Whereas *jurisprudence* has to do with the conditions for reporting true propositions of a legal system, *philosophy of law* – or, *perhaps*, *legal ethics*[27] – asks which true propositions of a given legal system can be taken for just or good.

Dworkin's critiques on Hart's project became the pivotal case for the third sense of *normative jurisprudence*. It is possible to say that the sharp distinction between *descriptive* and *normative jurisprudence* is a product of Dworkin's first critiques on Hart's theory, especially after Hart's Postscript, and it makes sense only in this context.

The most profound disagreement between Hart and Dworkin consists in their methodological characterisation of jurisprudence. Both philosophers agree that jurisprudence has to do with the identification of valid or true legal propositions, and that understanding law implies an internal point of view of legal practice. There is no divergence on this level.[28] The controversy is about the character of this act of identifying the content of the law from an internal point of view. In Dworkinian terms, they share the concept of jurisprudence, albeit they disagree on a deep level regarding its better conception.

Hart advocates a descriptive conception of jurisprudence. He believes that one can identify the determinants of content of the law from a theoretical point of view, that is, without making any statement about the *point* or *value* of law as legal practice:

> But the descriptive legal theorist may understand and describe the insider's internal perspective on the law without adopting or sharing it. Even if … the participant's internal perspective manifested in the acceptance of the law as providing guides to conduct and standards of criticism necessarily also included a belief that there are moral reasons for conforming to the law's requirements and moral justification of its use of coercion, this would also be something for a morally neutral descriptive jurisprudence to record but not to endorse or share.[29]

[27] D von der Pfordten, *Rechtsethik* (Beck 2011).

[28] In this context, it is important to observe that Dworkin does believe that it is possible to make descriptive statements about the law. His disagreement with Hart is not that there are no descriptive propositions about the law, but rather that there are no descriptive propositions about the law in jurisprudence: '[A]s I have said I conceded that an account of the "internal perspective" can be descriptive if it takes the form of a description of propositional attitudes toward the law: if it describes nothing more, that is, than human beings have thought or think. So I do not deny that a legal theorist can "describe" a judge's "acceptance" of a particular rule without the theorist himself "accepting" it. But when a theorist says, not that the judge does or does not accept a particular rule, but that the law contains or validates that rule, the theorist does more than describe someone else's attitude. He *accepts* a rule himself, in the particular sense of confirming that it really is a rule of the system in question, and that plainly goes beyond describing other people's attitudes.' R Dworkin, 'Hart's Posthumous Reply' (2017) 130 *Harvard Law Review* 2096, 2103.

[29] HLA Hart, *The Concept of Law* (2nd edn, Oxford University Press 1997) 243.

Accordingly, the task of legal theory consists in explaining the necessary – but perhaps not sufficient – conditions for someone having a right, and this can be done in a pure descriptive or value-neutral way.

Dworkin, on the other hand, states that it is impossible to determine the content of the law without *doing* law, that is, it is impossible to identify the content of the law without making a statement about the *point* or *value* of law as legal practice. In this context, Dworkin claims that legal reasoning is normative, and not merely descriptive: 'In *Law's Empire* I argued … that legal theory cannot be Archimedean with respect to law: that describing law is doing law, so that, to the extent and in the way that ordinary legal reasoning is normative, legal theory must be normative, too.'[30]

The debate between descriptive and normative jurisprudence is a debate between non-evaluative and evaluative character of legal reasoning, and it runs somehow in the following way: (i) Law is taken for a social practice. (ii) Law as social practice entails innumerable raw data or brute facts, like, for instance, statutes, Constitution, court decisions, etc.[31] (iii) A true or false statement related to this social practice depends on an adequate reference to some of these data or brute facts. (iv) Whereas Hart believes that the identification of these data or brute facts and its relation to true legal propositions can be made through mere observation of the social practice, Dworkin maintains that it is necessary to presuppose a sense, point or value for identifying correct data or brute facts in order to justify true legal propositions. For instance, according to Hart, to say that the preface of the Brazilian Constitution determines the truth of proposition X implies a correct observation of social facts of legal practice – for instance, the rule of recognition – that recognises the normative force of the preface. An opposite view is offered by Dworkin, who would argue that the preface of the Brazilian Constitution as social or brute fact determines the truth of proposition X if, and only if, there is a value, principle or point of legal practice that gives normative force to the preface.

III. POSTEMA'S AND DWORKIN'S PROJECTS FOR JURISPRUDENCE

Postema's project to overcome the methodological dispute in jurisprudence consists, first, in approaching the theory of law to the other social sciences, in particular, through methodological models that include empirical research. Such an approach, in his view, should enable a more comprehensive explanation of the law in its connection with other practices and social phenomena. This can be seen in some parts of his work, as for example in his text 'Morality in the

[30] Dworkin (n 28) 2097.

[31] Brute facts are defined in opposition to normative facts. About this concept: GEM Anscombe, 'Modern Moral Philosophy' (1958) 33 *Philosophy* 1, 3–4.

first person plural',[32] in which the social character of law – understood on the basis of the idea of a person that leaves his individual vision for the benefit of a common or inclusive view of others at the time of his judgment – is explained through a long psychological debate about how cooperation is possible between individuals without presupposing collective entities.

This openness of law towards other models of investigation and other phenomena can, on the other hand, be made more fruitfully through what is known as *synechist methodology*, which consists, ultimately, of the answer to the question 'How is law like?' Contrary to what Postema calls an analytical methodology, *the synechist methodology* does not aim to identify the necessary and sufficient properties of a concept ('What is law?'), but rather seeks to trace similarities between typical characteristics of various social phenomena, which, however, cannot be considered necessary (although they can elucidate the legal phenomenon even more efficiently). The point of this methodology is not to differentiate the law from other social phenomena, but rather to provide an approach to the basis of these typical characteristics.

Postema's double proposal for the future of jurisprudence is also advocated in some recent works of other legal theorists. The most representative of these works, in my view, is Frederick Schauer's *The Force of Law*.[33] In this work, Schauer seeks to bring new light into the phenomenon of law by means of the debate about a subject insufficiently discussed in the analytical theory of law of the last century, namely, the phenomenon of coercion. His book begins by bringing the history of the treatment of the subject of coercion within the framework of the analytical theory of law from Austin. Like the historical treatise of Postema,[34] the central point of the work is the methodological or hermeneutic turn in legal positivism through the model proposed by Hart, already explained in section II.A. Schauer argues that the subject of coercion becomes invisible in the theory of law of the second half of the twentieth century, mainly because of Hart's criticisms of Austin and Kelsen, and therefore of the adoption of a conceptual analysis as the methodological standard of philosophy of the law. In other words, Hart's claim that there are legal rules without sanctions (as is the case of secondary rules) and that coercion cannot be considered as a necessary feature of legal rules, led the philosophy of law of the twentieth century to slowly abandon the issue of coercion as central to the explanation of law.

This thesis of Schauer corroborates Postema's reluctance to adopt conceptual analysis as a methodological standard for the theory of law. Like Postema's methodological proposal, Schauer shows that his discussion of coercion is only possible if the theory of law abandons its classical methodology of conceptual analysis and begins to think from typical conditions, which can bring it

[32] GJ Postema, 'Morality in the First Person Plural' (1995) 14 *Law and Philosophy* 35.
[33] FF Schauer, *The Force of Law* (Harvard University Press 2015).
[34] Postema (n 2).

closer to several other social phenomena, making its analysis more complex and integrated. Schauer calls this methodology 'differentiation' as opposed to the classical methodology of analytical theory of law, which, in essence, seeks limits or boundaries between concepts from necessary and sufficient properties.[35] Again, there are strong similarities between the proposals of Postema and Schauer, in that Postema also defends the need for a closer approximation between the phenomenon of law and other social phenomena.

Both Postema and Schauer, therefore, point to the necessity of overcoming the traditional methodology of conceptual analysis in the philosophy of law. Traditional conceptual analysis presupposes the idea of analytic truths,[36] that is, it presupposes the search for necessary and sufficient properties that are part of the meaning of the word or are constitutive of the concept. A classic example is the definition of 'single' as 'unmarried'. In it, it is possible to observe the two features of the idea of traditional conceptual analysis: (i) the definition is *a priori* and (ii) it is made by a reduction of a concept to a more basic concept ('single' → 'unmarried'). When this analysis is extended to the concept of law, the idea is to identify the necessary and sufficient properties of the concept of law in an *a priori* manner, that is, without an *a posteriori* foundation, and from a reduction of the concept of law to more basic concepts like, for example, rule or authority, which should refer to ordinary social practices. Hart's methodology, or at least the way it was received in the analytical theory of law, seems to be interpreted by Postema and Schauer in the wake of this form of conceptual analysis.[37]

Overcoming of this way of doing legal theory requires a search for typical but not necessary properties of the law. An example would be the very concept of 'coercion', which is typical of a series of social phenomena, such as the mafia, democracies and tyrannies, but which, in the prevailing view of post-Hart analytical jurisprudence, is not a necessary property of the concept of law. In this way, it would be possible to integrate the legal phenomenon into a series of other social phenomena, which do not share the same necessary properties but nevertheless share certain features typical of the historical instances of law.

It is obvious that, as Greenberg well observes, the adoption of synechist methodology or differentiation does not necessarily mean the complete abandonment of the classical methodology of conceptual analysis.[38] Classical conceptual analysis can be extremely useful if, for example, the philosophical project in question is classificatory, as when one seeks to identify the belonging of an institution to law or politics.[39] In addition, it is possible to combine conceptual

[35] Schauer (n 33) 154–68.

[36] M Greenberg, 'How to Explain Things with Force' (2016) 129 *Harvard Law Review* 1932.

[37] On the methodology on Hart's juridical positivism, see generally J Gardner, *Law as a Leap of Faith: Essays on Law in General* (Oxford University Press 2014); and Stavropoulos (n 10).

[38] Greenberg (n 36).

[39] The classic discussion about the juridical or political character of the 'Constitutional Tribunal' seems to be a good example of that way of philosophical investigation.

analysis and explanation of typical characteristics of the legal phenomenon. In any case, Postema's critique goes much further towards re-opening the theory of law for other methodologies, as a way to definitively overcome the methodological conflict that still persists in the theory of law and to make philosophical research in the field of *jurisprudence* successful again.

Moreover, in order for this approximation based on typical characteristics between law and other social phenomena to be successful, philosophy of law should be carried out with support in modes of investigation of the social sciences, especially empirical analysis. In short, the explanation of the law happens to be conducted by means of a fuzzy method of approximation between common characteristics of several social phenomena and, in addition, by means of empirical studies, that corroborate to a more inclusive understanding of the law.[40]

The silence of Schauer's work about perhaps the most relevant proposal of the treatment of law in relation to coercion in the twentieth century, namely the work of Ronald Dworkin, is puzzling.[41] As is well known, Dworkin defines the law as a model of justification for the use of coercive power by the state through reference to political decisions of the past.[42] Likewise, Postema, in his programmatic writings to overcome the current methodological conflict in the theory of law, does not comment on the extent to which his proposal finds (or not) an echo in Dworkin's proposal for the analytical theory of law.

In that sense, Stephen Guest comments that one of the main issues that bothered Dworkin was precisely the fact that the methodology employed in the analytical theory of the law of his time seemed to be extremely unsuccessful.[43] This fact seems to be directly related to the criticisms made by Postema and Schauer against the classical conceptual analysis of what the law is. In effect, Dworkin argues that what is most important in an explanation of law is not the identification of the necessary and sufficient properties of the concept of law but rather an explanation of typical elements that characterise the phenomenon of law as an institutional practice and which, in many cases, can bring the law closer to other social phenomena. It is for this reason that in his work his examples arise from the manner in which lawyers, judges and so forth apply concepts in their arguments against or in favour of a thesis. That is to say: what is central to his jurisprudence is not to identify the necessary and sufficient properties of a concept, but rather to understand the way ordinary people apply certain concepts in their arguments and, from there, to identify which are the typical

[40] As Greenberg (n 36) points out, it is not clear how that fuzzy methodology of phenomenon analysis could work adequately, given that the law could be related to diverse social phenomena in shuffle mode without necessarily having been productive.

[41] ibid 1952–53.

[42] R Dworkin, *Law's Empire* (Belknap Press 1986).

[43] S Guest, *Ronald Dworkin* (Stanford Law Books 2013) 19.

characteristics of such concepts.[44] The way a concept is applied indicates how people typically understand a certain concept, regardless of its possible *a priori* content. Thus, in all his writings, Dworkin maintains that the task of the philosophy of law consists in understanding legal phenomenon as an institutional practice relative to other social practices (institutional or otherwise), always emphasising that the legal phenomenon must be understood as a phenomenon collective or in the first person plural: 'We live in and by the law. It makes us what we are …'[45]

At this point, there is no significant difference between the methodology proposed by Postema (or even Schauer) and Dworkin, in that they all are concerned with understanding the legal phenomenon in its typical characteristics, as a response to the question 'How is law like?' In fact, this question corresponds to the title of one of its main articles: 'How Law is like Literature',[46] The importance of this text, if well understood, lies precisely in the fact that Dworkin seeks to present what can be understood as law in a possible comparison between the practice of law and literary criticism. This approximation between legal and literary judgment presents a new way of doing legal theory, unconcerned with analytical truths and open to illuminate contingent but common aspects of legal practice.

From this, we can perhaps conclude that there is no substantial difference between the *synechist* methodology of Postema and the way in which Dworkin understands the methodology of legal philosophy. Both condemn the classical conceptual analysis that seems to be the main legacy of Hart's theory of law. If there is one, the fundamental difference between the proposals of Postema and Dworkin lies precisely in the second part of his thesis, that is, in the external form of approximation between the legal phenomenon and the other social phenomena through empirical studies of the social science. In effect, Dworkin clearly favours another way of understanding the law allied to the *synechist* methodology, which seems not to have been taken into account in the considerations of Postema – and also of Schauer.

Dworkin argues that it is possible, through the same methodology used by Postema, to identify typical characteristics of the legal phenomenon related to the purpose, functionality or standard of correction of institutional practices.

[44] Stephen Guest (ibid 8) highlights this characteristic of the way Dworkin thought about law: 'One thing I've always admired in Dworkin is his ability to "talk straight," and to say it "like it is." He does not accept implausible claims. He doesn't use jargon, or do large diagrams on the blackboard, or the 101 other academic tricks. A leading UK public law scholar once exclaimed to me with irritation when I'd mentioned Dworkin, "I don't do Dworkin talk!" The irony is that "Dworkin talk" in public law is nothing other than "rights," "morality," "equality," "freedom," "principles," "rules," "legality," "policy," "integrity," and "discretion," which are jargon-free, normal words of public law discourse.'

[45] Dworkin (n 42) vii.

[46] RM Dworkin, *A Matter of Principle* (Harvard University Press 1985) 146.

In this sense, its interpretative methodology cannot avoid the attitude of seeking typical but not necessary features of law, and one of these possible features is the value or points presupposed by social practices, including law. In this way, it also seems possible to approximate the law to other social phenomena through accepted standards of correction. It is in this way that Dworkin will seek to present an integrated system of values constituted by ethics, personal morality and institutional morality, which are unified through the value of dignity.[47] It is not a question of asserting that dignity is an absolute value or a necessary property of every concept of ethics – morality and politics – but rather of saying that it is possible to observe this value as typical in ethical, moral and social practices of our form of life.

It is important, however, to stress that Dworkin's approach has its focus on a doctrinal concept of law,[48] which can be understood as an enquiry into the identification of true legal propositions that can legitimate the state's use of coercion. Thus, Dworkin's methodology should be regarded as a model for identifying the content of the law regarding interpretative concepts. Postema's jurisprudence as sociable science is better described as an attempt to grasp a sociological concept of law, which can be understood as an inquiry into the identification of basic elements of institutional phenomenon or action.[49]

In other words, the final version of Dworkin's legal theory is grounded in two main theses: the so-called *one-system thesis*, and the *interpretative thesis*.[50] According to the interpretative thesis, legal propositions can be true or false depending on the internal point attributed to a particular institutional practice. The very idea of this way of understanding legal practice, and consequently legal propositions or concepts, was the main part of my argument. In this sense, the point of institutional practice cannot be deducted from an external point of view (or Archimedean point in Dworkin's terminology), and it always depends on an internal inferential understanding of the practice. According to the second thesis, the one-system thesis, law should be understood as a branch of political morality, which is beside ethics and personal morality, one part of morality in general. Therefore, Dworkin's theory can indeed be read as a kind of *synechist* methodology, since the association between law and morality should not be understood according to the classical methodology of conceptual analysis but furthermore as a kind of approximation between some common aspects between law and morality based on an internal point or purpose of the practice.

[47] R Dworkin, *Justice for Hedgehogs* (Harvard University Press 2011).

[48] '[T]he doctrinal concept that we use in stating what the law of some jurisdiction requires or forbids or permits ("Ignorance is no defense under the law")' (RM Dworkin, *Justice in Robes* (Harvard University Press 2008) 223).

[49] '[T]he sociological concept we use to describe a particular form of political organization ("The Romans developed a complex and sophisticated form of law")' (ibid).

[50] T Bustamante, 'Law, Moral Facts and Interpretation: A Dworkinian Response to Mark Greenberg's Moral Impact Theory of Law' (2019) 32 *Canadian Journal of Law & Jurisprudence* 5.

Regarding the very idea of both projects, the facts that Postema believes that jurisprudence should give more importance to studies on sociological aspects of law and that Dworkin's account is constructed based on a doctrinal concept of law, in practice represent two different important ways of understanding the subject of jurisprudence. For Dworkin, jurisprudence is an enquiry into the models of determining true legal propositions, which is part of morality due to the fact that legal validity depends on political obligation.[51] Accordingly, it is of course possible to pursue other scientific objectives considering law, as for instance to understand how modern legal institutions are dependent on certain aspects of the Christian religion (sociological concept of law in Dworkin's terminology) or how people react psychologically to legal rules (natural kind concept of law in Dworkin's terminology). Jurisprudence remains, however, according to Dworkin, untouched by these other approaches, since the realm of jurisprudence is autonomous in relation to other possible realms of scientific inquiries about law.[52]

Thus, it can be said that there is no primary incompatibility between the methodological proposals of Dworkin and Postema to overcome the form by which the analytical theory of law from Hart came to be characterised. In fact, the two proposals are complementary while distinguishable. On the one hand, they are complementary because they both favour a *synechist* methodology, but on the other hand they distance themselves in the way of identifying and analysing the typical characteristics of the legal phenomenon and its integration with the phenomena of social rights. However, at the same time, both projects differentiate themselves regarding the very idea of jurisprudence. Dworkin's theory sets a thick limit on the meaning of jurisprudence, confining its purpose to questions on legal validity and its connection to political obligation, whereas Postema's approach is much more open to other modes of inquiry and developments of social sciences.

IV. FINAL COMMENTS

One of Postema's main works, *Legal Philosophy in the Twentieth Century: The Common Law World*, concludes with a programmatic writing about the future of the analytical theory of law. In it, Postema presents a methodological proposal for the analytical theory of law to overcome the dispute of method, understood as a legacy of Hart's work and in which it is steeped from Dworkin's early criticisms of Hart's work. This methodological dispute at the heart of the analytical theory of law is characterised by the debate between a descriptive and

[51] ibid.
[52] Dworkin (n 47).

normative or other normative way of identifying the content of law, that is to say, legal rights in the Hohfeldian sense.

Postema's project to overcome this paradigm consists, on the one hand, in moving away from the traditional method of conceptual analysis, characteristic of Hart's work, and, on the other hand, in dialogue with other social sciences, especially empirical studies. In this sense, Postema criticises the classical conceptual analysis, based on the search for the identification of necessary and sufficient properties of the concept of law, and affirms that the theory of law should adopt a *synechist* methodology, which deals with the identification of characteristics typical of the law, without concern for its nature. In addition to this, it is necessary to integrate the legal phenomenon with other social phenomena through an approximation of such characteristics contingent on or typical of the legal phenomenon, as a way to improve their understanding in the midst of social reality.

In the end, this chapter points out that this methodological proposal of Postema does not differ fundamentally from Ronald Dworkin's proposal in his main works, since it was precisely against the classical conceptual analysis attributed to Hart that Dworkin developed his methodology, known as interpretativism. The difference between the two proposals consists above all in the way in which the two authors approximate the law to other social phenomena, inasmuch as Dworkin favours such an approach by identifying patterns of correction or common points, even in a contingent way to several social phenomena, in order to identify the content of the law (doctrinal concept of law) in relation to political obligation, while Postema bets on the approximation through empirical characteristics of the phenomena compared for grasping a sociological concept of law.

Part V

Postema's Analysis of Contemporary Legal Theories

12

In Defence of a Thin Concept of Law

ANDREA FAGGION

I. INTRODUCTION

IT IS AN honour and a privilege to participate in dialogue with one of the most important legal philosophers of our time.[1] I have chosen to focus on an issue that, according to Gerald Postema, is central to legal philosophy: the normativity of law. Postema's first famous endeavour to account for the normativity of law was a conventionalist reconstruction of Hart's rule of recognition. At a later stage, however, he moved away from Hart, thoroughly rejecting the Hartian concept of normativity. Indeed, it is safe to say that only a minority of legal philosophers now share Hart's position, according to which legal obligations do not imply reasons to comply on the part of legal subjects. Nevertheless, I wish to join that minority. Section II of the chapter presents an outline of the problem. In section III, I introduce Postema's first approach to the problem and what I take to be the main reason for his departure from it. Section IV is dedicated to Postema's arguments against Hart and my defence of Hart's thin concept of law.

II. THE HARTIAN CONCEPT OF LEGAL OBLIGATION

A. The Internal Point of View

The major ambition of HLA Hart's jurisprudence is the development of a theory of normativity capable of accounting for the normative language of law without reducing its meaning to bare coercion or moral normativity. The success of Hart's endeavour depends heavily on the concept of an internal point of view, by which he distinguishes between mere habits or regular social

[1] This would not be possible without Postema's generous help. I am especially grateful for his reading recommendations.

behaviour and social rules. For Hart, the law's normativity is a form of social normativity.

From the internal point of view, social practices function as rules; they are accepted as reasons for action and for appraisals of actions inside a social group.[2] This being so, the internal point of view concerns the attitudes involved in practical reasoning. It does not refer to feelings or other mental states.[3] It needs for its expression propositions related to the *acceptance* of norms as such, for instance 'I have an obligation', or 'they ought to do it'. For Hart, propositions such as 'I am obliged to do it' or 'you will suffer for it if …' are not able to express the internal point of view.[4]

An agent can consider information about the likely consequences of a decision in her practical reasoning. Such propositions serve as theoretical premises in her reasoning (not every premise in practical reasoning must be normative). This being so, it seems to be faithful to Hart's theory to claim that a pattern of behaviour has not been accepted as a rule or practical premise if the agent's reasoning only takes into account the sanctions that other agents are willing to impose on her because of *their* acceptance of that pattern as a rule or norm. In this case, the practical reasoning might take the following form:

> Practical reasoning 1:
>
> 'I ought to avoid sanctions *x*' (practical premise).
>
> 'Agents *A* are likely to enforce *x* against me if I violate their social rule *r*' (theoretical premise).
>
> 'I ought to avoid violations of *r*' (practical conclusion).

It is possible for a pattern of behaviour to function not as a rule but as a theoretical premise in the agent's practical reasoning when the following conditions apply: (i) the agent fails to understand the reasons for accepting the rule; (ii) the agent understands the reasons behind the rule but has stronger reasons against the rule; (iii) the agent is in favour of the rule in general but does not view herself as being bound by it, because she wants to escape the burden of being held to it while nonetheless benefitting from its general observance (she is a *free rider*); (iv) there is no reason for the agent to accept the pattern of behaviour as a rule (she is a *victim* of a coercive system).

On this practical reasoning, when it comes to determining whether the agent takes the external point of view, it does not matter why she does not accept a pattern of behaviour as her own rule. What matters is that the rule is not accepted as such. In order to accept a social pattern as a normative rule – and thus to take up the internal point of view – the agent must use that social

[2] See HLA Hart, *The Concept of Law* (2nd edn, Oxford University Press 1994) 98.

[3] See ibid 88; GJ Postema, *Legal Philosophy in the Twentieth Century: The Common Law World*, vol 11 (Springer 2011) 296.

[4] See Hart (n 2) 90.

pattern as a practical premise in her practical reasoning, as in the following example:

> Practical reasoning 2:[5]
>
> 'People ought to take off their hats when entering a church' (social rule/practical premise).
>
> 'I am entering a church' (theoretical premise).
>
> 'I ought to take off my hat (if I am wearing one)' (practical conclusion).

According to Hart, it is impossible to account for the normativity of law if officials in a given system do not take the internal point of view on legal rules.[6] Officials can use legal rules in their practical reasoning without necessarily morally endorsing them, however.[7] Thus the core of a key debate between Hart and Joseph Raz lies in the fact that Hart is willing to admit – while Raz is not – any kind of reason for norm acceptance. Before exploring the debate between

[5] Stephen Perry has argued that Hart has no good reason to exclude the bad man's perspective from the internal point of view. According to Oliver Wendell Holmes, Jr, a bad man pays attention to the law and complies with it only to avoid unpleasant consequences. Thus, for Perry, 'the bad man also regards the social practices Hart calls "rules" as reason giving'. SR Perry, 'Holmes versus Hart: The Bad Man in Legal Theory' in SJ Burton (ed), *The Path of the Law and Its Influence: The Legacy of Oliver Wendell Holmes, Jr* (Cambridge University Press 2000) 165; see also SR Perry, 'Interpretation and Methodology in Legal Theory' in A Marmor (ed), *Law and Interpretation: Essays in Legal Philosophy* (Oxford University Press 1995) 100. Postema makes a similar point. See GJ Postema, 'Jurisprudence as Practical Philosophy' (1998) 4 *Legal Theory* 329, 338–41. Certainly, the bad man or an agent reasoning from the external point of view in Hart's sense can engage in practical reasoning about law. What I intend to show by comparing the two examples of practical reasoning above is that the relevant difference between the internal and the external points of view is the role played by the rule in practical reasoning, ie the type of premise in which the rule appears in each type of practical reasoning. As Matthew Kramer has said in reply to Perry, it is possible for a legal rule to operate like a rain cloud in practical reasoning, providing theoretical premises for the agent because of its activity. See MH Kramer, *In Defense of Legal Positivism: Law without Trimmings* (Oxford University Press 1999) 242. However, Postema refers to a difficulty regarding the possibility of viewing social rules from the outside. According to this criticism, viewed from the outside, 'there is no non-arbitrary way to identify the rule-relevant data': GJ Postema, 'Conventions at the Foundations of Law' in P Newman (ed), *The New Palgrave Dictionary of Economics and Law*, vol 1 (Macmillan 1998) 467. That is, social rules are always indeterminate from the external point of view. It is perhaps possible to handle this objection by appealing to a version of Joseph Raz's distinction between detached and committed statements (which Raz ascribes to Hans Kelsen). See J Raz, *The Authority of Law* (2nd edn, Oxford University Press 2009) 306. For Raz, detached statements are statements from a point of view (they are made on the assumption that a basic norm is valid but without commitment to that assumption), whereas committed statements are ordinary moral statements. In applying this distinction to Hart's theory, we should admit prudential commitment as well. Thus, from a Hartian internal point of view, all statements are committed. Detached statements are the statements of an outsider who is attempting to figure out the rules that are accepted by a community in order to avoid unpleasant consequences when interacting with members of that community. This outsider reasons in much the same way that a philosophy teacher reasons when she puts herself in the place of a certain philosopher in order to answer her students' questions.

[6] See Hart (n 2) 116.

[7] This is why Perry is also wrong when he opposes what he calls a 'socialized' point of view, meaning the point of view of one who accepts a social pattern as a norm, to a 'prudential' point of view. See Perry, 'Holmes versus Hart' (n 5) 169; see also SJ Shapiro, 'The Bad Man and the Internal Point of View' in Burton (ed) (n 5) 201, for a reply to Perry.

Hart and Raz on this point, however, we must deepen our understanding of Hart's jurisprudence by introducing another concept that is just as central as the concept of an internal point of view: the rule of recognition. This is essential, inasmuch as the debate is, above all, a debate about appropriate reasons for accepting the rule of recognition on the part of the officials of a legal system in their public capacity.[8]

B. The Rule of Recognition

The rule of recognition is a social rule by which a society distinguishes between legal rules and its other social rules. This is why it is so important. As is well known, according to Hart, the key to jurisprudence is a connection between what he calls primary and secondary rules.[9] Primary rules require subjects to perform or abstain from certain actions, despite their wishes. Secondary rules confer powers to introduce, extinguish, change, apply and identify rules. The rule of recognition is a secondary rule.

The rule of recognition provides a test for determining the rules of a legal system, which purport to guide the actions of a group. It is supposed to settle doubts as to what the legal rules are (ie membership in the system) and their precise scope. The acknowledgement of legally authoritative texts and persons as such also requires a rule of recognition.[10] This amounts to saying that legal validity is validity in accordance with a system's rule of recognition.

Hart is explicit about the fact that concepts such as validity 'demand a reference to the internal point of view for their analysis'.[11] However, according to Hart, the rule of recognition is seldom expressly formulated. From the internal point of view, its existence is not stated as a fact but is shown in the way in which it is accepted as a guiding rule by courts and others to identify legally valid rules.[12] As Hart argues, employing one of his standard game metaphors, shouting 'goal' in a stadium is 'the language of one assessing a situation by reference to rules which he in common with others acknowledges as appropriate for this purpose'.[13]

[8] Indeed, Hart may have been referring to private reasons for norm acceptance, whereas Raz was referring to law's claims. To be relevant, however, that debate should be reconstructed as a debate regarding law's claims, ie claims that officials are supposed to make in their capacity as legal officials. One of the best analyses of the sense in which law can make claims is the analysis offered by J Gardner, 'How Law Claims, What Law Claims' in *Law as a Leap of Faith: Essays on Law in General* (Oxford University Press 2012).

[9] It is always good to remember that such a claim should not be understood as a semantic thesis, as if the union between primary and secondary rules were a necessary condition for the correct use of the word 'law'.

[10] See Hart (n 2) 94–95.

[11] ibid 98.

[12] ibid 101.

[13] ibid 102.

In the legal 'game', a rule that satisfies the validity tests provided by the rule of recognition is a reason (a practical premise) for a judicial decision.[14] For Hart, the rule of recognition is an 'ultimate rule'; where there are several, hierarchically organised criteria of legal validity, one of them is supreme.[15] This means that in situations where a legal rule that is used as a judicial reason is challenged, the rule of recognition may need to be expressly formulated.

Indeed, Hart traces a chain of challenges and answers that begins with the question of whether some suggested rule is legally valid.[16] However, such a chain of reasons ends in the rule of recognition – a rule that, while providing criteria for the assessment of the legal validity of other rules, is not legally valid or invalid, since there is no rule providing criteria for the assessment of its own validity.

According to Hart, there are two kinds of questions to be asked about the rule of recognition. On the one hand, is it a rule the existence of which produces more good than evil? Do I have a moral obligation to support it? Is it at least prudential to follow it? On the other hand, is that rule actually used by officials and ordinary citizens as the ultimate rule of that legal system?[17] With the first kind of question, we have moved from the domain of legal validity to a statement of value. With the second kind of question, we have moved from the internal point of view to an external statement of fact.[18] Since neither statements of value nor statements of fact can provide the legal validity of a rule, Hart concludes that 'No such question can arise as to the validity of the very rule of recognition which provides the criteria [of legal validity]; it can neither be valid nor invalid.'[19]

C. Legal Obligations and Reasons for Action

Readers who follow Hart up to this point might be left with an uneasy feeling.[20] Hart describes an internal point of view with legal rules as reasons for judicial decisions; at the end of the day, however, a chain of legal reasons offered by a judge who is enforcing a legal obligation is left hanging in the air, as it were. It seems perfectly reasonable to ask that judge a further question: why ought I, an ordinary citizen, to accept the obligations that are ultimately grounded in the rule of recognition, which is itself unjustified?

As Hart is famous for stressing, law does not merely oblige me to act in certain ways or to refrain from certain actions, like a gunman threatening me to

[14] ibid 105.
[15] ibid.
[16] ibid 107.
[17] ibid.
[18] ibid 108.
[19] ibid 109.
[20] See, for instance, Postema, 'Jurisprudence as Practical Philosophy' (n 5) 337; Postema (n 3) 317–18.

make me do what he says.[21] Law claims to create obligations for me, and it justifies its coercion against me by appealing to those obligations. Hence, is it not the case that legal obligations can justify coercion only if law necessarily claims that the rule of recognition is morally justified? Otherwise, how can we understand the normativity of law? Would not law be a system of mere coercion after all?

As noted, the matter at issue here was debated by Hart and Raz. In his *Essays on Bentham*, reacting to an objection in a footnote in Raz's *The Authority of Law*,[22] Hart offers a non-cognitive account of citizens' legal obligations. According to this account, having an obligation is different from merely being obliged, insofar as if A claims that B has a legal obligation, A means that:

1) There are actions which are due from or owed by B.
2) These are actions that may be properly demanded of B according to legal norms *n*, which regulate demands for action.
3) A accepts (in common with others, but not necessarily in common with B) a rule of recognition *r* that includes a criterion *c*, which identifies *n* among the laws which A (and others) must apply and enforce.[23]

For Raz, the crucial question in this debate seems to be why the acceptance of *r* by A (and others) could justify a demand for action from B. Hart in turn defends his old account of voluntary acceptance of a rule of recognition.[24] At first, he admits that it would be extraordinary if judges could not provide an answer as to why they accept a rule that is responsible for determining the standards of correct judicial behaviour and for providing reasons for applying and enforcing particular rules.[25] With this noted, however, he then claims that 'all that is required is that judges should have some comprehensive motives for behaving as they do'.[26] Hart goes on to list examples of comprehensive motives, '[judges] simply wish to continue in an established practice or … they had sworn

[21] See Hart (n 2) 82–91.
[22] See Raz (n 5) 155, fn13.
[23] HLA Hart, *Essays on Bentham: Studies in Jurisprudence and Political Theory* (Clarendon Press 1982) 159–60. Philip Soper claims that this Hartian account of legal obligation is a retreat from Hart's distinction in *The Concept of Law* between having a legal obligation and being obliged. See P Soper, *The Ethics of Deference: Learning from Law's Morals* (Cambridge University Press, 2002) 58, fn12, 68–69; Hart (n 2) 82–87, 167–80. Indeed, Soper believes that this alleged retreat came in two stages, starting with the admission, in *The Concept of Law*, of self-interested reasons as reasons for acceptance of a system's rule of recognition. However, there is no reason to believe that Hart once aimed to explain the difference between the enforcement of legal obligations and a gunman situation writ large with an explanation that differed essentially from the account offered for legal obligations in the *Essays on Bentham*. To be sure, Hart never intended the difference to be moral. From what I can see, the point was always only that the gunman is not applying a rule, even less applying a rule identified by criteria recognised in a social practice. The gunman is merely giving an order to a particular individual or group of individuals, whereas a legal obligation is not a mere particular order to a multitude of individuals.
[24] See Hart (n 2) 203 for this account.
[25] See Hart, *Essays on Bentham* (n 23) 265.
[26] ibid.

on taking office to continue it or ... they had tacitly agreed to do so by accepting the office of judge'.[27]

For Raz, the above motives are the wrong type of reasons for accepting *r*; if A enforces an obligation on B, *what is required of A from the internal point of view is an appeal to reasons for B's acceptance of such an obligation.* This point was made by Raz in *The Authority of Law*, but it is clearer in Raz's reply to the *Essays on Bentham*:

> I have contrasted accepting a rule concerning the behaviour of the agent ('I ought not to buy sweets') and accepting a rule concerning the behaviour of another ('He ought not to buy sweets'). I can believe in the validity of the first for reasons of self-interest or convenience. But I cannot justify a belief in the validity of the second by such reasons. That it may be to my advantage if I refrain from having sweets is a reason for accepting that I ought not buy them. But that it is to my advantage that you refrain from buying sweets is not a reason for me or for anyone else for accepting that you ought not buy them (unless you ought to promote my interest).[28]

On Raz's account, a legal obligation is thus necessarily an obligation the enforcement of which law claims to be morally justified (even though such a claim can be false), which means that, in the practice of law, the rule of recognition is always (implicitly) claimed to be morally justified.[29] For Raz, since Hart is not willing to admit any kind of necessary connection between legal validity and a claim to the moral justification of the rule of recognition, he is unable to account for the normativity of law after all. In this context, Gerald Postema has endeavoured to develop an alternative account of the reasons behind judicial acceptance of the rule of recognition – one that avoids appealing to political morality as a foundation of law but still provides an account of law's normativity.[30] It is to this account that I now wish to turn.

III. THE CONVENTIONALIST APPROACH TO NORMATIVITY

A. Conventions and Coordination Problems

In his famous paper 'Coordination and Conventions at the Foundations of Law', Postema considers some of the objections to Hart's account of the normativity

[27] ibid.

[28] J Raz, 'Hart on Moral Rights and Legal Duties' (1984) 4 *Oxford Journal of Legal Studies* 123, 130.

[29] According to Raz, every time judges apply legal norms, they present themselves as believing that there is a doctrine of political morality from which it follows that they ought to apply these legal norms: '[t]heir decisions are moral decisions in expressing a moral position'. J Raz, *Ethics in the Public Domain: Essays in the Morality of Law and Politics* (rev edn, Clarendon Press 1995) 223.

[30] GJ Postema, 'Coordination and Conventions at the Foundations of Law' (1982) 11 *The Journal of Legal Studies* 165.

of law discussed in section II.[31] He claims that a conventionalist interpretation of Hart's rule of recognition can bridge the gap between social fact and genuine normativity. On his view, Hart did not cut off questions of justification at the level of the rule of recognition but merely required a certain type of justification that he himself had not developed.

According to this interpretation, a legal system's supreme rule of recognition is not justified by an inductive inference from the brute fact that many officials (for whatever reason) actually apply that rule to identify membership in the normative system. With this said, it is not justified by political morality either. The main idea is that sharing a rule of recognition is a convention that solves coordination problems among officials on the one hand and between officials and ordinary citizens on the other.

First, a coordination problem is a special case of strategic interaction. According to Postema, strategic interactions are defined by two properties: (i) the actions of all parties jointly determine each party's outcomes, and (ii) the best choice for each party depends on expectations about others' behaviour, where each party is trying to guess what the others will do and where each party knows this.[32] According to Postema, however, three features distinguish coordination problems from other types of strategic interaction:

> [a)] Rough Coincidence of Interests: Each party is likely to benefit more by cooperation than by noncooperation. …
>
> [b)] Mutually Conditional Preferences: Certain actions are preferred to others if, but only if, other parties also prefer them (or appropriately corresponding actions) …
>
> [c)] Ambiguity: There are at least two combinations of the actions of all the agents which each agent would count as 'successful' coordination.[33]

Thus, problems of coordination are marked by 'coincidence of interest' (a) and 'interdependence of decision' (b). What makes the situation problematic is property (c): the deficit of information. If there is more than one coordination possibility, agents cannot know what the others will decide or what those others will expect them to decide. Conventions solve this kind of informational problem. Postema lists the following conditions for counting as a convention:

> A regularity R in the behavior of persons in a population P in a recurring situation S is a *convention* if and only if in any instance of S
>
> (1) it is common knowledge in P that
>
> *(a)* there is in P general conformity to R;
>
> *(b)* most members of P expect most other members of P to conform to R;

[31] ibid 166, 169–71.
[32] ibid 173.
[33] ibid 174.

(*c*) almost every member of P prefers that any individual conform rather than not conform to some regularity of behavior in S, given general conformity to that regularity;

(*d*) almost every member of P prefers general conformity to some regularity rather than general non-conformity (ie, general conformity to no regularity);

(2) part of the reason why most members of P conform to R in S is that 1*a*–1*d* obtain.[34]

Given the above definitions of coordination problems and conventions, it is difficult to see why there would be any *obligation* to adhere to any convention and thereby solve a coordination problem. After all, it is part of the definition of the problem that its solution is in each agent's interest. In other words, the solution to the problem is the mere provision of information that each agent is looking for; if one agent loses interest in the solution to the problem, she has no reason to adhere to the convention.[35] This is why Postema relies on the idea of detrimental reliance to explain the obligation at issue.[36]

B. Detrimental Reliance and Obligations

Postema admits that cases of detrimental reliance that grounds obligations to adhere to conventions are rare in problems of coordination, for the detrimental reliance needs to be *induced* in order to ground an obligation. He argues, however, that the legal activities of both officials and ordinary citizens have the structure of a network of coordination problems, and in this legal context Postema attempts to show that conventions do give rise to genuine obligations due to detrimental reliance.

The obligations that Postema has in mind are not held by ordinary citizens. The main reason for excluding ordinary citizens appears to be precisely the fact already mentioned, 'law-subjects who will be no better off having successfully coordinated their activity under the law than if they had failed, will have no reason to conform'.[37] For Postema, however, this outcome is not unwelcome, because 'Although we are inclined to hold that officials have obligations to respect the expectations of citizens regarding the officials' activities, we are less inclined to hold that citizens owe a similar obligation to officials.'[38] Thus, Postema claims to have shown that there is a genuine judicial obligation

[34] ibid 176.

[35] For a deeper development of this type of argument against the conventionalist approach to legal reasons, see L Green, *The Authority of the State* (Clarendon Press 1990) ch 4; L Green, 'Positivism and Conventionalism' (1999) 12 *Canadian Journal of Law and Jurisprudence* 35.

[36] Postema (n 30) 180.

[37] ibid 195.

[38] ibid 196.

to comply with conventions at the foundations of law, since courts '*induce* … expectations (and reliance on them) on the part of citizens'.[39]

In sum, the rule of recognition is a convention that lies at the foundation of law. Coordination in law is possible if ordinary citizens adjust their behaviour to fit the norms that they expect officials to identify and apply to them, and if officials who identify and apply those norms adjust their activity to fit ordinary citizens' expectations. The rule of recognition is then a convention, adherence to which satisfies these induced expectations. Thus, Postema grounds in this conventionalist account of Hart's rule of recognition a judicial obligation to adhere to such a rule.

We have seen that the gist of the argument for judicial obligation is the idea of detrimental reliance. Nonetheless, Hart's jurisprudence allows for a minority's (or even a majority's) being exploited by an elite who run the legal system, in which case certain judicial departures from the rule of recognition may be detrimental only to officials themselves and the class of those who generally benefit from the unjust system.[40] In this context, it makes no sense to talk of even a prima facie or defeasible moral judicial obligation to identify and apply legal rules in accordance with the system's rule of recognition.[41]

In such an unjust legal system, those who suffer as a result of the enforcement of legal obligations are likely to hope for benign judicial departures from the rule of recognition, although they are unlikely to expect such departures. By contrast, those who benefit from rigorous judicial acceptance of the rule of recognition are likely to expect judicial adherence to that rule, but they would not have a *legitimate* expectation capable of grounding a moral judicial obligation. At most, we can say that officials in that system ought to accept their system's rule of recognition because they need to coordinate their actions to sustain a system that is in their interest. But this would be a merely prudential 'ought' for those who enforce the law, which would not imply that legal norms themselves provide practical premises for norm-subjects.[42]

C. The Normative Force of Customary Norms

A merely prudential (self-interested) reason is the type of reason for rule acceptance that Hart has been willing to accept, although his critics have not. An exploitative arrangement in the interest of the rulers, on Hart's view, is consistent with the normativity of law, and there would therefore still be

[39] ibid 197.

[40] Hart (n 2) 117, 201–02.

[41] As Kramer notes, where legal rules are substantively unjust, they can function as standards for a minimum of decency in the treatment of ordinary citizens, but the courts are under an obligation not to treat such a minimum as a maximum and are therefore under an obligation to depart from the rule of recognition. See Kramer (n 5) 26.

[42] Regarding this analysis, I am especially indebted to Kramer. See Kramer (n 5).

legal obligations in such a context. No judicial moral obligations to accept the system's rule of recognition would arise, however, precisely because the norm-subject would have no reason to accept the norm as such. In his 'Custom in International Law: A Normative Practice Account', Postema seems to be well aware of this last fact, detaching himself from his former position, according to which there can be situations in which judges have a genuine obligation to apply the law while citizens do not have an obligation to comply:

> [T]here may be conditions in which the defector can justify his defection by pointing to some load-bearing difference between his situation and that of most other parties. He might argue, for example, that he does not stand to benefit (or benefit enough, relative to the benefits others will reap) from successful cooperation. If the defector can successfully make this argument, then fair-minded participants must acknowledge that it is not the defector who exploits the cooperation of the others, but rather the cooperators who exploit this individual. His defection is not free-riding, and holding him to his alleged 'obligation' in the cooperative enterprise is unwarranted. ... A fairer cooperative enterprise would recognize in some systematic way the legitimacy of such defections.[43]

Here, Postema is discussing the normative force of customary norms, which matters for us because the rule of recognition would be a customary norm. Postema makes the normative force of customary norms depend on mechanisms of recognition of conscientious defections within the community, with two exceptions: (i) the customary norm is thought to serve common values rather than convergent interests (values that are regarded as essential to community membership); and (ii) the customary norms articulate abstract moral principles that depend on customs for their concrete force.[44]

Hence, Postema has a way out of the objection to his earlier use of the idea of detrimental reliance in the construction of a genuine judicial obligation. This way out consists in denying the legal validity of any system that is openly based on the rulers' self-interest as previously described. In short, in order to avoid the objection, Postema must avoid severing the concept of legal obligation from the presumption of the legal norm's being a practical reason for the norm-subject (and indeed he was ultimately willing to connect the two). I shall now turn to Postema's arguments against Hart's thinner concept of

[43] GJ Postema, 'Custom in International Law: A Normative Practice Account' in A Perreau-Saussine and JB Murphy (eds), *The Nature of Customary Law: Legal, Historical and Philosophical Perspectives* (Cambridge University Press 2007) 298. In 'Coordination and Conventions at the Foundations of Law', Postema had loosened the concept of a coordination problem to make room for the doctrine of fair play, according to which an agent may have an obligation to take part in a fair cooperative enterprise rather than free riding. See Postema (n 30) 182. Later on, he adopted the concept of cooperation problems, which includes not only pure problems of coordination but also iterated situations in which conflict predominates. According to Postema, what these cooperation problems share is the fact that agents are usually better off if they cooperate. See Postema, 'Conventions at the Foundations of Law' (n 5) 468; GJ Postema, 'Salience Reasoning' (2008) 27 *Topoi* 41, 42.

[44] Postema, 'Custom in International Law' (n 43) 299.

law's normativity. These arguments reinforce the objections to Hart voiced by Raz that were outlined in section II.C.

IV. THE NORMATIVITY OF LAW

A. The Gunman Situation Writ Large?

In 'The Normativity of Law', Postema challenges Hart's view of legal obligation by arguing that it implies that there are reasons for judges to enforce obligations but no reasons for norm-subjects to accept the norms under which those obligations are enforced.[45] In the context of wicked legal systems, Postema notes that it is not obvious that the victims of political and institutional violence have legal obligations to comply with the law. An interesting point made by Postema is that Hart's theory of law leads to this outcome because it describes the point of view of the officials but disregards that of the victims:

> The victim has an intelligible *participant* view of the situation as well. The committed judgement, that demands imposed on victims by the organized powers in a territory generate no obligations whatsoever and therefore cannot be regarded as valid or binding, is a perfectly legitimate, intelligible judgement. If there cannot be found even minimally persuasive reasons for victims voluntarily to comply with the dictates of those in power, then those dictates cannot be regarded as binding.[46]

The inclusion of victims under the category of *participants* of that system is counterintuitive, however. To what extent do victims participate in such systems? Do they participate by suffering the consequences of others' decisions? It is clear that any such victim's claim that the demands imposed on her are not binding or valid are legitimate. But is this not because we agree that those demands are not *morally* binding or valid? To say that the same demands generate no *legal* obligation and cannot be regard as *legally* valid or binding because they are not *morally* valid or binding is to beg the question.

Postema's concept of legal obligation embraces a legitimate inference, in normal circumstances, from subjection to a valid law to a moral obligation to comply. Such a moral obligation, and with it any legal obligation, is extinguished if the relevant formally valid law does not meet certain conditions of justice.[47] Postema's defence of this concept of legal obligation, according to which 'there is no law for those systematically excluded',[48] rests on three premises. I will consider the first two in this section and the last one in the next section.

[45] See GJ Postema, 'The Normativity of Law' in R Gavison (ed), *Issues in Contemporary Legal Philosophy: The Influence of HLA Hart* (Clarendon Press 1987) 81, 88–93. I will not here consider Hart's own defence of his position on legal obligation in *Essays on Bentham*; I am not convinced of the soundness of his arguments, and explaining why would take me well beyond the scope of this chapter. With this said, I do intend to provide a Hartian defence of Hart's position.

[46] Postema (n 45) 90.

[47] ibid 91.

[48] ibid 92.

According to the first premise, law 'seeks to guide the behaviour of rational beings through rational means, that is, through addressing to them public general rules to which they are expected to conform in their behaviour'.[49] We should clearly accept this premise. This does not take Postema's argument very far, however, since even the gunman guides the behaviour of a rational being through rational means. After all, a threat only makes sense if it is made against a deliberating being – an agent capable of balancing reasons. The gunman makes a specific threat on the basis of the types of reasons that are likely to top his victim's balance of reasons. Besides, even gangs of bandits can decide to address general rules to their victims, allowing them to control large territories and reasonably sized populations indefinitely (eg cartel-imposed curfews in Rio de Janeiro).

The second premise is a claim that will be familiar to those who have read 'Coordination and Conventions at the Foundations of Law'. This is the claim that 'it is necessary for [law-making and law-applying officials] to look at the rules and directives from the point of view of law-subjects, to understand the role the rules can be expected to play in the practical reasoning of law subjects'.[50] Thus the question is why officials cannot simply understand these rules as playing the role of an imperative in the practical reasoning of law-subjects. At this point, Matthew Kramer's analysis of the difference between imperatives and prescriptions is very useful.[51]

Let us understand a prescription as a practical 'ought' judgment that sets forth or presupposes reasons for action.[52] A prescription can be moral or prudential. Thus, the first point to be made about Hart's theory of legal normativity is that legal rules can be prudential prescriptions for officials who need to coordinate their actions with other officials in order to maintain a regime. As is well known, Hart thought that the internal point of view required of officials could be taken up without their morally endorsing those rules.

A second well-known point about Hart's view is also essential in this regard: legal rules do not need to be (prudential or moral) prescriptions for law-subjects, since it is consistent with the Hartian concept of a legal system that law-subjects can consider legal rules from the external point of view.[53] Hence legal rules defining legal obligations can be bare imperatives for law-subjects. Imperatives are 'must' – not 'ought' – statements.[54] In the terms of this chapter, imperatives provide theoretical premises for practical reasoning. This is why

[49] ibid 91–92.
[50] ibid 92.
[51] See Kramer (n 5) 83–89, 221–25.
[52] ibid 84.
[53] For Postema, it is a defining feature of rules 'that they provide, or claim or are intended to provide, compliance reasons': Postema, 'Jurisprudence as Practical Philosophy' (n 5) 348. This definition is not shared by Hart. Indeed, such a controversy regarding the normativity of legal rules is the main concern of this chapter.
[54] See Kramer (n 5) 80.

coercion gives effect to imperatives.[55] From the ruler's perspective, it is irrelevant whether the norm itself serves as a practical (prudential or moral) premise in the law-subject's reasoning: '[imperatives] demand acts or abstentions that essentially serve only the interests of the officials who imposes the demands'.[56] Thus, taking for granted Postema's second premise that rulers need to look at the rules from the point of view of law-subjects, what would prevent rulers from considering their rules imperatives addressed to law-subjects?

At this point, it should be noted that the Hartian view does not imply that it is impossible to distinguish raw evil from legal evil,[57] as if Hart had fallen prey to the same mistake he attributes to John Austin. As Kramer convincingly argues, we can grasp the difference between law and raw force without appealing to moral claims of legal systems or moral facts about legal systems: 'Whereas the ascendance of a gunman over his victims typically involves situation-specific orders rather than any general decrees or standards, a regime of law must involve the reign and application of general norms.'[58] This means that if a criminal organisation like the Mafia is able to control a large territory with a reasonably sized population indefinitely, we may well designate it a legal regime. Whether we do so will depend on morally neutral issues such as efficacy and comprehensiveness. The regime's lack of moral legitimacy (or any claim to such legitimacy) does not prevent us from using the concept of law to describe it.[59]

B. In Defence of a Thin Concept of Law

What I am defending, following Kramer's lead, is what Frederick Schauer has called a thin concept of law.[60] If such a morally neutral concept is actually

[55] This being so, the fundamental difference between imperatives and prudential prescriptions is the fact that avoiding sanctions is a primary reason to comply with imperatives but only a secondary or auxiliary reason to comply with prudential prescriptions. With a prudential prescription, the agent is supposed to accept the rule as such because it is in her interest. With an imperative, the agent is supposed to view the rule as being in the interest of others and to comply with it only to avoid sanction. In Hartian terms, imperatives are rules that agents agree to comply with from the external point of view (as the rules of others), whereas prudential prescriptions are rules that agents agree to comply with from the internal point of view. Therefore, for Hart, legal rules cannot be imperatives for officials; they can only be imperatives for ordinary citizens.

[56] Kramer (n 5) 222.

[57] ibid 92–101.

[58] ibid 94. Since at least Raz and Postema have accused Hart of retreating to a Kelsenian concept of legal obligation, it is important to emphasise that imperatives are directed at citizens, even though the incentive to comply with them is the sanction. Without the imperative, and with the raw use of force, the citizen cannot know what to do to avoid sanction, and officials cannot compel the desired behaviour. Therefore, imperatives do provide 'rational guidance, guidance at a distance, as it were, to citizens'. For such accusations against Hart, see Raz (n 28) 131; GJ Postema, 'Norms, Reasons, and Law' (1998) 51 *Current Legal Problems* 149, 166–67.

[59] Kramer (n 5) 96–97.

[60] See F Schauer, 'Positivism Through Thick and Thin' in B Bix (ed), *Analyzing Law: New Essays on Legal Theory* (Clarendon Press, 1998).

sufficient to allow for a distinction between legal regimes and the raw use of force, why would we make the concept stricter by introducing moral conditions? What is to be gained by excluding openly immoral systems from the concept of law? Postema's third premise addresses this issue. Postema argues that 'We are forced to deny even *de facto* authority to imperatives backed by threats if those who issue them cannot themselves claim legitimacy without contradiction or self-deception.'[61] According to Postema, law is to be distinguished from other forms of social power because officials claim authority to issue directives and back them up with force.[62] However, our question consists precisely in knowing whether a claim to *moral* authority is necessary for the identification of a legal system as such. Supposing that a system of rules can be distinguished from the sheer use of force as a means of social control by the application of Hart's concept of legal obligation, why should we still insist on the necessity of a claim to *moral* authority? Could the empirical fact that most legal regimes do claim moral authority not be understood as a parochial matter, as a fortunate coincidence, or as a strategy for maintaining power without the recurrent use of force?

I am not arguing that all (or even most) legal system(s) are actually systems of sheer imperatives, where officials accept the rule of recognition for prudential reasons alone. The point at issue is the conceptual possibility of such an arrangement's counting as a legal system. To avert that possibility, what needs to be proven is that a (warranted) claim to moral legitimacy is conceptually related to the nature and function of law. Nevertheless, there is no theoretical agreement about the nature and function of law, or even about the question of whether law has a fixed nature and a single function. The formation of the concept of law is at stake.

Defenders of the inclusion of (at least a claim to) moral legitimacy in the concept of law tend to argue from supposedly indisputable data regarding legal phenomena. Above all, their starting point is that legal rules 'provide a framework for public justifications of actions'.[63] Apparently, the main idea is that the mere conformity of an official action to a rule recognised by the system's criteria of validity is not enough to provide the type of justification that is called for when officials in their public capacity justify their use of force against citizens by subsuming their actions under legal rules. In short, the practice of justification would not make sense if the rules themselves were not considered morally justified. This is why, according to those who defend this view, a moral claim can be thought to be intrinsically related to all applications of law. In Postema's words, lawyers, citizens and judges are active parties in activities in which others' rights and interests are at stake, but 'it is not enough for them to be able to show how

[61] Postema (n 45) 92.
[62] ibid.
[63] Postema (n 58) 165.

the "justification" might go within some system of norms. They must regard (or at least pretend to regard) that justification as applicable to their activities, as vindicating their actions.'[64] Therefore, even though Hart's list of reasons for judges' engagement in judicial practice can explain their personal motives, those motives will not fit the public practice of legal justification because they cannot vindicate those judges' actions. The rule of recognition, so the argument goes, should be publicly accepted for moral reasons.

Faced with the problem of concept formation mentioned above, some legal theorists seek help from political theory to justify their choice between a thin (wider, morally neutral) and a thick (narrower, morally loaded) concept of law.[65] We can understand the appeal of this kind of argument. Postema's thesis leads us to consider the claim 'it is legal' as embracing the claim 'it is morally justified' in normal circumstances. Under wicked regimes such as Nazi Germany, it is impossible to view this as being the case. The circumstances are too abnormal. Thus, it is also impossible to claim that the Nazi coercive order was properly legal or that Jewish people had legal obligations under that system.[66]

The view that the Nazi legal system lacked legality is held by many; let us consider, however, a less wicked legal system in order to bring the relevant aspects to light – for example, the legal system in Brazil. Most people would say that Brazil has a legal system. This is why Brazil is a good case when it comes to illustrating a possible political problem faced by Postema's position. In Brazil, it is common for judges to justify their exorbitant salaries (and the public expenditure on which these salaries depend) with the simple observation that the arrangement is legal. The same applies to Brazilian politicians who increase their own salaries in times of deep economic crisis. What remains remarkable is how common it is to hear ordinary Brazilian citizens reply to this kind of claim by saying that although such arrangements are legal, they are immoral. Ordinary citizens do not seem to accept that a legal claim can vindicate an attitude that is inconsistent with community interests and concerns. For the purposes of this chapter, the point is that a thin concept of law can help their case against the official argument. On the other hand, Postema's thick concept of law seems to support the Brazilian officials' political discourse.

Certainly, Postema could reply that legality is not an excuse to follow any morally undesirable course of action, since one can have strong moral reasons

[64] Postema (n 45) 98.

[65] For instance: N MacCormick, 'A Moralistic Case for A-Moralistic Law' (1985) 20 *Valparaiso University Law Review* 1; F Schauer, 'Positivism as Pariah' in RP George (ed), *The Autonomy of Law: Essays on Legal Positivism* (Oxford University Press 1996); L Murphy, 'The Political Question of the Concept of Law' in J Coleman (ed), *Hart's Postscript: Essays on the Poscript to the Concept of Law* (Oxford University Press 2001); Hart (n 2) 210. According to Will Waluchow, however, Hart retreated from his political arguments in favour of a wider concept of law in private correspondence. See WJ Waluchow, *Inclusive Legal Positivism* (Clarendon Press 1994) 98, fn 29.

[66] See Postema (n 45) 92.

to voluntarily give up a legal right.[67] Nonetheless, the view according to which legality amounts to at least a presumption of moral vindication is more favourable to the self-interests of the elites who run certain legal systems than the idea that a legal reason in itself has no moral weight at all. Be that as it may, I am not certain that political theory should come to the rescue of legal theory when the issue is concept formation.[68] Perhaps there is a way to choose between a thin and a thick concept of law from within legal theory.

C. The Rule of Law in a Nation of Devils

Our question is: if a system requires that any use of force be justified according to public rules identifiable by criteria provided by a higher rule shared by the system's officials, is it true that such a practice necessarily implies a claim to moral legitimacy even if the officials themselves do not believe that their practice is morally justified? In other words, is it impossible for law to avert the moral claim? Theorists engaged in the question of whether there is a conceptual connection between law and coercion commonly ask us to imagine a society of angels.[69] Angels can make use of a system of adjudication based on rules to authoritatively determine issues left open by practical reason alone. Therefore, it is possible to conceive of law without coercion, for angels would not need to be threatened in order to comply with their system's determinations. In order to resolve our conceptual issue, however, let us imagine the opposite scenario – a nation of devils:

> The problem of establishing a state, no matter how hard it may sound, is soluble even for a nation of devils (if only they have understanding) and goes like this: 'Given a multitude of rational beings all of whom need universal laws for their preservation but each of whom is inclined covertly to exempt himself from them, so to order this multitude and establish their constitution that, although in their private dispositions they strive against one another, these yet so check one another that in their public conduct the result is the same as if they had no such evil dispositions'.[70]

[67] *Mutatis mutandis*, there may be strong moral reasons not to discharge legal obligations even if legal obligations are also moral obligations. It is common for theorists for whom legal obligations are moral obligations to consider legal obligations mere prima facie moral obligations.

[68] For arguments against this approach, see for instance P Soper, 'Choosing a Legal Theory on Moral Grounds' (1986) 4 *Social Philosophy & Policy* 31; Waluchow (n 65) ch 4; Postema, 'Jurisprudence as Practical Philosophy' (n 5) 351.

[69] See, for instance, J Raz, *Practical Reason and Norms* (2nd edn, Oxford University Press 1999) 15.

[70] I Kant, 'Toward Perpetual Peace' in MJ Gregor (ed), *Practical Philosophy* (first pub 1795, Cambridge University Press 1996) 335. To the best of my knowledge, Plato, in Book II of *The Republic*, was the first philosopher to develop an argument according to which law serves egoistic purposes. See Plato, *The Republic*, ed GRF Ferrari, tr T Griffith (Cambridge University Press 2000) 38–39. I cannot develop this traditional line of reasoning here, but we can understand Hart's conception of the minimal content of natural law, as well as his conception of secondary rules as

Interestingly, it appears that Kant goes further than Hart, conceiving of the possibility that legal rules are mere imperatives (in Kramer's sense and not in the Kantian sense) even for officials. After all, in Kant's thought experiment, the devils want to exempt themselves from the law; therefore, in this sense, laws are not even prudential prescriptions for them. They do not want laws to cease to exist; they merely want those laws to function as norms in practical reasoning only when it comes to others, not themselves.[71] Thus, the devils coerce each other to obey legal rules ('check one another that in their public conduct the result is the same').

However, since their intention to exempt themselves from law must remain hidden, these devils must purport to accept laws as prudential prescriptions in their public practical reasoning. This being so, every devil can tell others how foolish they are for breaching rules that they freely admit are in their interest. In this sense, public official statements are made from the internal point of view, as prudential prescriptions, even though they are insincere. Above all, there is no place for moral claims in this scenario.

With this said, we must go even further if we are to prove Hart's point regarding the possibility of a legal system in which most ordinary citizens have no reason to view the law from the internal point of view. After all, in the Kantian devil scenario, all citizens can take up the (prudential) internal point of view, even if all (officials and citizens) merely purport to accept norms as prudential prescriptions since they want to exempt themselves from them. This being so, we must consider whether a race of devils ruling over human beings would sensibly justify the use of force through a public system of rules. In this new thought experiment, unlike the devils, human beings have no reason to want the rules to obtain.[72]

First, it must be clear that our devils would not be in disguise. They would not be pretending to run a benign regime. Even then, can the explanation of their heinous decisions by reference to human beings' legal obligations (as described by Hart) only be understood as a presumption of moral warrant? The answer is 'no'; such devils would emphasise the causal connection between the breaching of rules by human beings and the application of sanctions in order to sustain human beings' incentives to conform to the rules that are suited to the

remedies for defects in social arrangement based only on primary rules, as equally valid for a nation of devils, provided that those devils are rational ('they have understanding'), that their interest in survival is stronger than their wish to exterminate others, and that they share with human beings certain morally neutral characteristics, such as our physical vulnerabilities, approximate equality and resource scarcity. See Hart (n 2) 191–200, 91–97.

[71] In section II.A of this chapter, I noted that as a third explanation for an agent's failure to accept a rule from the internal point of view: '(iii) the agent is in favour of the rule in general but does not view herself as being bound by it, because she wants to avoid the burden of being held to it while nonetheless benefitting from its general observance (she is a *free rider*)'.

[72] In the terms of section II.A of this chapter, this situation would give rise to a different kind of motive for refusing to accept a rule from the internal point of view: '(iv) there is no reason for the agent to accept the pattern of behaviour as a rule (she is a *victim* of a coercive system)'.

devils' own interests.[73] Those devils would not want human beings to believe that penalties would be applied randomly.

Therefore, moral vindication is not the only intelligible purpose behind the justification of force based on a system of rules. The efficacious functioning of a scheme of imperatives is another candidate, which allows Kramer to conclude that 'even if we allow that publicly accessible explanations of official decisions are an integral feature of anything that counts as a full-fledged legal system, we should recognise that the explanations need not be presented as moral justifications'.[74] From this follows an even more important conclusion: 'the very fact that those statements [of legal obligations] can quite intelligibly be free of such pretensions is sufficient to dispel the notion that officials who explain their judgments through references to legal duties are perforce thereby announcing moral duties'.[75] In other words, there is no conceptual relation between an appeal to a system of rules to justify the use of force and a moral claim.[76]

Those who advocate a thicker concept of law can of course still refuse to apply the label 'law' to the devilish order described here.[77] It seems that there is a strong inclination to do so, for, from a moral point of view, law requires justification that goes beyond the rule of recognition, and it requires that justification to be moral precisely because law amounts to coercive[78] interference in others' interests. In short, a morally conscious agent cannot be a legal official without believing that moral reasons underpin the rule of recognition of her system. Hart's important observation, however, is that law is not only the business of morally conscious agents. It can also exist in a nation of devils.

[73] At this point, I am again following Matthew Kramer. See Kramer (n 5) 90.

[74] ibid 91; see also MH Kramer, 'Legal and Moral Obligation' in MP Golding and WA Edmundson (eds), *The Blackwell Guide to the Philosophy of Law and Legal Theory* (Blackwell Publishing 2005) 183–84.

[75] See Kramer (n 5) 91–92.

[76] Postema believes that Kramer is confusing 'a claim about what particular officials or law-subjects say or believe' with the question 'about how law, in virtue of what it is and does, implicitly presents itself and thus what a society is committed to when it establishes a legal system'. Postema (n 3) 354, fn 9. I do not think that this is the case. Kramer is making a conceptual point about how to make a practice that is an essential feature of any legal system intelligible without moral claims. Kramer's formulation of the question is very precise, '[r]egardless of whether the duty-imposing laws do in fact engender moral obligations of obedience, and regardless of whether the jural officials believe that such laws engender such obligations, do the officials' authoritative pronouncements on legal requirements imply that those requirements are morally binding?' Kramer, 'Legal and Moral Obligation' (n 74) 179.

[77] Compare this to the predatory order that, for Robert Alexy, cannot be law for conceptual reasons alone; cf R Alexy, 'On Necessary Relations between Law and Morality' (1989) 2 *Ratio Juris* 167, 176.

[78] Except for angels.

13

Philosophical and Psychological Distinctions between Presumptive Positivism and Rule-Sensitive Particularism

GUILHERME DA FCF DE ALMEIDA AND NOEL STRUCHINER*

I. INTRODUCTION

IN 1991, A special edition of the *Harvard Journal of Law and Public Policy* collected reactions to the ideas discussed by Schauer's contribution, 'Rules and the Rule of Law',[1] which offered a taste of the theory set out on his book *Playing by the Rules*.[2] One of the edition's articles was a response, by Gerald Postema,[3] to Schauer's suggested typology of legal decision-making models. In summary, Postema suggested that presumptive positivism and rule-sensitive particularism are indistinguishable from each other in two different ways. First, they are extensionally equivalent: equally well-informed, well-meaning and competent judges, operating under both models, would judge identical sets of cases identically. Not only that, Postema argues that they are also psychologically equivalent. We take that second claim to mean that the processes underlying each decision-making model are indistinguishable.

In this chapter, we challenge Postema's critiques: there are extensional and psychological differences between the models. Presumptive positivists would accept suboptimal application of a rule's text on more occasions than

* We are grateful for the careful reading of and illuminating critiques made to a previous version of this chapter by Bartosz Maciej Janik, Maciej Próchnicki and Piotr Bystranowski.

[1] F Schauer, 'Rules and the rule of law' (1991) 14 *Harvard Journal of Law & Public Policy* 645.

[2] F Schauer, *Playing by the Rules: A Philosophical Examination of Rule-Based Decision-Making in Law and in Life* (Oxford University Press 1991).

[3] GJ Postema, 'Positivism, I presume? … Comments on Schauer's "Rules and the rule of law"' (1991) 14 *Harvard Journal of Law & Public Policy* 797.

rule-sensitive particularists, therefore rendering the models extensionally divergent (as suggested by Schauer's response[4]). Psychologically, the gulf between decision-making models seems to be even larger, as each model seems connected to fundamentally different cognitive processes.

In section II, we briefly review Schauer's argument, laying out the distinction between formalism, presumptive positivism, rule-sensitive particularism and (simple) particularism. Next, in section III, we set out Postema's rebuttal. His position centres around two theses: the extensional equivalence thesis and the psychological equivalence thesis. In section IV some definitional issues around rule-sensitive particularism are sorted out, clearing the path for the next three sections, which discuss the psychological differences between presumptive positivism and rule-sensitive particularism. Section V describes dual-process theories, while section VI makes the case that the distinction between presumptive positivism and rule-sensitive particularism is rooted in different cognitive foundations. Section VII transitions towards the extensional equivalence thesis, trying to show how the psychological difference implies the possibility of extensional divergence. Section VIII explores how some evidence about human behaviour seems to support Schauer's suggestions about divergence. In the conclusion (section IX), we discuss how our responses to both theses interact with each other and how an empirical approach may shed light on important questions about jurisprudence.

II. MODELS OF JUDICIAL DECISION MAKING

Schauer[5] describes judicial decision-making models as possible attitudes we can have when facing suboptimal cases of rule application. Any description of Schauer's theory needs, therefore, to start with a (very) brief examination of rules and the relationship between a rule's canonical formulation (usually, but not necessarily, its text[6]) and the underlying justification that leads to its adoption.

A rule's canonical formulation is always currently or potentially in disagreement with its underlying purposes or justification. Schauer's pet example is the rule prohibiting dogs from entering a restaurant. We may assume that the rule was adopted with the purpose of avoiding nuisances to the restaurant's clients. The rule textually applies to guide dogs, even though they are not nuisances, and does not textually apply to bears, even though they could seriously harm clients. It is, therefore, suboptimal vis-à-vis its purposes.

[4] F Schauer, 'The rules of jurisprudence: A reply' (1991) 14 *Harvard Journal of Law & Public Policy* 839.

[5] Schauer (n 2).

[6] This qualification is necessary, as some implicit, unwritten rules might be completely clear and suboptimal. See F Schauer, 'Prescriptions in Three Dimensions' (1997) 82 *Iowa Law Review* 911.

What should we do when text and purpose disagree? This is the question answered differently by distinctive decision-making models. Two extreme answers are given by formalism and simple particularism.

Under the first, we should always abide by the rule's text, no matter how strongly we disagree with the results from the moral point of view, and regardless of whether or not a different result would have been dictated by the rule's underlying purposes. On the bright side, we spend almost no time or cognitive resources mulling over what decision to make: it is (usually) very easy to find out if something is or is not a dog.

Simple particularists, in contrast, argue that a rule's purpose always has precedence over its text, with the rule's canonical formulation being treated as a mere suggestion, with no intrinsic normative force. While directly applying the underlying purposes may lead to more just results, it demands a lot of time and consideration from the decision-maker, as every new case must be analysed in full. It can also be deemed unfair and unpredictable by the people subject to the rule.

Formalism and simple particularism are too extreme. Even though we value formalistic virtues such as predictability, minimising application error[7] and efficiency,[8] we find that sometimes it is necessary to deviate from a rule's entrenched formulations for moral, purposive reasons. However, we cannot *always* deviate, as a simple particularist would have it, or none of the rule-related virtues would obtain.

Because of this extremism, most people neither theoretically nor pragmatically adhere to these models. However, each model might be formulated under more palatable variations, giving rise to the protagonists of our discussion: presumptive positivism and rule-sensitive particularism.

[7] Formalist models are presumably less subject to application errors than particularism. Using the no-dogs rule example, imagine a restaurant owner who wants to be a particularist. He needs to think about each dog long and hard to determine whether that particular dog would be a nuisance to his clients or not. He may be wrong about some dogs. Sometimes, it might seem that a given dog would be calm and well behaved but, 15 minutes through the meal, reveals itself to be a loud and intimidating dog. This would be an application mistake under particularism. The correlate of this type of error under formalism would be cases where something is not a dog but is mistakenly banned from the restaurant with reference to the no-dogs rule, or where a dog is allowed in under the mistaken impression that it is something else entirely. The examples speak for themselves. It is much harder and unnatural to think of application errors under formalism than under particularism, which hopefully tracks the real-life performance of these models. It is important to note that all decision-making models are preoccupied with minimising overall errors in some sense. They disagree, however, about the most efficient way to bring about this goal. Particularists tend to believe that most errors are a product of the suboptimality of rules, ie the inevitable under- and over-inclusion of all rules given their generality, while formalists think that we will commit fewer mistakes overall by blindly following rules, rather than trusting the unconstrained reasoning employed by particularists. Formalists, therefore, are willing to tolerate the errors of under- and over-inclusion responsible for rules' moral suboptimality in order to avoid what we have called application errors.

[8] By doing our thinking upfront and coming up with simplified entrenched heuristics that can be then easily applied to cases on the fly, we optimise the usage of cognitive resources: after one single conceptual instance of careful and thoughtful deliberation we devise a simple, yet imperfect rule that can then be applied instantaneously to all relevant cases. Under particularism, all the thinking must be redone all the time, at each and every new case (for a more thorough exploration of this virtue, see Schauer (n 2) item 7.3).

Rule-sensitive particularism is a decision-making model that stems from a distinction between two different kinds of underlying justifications: substantive justifications and rule-generating justifications.[9] Avoiding annoying behaviours in the restaurant is a substantive justification for the rule that prohibits dogs in the restaurant. But there are other justifications for the rule that are not substantive but more formal, that is, reasons for positing a directive in the form of a rule. Virtues such as certainty, predictability, separation of powers, minimising application errors and efficiency[10] belong to this second, rule-generating kind of justificatory reason. While simple particularists care only about substantive justifications, deviating from entrenched formulations in every recalcitrant case, rule-sensitive particularists are also concerned with rule-generating justifications, therefore deviating less often from a rule's text.

Note that rule-sensitive particularism requires fairly complex reasoning: you need to determine the substantive reasons behind a given rule, then consider the weight rule-generating justifications should have on this occasion, and then balance these two sets of reasons before making a decision. What is more, you need to do this for every new case, as each case brings a new unique set of potentially morally relevant features to the table.

Finally, presumptive positivism, as a theory of adjudication, preserves rule-generating virtues by allowing decision-makers only a glimpse behind the rule's entrenched formulation: if the results dictated by canonical application are clearly morally absurd, we should deviate, but otherwise, we should not. This model recommends great deference towards rules, but allows for flexibility on a special subset of suboptimal cases, those presenting 'particularly exigent circumstances'.[11]

It is important to underline that the kind of moral evaluation engaged in by presumptive positivists is superficial. Schauer sums up this aspect as follows:

> Against this possibility, I tentatively offer the idea of a casual look, a glimpse, a peek, a preliminary check, pursuant to which a decisionmaker follows the recognized rule unless some other factor overtly intrudes on her decisionmaking process. Implicit in presumptive positivism is a phenomenology such that the decisionmaker is open to the possibility of the presumption being overcome, but does not actively pursue it, or can do a quick check short of a thorough inquiry. If I am correct, if presumptions do serve as psychological simplifiers as well as analytic decisionmaking devices, then presumptive positivism does not fail, even though it requires the decisionmaker to examine in some way the larger range of potentially overriding factors.[12]

[9] ibid item 5.4.

[10] Schauer (ibid 98–99) is not entirely clear about whether those two latter rule-justifying reasons are taken into account by rule-sensitive particularists. Once we consider possible responses to Postema's extensional equivalence claim, we will discuss how these two slightly but significantly different versions of rule-sensitive particularism come into play.

[11] ibid 196.

[12] Schauer (n 1) 677.

III. POSTEMA'S CRITIQUE

The 'casual look' behind a rule's justification advocated by presumptive positivism, according to Postema,[13] is enough to collapse 'serious rules' into rules of thumb, completely blurring the lines between rule-based and particularistic decision making. After all, the glimpse can be seen as a way to allow the decision-maker to balance substantive reasons against rule-generating reasons. If both models are concerned with the same sets of reasons then they should be extensionally equivalent. Not only that, but the psychological procedures underlying each model cannot be substantially different from each other. Those are the claims that make up Postema's theses, which we investigate further in the present section, starting with the extensional equivalence thesis. In order to get to extensional equivalence, we must first discuss what Postema takes to be the logical equivalence between models.

We have to concede that presumptive positivism and rule-sensitive particularism are similar in one respect. They are both concerned with the same inquiry about the same values. In every case, they ask whether rule-generating or substantive reasons should prevail. In doing so, both models think that the right answer is a function of those two kinds of reasons, and only of those two kinds of reasons. There is no difference between the sets of reasons deemed relevant for each model and no difference in the question being asked by each model about the relationship between those sets of reasons. This important similarity is what Postema calls the *logical* equivalence between models.

If we take this similarity seriously, we see that the importance assigned to rule-generating justifications by rule-sensitive particularists should be equal to the weight of the presumptiveness of a rule's text under presumptive positivism. Therefore, given an identical set of cases, equally well-intentioned, well-informed and competent presumptive positivists and rule-sensitive particularists should render an identical set of judgments. This is the extensional equivalence thesis: because there is no underlying logical distinction between both models, there is no difference between the judgments commanded by each of them. If this thesis were correct then the distinction between rule-sensitive particularism and presumptive positivism would be, at best, a psychological one.

But Postema is not satisfied with this. He wishes to deny even this second difference, purporting to show that there is not any possible distinction between both models:

> Schauer also claims that there is an important psychological (or 'phenomenological') difference between the presumptive rule-based model and the rule-sensitive model – a difference in the way judges following the two different models would typically look at rules. Again, I fail to see the difference. The difference seems to be that under the presumptive rule model, decisionmakers need to examine the set of excluded considerations only casually, whereas under the rule-sensitive model, decisionmakers

[13] Postema (n 3).

> need to inspect and balance out the reasons in every case. In the former model, only 'a casual look, a glimpse, a peek, a preliminary check' is necessary, Schauer maintains.
>
> This ignores the role of genuine rules of thumb in rule-sensitive particularist practical reasoning. Rule-sensitive decisionmaking need not be fanatically calculating. It requires only that decisionmakers be sensitive to those cases in which the relevant rule-dictating values are weak relative to conflicting considerations. There is nothing in the rule-sensitive approach, or its treatment of rules as rules of thumb, that requires decisionmakers to ignore the practical advantages of 'a casual look, a glimpse, a peek, a preliminary check'.[14]

This is the 'no psychological difference' thesis. It states that there is no difference in the ways rule-sensitive particularists and presumptive positivists approach the task of decisionmaking. 'Psychological', here, refers to the mental processes used by decision-makers to make decisions. Saying 'there is no psychological difference between models A and B' is shorthand for 'models A and B are carried on in the mind of decision-makers by the same mental processes'.[15] Throughout the chapter, we refer to the psychological equivalence thesis with this meaning of 'psychological' in mind.[16]

We consider the theses on reverse order, first arguing against the 'no psychological difference' thesis and then against the extensional equivalence thesis. This will allow us to see how presumptions may indeed perform the work that is required of them by Schauer's presumptive positivism, despite Postema's doubts. This step is crucial, because the existence of a psychological difference is a necessary condition for extensional divergence if we accept Postema's characterisation of presumptive positivism and rule-sensitive particularism. Schauer indeed accepted this characterisation, stating that the difference between models was never logical but psychological in nature. We believe that he was right about the existence of important psychological differences between presumptive positivism and rule-sensitive particularism, as they map onto distinct psychological decision-making models.

Successfully arguing against the psychological equivalence claim, however, is not enough. Postema could say that, at best, our efforts would establish an

[14] ibid 816.

[15] Postema is not entirely clear whether the mental process that is given priority is the one Schauer would associate with rule-sensitive particularism, or the one Schauer would attach to presumptive positivism. At times he seems to imply that presumptive positivism collapses into the more explicit calculus involved in Schauer's version of rule-sensitive particularism, while at others (such as the one quoted) he suggests that it is the other way around. While deciding between these two possibilities is important to evaluate the merits of Postema's own theory, we do not need to decide it in order to argue against the claim that the processes are the same.

[16] At times Postema uses psychological and 'phenomenological' as synonyms. If phenomenological were to mean only the subjective experience judges have while judging, this would hardly be interesting in discussing extensional equivalence and philosophically interesting differences or similarities between presumptive positivism and rule-sensitive particularism. Because of this, we believe that the right way to construe Postema's psychological equivalence thesis is to construe it as a claim pertaining to mental processes.

irrelevant difference. It may well be that, no matter the psychological route we take – that attached to presumptive positivism or the one related to rule-sensitive particularism – we shall always converge to the same set of decisions, given the same set of cases. We do not believe that this is the case: in fact, we believe that the best available evidence regarding human behaviour strongly suggests that presumptive positivism and rule-sensitive particularism are extensionally divergent.

IV. DEFINITIONAL ISSUES

Postema[17] provides his own account of Schauer's distinction between presumptive positivism and rule-sensitive particularism. While both authors certainly have the same thing in mind with regards to the first decision-making model, there is room to doubt whether their rule-sensitive particularists are sensitive to the same set of values. Postema's version of rule-sensitive particularism takes into account every rule-generating justification, including the least orthodox ones such as minimising application errors, while Schauer is less clear about it.

Under one possible reading, Schauer's account of rule-sensitive particularism is concerned only with a subset of all possible rule-generating justifications. Specifically, it is sometimes implied that rule-sensitive particularists could not possibly assign the adequate weight to separation of powers considerations, for '[t]o have an agent operating in one jurisdiction determine if this is a case in which she should invade the decision-making jurisdiction of another is in substantial tension with the very ideal of jurisdictional separation'.[18] Similar lines of argument could be discerned regarding judges' fitness to make calls about decision-maker disability (application errors) and efficiency.

If we take rule-sensitive particularism in this restricted sense, both claims would be false, as the models would be – to use Postema's terminology – logically distinct. After all, each model would demand the consideration of different sets of reasons, possibly indicating divergent results. In other words, it would be trivially true that equally well-intentioned, well-informed and well-meaning judges operating under each model would render different judgments given an identical set of cases to decide.[19] That is why Postema says Schauer is successful

[17] Postema (n 3).

[18] Schauer (n 2) 98–99.

[19] Readers pointed out that the paragraph mentions both possibly ('possibly indicating divergent results') and actually different results ('equally well-intentioned, well-informed and well-meaning judges operating under each model would render different judgments given an identical set of cases to decide'). That is intentional: in some cases, presumptive positivism and rule-sensitive particularism *will* converge, no matter which perspective we take on the Schauer v Postema debate. This will be the case when rule and purpose converge, for instance. The question is whether they *may* diverge or not. We wish to point out that this is indeed possible if each model is concerned with its own, distinct, set of values. In the second excerpt, our intention is to point out that given an identical set of – presumably diverse – cases, there will actually be conflicting rulings. This is, of course,

in distinguishing his theory from 'the simple particularism of some realist (and neo-realist) theories', but not against 'a sophisticated rule-sensitive particularism that takes into account the value of local priority, separation of powers, and other rule of law values'.[20]

Regardless of what is the best reading of Schauer's work, it is interesting to consider the version of rule-sensitive particularism proposed by Postema, one that shares the concern with the full set of rule-generating values with presumptive positivism. In the first place, it would be interesting to do so because, as Schauer makes clear, the judicial decision-making space is a continuum. As such, Postema's flavour of rule-sensitive particularism would be another point on this spectrum, and arguably one worth exploring by virtue of the interesting claims Postema made about its relation with presumptive positivism. In the second place, Schauer[21] himself could have objected to Postema's characterisation but did not, indicating that their discussion was not contingent upon this ambiguity. With all of this in mind, we will focus on this second kind of rule-sensitive particularism, trying to show how even it might still be psychological distinct from and extensionally divergent with presumptive positivism.

V. PSYCHOLOGICAL MODELS OF MORAL DECISION MAKING

The first and more challenging suggestion of Postema's critique is that presumptions are not really a thing. According to Postema, to say that a rule's text should be followed up until the point where it leads to absurd results is only a shortened way of saying that a rule's text should be followed up until the point where rule-generating reasons are overcome by particularly exigent substantive reasons. Balancing substantive and rule-generating reason, however, is precisely what rule-sensitive particularists do. When we frame the question this way, it seems reasonable to assume that the mental process required to decide whether substantive or rule-generating reasons should prevail in each case would be the same.

Postema is not clear about how this mental process underlying both presumptive positivism and rule-sensitive particularism works: is it cursory in nature, or does it demand that we carefully and explicitly weight each set of reasons?[22] However, one thing is clear: indistinguishable mental processes that balance the same set of reasons should render an identical set of results. Thus, this overarching challenge is central to both the psychological and extensional equivalence theses. If we concede – as we already did – that presumptive positivism and

conditional on the set of cases' containing cases where the models diverge, ie, cases where the greater domain of rule-generating reasons attended to by presumptive positivists come into play.

[20] Postema (n 3) 813.

[21] Schauer (n 4).

[22] See n 16.

rule-sensitive particularism are indeed trying to do the same kind of operation upon the same sets of values, the psychological difference becomes a necessary (albeit, as we shall see, not a sufficient) condition for extensional divergence.

Schauer offers an argument to show that presumptions are indeed a thing, for we can think of at least some thought experiments where presumptions behave differently than a rule-sensitive approach:

> Suppose then that a decisionmaker is instructed to operate in a strictly rule-based manner. Further suppose that there is an array of sanctions supporting those instructions, such that the decisionmaker would be punished when she did not follow the rule, even if it appeared to her best at the time of the decision to ignore the rule, and even if it turned out best in the end to have ignored the rule. All agree that this is a different procedure from one in which the decisionmaker decides in each case whether to follow the rule, taking into account the value of having a rule. But now suppose we add what we might call the 'Nuremberg rider'. Suppose the decisionmaker is instructed and sanctioned to follow the rule in all cases, except when following the rules would produce moral horrors equivalent to those that led to the rejection of the 'I was only following orders' defense in the Nuremberg trials.
>
> Obviously, this is a presumption of enormous strength. Indeed, I would expect that in a normal operation it would produce the same outcomes as strict rule-based decisionmaking. But it is a presumption nevertheless, rather than a strict rule; and if total opacity and rule-sensitive particularism are different, it is implausible to suppose that the mere addition of this quite remote qualification produces extensional equivalence where before none had existed. And if the Nuremberg rider does not produce extensional equivalence, then there is nothing about the change from opacity to presumptions of lesser strength that necessarily produces extensional equivalence.[23]

The suggestion is that there is some structural difference between all-things-considered, particularistic reasoning and reasoning according to presumptions, and even if this difference is not logical in nature, it can still produce distinct results in practice. Is this suggestion psychologically feasible? Does the literature on cognitive and moral psychology offer some distinction consistent with Schauer's?

Since the beginning of the 2000s, there has been relatively widespread consensus on psychology about the existence of two fairly distinct psychological moral decision-making models.[24] Those systems are characterised, on the one hand, by intuitive, automatic, emotional and fast decision making, and, on the other, a conscious, effortful, detached and slow procedure. Kahneman[25] popularised the names 'System 1' and 'System 2' to refer to these models.[26] Throughout the years, different authors explored different aspects or dimensions of the

[23] Schauer (n 4) 846–47.

[24] J Haidt, 'The New Synthesis in Moral Psychology' (2007) 316 *Science* 998.

[25] D Kahneman, *Thinking, Fast and Slow* (Farrar, Straus and Giroux 2011).

[26] Kahneman was primarily concerned with cognitive psychology, but the terminology extends to moral psychology.

dichotomy. Haidt's social-intuitionist model,[27] for instance, focuses on the affective and intuitive versus detached and reflective aspects of the distinction. Other approaches focus more on the cognitive mechanisms underlying moral decision-making, trying to describe the structure of these mechanisms,[28] while others still dismiss the dual-process approach altogether.[29]

Despite thinking all of these dimensions of dual-process moral psychology are relevant for legal theory,[30] we will focus on the cognitive approach, and especially on the distinction between model-free and model-based decision making.[31] These models originated in artificial intelligence research, specifically in the field of reinforcement learning, a method of machine learning that rewards certain actions and punishes others.

Model-based decision making involves the exhaustive computation of the consequences attached to each available option, in order to find the most valuable one. Imagine, for instance, a game where you have five moves available and can straightforwardly assign a different value to each move. Let us say three of the moves add two units of value towards your score, one of them subtracts a point from it and the final one adds five points. We can compare the values attached to each move and choose the one that maximises our score (the last one). So far, our 'model' of the decision-making space is not modelling anything, since there is a perfect representation of the payout structure available. More frequently, we will not have all the information, and thus will need a proper statistical model of some sort in order to estimate each move's value. Hence, we speak of 'model-based' decision making.

Model-based decision making is a good decision-making procedure insofar as it can yield demonstrably good results. It is, however, extremely cognitively costly. Imagine you have not five available moves but 5,000, or that you need to make non-trivial calculations in order to estimate the value attached to each move. It suddenly becomes paralysingly hard to be a model-based decision-maker.[32]

In contrast, model-free decision making evaluates actions based on previous experience. If an action produced good consequences in the past, it should be

[27] J Haidt, 'The emotional dog and its rational tail: a social intuitionist approach to moral judgment' (2001) 8 *Psychological Review* 814.

[28] F Cushman, 'Action, outcome, and value: a dual-system framework for morality' (2013) 17 *Personality and Social Psychology Review* 273; M Crockett, 'Models of morality' (2013) 17 *Trends in Cognitive Science* 363.

[29] DE Melnikoff and JA Bargh, 'The mythical number two' (2018) 22 *Trends in Cognitive Sciences* 280.

[30] In two papers with Ivar Hannikainen, we are concerned with the intuitive/reflective (N Struchiner, I Hannikainen and GFCF Almeida, 'An experimental guide to vehicles in the park' (2020) 15 *Judgment and Decision Making* 312) and emotional/detached dimensions of the distinction (under review).

[31] Cushman (n 28); Crockett (n 28).

[32] Actually, the options may be so many and so complex that it becomes impossible to apply such procedure. See G Gigerenzer, *Adaptive Thinking: rationality in the real world* (Oxford University Press, 2002).

perceived as a good option. If it has led to bad outcomes, it should be avoided.[33] This makes the model remarkably efficient on a computational level. There is no need to painstakingly calculate the expected outcome of every action. You simply rely on past experience and choose those actions that led to good results, while avoiding the ones that did not. Though computationally simple, the model has its own set of shortcomings. In Crockett's words, 'Because the model-free system lacks access to current action-outcome links, it is retrospective rather than prospective and can make suboptimal recommendations in settings where traditionally good actions leads to undesirable outcomes, or *vice versa*.'[34]

These psychological decision-making procedures track two distinct neural bases,[35] further reinforcing the conceptual and behavioural evidence that indicates we are dealing with qualitatively distinct procedures. We hope the parallels with legal decision making are obvious by now, but in the following section, we are going to spell out the connections between psychological and judicial decision-making models.

VI. THE PSYCHOLOGY OF JUDICIAL DECISION MAKING

Model-free decision making is easy. All you need to do is look up whether or not previous experiences were good or bad. Formalism is also easy. You do not need to think long and hard about purposes and moral questions, you simply apply a rule's text.

Formalism and model-free decision making are also silent about what to do when facing novel, unanticipated cases, prompting agents to fill the gaps with other decision-making methods. Model-free reinforcement learning agents will use exploratory techniques, choosing random actions,[36] while formalistic oriented agents will generally resort to particularistic methods or some meta-rule regarding gaps.

Finally, they are strikingly similar on a normative level. Both offer satisfactory and consistent, albeit suboptimal, results at very low computational costs.[37]

[33] Naturally, it is more complex than this. For a quick but thorough overview, see Cushman (n 28).

[34] Crockett (n 28) 363.

[35] Cushman (n 28) 279; Crockett (n 28) 363. Both authors bring a number of sources to their claims. We do not think it is necessary or convenient to reproduce such sources here. It is sufficient to hedge our bets on Cushman and Crockett and make our claims contingent on theirs.

[36] LP Kaelbling, ML Littman and AW Moore, 'Reinforcement learning: a survey' (1996) 4 *Journal of Artificial Intelligence Research* 237.

[37] Note that the costs are low at the moment of application, but may be high at other moments. In the case of model-free decision making, there may be costs during the training of the agent, ie there is a cost to the suboptimal and random decisions the model-free agent takes while learning what are the courses of action associated with good and bad outcomes. There is little cost, however, at the moment of decision making, ie after you go through the training stage and have learned which actions are associated with which outcomes. A similar story is true with presumptive positivism. Although making good rules is costly, following them is cheap. We thank Piotr Bystranowski for pointing out this possible objection.

Just as a rule's text might apply to a situation where its underlying purposes would not, a model-free decision-making procedure might recommend an action that has generally been good in the past but is not in that particular context.[38]

In contrast, model-based decision making is hard. It requires one to explicitly calculate the expected value of each available course of action. Similarly, simple particularism demands that decision-makers take into account all the morally relevant kinds of justification pertaining to each case. This approach might, in both cases, lead to very real pragmatic difficulties when the complexity of the problem scales up. In these cases, decision-makers might be forced to simplify and resort to some heuristic decision-making method.

Model-based and particularistic decision-making models, however, have no theoretical problem with unanticipated cases. In theory, you can always estimate the value of a given option, even if this means you will assign some standard value to it or that you will have to keep calculating long after all humans are dead. There is no theoretical need to deviate from the decision procedure in such cases, even if it is pragmatically necessary.

Again, there are normative similarities. They are both means of achieving theoretically optimal results through expensive computation that takes into account highly contextual information.

Perhaps Postema would look at these parallels and concede that they are valid with regard to formalism and simple particularism, but not with respect to the logically and psychologically indistinguishable presumptive positivism and rule-sensitive particularism. We would like to propose that model-based and model-free reinforcement learning are also extreme points in a continuum, and that their core characteristics are representative of slightly less strict, but ecologically more frequent, variations. Crockett puts it this way:

> There is now substantial evidence that model-based, model-free, and Pavlovian systems are situated in at least partly distinct brain circuits, although behavioral outputs likely reflect their combined influence, and recent evidence suggests that certain regions integrate model-based and model-free evaluations.[39]

We would like to propose that hybrid, but mostly model-free, models might 'peek' behind normative reasons in the same way presumptive positivism does. To show how this may be the case, let us start with a simple, purely model-free agent, and then make it hybrid: imagine a simple model-free procedure that simply tallies the outcomes associated with each available action in the past and

[38] In stating that the results of formalism are satisfactory, we presume that the rules being followed are satisfactory. If the rules are awful vis-à-vis a given moral system (ie they are pervasively under- and over-inclusive) then the results of using formalism as a decision-making method will be awful. However, here too there is a parallel with model-free learning: if the training phase takes place in absolutely abnormal circumstances where payoffs are, for some reason, flipped, the results of the model's application will also be awful. Again, this possible difference between formalism and model-free decision-making was brought to our attention by Piotr Bystranowski.

[39] Crockett (n 28) 363.

chooses the higher-value action. This is all there is to the life of this simple agent. It does not matter how small the gap is between two courses of actions, or how bad the outcomes associated with the best action might be;[40] the agent will always let the past rule his decision. This simple agent is analogous to a formalist, in that both look only for one cheap source of guidance and follow it wherever it might lead.

Our simple agent may achieve better results if we add a provision stating that, whenever the total tally is below a given number,[41] an auxiliary, model-based procedure should be engaged. This way, we still drastically reduce the computational cost of making decisions compared to a pure model-based alternative, while mitigating the suboptimal results of the model-free approach.[42] Crucially, however, the hybrid nature of our improved agent does not strip from it the advantages of model-free decision making. In most cases, the solution is still inexpensively provided by past decisions. The only added cost is that required to check, at every step, whether the expected outcome is too low. This cost is not enough to collapse model-free into model-based decision making. If this is true, there is no reason to imagine that the cursory glimpse suggested by Schauer is enough to collapse presumptive positivism into rule-sensitive particularism. Just as we can hybridise a model-free agent without making it indistinguishable from model-based agents, we can introduce the idea of an overridable presumption into formalism without making it indistinguishable from particularism.

If we approach the problem the other way around, starting with a simple model-based agent, will we get to the exact same end-point? We do not think so. Feeding rule-generating reasons to a model-based agent does not make it presumptive in nature, even if some of the rule-generating reasons concern efficiency.

[40] By stipulation, our simple model-free agent chooses the best among competing courses of action. If all courses of action are bad, he will pick the least worse, no matter how bad the net result.

[41] There are other ways to make an agent presumptive, eg, through rules like 'whenever the difference in expected score between the best and second-best course of action is below a given threshold, engage in a model-based inquiry'. This would make the agent presumptive in nature, but perhaps not analogous to presumptive positivism. If both courses of action are really good but the difference between them is small (hence making it, in some sense, a difficult decision), presumptive positivism would still not engage in the complex reasoning required to dissolve all doubts. With presumptive positivism, it is only when the decision is hard *and* the results of applying a rule's text are bad that we must either deviate from or engage in more complex decision-making methods.

[42] In one reading of presumptive positivism, it is never the case that we need to resort to some form of particularism, since on the occasions where the result appointed by the rule's text are normatively absurd, we should clearly act according to the moral considerations that make it absurd. This might be a difference between psychological and judicial decision-making models. Another possibility is that it is merely a function of the number of alternatives available to each decision-maker. Judicial decision making is prototypically restricted to binary decisions about whether a rule should or should not be applied (but see LA Kornhauser and LG Sager 'Unpacking the court' (1986) 96 *The Yale Law Journal* 82). Under such restricted conditions, however, model-free decision making would arguably never give place to hard decision-making methods, relying instead on some heuristic meta-rule, such as 'everything that is not forbidden is allowed'.

To see this, imagine a chess-playing model-based agent. It is true that its decisions must be made in a finite amount of time, and therefore it cannot be 'fanatically calculating'. To avoid this, the programmers establish that if the agent does not arrive at an optimal solution in 20 minutes, it must play the best move it has found up to that point, no matter how bad. This hybrid model-based learning agent, in contrast to the previously discussed hybrid model free agent, incurs significant costs at each and every turn, no matter how easy or hard the decision. The structure of reasoning underlying both approaches is clearly different, even though both are concerned with efficiency as well as with their final goals. Neither model collapses onto its opposite once we introduce hybrid elements into it.

Although not perfect, these analogies are very straightforward and natural. They suggest that each judicial decision-making model is associated with a distinct psychological model. It is hard to argue the 'no psychological difference' thesis on the face of the list of similarities between psychological and legal decision-making models.

VII. EXTENSIONAL DIVERGENCE AND PSYCHOLOGICAL MODELS

The argument set out in the preceding sections suggests that presumptive positivism and rule-sensitive particularism rely on different psychological mechanisms. Does this imply anything with regards to Postema's claim about extensional convergence? Both Cushman and Crockett note that both models tend to converge, but that crucial differences between them remain. Cushman is the better spokesman here:

> Over time, a model-free algorithm will lead an organism to make adaptive choices, just like a model-based algorithm. Yet, the two algorithms differ in very fundamental respects. Unlike a model-based agent, a model-free agent cannot make flexible choices, in the sense that a local change to a specific value representation cannot immediately be used to adjust behaviors globally. This is impossible because the model-free learner has no representation of the causal structure that links one value representation to another. The links are forged only through trial-and-error learning, as an agent notes the value representations that follow on each of its behavioral choices. Moreover, a model-free agent cannot be goal-oriented, in the sense that the agent cannot select a particular goal to be obtained and then select the necessary sequence of actions to obtain that particular goal. Again, goal-oriented planning demands a model of the environment that a model-free learner simply lacks.[43]

The basic claim here is that even though the extensions of both models might be similar, they are not identical. Because of the differences between both algorithms, there is always the potential for divergent cases. This implies that, as an

[43] Cushman (n 28) 278.

empirical matter, even if not as a conceptual matter, the psychological difference may already entail extensional divergence. Namely, model-free decision making, just like presumptive positivism, will have to accept a larger number of suboptimal results than its counterpart. This disadvantage, however, is compensated by the comparative computational cost:

> However, along with these costs comes one tremendous benefit: Model-free algorithms can be extremely computationally light. At no point does an agent's decision to act involve anything more than querying the value representation associated with each immediately available choice. This stands in contrast to the model-based algorithm, which demands a computationally intensive search …[44]

Put in a simpler way, the passages quoted above state that good implementations of the two models are always potentially divergent but will probably yield similar sets of results. This convergence, in turn, captures the most intuitive part of Postema's argument about the extensions of judicial decision-making models. His intuition that equally good decision-making models that take into account identical sets of normatively relevant cases should converge, no matter what mental processes are at play, is sound. We take issue with the extensional equivalence thesis only insofar as we understand it to be too strong.

We can use chess-playing agents to illustrate the ideas of the last two sections and clarify the relationship between the psychological differences and extensional divergence. Chess is a good example because it satisfies Postema's condition of 'logical' equivalence: players need to make the same kinds of decisions (what piece should I move now?) and are concerned with the same set of values (which is the play that most improves my chances of winning?) no matter the procedure they use to select plays. To make chess an apt example, imagine that the players are time-constrained. This way, agents have to take into account not only first-order values regarding what is the best move available, but also efficiency.

Given these constraints, which, in Postema's parlance, amount to logical equivalence, two agents using the same non-random decision-making procedure would render extensionally equivalent sets of plays. In these circumstances, it is only by changing the decision-making procedure that we can introduce extensional divergence. Hence, our assertion that psychological divergence is a necessary condition for extensional divergence, given that we accept Postema's formulations of presumptive positivism and rule-sensitive particularism.

Divergence between decision-making procedures, however, is not sufficient for extensional divergence. Different procedures can conceivably yield the same results reliably. Whether or not they diverge is a matter of working out the particular implications pertaining to each model.

We have already described the model-based-learning hybrid model: it tries to find an optimal solution for 20 minutes, but when the time is up it must play the

[44] ibid.

best move it has found up to that point, no matter how bad. Let us call this the rule-sensitive particularist agent. The agent takes into account both efficiency-related and first-order values in order to make its play. Contrast this with a model-free-leaning hybrid model that plays whatever move it associates with the highest outcome, unless some absolute or relative threshold is met, in which case it engages in model-based reasoning until time is up. Call it the presumptive positivist agent. Should we imagine that these agents would come to make identical sets of moves given identical boards? We hope our readers would agree that this hypothesis is highly unlikely.

Note that it may very well be the case that the rule-sensitive particularist agent turns out to be a better chess player than the presumptive positivist agent. This is not at play here. It is reasonable to assume that, just as it happens in law, in chess also the preferred decision-making model is contextual. If we manipulate the time constraint, for instance, at some moment the presumptive positivist agent would have the upper hand. No time manipulation, however, can feasibly make these agents extensionally equivalent.

VIII. EXTENSIONAL DIVERGENCE AND HUMAN BEHAVIOUR

How can we know if actual decision-makers using presumptive positivism and rule-sensitive particularism would diverge?[45] Schauer's response, once more, provides an excellent starting point. He seeks to establish that even if we were to admit that morally perfect agents would allocate equal weight to rule-generating justifications under both models (and hence make an extensionally equivalent set of decisions), this is not the case in practice: human beings are not ideal moral agents and our knowledge of human behaviour shows that they would not behave as predicted by Postema. They are, in fact, subject to some failings or biases. In as much as those biases affect presumptive positivists and rule-sensitive particularists in different ways, there is reason to believe their decisions will not be extensionally equivalent.

Our claims about the effects of biases on judicial decision making might be fairly limited. In order to support extensional divergence, we need to show only that *some* rule-generating reasons are systematically undervalued by rule-sensitive particularists. For even if *most*, but not all, rule-generating reasons are properly weighted, the remaining residue can cause divergent results. This follows the lead of Schauer's own defence, which argues that rule-sensitive

[45] Much of the evidence discussed in this section is drawn from literature published by psychologists in psychology journals. We choose to refer to them as studies on human behaviour to avoid confusion with earlier claims about the psychological mechanisms fundamentally involved in judicial decision making. We believe this is a justified choice, since in the current section we are concerned with the behavioural outcomes that result from psychological processes without regard to the processes themselves, which were the focus of last section.

judges will not be able to give proper weight to separation of powers considerations and the decision-maker's propensity to commit application mistakes,[46] while giving room to the possibility that other rule-generating justifications will be adequately considered by them. Schauer, however, offers no evidence for these empirical claims. Our main goal in this section is to fill this evidential gap.

Let us begin by looking at the specific claim according to which judges would be likely to underestimate their own propensity to commit application errors, or decision-maker disability. It turns out that there is a consistent body of evidence for this idea, in the form of the better-than-average effect.[47] According to it, people consistently and across domains rate themselves better than their peers at all kinds of different tasks and traits, including susceptibility to biases,[48] which necessarily includes mistakes.[49] Guthrie, Rachlinksi and Wistrich found that the better-than-average effect also affects federal judges in the USA: when asked to rank themselves in the quartiles describing reversal rates from lowest (<25%) to highest (>75%) among their peers, 87.7 per cent of the judges surveyed 'believed that at least half of their peers had higher reversal rates on appeal'.[50]

Based on these results, it seems fair to conclude that judges are likely to undervalue the error-avoiding virtues of rule-based decision making. If judges think they commit fewer mistakes than they actually do, presumably they will not give as much importance as they should to error-minimising strategies such as formalism. This seems to put on firm empirical grounds Schauer's scepticism towards judges' ability to properly evaluate their own propensity for application mistakes.

In that scenario, we expect that rule-sensitive particularists will assign less weight to these rule-generating justifications than their presumptive positivist counterparts. Why? They routinely engage in judgments about the likelihood of committing mistakes, while presumptive positivists do not.[51] The presumptive

[46] The rule-generating justification regarding efficiency is not covered in Schauer's response and will not feature in this part of our defence of Schauer's distinction. It does, however, play a role in our argument, because if we were to accept the extensional convergence thesis, the greater efficiency found in presumptive positivism would be a decisive advantage. This is a topic we shall come back to in the conclusion to this chapter.

[47] E Pronin, DY Lin and L Ross, 'The bias blind spot: Perceptions of bias in self versus others' (2002) 28 *Personality and Social Psychology Bulletin* 369.

[48] For a comprehensive overview of the literature, E Pronin. 'How we see ourselves and how we see others' (2008) 320 *Science* 1177.

[49] A bias is generally defined as a systematic deviation from a normative model (J Baron, 'Heuristics and biases' in E Zamir and D Teichman (eds), *The Oxford Handbook of Behavioral Economics and the Law* (Oxford University Press 2014) 5). By this definition, if you think that you are less susceptible to bias, you think that you commit fewer mistakes than others do.

[50] C Guthrie, JJ Rachlinksi and AJ Wistrich, 'Inside the judicial mind' (2001) 86 *Cornell Law Review* 814. We are grateful to Piotr Bystranowski for drawing our attention to this study.

[51] Postema could very well retort that presumptive positivists might also overestimate their own capacity for identifying 'particularly exigent' cases, in fact incurring the same number of mistaken/biased results as rule-sensitive particularists. While this is a fair point, we believe it relies on a overly pessimistic view about presumptions. Rule-generating reasons are not as readily available

force assigned to rules is not open to reevaluation in every case, thus drastically reducing the opportunities presumptive positivists have to be affected by the better-than-average effect. As such, the bias should affect presumptive positivists and rule-sensitive particularists in different ways, affecting at least some judgments and rendering the models divergent.

What about separation of powers? Is the better-than-average effect enough to show that here too rule-sensitive particularism would fare worse? It may be the case that a judge, despite thinking of himself as a moral lighthouse in a world of pettiness, recognises the value of deferring towards the will of a morally less perfect majority, expressed through representative legislative power, even when he believes the majority is wrong. In other words, a judge may be subject to the better-than-average effect and still abide by the separation of powers.

There is, however, a bias blind spot, a special, higher-order case of the better-than-average effect that applies directly to this problem: people not only judge themselves as better than average, but they are oblivious to this fact, even when we point it out to them. In one experiment, Pronin, Lin and Ross[52] asked subjects to rate themselves relative to their peers in a range of personality dimensions. Afterwards, subjects were informed about the better-than-average effect and asked to indicate whether their own ratings were subject to bias, purely objective or biased towards modesty. Despite showing just as much bias as other subjects, the vast majority of participants either denied being subject to the effect (63 per cent) or claimed to have been too modest (13 per cent).[53] Guthrie, Rachlinsky and Wistrich show that American administrative law judges are also subject to a bias blind spot. Asked about how they would rank themselves among judges as to 'their capacity for avoiding bias in judging, a whopping 97.2 percent of [judges] placed themselves in the top half'.[54]

How can this affect legal decision making? A judge might deviate from a rule's entrenched formulation through biased textual interpretation, for instance. In such event, he will be undermining the separation of powers, while being completely oblivious to this fact. In contrast, he might be the first to charge with activism any disagreeing judge.

Consider the example of a rule prohibiting vehicles in the park. Is a modern hoverboard a vehicle? A judge may decide that it is. Maybe the true causal explanation behind his decision is a generally bad disposition towards young people and not any valid juristic reason. He might, however, justify the prohibition by

for presumptive positivists as they are for rule-sensitive particularists, and this should entail some higher level of resistance towards bias.

[52] Pronin, Lin and Ross (n 47).

[53] This could be due to scepticism about the existence of the 'better-than-average effect'. But it does not seem to be the case, as another study reported in the same paper shows how good people are at finding this bias in others.

[54] C Guthrie, JJ Rachlinksi and AJ Wistrich 'The "hidden judiciary": an empirical examination of executive branch justice' (2009) 58 *Duke Law Journal* 1529. Again, we are indebted to Piotr Bystranowski for the suggestion.

reference to the no-vehicles rule and its creators. He believes himself to be a rule-enforcing judge, abiding by the doctrine of the separation of powers.

A second judge may hold the opposite view, ruling that hoverboards are not vehicles under the no-vehicles in the park rule. Hoverboards, he may argue, were not a 'thing' when the rule was invented, and it is foolish to prohibit something that was not intended by the rule's creators. He might even accuse the first judge of being an activist. To the second judge, the separation of powers in this case would mandate judicial restraint and an attitude consistent with the idea that whatever is not prohibited is allowed. Now imagine that the second judge's son is one of those hoverboard-loving young people loathed by the first judge. If the desire to make his son happy, instead of the justificatory argument about intentionalism, is the true causal explanation for his judgment, he is just as biased as the first judge.

It does not matter who is right and who is wrong on the justificatory level. It seems that the bias blind spot would make both judges ignorant of their own investments in each line of argument. Clearly, they are not in a position to carefully consider the requirements of the separation of powers in this case, and would probably decide differently (and, though this is not relevant for our current argument, better) when relying on a presumption of some kind.[55]

When we look to behavioural evidence about how humans – including judges – make decisions, we can see that people are not the best judges when it comes to their own shortcomings. Given this – and that presumptions are, indeed, a thing – it is hard to see how rule-sensitive particularists could give the same weight to avoiding application mistakes and to separation of powers as someone using a presumption. Thus, it seems that extensional divergence obtains.

IX. CONCLUSION

Presumptive positivism and rule-sensitive particularism are both psychologically distinct and extensionally divergent. Schauer was right all along and the theses of Postema's critique are false.

As we have seen, however, some might be sceptical about our arguments towards extensional divergence. They may, for instance, take issue with the

[55] This example is arguably a hard case. This could be a blow to our argument, since hard cases are not totally decided by pre-existent rules, and therefore separation of powers arguments would not apply. Note, however, that each judge has used the separation of powers argument to ground his judgment in ways that are not obviously fallacious. If we grant that they actually believe that these arguments are causally responsible for their judgments and normatively sufficient to justify them, we can see that to each of the competing judges, the case is not hard at all. The first judge thinks the rule clearly includes hoverboards, while the second judge firmly believes that it does not. This may show, at the very least, that the bias blind spot is psychologically relevant to separation of powers arguments. In other words, maybe the fault is more with the example and less with the conceptual point.

poor replication record of heuristics-and-biases findings and reject this part of our argument. This die-hard sceptic, a zealot for methodological accuracy, would presumably be more inclined to believe the neurological evidence brought forward by Crockett and Cushman. If this is the case, he may believe that the models are structurally/algorithmically different but extensionally convergent. So, one point for Schauer, another for Postema, right? On a descriptive level, maybe, but on a normative level, this would mean a decisive win for presumptive positivism.

If the results delivered by each model are the same, we have to look for other characteristics that may help differentiate them. The most prominent and well-supported factors would be those regarding time and effort: presumptive positivism and model-free decision making are decisively faster and easier.[56] If this is the case, there is no question. We should prefer presumptive positivism over rule-sensitive particularism.

While we believe that this is a meaningful contribution towards the philosophical understanding of legal decision making, future research should be able to go even further than we did. While we extended Schauer's insights and defended him against Postema's critique using the psychological literature, this is still predicated upon a lot of untested assumptions. We are assuming, for instance, that legal decision making maps onto the same structures in the brain as moral decision making and that the better-than-average effect would not be relevant to a presumptive positivist. And there are surely more assumptions such as these sprinkled throughout the text that may have come to the attention of the sceptic reader. Research in jurisprudence should no longer be satisfied with this. We should strive to test our own hypothesis with the rigour of contemporary psychology, while retaining the philosophical sophistication that is necessary to fully grasp the complexities of law.

[56] Efficiency was one of Schauer's rule-generating justifications precisely because of this point.

14

Interview with Professor Gerald Postema

THOMAS BUSTAMANTE, CÉSAR SERBENA AND NATALINA STAMILE*

Interviewers: First of all, thank you so much, Professor Postema, for accepting this invitation. Could you start, please, by giving a brief introduction? Who were your main influences? Why have you chosen to study Legal Philosophy? What defines you as a legal philosopher?

Gerald Postema: I regard myself as a philosopher, first of all, and then a philosopher of law. Early on, I focused on political, moral and especially legal philosophy. There is a slightly curious story about how I got there. I began my graduate study at Cornell University, planning to work in the philosophy of religion. I hoped to work with a philosopher of religion, Nelson Pike. After I had already enrolled, I discovered that Nelson Pike had left Cornell seven years earlier. So, I suddenly had to think about what I wanted to focus my work on. Over the summer before beginning graduate study, I had read Hart's *The Concept of Law* for the first time. Mind you, this is in 1970, just a few years after *The Concept of Law* was published. (It was published in '61, I believe.) I read Hart's book and I thought, 'this is really interesting! Perhaps I can study legal philosophy'. So I fell

* The authors would like to thank the Academic Publishing Advisory Center (Centro de Assessoria de Publicação Acadêmica, CAPA – www.capa.ufpr.br) of the Federal University of Paraná (UFPR) for assistance with English language editing. The authors give special thanks to Daniel Persia, Fulbright English Teaching Assistant at UFPR, for helping with the transcription of the interview.

into philosophy of law – I didn't choose it with any kind of careful deliberation, I fell into it. When I got on campus, I talked to various people who said Professor David Lyons was a very good thesis director and that he was interested in philosophy of law. When I sought him out, I discovered that he was on leave that year. So I had to think again. However, I was introduced to a professor in the law school named Robert Summers. Professor Summers welcomed me with open arms. He worked out an informal programme for me so that I could study law and philosophy at the same time. I didn't intend to earn the law degree, I just wanted to learn law. So I learned as much of law as one would expect a first or second year law student to learn, while I was working on my PhD in philosophy. First I studied moral and political philosophy and then I focused on the philosophy of law. That's how I got started.

I began my career at Johns Hopkins University, teaching all sorts of topics in ethics and political philosophy. I also taught part-time at the University of Maryland Law School, In 1980, after teaching for five years at Hopkins, I was invited to take a post at the University of North Carolina at Chapel Hill. At UNC I was able to focus my attentions much more sharply on legal and political philosophy and the history of both.

My work has been in the philosophy of law and political philosophy more generally. I have written a good bit on various figures in the history of philosophy as well, most notably David Hume, and Hume's moral psychology. Also, of course, a lot of work on Bentham, mainly his legal philosophy. Early on, I was also interested in the professional ethics of lawyers, and I did some writing on that subject. I've always regarded philosophy of law as an integral part of philosophy. I believe that one can do philosophy of law well only if one can do philosophy well, and I believe that one can do philosophy well only if one is immersed in the history of philosophy.

Interviewers: You mentioned here, and in the colloquium, this interface between legal philosophy and the history of ideas. You also mentioned something about what you call the 'tyranny of intuitions', which seems to be linked to contemporary legal philosophy. What do you think are the most important problems of contemporary legal philosophy, and what method of legal philosophy should be used?

Gerald Postema: I can answer the latter question first and then I will try to come around to the other question. I think, a method – or I might call it rather a preferred approach – to thinking about the classic problems of philosophy of law, at least in my view, is to take a wide view of the kind of things that we might think the object of our study to be. We need first to gather the data regarding the phenomena that we want to theorise about. We do not start our philosophical theorising already believing we understand what law is, and then just try to represent it more abstractly and perhaps make our understanding of it more coherent. I think we have to start with the assumption that we have a rough idea of what we want to identify as law and what we think is important about it. But that idea must be enriched by looking beyond the boundaries of our own local and familiar practice. To do so requires two things. First, it requires that we look beyond the local activities of practising lawyers to the way in which law interacts with the lives of ordinary people – the people who are keen to follow law, what John Finnis once called 'The Good Man', but also those who are alienated from it, those who are cut off from it, and those who just want to get on with their own business and don't want to pay a whole lot of attention to law. Second, we have to broaden it beyond the scope of our concern with twenty-first-century, highly sophisticated, state-orientated law. That may be our final focus, but we need to take into account a much broader range of experience, ways in which law has interacted with human experience over time. That requires us to look more broadly in other kinds of social circumstances, other historical periods, and the like.

So as far as the approach to philosophy of law goes, for us as a scholarly community – not for me as an individual, but for us as a scholarly community – the approach, I think, needs to be broadly focused, gathering as much important information as we can. Later, perhaps, we can say, 'well, we took this kind of experience into account, but it really doesn't fit our best understanding of law over time and so we shouldn't really count it'. We must not start here, but we might end up with a view that certain kinds of things that we thought fell within the concept of law really are not good examples of what we want to treat as central to our understanding of law. Thus, I want to take a fairly wide and encompassing view.

Interviewers: If we use, for instance, Hart's vocabulary, do you think that legal theory is constructed from the internal point of view?

Gerald Postema: It always must be constructed from the internal point of view, in at least one sense of that phrase. One orienting assumption of legal theory is that law is a social phenomenon, practised by people, which has some impact on their day-to-day lives. In consequence, we can't begin to understand law in any of its various forms that have appeared over time, unless we understand it from the point of view of those who are engaged in it, practising it, or are critics of it.

So, yes, you're right, we must start there. But one of the interesting things about the way in which law, and participation in law, work is, first, that people can engage with law and practise law on a relatively unreflective level, and we need to get an understanding of what they're doing, if you will, from the inside of that extended activity. But, as time goes on, and some participants in the practice have enough leisure to be reflective about their activity, the judgments they make – the way in which they go about saying that this is a good exercise of the practice – get articulated, not just acted on, in more and more sophisticated forms. After a point, theorists/philosophers start thinking about those things. Over time, those forms of self-understanding in the practice are then more abstractly theorised. So, if we want to understand law, we have to understand how those various philosophical or theoretical articulations of law developed, what their content is, and how they developed over time. That is the history of philosophy dimension of law that I think is an important component of the scholarly enterprise of philosophical jurisprudence.

That means, I think, that we philosophers of law need to gather data for reflection of two kinds.

We need to look across time to see what forms of interaction are enough like the law we are familiar with that we are willing to include them in our database, and seek as best we can to understand that practice from the inside. But also we must recognise that this is the kind of practice that lends itself to and invites theoretical reflection on it, and thus over time more or less sophisticated theoretical accounts of the practice will be available. On my conception of philosophical jurisprudence, we must take the second kind of data into account, too. Finally, we must realise that those philosophical or theoretical accounts are always shaped in the context of, and with respect to, social circumstances and the politics of the time. One cannot really do an adequate job of understanding those theoretical accounts without looking at the historical context in which they were embedded. There is, then, an inescapable historical dimension to philosophical jurisprudence – not just a history-of-philosophy dimension, but a dimension of the historical setting of those theories. Understanding those forms of law requires understanding the context in which they developed and the way they have changed.

On this view, the philosophical enterprise we engage in as a community of scholars is wide; it is even wider because it joins in partnership with other forms of rational inquiry into the same social phenomenon, for example, sociology, psychology, history, and even perhaps theology. These various forms of reflective inquiry into this phenomenon are potential partners. They are not part of the philosophical enterprise itself, but they are potential partners at various points. Thus, on my conception of the enterprise, the desirable approach that a philosopher should take is, as Sir Edward Coke put it, 'sociable'. It is open to interaction with, and partnership with, other rational sciences.

Interviewers: Much of twentieth-century legal philosophy is about the necessary and sufficient properties of law, of how to identify legal facts. One might think of this way of theorising as asking a metaphysical question about the nature of law. Nonetheless, from what we got from your keynote address 'Fidelity, Accountability and Trust', we believe you assume some connection between law and politics. Should jurisprudence be 'political' rather than 'metaphysical'?

Gerald Postema: It is true that latter twentieth-century and early twenty-first-century Anglo-American legal philosophy, or better yet Anglo-American analytic legal philosophy, has turned very much to metaphysics to give answers to recurring questions about the nature of law. I don't want to say that that is something we shouldn't be doing; I want to say that it is something we shouldn't be doing exclusively. My view is that philosophy of law must be open to all dimensions of philosophy – metaphysics, epistemology, philosophy of action, philosophy of mind, etc – all those dimensions of philosophy that we practise as philosophers. They are all fair game, but not the whole game. It is important to keep in mind the way in which, over time, philosophical reflection on law was incorporated into the more systematic approaches to what we might call very broadly 'explanations of human experience', by philosophers from Plato and Aristotle to Aquinas, Kant and Hegel, and beyond. They always found a place for law in their attempts to understand more generally the nature, and scope and limits of human experience.

So, I'm inclined to say: go ahead and do your metaphysics, but just don't exclusively do the metaphysics. And make sure that your metaphysics is fully and deeply informed by the history of doing that metaphysics. Here's my point about intuitions: a lot of our current metaphysics, and a lot of our analytic legal philosophy, is done by saying, 'does this or that property or features fit our intuitions about law'. That kind of question is bound to be *very* present-oriented, because our intuitions are intuitions about how we sort of get on with the business of law now. If we are to have a truly critical and philosophical approach to understanding law, we cannot be bound by the tyranny of intuitions – we need a point from which we can stand outside of them and challenge them. They will oftentimes be perfectly legitimate, but they are not legitimate by virtue simply of being our intuitions. To think that, I think, is philosophically irresponsible.

Interviewers: What is your position on American legal realism?

Gerald Postema: Legal realists brought a certain important perspective to twentieth-century legal theorising. They really focused on how law works in daily life and were less interested in grand theorising. They wanted to explore law 'where the rubber hits the road'. Different strains of legal realism were more or less open to strictly empirical, sociological or psychological investigations. As a matter of fact, much of the work that was done by the legal realists was not very good. It was highly questionable from the point of view of sociological or psychological method. However, children and grandchildren of that school, as you might call them, developed much more sophisticated psychological theory and sociology of law. It seems to me that the descendants have developed the tools and the capacity to use them in ways the Realists in the 1930s and 1940s wished they could have done. So, I think there is a dimension of their project that I'm perfectly willing to take seriously, and encourage other philosophers to take seriously. I say this not because I think philosophers can do sociology, and not because social theorists can do philosophy, but because there are points at which the central questions that we want to ask and get answers to *need* the help and partnership of sociologists, psychologists, and the like. We need their insights, their constraints, their information, and their criticisms, if we are going to do our philosophical job responsibly.

Interviewers: Here's a question related to your point about legal positivism, at least the Hartian methodology. Can legal validity be understood –can questions of legal validity be understood – apart from questions of legal legitimacy?

Gerald Postema: Probably not, I believe, though we have moved now in our conversation from rather high-level descriptions of an ambition for what I call philosophical jurisprudence to a specific question within current philosophy of law. My view is that, because law is intensely practical, the questions that we want to answer must ultimately fit into a larger context of practical reasoning and the way it works in ordinary daily life in the present as well as in the past and other legal cultures. The result is,

I think, that while it might be possible to carve out a concept without paying much attention to background practical principles (and we might make some progress on that), in the end, we have to see that answer in the context of practical reasoning generally, if we are going to be able to convince ourselves of the adequacy of that account. If so, then it seems to me that when we talk about practical reasoning with respect to law and what is at stake in recognising a law as valid or not, the stakes are high enough that concerns of normative political principle will be implicated. I do not think, in the end, that legal validity can be divorced from concerns about legitimacy, but I may be wrong about that.

I want to emphasise this point with respect to my overarching picture, too. Some have challenged me in this kind of ambition. They say, 'But you know, philosophy is not like that, philosophy is about making careful analytic distinctions within a narrow domain. That's what we do. We're distinction mongers.' I want to reply, 'Yes, that's right,' and the standards of clarity and precision and logically persuasive, logically powerful argument are crucial to the enterprise. However, they are just not the whole thing. It is possible for us to indulge in what my friend, Fred Schauer, calls 'analytic isolation'. You take a little bit and you just do an analysis on that, and I say, 'yep, that's good'. I understand that modest ambition, but that can't be the whole philosophical enterprise. In fact the history of analytic philosophy in the twentieth century – which I wrote about in that rather-too-long book – is the history of that kind of modest ambition. The prevailing thought was that jurisprudence has one task and that is to subject what are thought to be the core concepts in the practice of law to relatively narrow conceptual analysis. By what standard were the core concepts picked out? By a standard that tells us what the law is. What was the standard? The standard proposed was: those rules that are identified as commands of a sovereign backed by sanctions. Austin told us what the domain, what the province of jurisprudence is. But, as post-Austinian English legal theorists insisted, what he was doing was not jurisprudence; he was stipulating the boundaries of the enterprise he had in mind. The idea governing the jurisprudential enterprise was that once we have a clear view of the boundaries of our province, we can start doing jurisprudence. We just subject to analysis the concepts that play a key role in this province. Jurisprudence was limited to this enterprise of analytic isolation. A lot of twentieth-century Anglo-American analytic legal philosophy was done without fully realising how the beginning of the century had carved out this narrow task. Philosophers thought they could engage in their modest task, and do it well, without having to look at how restoring the analysed concepts to their larger context affected those very concepts. They seemed to think that, if you could take a little module, and work on it, and then you plug it back into the machine, the module won't be affected at all by the role it plays in the machine. In general, that is not likely to be true. The assumption that there are conceptual modules that are discrete and unconnected with the whole mosaic of law, is, it seems to me, just false. Thus, there is value in working in analytic isolation, real progress in understanding law can be made in this way, but eventually you look to the place of the analysed concepts in their larger context.

Interviewers: One of the topics that connects these ideas you mentioned is the rule of law. And you have done some quite important work on this subject recently. You mentioned that the rule of law supposes a discursive environment. If law is an argumentative practice, the idea of rule of law should be understood differently. So here are two questions. We think that you seem to assume some equality of the participants in the social practice in order for it to comply with the requirements of the rule of law. Can there be rule of law where there is no democracy? Can there be rule of law where there is no economic equality?

Gerald Postema: Wonderful questions. What we must keep in mind is, first of all, that the term 'rule of law' refers to a political principle and that recommends or requires that power be exercised only in certain ways. That demand is understood to apply to ruling power – that is, governments – but also power exercised in a civic context. Power can be exercised in both 'vertical' and the 'horizontal' dimensions. The rule of law is a recommendation for – or a demand that – governance take a certain shape *and* our civic associations take a certain shape. It is an ideal for both dimensions. And it is an ideal that can be realised in greater or lesser degrees. You asked, 'is it possible for there to be a rule of law under conditions of economic inequality?' The answer must be that at *some point* it may become impossible, but we can have more or less fully realised rule of law in a political community. The realisation of the rule of law is not an on/off matter; rather, it is scalar, a matter of degree. The rule of law can be more robust in a community or less, and how robust it is will depend on the circumstances under which those who are engaged in its distinctive activities live.

Now, it does look like really robust rule of law presupposes a kind of equality at least to the extent that each participant, each layperson or official, has the capacity (perhaps in concert with others) to stand and hold others accountable. If you begin thinking about it just a little bit that requires intellectual capacity and character on the part of individuals. It also requires a social framework, and if the intellectual capacity is not there, if the character is not there, or not there enough, or if the circumstances are such that it becomes difficult to exercise these capacities, then we have a less robust rule of law. If the deficiency is great enough we may see only marginal rule of law, or even no rule of law at all.

Two things can be said about this feature of the rule of law. One is that it might be true that, under some circumstances, the rule of law has not been achieved or cannot be achieved. That may be a reason itself to say that there is something fundamentally wrong with that mode of association or that mode of government. If it fails the rule of law, that is a serious moral/political failure. It is not just something that, unfortunately, we can't bring about; it's a failure. So somewhere along this line it might turn out that circumstances are such that the rule of law is failing, or perhaps the rule of law has failed. There are certain kinds of attitudes that people take with respect to law that are inconsistent with there being a robust rule of law in a political community. Martin Krieger likes to quote what he tells me is a

Bulgarian commonplace that goes something like this: 'Law is like a door in the middle of a meadow. You can walk through it if you like, but what's the point.' If *that* attitude is prevalent in a community, it is unlikely that the rule of law is robust there, because certain kinds of attitudes are required for the rule of law to get rooted and to be active and robust in a community. In that case, the society falls short of what the rule of law demands – it is a failure of the rule of law. It's a failure of the rule of law not because the rules are not general, or prospective, or the like. Rather, it is a failure because there are not adequate, as it were, resources for the ethos of the rule of law to take hold. I take that to be a failure of the rule of law, not an impossibility.

It might turn out, however, that there are some circumstances such that there would be no point in talking about the rule of law. There might be something akin to Hume's idea of 'the circumstances of justice' – we might call them 'the circumstances of the rule of law'. I don't know exactly what they might be. It might turn out that under some circumstances the inequalities are so great that at that point thinking about implementing the rule of law is just the wrong place to put our energies. We might think that we have to put our energies into something else first; implementing the rule of law will have to come later. I can understand that, because the rule of law is, after all, just one principle among others in our political theory, in our political morality, and we have to think about other political-moral values too if we are serious about our political morality. However, I worry a bit about that idea, because it may be used to excuse, and even encourage, those who want to exercise arbitrary power for their own benefit. Nevertheless, it is entirely conceivable that we can face circumstances in which it is reasonable to say that there is another job that has to be done first before our society has the resources and capacities for a robust rule of law.

Of course, that is true about democracy as well. Democracy is not a viable way of organising political life under all circumstances. Democracy can be robust only in some social/economic circumstances. Sometimes we have to work on improving or enhancing the necessary background conditions first before we can hope to have a robust democracy. Democracy and the rule of law, as I understand the rule of law, are in this respect like cousins or maybe partners. They are not the same thing and they may not serve exactly the same values, but they need to work together. It should not be surprising, then, that they might have maybe similar sets of conditions that make them possible or robust or not.

Interviewers: So, following up, you mentioned in the colloquium that you might have changed some of your views about the role of conventions in law. Can you tell us: what are the main changes in your conception of law over time, over your career?

Gerald Postema: My understanding of law is partial, and incomplete, and under construction. It will be still partial, incomplete and under construction when I die. I don't regard philosophical jurisprudence as something that one can complete, and furthermore, I don't regard it as just my project. Although philosophy tends to be done (and especially the way I do it) in one's study, I never regard it as a task for myself alone. I like to think of it as a task for many hands, a work of many hands. That being so, just let me say a little bit about the dimensions and the development of my own views on social rules, conventions and customs.

Early in my career, when I started thinking about distinctively analytic legal philosophical questions, in particular those posed by Hart, what worried me was that Hart had not adequately explained how it is that law could be normative. It was very important for Hart, too, because he didn't want to go the route of some of the American legal realists or especially the Scandinavian realists who reduced law to certain psychological facts. But also he didn't want to go the Kelsenian route that grounded law's normativity in something like a transcendental or abstract norm that somehow underlies law. He wanted the explanation of law's normativity to be intrinsic to the practice of law, not something transcendental and outside it. So – it was a brilliant move actually – he put at the core of his whole theory the idea of a social rule, and he gave an explanation of what it is for a social rule to exist. I thought at the time that the project he had in mind was just right, and yet I started asking questions about the adequacy of his analysis of social rules and his use of them as the foundation of his legal theory. What he wanted to do was to give an account of social rules that could explain law's normativity only in terms of certain social facts. How could he do that? I wondered. He analysed social rules as a combination of regularities of behaviour – an observable social phenomenon – and an internal attitude – a matter of psychological fact. So, he argued, a combination of a sort of behavioural fact and a psychological fact can do the work of explaining law's normativity. I came to the view that he didn't succeed, but I thought that something in the neighborhood of these ideas might work.

About this time I looked into David Lewis's book *Convention*, and game theoretic accounts of coordination. I began to think that one could perhaps capture a good bit of what Hart was trying to do by thinking about it in terms of coordination and the reasons for action that setting certain kinds of behavioural facts into a network of expectations can actually generate. I thought the concept of a convention, understood largely in ways that Lewis had put into the philosophical lexicon, could supply what was missing in Hart's account. So, in an early paper I argued that Lewis-type conventions lie at the foundations of law – that we could understand the 'rule of recognition' as a kind of Lewis-type convention. Mere regularities of behaviour (that component of social rules), set into the deliberative context of a coordination problem, I thought, could provide the salience needed to solve the problem and this could give officials/judges reasons to identify certain rules as valid rules of law. This, I thought, provided an explanation of the normative, reason-giving force of what Hart called the 'rule of recognition', which in turn accounted for the normativity of the rest of the legal system.

One nice thing about Hart's picture was that he could say the rule at the foundation of law is just a pattern of behaviour. You get to a certain point when asking what a given legal rule rests on for its validity and you reach the rule of recognition, and the rule of recognition is just a social rule, a matter of observable behaviour plus presumed attitudes. They are matters of social fact – no moral or transcendental principles are needed for the account. On the Lewis-convention account, some such social facts have normative significance precisely because they fit into a context of coordination. The known, observable pattern of behaviour has the kind of salience that allows us to solve coordination problems. 'Boy, that just does what Hart wanted to do,' I thought.

For various reasons people began to challenge that approach. Some of those reasons I thought could be answered; but I came to realise that some of them could not be answered. People began to say, and I began to think too, maybe it is not correct or plausible to think of the rule of recognition or other activities of law-applying officials in terms of coordination games. That focus is too narrow. I tried my best over the following many years to broaden that idea. Doing so, I became aware of three significant problems with the game theoretic attempt to give an answer to the question 'What is a social rule?'

One was that this basis of understanding normativity is radically individualist, and the reasons that are generated are reasons of each individual participant's own strategic position within a coordination game. Consequently, what emerges from the game theoretic framework are individual practical strategies for an individual's achieving certain ends in contexts in which the individual must work with others and seek to coordinate with them. I thought that this doesn't give us a plausible answer to the question, 'What makes it a *social* rule?' These 'rules' are just a collection of accidentally coinciding individualised strategies adopted by various parties. This account does not give us any sense of how this collection could add up to a social rule – that is, a rule *for* and *of* the group. Of course, it was very important for Hart to portray the rule of recognition as a proper social rule. Hart said judges don't decide just for themselves, for their own part only; they do it as a collectivity, a group. Recognition of this inadequacy of the standard Lewis-type analysis of conventions forced me to think more about what could make a rule a *social* rule.

Second, I had done some work thinking about the phenomenon of salience that lies at the core of Lewis's convention story. I came to the view that salience, if it was to underlie social rules, could only be understood as the product of the exercise of a kind of social or common reasoning process, not merely the reasoning process of individuals. So I begin to think more seriously about what common reasoning might look like, what public reasoning might look like.

Third, upon thinking more about Dworkin's view (and what the Hartian positivist picture leaves out of an account of essential features of law), I became convinced of the importance of the 'argumentative' or the 'discursive' dimension of law. That seemed to me to be an important feature of law that is left out if you think of law simply as (isolated) norms or rules. The way in which the components of law work together in practical reasoning has a very important discursive character. That came to me in large part not just through reading Dworkin, but through my study of seventeenth-century common law jurisprudence. The classical common law view was that, fundamentally, law is not a set of rules but rather a discipline of practical reasoning – a public discipline, or a discipline of public practical reasoning.

So these considerations – the common or public nature of some practical reasoning, especially that associated with social rules and the fundamentally discursive nature of law – forced me to think more broadly and to give up the idea that we could explain the normative foundations of law using the coordination game model. I undertook to look more broadly at customs or social norm as rules *of* a community in which their social character is intrinsic to the kind of rules they are. They are not necessarily discursive, of course, but adding the discursive element to this more distinctively social character of rules, I came to think that we have resources we can explain core elements of the law with. These resources are not likely to be all we need, but they provide a good starting point.

That, in rough outline, is the trajectory of my thoughts about conventions at the foundations of law.

Interviewers: To conclude, what are the fundamental texts of legal philosophy for you, if there are any? What do you think should be the future of legal philosophy? What problems still are there to be addressed?

Gerald Postema: Fundamental texts: I think we must include Plato and Aristotle – Plato's *Statesman* and *Laws* and portions of Aristotle's, *Nichomachean Ethics* and *Politics* – those are terribly important. I'm inclined to think some very important but little-read medieval texts are important; for example, some of the political works of William of Ockham and *Defensor Pacis*, by Marsilius of Padua, are important. Aquinas obviously should be added – not just his so-called 'Treatise on Law' in *Summa Theologiae*, but other parts of his *Summa Theologiae* in which he discusses justice and property, and other parts where he develops his view of human psychology and the role it plays in practical reasoning are important. One text I think should be in the canon is a work by Johannes Althusias written at the turn of the seventeenth century, called *Politica*. He develops a very interesting view of both the rule of law and federalism in an interesting way. We have not yet brought his ideas into a twenty-first-century context to see what we learn from them. Other very important figures writing a bit later in the seventeenth century would be Grotius, *On the Law of War and Peace* and *Freedom of the Seas*; Francisco Suárez's *On Laws and God as Law-Giver* is also important. Then some of the more familiar ones: Thomas Hobbes, maybe Locke, but Hobbes is much more fundamental here. I would also add, but in this I am probably idiosyncratic, the work of the great seventeenth-century English jurist, Sir Matthew Hale. From the eighteenth and nineteenth centuries I would urge close study of Bentham, Kant, and Hegel. From the twentieth century, the giants are Hart and Kelsen; their work is absolutely critical. I don't want to say anything about more contemporary things because who knows what would be classic.

Though that is the kind of syllabus that I would put together; in fact, that's the syllabus I put together. Typically, I start from the medievals, and I read Ockham, Scotus, Marsilius and Aquinas and the early seventeenth-century Europeans and the like. I also think it is important to look at Islamic philosophy, there's a lot there yet. Medieval Islamic philosophy is very useful in this context. That's how I build my introduction to modern legal and political philosophy – to start with Plato and Aristotle and proceed to the story of the reception Roman law in the eleventh century and then work from there. So those are the great texts, in my view. I'm sure I've left out some, and I'm sure a couple of them there are entirely idiosyncratic, but those are the ones I would focus on.

Interviewers: Would you include Kant?[1]

Gerald Postema: Kant yes, absolutely. Kant has to be there and Hegel has to be there, it seems to me, if we are going to understand the kind of framework we ought to have in thinking about law. Bentham also plays a big role there: not because I accept much of Bentham's theory, but he brings to the table a combination of close analysis and a very wide view about what is relevant to thinking about law, about the scope of the jurisprudential enterprise. It is not enough to read just Bentham's *Of Laws in General* (now called *Of the Limits of the Penal Branch of Jurisprudence*). One should read some of his work on the constitutional code and his discussion of 'securities against misrule'. So Kant, Bentham, up to Hegel. There's more after that, but that was a good start.

What problems for the future? I think we still need to understand how practical reasoning works, and how law as a mode or discipline of practical reasoning relates to practical reasoning generally. There is a psychological dimension, a political, and a moral dimension of this inquiry. As a part of that, I think, is a crucial task that we have not yet tackled: we must ask the question how it is that ordinary people come to learn law, and how better understanding how people learn the law could then influence our understanding of the practical reasoning on which law depends. I think that it is likely to be true that we come to learn law not by learning particular rules, but by learning how to engage in certain kinds of interactions that are infused with and reflect the law. But it's not a matter of knowing what those rules are in a kind of straightforward, 'no dogs allowed' kind of model. If this is right, then it would seem that law must find a way to integrate itself

[1] Although the question had been already answered, the interviewers decided to maintain it to keep this record as faithful as possible to the actual interview.

into ordinary practices of people. Yet we only learn, at that point, a fairly small amount of the law; the rest of the law that bears on our lives and that should or even must interact in some way with our practical reasoning has to be brought to us through intermediaries. The question, then, is what is the nature of those intermediaries, what sort of constraints should be placed on them, and is 'mediated law' adequate for the purposes of respecting and supporting the rule of law? How is it possible to realise the objectives of a rule of law, if the access people have to the law is inevitably mediated? We have to understand a whole lot better the relationship between actually functioning law in all of its twenty-first-century complexity, on the one hand, and the practical reasoning of ordinary people on the other. This is one inquiry in which we must join hands with scholars trained in psychology and sociology to understand how social norms are learned and handed on; how those social norms connect up with more formally structured rules and principles of law; and what role intermediaries play in that process of learning. Legal philosophers have not paid much attention to these questions. Our model of the way in which law has a practical effect is that it addresses each individual citizen or subject of law directly. It seems to me that this assumption has to be wrong. We need to work out a richer and more complex picture. This primary question has not yet been addressed adequately.

Another issue concerns the relationship between the value that law provides us, perhaps represented in the idea of rule of law, and other fundamental principles of our political morality like justice, equality or liberty. The relationship of law and the rule of law to democracy is another such question. Of course, these questions have been addressed, but they are perennial, and we must continually address them. Also we must ask the question that you asked earlier: what are the conditions that make those principles important for us, and when do they take second place to other vital concerns of political morality. Those are fundamental questions and we still need to think about them.

Interviewers: Thank you very much!

Index

Introductory Note

References such as '178–79' indicate (not necessarily continuous) discussion of a topic across a range of pages. References to footnotes are in italics. Wherever possible in the case of topics with many references, these have either been divided into sub-topics or only the most significant discussions of the topic are listed. Because the entire work is about the 'philosophy of law', 'jurisprudence' and 'Gerald Postema', the use of these terms (and certain others which occur constantly throughout the book) as entry points has been minimised. Information will be found under the corresponding detailed topics.

www.ingramcontent.com/pod-product-compliance
Ingram Content Group UK Ltd.
Pitfield, Milton Keynes, MK11 3LW, UK
UKHW020238290926
15470UKWH00002B/595

9 781509 933884